Lexis and Creativity in Translation

A Corpus-based Study

Dorothy Kenny

Routledge
Taylor & Francis Group
LONDON AND NEW YORK

First published 2001 by St. Jerome Publishing

Published 2014 by Routledge
2 Park Square, Milton Park, Abingdon, Oxon OX14 4RN
711 Third Avenue, New York, NY 10017, USA

Routledge is an imprint of the Taylor & Francis Group, an informa business

ISBN 13: 978-1-900650-39-7 (pbk)

Cover design by
Steve Fieldhouse, Oldham, UK

Typeset by
Delta Typesetters, Cairo, Egypt

British Library Cataloguing in Publication Data
A catalogue record of this book is available from the British Library

Library of Congress Cataloging-in-Publication Data
Kenny, Dorothy.
Lexis and creativity in translation : corpus-based study / Dorothy Kenny.
p. cm.
Includes bibliographical references and index.
ISBN 1-900650-38-X (alk. paper) — ISBN 1-900650-39-8 (pbk. : alk. paper)
1. Translating and interpreting. 2. Linguistics. 3. Machine translating. 4. German language—Translating into English—Data processing. I. Title.
P306.2 .K46 2001
418'.02—dc21

00-011905

for my father
Ernan John Kenny
and in memory of my mother
Monica Kenny

Contents

List of Tables

List of Figures

Acknowledgements

Several individuals and institutions have helped to make the research reported on in this book possible. I am especially grateful to Prof. Michael Townson and my colleagues in the School of Applied Language and Intercultural Studies at Dublin City University for all they have done to create a supportive research environment in SALIS, and for enabling me to take sabbatical leave in 1997-98 to pursue doctoral research at UMIST. In particular, the assistance of Lynne Bowker, Angela Leahy, Cornelia Opitz, Jennifer Pearson, Barbara Rieger, Iris Schneider, Gabriele Schön, Annette Simon, and Jenny Williams is gratefully acknowledged. I am also grateful to DCU's Research Committee, who generously supported the purchase of printed books for inclusion in GEPCOLT, the electronic corpus compiled for use in this research.

My thanks are also owed to: Terry Hale, Hans-Christian Oeser, Malcolm Green, and Johan Drumbl, all of whom shared with me their vast knowledge of German literature, tapped liberally in the text selection phase of this project; Ray Keenoy, who made the *Babel Guides* database of German literature in translation available to me at a crucial moment; software developers Knut Hofland, and David Woolls, who were generous with their advice and time; Irmtraud Jüttner and her colleagues at the *Institut für deutsche Sprache* (IDS) in Mannheim, who gave me access to the collection of German language corpora held at the IDS; and Mona Baker, Ian Mason, and Maeve Olohan, all careful readers of most of the research reported on in this book, when it was still part of a doctoral thesis. My gratitude to them is immense. Any omissions or errors that remain in this work, are of course, my own.

The following publishers, authors, and translators, who granted permission for their copyright material to be included in GEPCOLT, are also gratefully acknowledged:

ÖBV-Klett-Cotta Verlagsgesellschaft mbH, for Konrad Bayer's *der kopf des vitus bering* (1965); Atlas Press, for Konrad Bayer's *the head of vitus bering* (1994, trans. Walter Billeter); Pieke Biermann, for *Violetta* (1990), published by Rotbuch Verlag; Serpent's Tail, for Biermann's *Violetta* (1996, trans. Ines Rieder and Jill Hannum), Elfriede Jelinek's *Wonderful, Wonderful Times* (1990, trans. Michael Hulse) and *Lust* (1992, trans. Michael Hulse); Ammann Verlag AG, for Georges-Arthur Goldschmidt's *Die Absonderung* (1991); Quartet Books Ltd, for Georges-Arthur Goldschmidt's *Worlds of Difference* (1993, trans. James Kirkup); Carl Hanser Verlag GmbH & Co, for Gert Hofmann's *Unsere Eroberung* (1984); Carcanet Press Ltd, for Gert Hofmann's *Our Conquest* (1987, trans. Christopher Middleton), and Dieter Wellershoff's *Winner Takes All* (1986, trans. Paul Knight); Rowohlt Verlag GmbH, for Elfriede Jelinek's *Die Ausgesperrten* (1980) and *Lust* (1989); Bodo Kirchhoff for *Infanta* (1990) published by Suhrkamp Verlag; Harvill Publishers, for Bodo Kirchhoff's *Infanta* (1992, trans. John Brownjohn); Linden Verlag, for Erich Loest's *Völkerschlachtdenkmal* (1984) and *The Monument* (1987, trans. Ian

Mitchell); Christoph Ransmayr for *Die Schrecken des Eises und der Finsternis* (1984) published by Christian Brandstätter Verlag und Edition; Weidenfeld and Nicholson Ltd, for Christoph Ransmayr's *The Terrors Of Ice And Darkness* (1991, trans. John Woods); S. Fischer Verlag, for Gerhard Roth's *die autobiographie des albert einstein* (1972) and *Am Abgrund* (1986); Malcolm Green for Gerhard Roth's *the autobiography of albert einstein* (1992, trans. Malcolm Green) and *On the Brink* (in press, trans. Malcolm Green), Unica Zürn's *The House of Illnesses* (1993, trans. Malcolm Green) and *The Man of Jasmine & Other Texts* (1994, trans. Malcolm Green); Kiepenheuer und Witsch, for Dieter Wellershoff's *Der Sieger nimmt alles* (1983); Reclam Verlag, and the author, for Natascha Wodin's *Die gläserne Stadt* (1983); Harcourt Brace & Company, for Natascha Wodin's *The Interpreter* (1986, trans. John Brownjohn); the Erbengemeinschaft Unica Zürn, for Unica Zürn's (1977) *Der Mann im Jasmin*, published by Verlag Ullstein GmbH.

Finally, I cannot thank Graham – and Niamh – enough, for their patience and support.

Introduction

Computers offer new perspectives in the study of language. They allow us to see phenomena that previously remained obscure because of the limitations of our vantage points. Corpus linguists often liken the computer to the telescope, or microscope, in this respect, but the kaleidoscope might be as fitting an image. Kaleidoscopes allow us to view patterns, and to change those patterns at will. In corpus linguistics, the words and characters of electronic texts act like pieces of coloured glass and paper, constantly forming new patterns, which then recede as others take their place. And while the telescope and microscope are scientific instruments, the kaleidoscope is most definitely a toy. Corpus linguistics is a serious business, but there are few corpus linguists who will not admit to playing with their corpora. We list words in arbitrary groups of ones, twos, or threes. We sort and re-sort concordance lines, to see what new patterns might emerge. We follow the fortunes of nodes as if they were characters in a soap opera. Corpus analysis can be time-consuming and painstaking, but there are also moments of sheer delight – and insight. One of the principal aims of this book is to invite readers to partake in the very real pleasure of playing with a corpus.

The corpus in question is GEPCOLT, the German-English Parallel Corpus of Literary Texts. GEPCOLT was constructed in the first instance to enable a corpus-based investigation of lexical normalization in translation, a study that is reported on in detail in the latter part of this book. But readers who are more interested in compiling their own translation corpora, and pursuing other lines of inquiry, should find plenty of encouragement and practical advice in the pages of this volume. No previous knowledge of computing or corpus linguistics is assumed, and the primary focus here is on what can reasonably be achieved by an individual researcher with a PC and scanner, standard corpus-processing software, an internet connection, and a taste for discovery.

Mindful of criticisms that have been levelled at linguistic approaches to translation in the past, the book starts by making a case for the use of corpus linguistics in translation studies. Corpus linguists and translation scholars share much theoretical ground, which this book seeks to explore. Attention is thus focused on the basic theoretical positions of both translation scholars – including those aligned with cultural studies – and corpus linguists, and the study of lexis is proffered as an area in which corpus linguists are seen to speak particularly to the concerns of translation scholars. The interaction so far of corpus linguistics with translations studies is discussed, as is the limited role investigations of lexis have played thus far in corpus-based translation studies. Long established, and more recently popular corpus linguistic approaches to the study of lexis are outlined, and special emphasis is put on their application to studies of lexical norms and creativity. Issues of corpus compilation and processing are addressed in detail, and the theory is then applied in a detailed investigation of how translators typically handle source-text lexical creativity in GEPCOLT.

No doubt some readers will find mine an odd, perhaps ill-advised, way to approach literary texts. Let me assure such readers that the analysis presented in this book is not intended as a replacement for the more holistic kind of aesthetic appreciation that individual texts, authors, and translators so richly deserve. I am also resigned to the fact that not all readers will agree with all the judgements made here about what is – or is not – creative in the source and target texts, and remain open to criticisms and comments in this regard. Some readers may even feel tantalized by the glimpses they get in the bilingual concordances in Chapters Six and Seven of interesting textual features that I have not discussed. Such readers are invited to make themselves known to me. They may just like to play with GEPCOLT themselves.

Dorothy Kenny
July 2000
Dorothy.Kenny@dcu.ie

1. Is 'Linguistics' Singular or Plural?

> In the final analysis, if linguistics is not about language as it is actually spoken and written by human beings, then it is about nothing at all.
>
> Peter Trudgill (1996:xi)

> However systematically you may talk, you do not talk systematics.
>
> J.R. Firth (1957:180)

Introduction

Linguistics has had something of a chequered history in translation studies. In the mid-twentieth century, linguistic analysis occupied what Lawrence Venuti (2000:69) has called the "optimistic extreme" in translation theory. In the face of philosophical scepticism, linguistically-oriented commentators cheerfully proclaimed that translation was possible, and outlined whole batteries of procedures used by translators to overcome target language lexical gaps, or problems caused by structural differences between languages. Several books were published on the subject, including Vinay and Darbelnet's (1958) *Stylistique comparée du français et de l'anglais*, Mounin's (1963) *Les problèmes théoriques de la traduction*, Nida's (1964) *Towards a Science of Translating*, Catford's (1965) *A Linguistic Theory of Translation*, and Wilss'(1977) *Übersetzungswissenschaft. Probleme und Methoden.* Translation theorists like Nida and Wilss were quick to adopt the "truly scientific perspective" that Chomsky had purportedly gifted to linguistics (Newmeyer 1980:20), and both included whole chapters on machine translation, a burgeoning field where the usefulness of formal descriptions of contrastive linguistic structures seemed incontrovertible. The confidence was palpable. Linguistically-oriented translation theory had set itself up on a scientific basis and was convinced that its results could be applied in the practices of human and machine translation. It was ready for a fall.

By the late 1980s, proponents of linguistic approaches to translation were coming under fire from several quarters (see, especially, Godard 1990; Hermans 1985a; Lefevere and Bassnett 1990; Snell-Hornby 1988a, 1990). They were criticized for their scientistic posturing and derided for restricting their analyses to lower linguistic ranks. They were described as doggedly clinging on to a naïvely representational view of language, one that could sustain the 'illusion of equivalence' between languages, but that necessarily effaced the role of the translator in creating meaning in the target language. They were caricatured as myopic drones, conducting painstaking analyses of source and target texts, but indifferent to any wider cultural import that translation might have. Linguistics was further considered inadequate to the task of dealing with "the manifold complexities of literary texts" (Hermans ibid:10). And, as if things weren't bad enough, the "triumph of machine translation" (Lefevere and Bassnett ibid:4) had turned out not to be just around the corner after all.

The onslaught against linguistically-oriented approaches to translation continued well into the 1990s, gathering momentum with the continuing rise of cultural studies in translation. Rosemary Arrojo (1998), Edwin Gentzler (1993) and Lawrence Venuti (1996, 1997) in particular used the philosophical apparatus of postmodernism to critique linguistically-oriented translation studies, questioning linguists' pretensions to objective neutrality, their promotion of scientific models, and their view of language itself.

But if linguistics was coming under fire in translation studies in the 1980s and 1990s, these decades are also remarkable for the volume of work that continued to be published by linguistically-oriented translation scholars. Baker (in press) lists Delisle (1980, 1993), House (1981, 1997), Blum-Kulka (1981, 1986), Wilss (1982), Hatim and Mason (1990, 1997), Mason (1994), Bell (1991), Baker (1992, 1993, 1995, 1996b), Neubert and Shreve (1992) and Harvey (1998) as examples of such work. It could also be added here that some earlier work never lost its appeal – Vinay and Darbelnet (1958) and its 1995 translation into English is one such volume – and Baker's own linguistically-oriented coursebook on translation (1992) became an academic best-seller.

The parallel development of two seemingly incompatible approaches to translation became the subject of much debate in the late 1990s. Mona Baker, who was to become something of a spokesperson for linguistic approaches (see Baker 1996a, 2000, in press), warned that the rift between the cultural studies and linguistic paradigms threatened "to reduce the discourse on translation studies into a series of fault finding exercises and divisive oppositions" (1996a:9) and argued for a place for both perspectives in translation studies. And Lawrence Venuti, whose sympathies clearly lay with cultural studies, nevertheless argued not that linguistic approaches be abandoned, but that they be supplemented in specific ways (1996: 104, 109). The tone of his landmark *Translation Studies Reader* (2000) is even more conciliatory: cultural, linguistic, and other approaches to translation sit side-by-side in the book, and even in some of the same articles.

So how can linguistic approaches to translation have been so right, and then so wrong, and then alright again? These questions have been addressed to varying extents by other writers, in particular Baker (1996a, 2000, in press) and Fawcett (1997). One picture that emerges from these critiques is that of a fledgling discipline – the one that became known as translation studies – attempting to secure its place in the academy by aligning itself with the 'science' of linguistics and initially focusing on the idealized, decontextualized and simplistic interlingual operations this seemed to entail. As time went on, linguistic approaches to translation began to recognise their own shortcomings and shift their focus to real translation behaviour, translation as communication, whole texts, and their ideological import. By chronicling the evolution of linguistically-oriented translation studies, scholars like Baker and Fawcett could counter criticisms of linguistics emanating from within cultural studies and even point to a convergence of interests between the two supposedly competing paradigms. But they did more than that. By highlighting the diversity not only within what could be considered linguistic approaches to translation, but also within linguistics itself, they began to undermine a basic position implicit in much of the postmodern critique of linguistics in translation: the assumption that there is an undifferentiated monolith called 'linguistics'.

That there is diversity within linguistics, and that linguists can occupy diametrically opposed positions when it comes to such basic issues as what their object and mode of inquiry should be, are points that have been well made by linguists themselves (see, for example, Beaugrande 1994, 1997; Sampson 1980). Michael Stubbs' (1993, 1996) treatment of the deep and systematic differences between Chomskyan and neo-Firthian linguistics is of particular interest here, as it juxtaposes the work of arguably the most influential twentieth-century linguist, Noam Chomsky, with that of the linguist whose legacy is felt in the work presented in this book, J.R. Firth. Below I follow Stubbs' lead in setting Firth off against Chomsky, but my analysis will have an added, translation studies dimension, in that it will attempt to show how the ideas of each were taken up in linguistically-oriented theorizing on translation. If more space is given to Firth's ideas, this is because they are more applicable to translation, and in particular corpus-based translation studies, than are Chomsky's. Ironically though, I will argue how ultimately it was mainly Chomsky's influence that was acknowledged, implicitly or explicitly, by critics of linguistics in translation studies.

Chomskyan linguistics

Chomsky's oeuvre is extensive, spanning nearly fifty years of publication and taking in linguistics, philosophy and dissident politics. I will not attempt to do his intellectual achievements justice here. Instead, the reader is referred to Smith's (1999) sympathetic survey of Chomsky's work to date. The technical details of his linguistic theory have also changed constantly over the last half century, so much so that Smith likens Chomsky to Picasso for his ability to overthrow his own established systems with "startling" frequency (ibid:1). But certain fundamental positions have remained constant in Chomskyan linguistics, and problematic for his detractors. These positions include Chomsky's stance on the goals of linguistic theory, the nature of linguistic evidence, and of language itself.

Chomskyan linguistics has long been concerned with native speakers' knowledge of their language, their linguistic 'competence' (Chomsky 1965) or 'I-language' (Chomsky 1986). Chomsky originally contrasted competence with 'performance', "the actual use of language in concrete situations" (1965:4), but noted that only competence could be the object of inquiry in a properly constituted linguistic discipline. From the outset, Chomsky has been far more concerned with the mental structures underlying human language than with the actual use of language:

> in the technical sense, linguistic theory is mentalistic, since it is concerned with discovering a mental reality underlying actual behavior. Observed use of language or hypothesized dispositions to respond, habits, and so on, may provide evidence as to the nature of this mental reality, but surely cannot constitute the actual subject matter of linguistics, if this is to be a serious discipline. (1965:4)

Coupled with Chomsky's mentalism is his staunch defence of innateness. Chomsky argues that much of what we know about language is hard-wired in our brains, part of our biological endowment (see, especially Chomsky 1988). Part of the evidence for this claim comes from Chomsky's conviction that there are structural properties that are common to all languages, linguistic universals that can only be explained with reference to a language acquisition device that is shared by all humans.

Chomskyan linguistics is further based on a number of idealizations that allow linguists to ignore speakers' idiosyncrasies, the nebulousness of speech communities, and irrelevant features of performance. This basic position is summed up in one of Chomsky's (1965:3) most famous passages:

> Linguistic theory is concerned primarily with an ideal speaker-listener, in a completely homogenous speech-community, who knows its language perfectly and is unaffected by such grammatically irrelevant conditions as memory limitations, distractions, shifts of attention and interest, and errors (random or characteristic) in applying his knowledge of that language in actual performance.

Despite objections from other quarters, which will be dealt with below, these idealizations continue to be underwritten by the Chomskyan commitment to linguistics as a natural science. In Smith's words, "all science involves idealization", and in order to see the principles that underlie linguistic behaviour, "it is necessary that some things be fruitfully ignored" (1999:12-13).

Like Saussure (1916) before him, Chomsky thus bases his linguistics on a dichotomy between an abstract system that underlies language use (Chomsky's competence; Saussure's *langue*), and real-life language as used by real people (performance; *parole*). There are differences however: Chomsky rejects the Saussurian notion of *langue* "as merely a systematic inventory of items" and advocates a return to "the Humboldtian conception of underlying competence as a system of generative processes" (1965:4); and whereas Saussure's *langue* exists perfectly only within a collectivity, Chomsky's competence resides very much in the minds of individuals. Nevertheless, both privilege the study of an abstract linguistic system, which is not amenable to direct observation, over real spoken and written language, which is. For Saussure this has the effect of insulating *langue* from the massive variability of *parole*, of maintaining *langue* as a well-defined object in the heterogeneous mass of speech facts. It also allows him to defend the autonomy of linguistics from the other disciplines that might be interested in the "heterogeneous mass of speech facts", including anthropology, sociology and psychology. And by fencing off synchronic from diachronic linguistics, he manages to fix *langue* as a stable, ahistorical entity.[1] Chomsky likewise, by constructing his object of inquiry so narrowly, carves out a niche for an autonomous discipline of linguistics. But nowhere in language does the idea of autonomy work quite as well as it does with syntax.

Beaugrande (1997, 1998) has suggested that by disconnecting linguistic theory from real data and the life-histories of speakers, formalist linguists – as exemplified by Chomsky – privilege syntax. While phonology and morphology typically retain contact with the reality of language, "by matching their theoretical units (phonemes and morphemes) against the practical units (sounds, inflections, etc.) discovered in fieldwork data" (1998:774), syntax can readily disengage from reality by assuming that word-order "can be most rationally accounted for by an independent system of deterministic 'rules' situated entirely on the side of 'language' [Saussure's *langue*]... and unaffected by the contexts of real speech, the motivations of real speakers, and perhaps even the meaning of utterances" (ibid:773). Beaugrande's final point here is an allusion to Chomsky's (1957:17) insistence that "grammar is autonomous and independent of meaning", a position that informed Chomsky's earlier work. Chomsky now holds that much conceptual information associated with words is contained in the entries of our mental lexicons, and constitutes a large part of our knowledge of language. He calls this conceptual information 'syntax' however, "because it has to do with mental representations and the structure of mental representations" (in Olson and Faigley 1991:93). What Chomsky is adamant about, however, is that linguistics cannot have anything to say about *reference*, the relationship between words and things in the real world. In Chomskyan linguistics, there is no bridging the internal structures of language with the outside world. *Ad hoc* extralinguistic contexts may be set up by hearers to enable them to interpret linguistic utterances, but this has little to do with linguistics, and everything to do with what Chomskyans regard as the separate discipline of pragmatics. (Verbal) communication in general may be parasitic upon language, but it does not determine language, and Chomsky has little to say about the issue (see Smith 1999:151-154). Likewise, speakers and writers may use language to act upon the world in certain ways, for example to impose authority, but this has little to do with the structures of language, and remains uninteresting to Chomsky, who claims the question has "no intellectual depth to it at all, like most things in the social sciences" (in Olson and Faigley 1991:88).

A final word will be said here about Chomsky's methodology: Chomsky's focus on competence, or I-language, has implications for how linguistic research is carried out, and for what constitutes evidence in a linguistic theory. Competence is

---

[1] The analysis of Saussure presented here draws on Beaugrande (1997, 1998), but see Lecercle (1990:29) for an alternative reading of Saussure, one that regards the latter's *langue* as "*radically* social and historical".

studied through introspection, and if the object language is the linguist's own native tongue, then the linguist's intuitive judgements about the well-formedness of particular sentences constitute valid data. The fact that the sentences invented by linguists to test their judgements are often outlandishly convoluted does not pose a particular problem for Chomskyans, who hold that there is "no requirement in science that the phenomena used as evidence should occur spontaneously under natural conditions" (Smith 1999:33).

Chomsky and translation theory

Given the universalist impulse in Chomskyan linguistics, its proponents may make appeals to cross-linguistic data to show that their analyses can be generalized to other, and ultimately all languages (see Smith 1999:75), but they have had very little interest in translation *per se*. Chomsky himself warned that even if all languages turned out to have certain deep-seated syntactic or semantic properties in common, this would not imply that there must be "some reasonable procedure for translating between languages" (1965:30), where "reasonable procedure" meant one that does not involve extralinguistic information (ibid:201-202, n.17). For Chomsky it was thus clear that translation was not an exclusively linguistic phenomenon, a lesson already learned by his colleagues working in machine translation. Nor was it something that his own transformational generative grammar could easily elucidate. Small wonder then that Louis Kelly (1979:23) could claim at the end of the 1970s that transformational generative grammar had had 'next to no influence on translation theory'.[2] Nevertheless, Chomsky did influence Nida's (1964) 'science' of translating.

Nida's debt to Chomsky revolves around his use – or abuse (Gentzler 1993:50) – of the notions of transformation and kernel sentence (Chomsky 1957) to underwrite precisely the kind of procedure for translating between languages that Chomsky denies is possible. In Nida's (1964:68) scheme, decoding a stretch of source text by undoing the transformations it has been subject to, reveals its structurally simple kernel sentences. Kernel sentences then become convenient pivots in translation, for two reasons: first, they are "remarkably similar" across languages, and second, at this level, languages display "a high degree of parallelism" between formal classes of words (e.g. nouns, verb, adjectives, etc) and their basic functions (objects, events, abstracts, and relationals). Nida thus finds support in linguistic theory for his contention that "that which unites mankind is much greater than that which divides, and hence there is, even in cases of very disparate languages and cultures, a basis for communication" (ibid:1). Such felicitous similarities allow Nida (ibid:68) to

---

[2] For similar views see Baker (in press), Fawcett (1997:72) and, ironically, given Gentzler's (1993:62-67) comments on Chomsky's influence on Wilss, Wilss (1982:68).

propose a translation method that is more satisfactory from a 'scientific' point of view than the kind of surface-structure oriented procedures advocated in comparative stylistics:

> Instead of attempting to set up transfers from one language to another by working out long series of equivalent formal structures which are presumably adequate to 'translate' from one language into another, it is both scientifically and practically more efficient (I) to reduce the source text to its structurally simplest and most semantically evident kernels, (2) to transfer the meaning from source language to receptor language on a structurally simple level, and (3) to generate the stylistically and semantically equivalent expression in the receptor language.

Nida thus offers a classic transfer model of translation without actually specifying what happens at the transfer stage: meaning is somehow transportable across languages, and therefore external to any particular language, though its passage from one language to the other is facilitated by simplifying the syntactic structures in which it is couched.

Edwin Gentzler (1993:43-60) has suggested that Nida's appeal to the science of linguistics is disingenuous, that Nida is really in the entirely unscientific business of spreading the word of God. He argues that Nida's basic position, revealed in his 1960 work *Message and Mission*, is that words are mere labels that can be replaced or adjusted as necessary to effect communication of the fundamental divine message, a message to which Nida, as translator-theologian, has privileged access. Gentzler's description of Nida is not unlike Beaugrande's depiction of Chomskyan linguists as "implicitly claiming a miraculous superhuman capacity to 'become aware of and report' an 'enormous mass of unquestionable data' that speakers themselves cannot – indeed to become aware of and report data about the 'competence' of the '*ideal* speaker-hearer' 'who knows the language *perfectly*'" (1997:177). Both Nida and Chomsky set themselves up as experts with access to a truth behind surface linguistic phenomena, though Nida still requires Chomsky to give his theory a scientific veneer. But if Chomsky was a 'Godsend' for Nida, as Gentzler (1993:46) puts it, then so were other linguists, and a number of theorists in related disciplines like communication theory, all of whom were pressed into service in Nida's science of translating.

For example, Nida also draws on the Bloomfieldian notion that the meaning of a linguistic form can be defined as "the situation in which the speaker utters it, and the response it calls forth from the hearer" (Bloomfield 1933:139). This decidedly un-Chomskyan, behaviourist position is described by Nida as "a healthy antidote to traditional mentalism, for language as a mode of action is described as a system of symbols which signal behavior, and not merely as countersigns of or indices to thought" (1964:37), and it is embraced by him in his favoured translation strategy of dynamic equivalence, which is directed at ensuring "equivalence of response rather than equivalence of form" (ibid:166). Yet Nida also embraces the mentalism of Katz and Fodor's (1963) semantic extension to Chomsky's transformational generative grammar. Katz and Fodor rely on mentally manipulated semantic features of problematic words and the words around them to explain how speakers can possibly understand each other in the face of pervasive lexical ambiguity. Having lent his support to this mentalist, semantic-features based approach to meaning (ibid:38-40), Nida goes on to reiterate an essentially empiricist, anti-mentalist tenet, namely that it is a mistake to think of the meaning of a word as isolated from the communicative events in which it is used, "for once we have isolated a word from its living context, we no longer possess the insight necessary to appreciate fully its real function" (ibid:40). We can thus begin to see Nida's science of translating as a pick-and-mix of contemporary, and often conflicting, linguistic theories. Nida's commitment to Chomsky's mentalist linguistics is not total, despite Gentzler's 'Godsend' theory.

Firthian linguistics

Much of what Michael Stubbs (1996:22) has described as the "enduring and distinctive vision of language study" in twentieth-century Britain has its origins in the work of John Rupert Firth (1890-1960). Firth's legacy lives on through the work of contemporary linguists like M.A.K. Halliday, John Sinclair and Stubbs himself, linguists whose collective work is often labelled 'Firthian', 'neo-Firthian', or, in Germany in particular, as adhering to the school of British Contextualism (Lehr 1996). Although Firth did not leave a "tidy and consistent body of writings" (Stubbs ibid:50), much of his work has been collated and published in two important volumes: papers from 1934 to 1951 appeared together in Firth (1957); and a posthumous collection of selected articles from the period 1952 to 1959 was edited by F.R. Palmer and published in Firth (1968). In tracing the main ideas of Firth's linguistics below, reference will be made to these two volumes, although the reader should keep in mind that the articles referred to may have been published much earlier than either 1957 or 1968. Firth's legacy is discussed in greater detail in Mitchell (1975) and Stubbs (1996), and Gregory (1980) outlines his ideas on translation.

If Chomsky's linguistics is essentially mentalist, Firth's is social. Firth maintained that linguists should take as their object of study "the speaking person in the social process" (1957:190). He held that linguistics should not concern itself with the study of Saussure's *langue*, a "system of signs placed in categories" (ibid:180) and divorced from the realities of actual speech, but rather should focus on "persons and personalities as active participators in the creation and maintenance of cultural values" (ibid:186). For Firth languages were essentially social and bound up with the contexts in which they are used and the cultures they perpetuate.

And if Chomsky focuses on syntax, Firth's central concern as a descriptive linguist was "to make statements of meaning" (1957:190), and to do so without recourse to "dualisms of mind and body, language and thought, word and idea, *signifiant et signifié*, expression and content" (ibid:227). Firth's distinctive approach to meaning draws on the basic postulate of 'context of situation', a schematic construct that links language very definitely with the outside world by relating to each other the following factors in a linguistic event:

A. The relevant features of participants: persons, personalities.
   (i) The verbal action of the participants.
   (ii) The non-verbal action of the participants.
B. The relevant objects.
C. The effect of the verbal action. (1957:182)

Firth (1968:175) stresses that contexts of situation are not the actual things, persons, etc, found in the immediate environment of speakers,[3] nor are they mere descriptions of the things and people involved in a particular utterance. Rather they are more generalised constructs abstracted from real linguistic experience and applicable to, and revisable in the light of, new instances of language in use. Such generalisations are possible because, despite the infinite variety of situations in which humans may find themselves, much of our linguistic activity is actually played out in routine contexts: "Speech is not the 'boundless chaos' Johnson thought it was. For most of us the roles and the lines are there, and that being so, the lines can be classified and correlated with the part and also with the episodes, scenes, and acts" (Firth 1957:28). The notion of routine in language use is one that has served neo-Firthian linguistics well, and will be taken up again below.

If the main task of descriptive linguistics is to make statements of meaning, and meaning is to be regarded as "situational relations in a context of situation" (1957:19), then the characterisation of these contexts takes on prime importance. Firth (ibid:27) suggests that the task of "describing and classifying typical contexts of situation within the context of culture" falls to "sociological linguistics". He acknowledges the difficulty of this task (ibid), but proposes some elementary categories that may be of use. These include whether participants are speaking or writing, listening or reading; whether the language used is of a familiar, colloquial or formal nature; whether the events are occurring in schools, law courts, or churches, etc (ibid:29-30). In this and later work (1968:177-8), Firth anticipates one of the foremost concerns of contemporary corpus builders, that is, the problem of text and corpus classification, which is still usually carried out on the basis of the kind of 'external' criteria suggested by Firth. Firth (ibid:31) also suggests that classifying linguistic functions might be easier than classifying situations, so that linguistic events could be classified according to whether, for example, speakers are agreeing or disagreeing,

[3] Although Firth borrowed the term 'context of situation' from Malinowski, his usage differed from that of Malinowski, for whom context of situation was not an abstraction, but rather 'in rebus' (see Palmer 1968:6).

encouraging or discouraging, etc, and along the broader lines of narrative types. Firth thus reveals a concern with context and function that distinguishes his linguistics sharply from the mentalist, formalist linguistics of Noam Chomsky, but links it to subsequent developments in Britain and to the functionalist tradition of the Prague School (see Beaugrande 1997).

Classifying contexts of situation is one problem; abstracting from actual experience is another. The linguist who studies meaning in relation to situational features is faced with the difficulty of somehow restricting those features to a manageable number. Firth suggests that this be achieved by focusing on texts.

> In dealing with language in the matrix of experience ... the actual language text duly recorded is in the focus of attention ... Relations are set up between the text and the other constituents of the situation, grouped and selected in attention as relevant. The linguist decides what is relevant ... (1968:173)

The insistence on the centrality of text is part of Firth's legacy to British linguistics and it is a basic position in corpus linguistics.[4] Like Firth (1968:112), corpus linguists insist that the language under description "must be exemplified by texts constituting an adequate *corpus inscriptionum*". But, as the above quote suggests, Firth's strongly empirical approach to linguistic data does not prevent him from acknowledging the role of intuition in selecting from "the mush of general goings-on" (ibid:199-200) features that are relevant to the task of making statements of meaning. There is no such thing as theory-free observation; what is important is that linguists do not impose pre-conceived theoretical categories on the data they encounter (1957:144), and also that the categories that they do use stand the test of re-application to "similar relevant events in renewal of connection with experience" (1968:199).

The first prong in Firth's method was to focus on real texts; the second to make statements of meaning about those texts with reference to relevant aspects of their context of situation. Such statements of meaning could not, however, be made in one fell swoop. Rather, meaning could be more tractably handled by its dispersion into a number of different levels, "rather like the dispersion of light of mixed wavelengths into a spectrum" (1957:192). Meaning was to be regarded as a complex of relations, with, phonetics, grammar, lexicography, and semantics each handling its own components of the complex (ibid:19). But although Firth refers to 'lower' and 'higher' levels and their arrangement in ascending order from phonetics to the rather vague notion of context of culture (ibid:198-199), he still maintains that "the total complex ... is a first postulate" (ibid:199). The interconnectedness of levels can be

---

[4] Note here though that Firth's insistence on the centrality of text may have been more aspirational than anything else. Stubbs (1996:30) reminds us that Firth "analyses little text, sometimes merely presenting texts as though their features were obvious".

seen, for example, in Firth's assertion that the phonaesthetic level – the level at which certain sounds, e.g. English word-initial *sl*, are associated with certain personal or social attitudes, in this case a pejorative one – correlates closely with features of contexts of situation, where such attitudes are most easily apprehended. Elsewhere, Firth makes the point even more strongly by insisting that "studies at one level must take into account findings at other levels" (1968:192), a position that was to take on particular importance in the work of Firth's successors, including corpus linguists such as Francis (1993), Sinclair (1991, 1996, 1997) and Tognini-Bonelli (1996a).

We have already seen that Firth rejected dualist approaches to meaning, in particular Saussure's (1916) idea of linguistic signs being made up of a *signifié*, a mental construct, the 'content' of the sign, and a *signifiant*, the acoustic noise or graphic form that stands for that concept. He did, however, make use of other concepts from Saussure's linguistics, in particular when describing linguistic structures and systems in terms of syntagma and paradigms:

> Structure, whether it be phonological or grammatical, is a syntagmatic relationship. It is an interrelationship of elements within the text or part of the text,[5] whereas a system such as a system of vowels or a system of grammatical forms is in the nature of a paradigm. The values of a paradigm are determined by the interior relations within the paradigm itself. (1968:103)

Linguistic structures and systems, Firth held, could be related to each other, and to structures and systems in the wider context of situation. This is how Firth proposed that translation be approached.

Firth and translation theory

It is well known that Firth drew heavily on the work of the anthropologist Malinowski. It was through his contact with anthropology, and its need to express in the anthropologist's language what had been observed in another, that Firth's attention was called to translation. His main ideas on the subject were outlined in two papers delivered in 1956 (reprinted in 1968:74-83, 1968:84-95). In these papers Firth takes a stand on a number of theoretical issues, claiming for example that although descriptive linguists had to draw on a common stock of grammatical terms, this did not imply any recognition of "grammatical universals" (1968:75). He also characteristically rejects the mentalist notion of "naked ideas" insisting that linguists "must always bear in mind that the English word 'kindness', for example, does not represent a 'naked idea' of any value to linguistics, and in that sense no other language in

---

[5] Note though, that although structures are attested within texts, like systems, they are abstractions. Structures are abstracted from textual form; they are more than mere segments of text and have an order "which is not merely a sequence" (1968:186).

the world has a word for 'kindness'"(1968:75). Nor could communication theory could be brought to bear on the problem of translation as it was "not concerned with meaning in any psychological or social sense" (1968:86). Firth was adamant that context of situation, although difficult to characterize, provided the soundest theoretical basis for translation (1968:91):

> You have the option of connecting structures and systems of language with structures and systems of thought or with structures and systems in situations comprising the human participants, their non-verbal behaviour, the relevant objects and other events and of these two alternatives, I suggest – difficult though it may appear – that the situational matrix is the more manageable one and more easily related to the problems of translation.

Shared experience, Firth suggests, allows us to set up "common human situations of an abstract nature' to form one of the 'bridges' between source and target languages. The abstract inter-situation thus formed could be considered to have common elements 'in everything but language text" (1968:82). As source and target language situations converge, for example in areas of activity that give rise to restricted languages, it becomes easier to build the translation "bridge" between the two (1968:109-110). But there will remain cases where elements of the source situation cannot find analogues in the target situation.

Finally, although Firth is adamant that (word-for-word interlinear) translations cannot be used as a basis for linguistic description, he is convinced that linguistic description can be used as a basis for translation: linguistic analysis at the grammatical, lexical, collocational and situational levels can be used as a basis for "total translation" (1968:76-78). And the more material levels of language also have consequences for translation: while phonological meaning, according to Firth, presents insurmountable difficulties for the translator (1957:193), graphological meaning can be translated using the resources of grammar and lexis, a feat Ezra Pound performed in finding metaphorical meaning in the structure of Chinese ideograms (see Firth 1968:92).

The above comments give some idea of the purview of Firth's linguistics. He was concerned with broad questions, such as how texts relate to their contexts of situation, how patterns of speech accumulate to form idiolects and sociolects, and how speakers use language to create and maintain cultural values.[6] But this often meant zooming in on the 'smaller' units of linguistic description – phonemes, and graphic and prosodic elements. And while he stressed the linguist's need to make statements of meaning, he was also acutely aware of the materiality of language, its "music" and "plastic form" (Oscar Wilde, quoted in Firth 1957:193). Indeed, he saw the phonological, prosodic and graphological levels as making their own con-

---

[6] For a sample of Firth's treatment of idiolects and sociolects see 'Modes of Meaning' (1957:190-215) where he discusses Walter Swinburne's poetic diction, and a collection of eighteenth- and early nineteenth-century letters. On cultural values, see Firth (1957:186).

tributions to the complex meaning of texts, including literary texts. We have also seen that Firth's approach to translation was holistic and contingent, relying as it did on the more-or-less nature of "inter-situation" rather than sure-fire "transcoding" operations or language-independent meaning atoms or "naked ideas". He was equally aware of the importance of contextualization in translation, distinguishing, for example, between the lawyer's and the historian's translation requirements (1968:88-89). And he adverted to the role of translation in "enriching" the target language (ibid:87), and to the differing careers of originals and translated texts in their respective cultures (ibid:109). Firth's writings on translation may not have been extensive, but they certainly were concerned with the big picture. His was hardly a case of linguistics-induced myopia.

It is probably because Firth had such a wide range as a linguist, because he refused to idealize "the speaking person in the social process" and to divorce languages from speakers and cultural values, because he was concerned with real texts and convinced that their complexities could not be handled by some elegant mechanism in one fell swoop, that Firth's linguistics is not rigorous in the mathematical or logical sense. The language use that Firth took as his object of inquiry simply did not lend itself to such a treatment. But in the academic environment of the second half of the twentieth century, when linguistics had come to be associated with formalisms and deterministic syntax-driven systems of rules, Firthian linguistics became eclipsed by Chomskyan linguistics, in translation studies as elsewhere.

There are, of course, problems with Firth's writings. They are often programmatic in nature, suggesting avenues for empirical research rather than engaging in it, and some of Firth's insights are fleeting, raising as many questions as they provide answers.[7] Contexts of situation and especially inter-situations can be difficult to pin down and make operational in studies of real translation, and the idea of a common human situation is not one that would find approval with all theorists (see, for example, Frawley 1984:163-164). Yet much of what Firth had to say was taken up in subsequent linguistically-oriented treatments of translation, initially by Halliday (1964) and Catford (1965).

Both Halliday and Catford relate translation to the notion of context of situation, with Catford claiming that "SL and TL texts or items are translation equivalents when they are *interchangeable in a given situation*" (ibid:49). Interchangeability relies on the fact that source and target language texts are relatable to at least some of the same features of the situation, as a complete match would be impossible (ibid:50).[8] Both Halliday and Catford are concerned with the notion of equivalence,

---

[7] See, for example, Firth's treatment of collocation discussed in Chapter Four.

[8] See also Halliday's (1964:124) claim that translation is "the relation between two texts playing an identical part in an identical situation", where the inappropriate word 'identical' is immediately qualified by saying that it does not represent an absolute concept as "two situations in which the language activity is in different languages are *ipso facto* not identical' and 'situations vary across cultures" (ibid).

a *bête noire* in translation studies, if ever there was one (see Snell-Hornby 1988a:13-22; and Gentzler 1993:4), but are careful to distinguish between equivalence as a hypothetical mapping between formal items in two abstract language systems, and as an empirical category, representing the relationship between SL and TL texts or portions of texts that are observed to be equivalent to each other. The first relationship Catford dubs "formal correspondence"; the second "textual equivalence" (1965:27).[9] The establishment of textual equivalence is logically and chronologically prior to that of formal correspondence for both authors,[10] although formal correspondence remains an important concept for Catford in that it helps to explain the nature of "translation shifts" (ibid:73-82). But although both Halliday and Catford appear to privilege actual matches between stretches of text over potential matches between abstract language systems, this is where their empiricism starts and stops: Halliday uses only a single sentence (from Colette's *Gigi* in French and English) to exemplify his ideas on translation, and the vast majority of the examples of 'translation' proffered by Catford are invented by the author.[11] For all of the Firthian preoccupation with real text, Firth and his immediate successors analyse precious little real translated text.

The sparsity of translation analysis in these writings is probably due to the fact that all three authors were more interested in trying out their favourite linguistic theory on translation, as Baker (in press) puts it, than in investigating translation in and for itself. And Halliday and Catford clearly were making territorial claims for linguistics, attempting to subsume translation under the rubric of 'comparative' or 'applied linguistics'.[12] But it is also the case that Catford, in particular, was putting theory before empirical research, attempting to develop an elegant, and as near exhaustive apparatus as possible, for the future analysis of translations (1965:vii). This he attempted by adopting wholesale a single theory of grammar – that of Halliday (1961) – to characterize translation in exclusively linguistic terms.[13] When Catford

[9] For a critique of Catford's and other approaches to equivalence in translation, see Kenny (1998a).

[10] See Halliday (1964:115) where he claims that if items in two languages "are not at least sometimes equivalent in translation", then "they are not worth comparing" and that only when we have decided that items are comparable in this way does it make sense to ask "to what extent they are formally equivalent". Catford is more tentative when he claims "It may be ... that formal correspondence can only be established ultimately on the basis of textual equivalence at some point" (1965:32).

[11] Catford uses the euphemism "decontextualized texts" (1965:27 n.1) to describe these invented examples. Mary Snell-Hornby is less charitable when she describes them as "absurdly simplistic sentences" and "isolated words" (1988a:20).

[12] See Halliday's assertion that "comparative descriptive linguistics includes the theory of translation" (1964:112), and Catford's claims that "the theory of translation is essentially a theory of applied linguistics" (1965:19) and "the theory of translation is concerned with a certain type of relation between languages and is consequently a branch of Comparative Linguistics" (ibid:20).

[13] Catford's approach thus differs considerably from Nida's (1964) linguistic eclecticism, or the "tool-kit" (Venuti 2000:340) pragmatism of contemporary linguistically-oriented writers on translation (see also Baker, in press).

does step outside the bounds of this linguistic theory to address the question of "cultural untranslatability" (ibid:99-101), he focuses on simplistic aspects of material culture – saunas and bath-robes, as they might impinge upon imaginary translations from Finnish and Japanese. And even then, cultural untranslatability, he claims, may be reducible to a form of linguistic, specifically collocational, untranslatability (ibid:101). Because Catford limits his discussion of translation to those aspects that can be elucidated with reference to a certain linguistic theory, and because he analyses, almost exclusively, invented sentences, designed to accommodate the theory rather than be indicative of real translation problems, his theory of translation is hopelessly restricted in its scope. It never engages with questions of ideology or the dynamics of the translation market-place. It ignores textual phenomena, and does not consider that translated language may have a specificity not accessible to the comparative linguist's intuitions. And apart from a brief admission that translation involves subjectivity (ibid:94), the translating subject is noticeably absent in Catford's theory.

It may come as no surprise then, that Catford's theory of translation came to be associated with a discredited linguistic tradition in translation studies (Baker, in press).[14] But there is much in Catford that is interesting, either because (1) it anticipates later developments in translation studies, or (2) it presents a view of language that some critics from within cultural studies would not necessarily associate with linguistics. On the first point, even if he does eschew any treatment of real translated text, Catford does foresee the use of corpora of source texts and their translations to monitor shifts in translation (1965:81-82), and to establish probabilistic translation rules for use in Machine Translation (ibid:31).[15] On the second point, by including a discussion of the potential of graphic and phonic form in translation, Catford draws attention to the materiality of language. He also insists that the concept of a whole language "is so vast and heterogeneous that it is not operationally useful for many linguistic purposes" (ibid:83) and therefore introduces language varieties to his discussion of translation, taking in concerns of dialect, sociolect, diachronic variation, and register (ibid:84-92). Finally, he takes a monist approach to meaning, claiming that meaning is a property of language, arising from a complex of 1) formal relations between items internal to a language and 2) relations between grammatical and lexical items and "linguistically relevant elements in the situations in which the items operate as, or in, texts" (ibid:36). Thus "An SL text has an SL meaning, and a TL text has a TL meaning" (ibid:35); and there can be no talk of texts in two different languages having the same meaning, or of meaning being extracted from a text

---

[14] See Baker (in press) and Fawcett (1997) for a discussion of other criticisms of Catford, and also answers to some of these criticisms.

[15] See Bakker *et al.* (1998) for an overview of shift analysis in translation studies and Munday (1998) for a discussion of how an electronic corpus of source texts and their translations can be used to study shifts. On the use of corpora in statistical Machine Translation, see Brown *et al.* (1990).

in one language and 'transferred' into a text in another language. This monist view of meaning also makes it impossible to theorize translation as a transcoding process. There can be no "pre-existent 'message' with an independent meaning of its own" that can be presented in one code, or language, and then in another (ibid:41). In all this, we can discern Firth's legacy. Firthian linguistics is highly empirical in its approach, allowing, if not requiring, the use of corpora in linguistic research, and probabilities in statements about language. It rejects the notion that meaning is external to language, and emphasises the role in creating meaning of both language system and the situational contexts in which utterances are made. Finally, it does not shy away from the materiality or heterogeneity of language. These are all features that separate Firthian from Chomskyan linguistics, and that characterise in part many of the approaches to translation that follow in the Firthian tradition.

The strength of the Firthian tradition in British linguistics can be seen in Stubbs's (1996) volume on text and corpus analysis. It also evident in much of the work conducted in translation studies in Britain in the 1990s, in which the emphasis has been on studying real texts using the tools of functionally oriented linguistics, and relating the features of these texts to their wider social and cultural contexts, often drawing on insights from critical linguistics. Baker (1992), Bell (1991), Hatim and Mason (1990, 1997) and Harvey (1998) are examples of such work, and studies in the emerging area of corpus-based translation studies also have the potential to continue in this tradition (see, for example, Kenny 1998b). But, as I will argue below, the Firthian tradition has often been overlooked by critics of linguistically-oriented translation studies, for whom Saussure and Chomsky still reign supreme.

The postmodern critique of linguistics in translation studies

This Chapter opened with a potted history of linguistics in translation studies and an indication of some of the criticisms levelled against linguistically-oriented approaches to translation. As already mentioned, some of these criticisms have been addressed by commentators like Mona Baker and Peter Fawcett, and it is not my intention to revisit ground that they have covered in detail. Rather, I have been more concerned with highlighting the differences between two competing conceptions of linguistics in order to give a small taste of the diversity within the area, and to prepare the ground for a discussion of corpus linguistics in Chapter Two. But I have made some comments about postmodern reflections on linguistics, and these comments now need to be fleshed out.[16]

[16] The term 'postmodernism' as used here and elsewhere is intended to be loosely synonymous with 'poststructuralism'. For a discussion of the similarities and differences between the two, see

Rosemary Arrojo (1998) criticizes linguistics for being implicated in the kind of essentialism that promotes the idea of stable meanings that are fully present in, and recoverable from, texts. This idea is said to underlie the view of translation as "a form of meaning recovery and transferral without essential loss" (ibid:28), and relies on a belief in the possibility of separating signified from signifier. Meaning, in this scheme, transcends form, so not only is it separable from form, it is also more important than form. The signifier is thus downplayed in a fashion that runs counter to the postmodern agenda (see also Venuti 1995). But although Arrojo claims to be reacting against linguistic approaches to translation (amongst others), her objection to the separation of form and content is one that is actually shared by some linguists. We have already seen that Firth and Catford objected to the view that meaning could somehow be fully outside language, but linguists who have followed in Firth's footsteps have made even stronger claims about the inseparability of meaning and form: the linguist and lexicographer John Sinclair has gone as far as saying that meaning and form are actually one and the same thing (1991:7), a point that will be taken up again in this book.

Sinclair's conviction comes from experience of dealing with an abundance of real texts. The volume of texts that contemporary linguists can cope with, and the speed at which these texts can be processed, are a direct result of the use of computers to support linguistic analysis. But the use of computers has another, perhaps unexpected consequence: insofar as the words contained in a 'raw' computerized corpus are simply uninterpreted strings of graphic symbols – as far as the software used to sort and display them is concerned – they are, in the first instance at least, signifiers and nothing else.[17] Even though the human analyst will almost inevitably interpret the word forms displayed by the computer, she or he is always aware that the tool in use, the computer, has access primarily to the materiality of those forms. This ensures that signifiers are not completely downgraded, as Arrojo fears they

---

Sarup (1988). Although 'postmodernism' is notoriously difficult to define, Cahoone (1996:2) offers the following useful compromise:

> When most philosophers use the word "postmodern" they mean to refer to a movement that developed in France in the 1960s, more precisely called "poststructuralism," along with subsequent and related developments. They have in mind that this movement denies the possibility of objective knowledge of the real world, "univocal" (single or primary) meaning of words and texts, the unity of the human self, the cogency of the distinctions between rational inquiry and political action, literal and metaphorical meaning, science and art, and even the possibility of truth itself. Simply put, they regard it as rejecting most of the fundamental intellectual pillars of modern Western civilization.

[17] I am concentrating here on the visual materiality of written words, but insofar as the spelling systems of languages like English and German are based on phonemic principles (with a number of important departures from these principles), we can also claim some correspondence between the visual and the acoustic.

might be. The corpus linguist is less in need than others of Lecercle's reminder that "Words do not only *do* things; they *are* things" (1990:47).

The postmodern critique of linguistic approaches to translation also questions the latter's supposed assumption that translation can somehow be indifferent to the circumstances in which it takes places, or unaffected by the subjectivity of the translator (see Arrojo 1998; Venuti 1996, 1997). Arrojo does, however, concede that linguistics and linguistically-oriented studies of translation have made progress in recent years, principally by embracing questions of ideology in language use, as evidenced in critical linguistics and discourse analysis (ibid:34). This concession shows an awareness of the more functionally, sociologically oriented linguistics that has flourished in Britain since Firth's time, and has also made a significant impact in Arrojo's native Brazil. But if Arrojo is aware of such developments, other critics of linguistics in translation studies have tended to assume that linguistics is an undifferentiated monolith fashioned along mentalist, formalist lines: witness Lawrence Venuti's claim that linguistically-oriented translation scholars see language as "a set of systematic rules autonomous from cultural and social variation" (1996:108), in other words through Chomsky-coloured glasses. And while Edwin Gentzler (1993:51) refers to doubts raised by "many creative writers, literary theorists, and translation practitioners" about the appropriateness of applying Chomskyan linguistics to the study of literature, he does not mention any objections to Chomsky's approach emanating from within linguistics itself, as if such objections did not exist. Gentzler even quotes Barbara Herrnstein Smith in an effort to undermine Chomsky's apparent monopoly on the study of language, but apart from a short reference to the linguistics of J.C. Catford (Gentzler 1993:96-98), he effectively ignores other linguists, thereby giving the impression that Chomsky is indeed the only linguist. Herrnstein Smith asks:

> Is linguistics a monolithic discipline? Specifically, is it equivalent to transformational-generative grammar? If not, is Chomsky's theory of language and the transformational-generative grammarians' pursuit of its study the only and/or the most suitable model for the theory of literature and the pursuit of its study? And, in any case, are the assumptions, procedures, concepts, and conclusions of linguistics themselves so well established, so free from internal problems or external criticism that the literary theorists are well advised to adopt and apply them unreflectingly? (1978:178, quoted in Gentzler 1993:51)

The answer to all of the above questions from within the Firthian school of linguistics is a resounding 'no', but this is a view that has not made as much impact in the United States as it has in Britain. That this should be the case is not surprising, given the vehemence with which Chomskyan linguists proclaim their domination: for Newmeyer (1980) linguistic theory in America is practically synonymous with transformational generative grammar, Chomsky's theory having become the "established" linguistic theory in the U.S. by 1970, if not before (ibid:20). The irony remains, however, that some of those who, in pursuit of a postmodern agenda, decry the promotion of scientific models in translation studies, seem to acknowledge only those flavours of linguistics that are self-consciously oriented towards the natural sciences, and that rely on what Beaugrande (1994:165) has playfully termed the "u-s-a hypothesis", that is, the assumption that language is a **u**niform, **s**table, **a**bstract system.[18] Seen in this light, Venuti's foreignizing translation may be a reaction to the global hegemony of English, and the political and economic ascendancy of the United States (1996:92), but his description of what linguistics is about does little to combat the hegemony of American, Chomskyan linguistics.

This is not to suggest that Venuti is unaware of, or indifferent to, other thrusts in linguistically-oriented translation studies. Indeed he makes a number of highly pertinent comments about the application to translation of Grice's (1975) theory of conversational implicature (Venuti 1996:104-108), but even here there is no challenge to Chomsky. The Gricean conception of communication, like Sperber and Wilson's (1986) competing model, is one that can sit happily on top of Chomsky's vision of language. It theorizes communication as relying on a system of inferences (belonging to the domain of pragmatics), made on the basis of clues supplied by a message in a particular linguistic code, the properties of which can be described and explained by the neighbouring discipline of (Chomskyan) linguistics. Grice and Chomsky are perfectly compatible because they investigate different, non-overlapping objects (Smith 1999:151-154).[19] What they have in common is that they both use invented, or 'purified' data (Lecercle 1990: 261, Stubbs 1996:29-30, Venuti 1996:105,108), thus maintaining the idealizations of speakers and speech situations on which their visions of language or language use are based. From a neo-Firthian point of view, Venuti is right to criticize 'autonomous' linguistics and Gricean models of conversation, but he would be wrong to assume that this is all there is to linguistics.

Nor is Venuti's focus on Chomsky and Grice peculiarly American. His view of linguistics tends to be reinforced by appeal to the work of French theorists Gilles Deleuze and Félix Guattari (1980/1987), and Jean-Jacques Lecercle (1990). Deleuze and Guatarri's 'rhizomes' are a reaction to Chomsky's trees; their agonistic view of communication a reaction to Grice's irenic one. Lecercle's 'remainder' is intended to cover the anachronistic, playful, and non-standard uses of language that fall outside of what mainstream, that is, Saussurian and Chomskyan linguistics can deal

---

[18] Beaugrande acknowledges in parentheses, however, that the u-s-a hypothesis is "by no means limited to or universally accepted in the real USA" (1994:165).

[19] Those working in the Firthian tradition, however, cannot make such an easy distinction between pragmatics and linguistics. When the focus of the linguist's inquiry is language in use, pragmatic factors will always impinge upon other, more formal aspects of language (see Chapter Four).

with. Venuti, Deleuze and Guatarri, and Lecercle all offer thought-provoking analyses of the shortcomings of much contemporary linguistic and pragmatic theory, but they might be surprised to find that their misgivings are shared by many in the functional linguistic tradition that I have linked here to Firth and his successors. By promoting a linguistically-oriented, corpus-based study of translation that (1) focuses on real texts rather than idealized translation situations, (2) attempts to link textual patterns to wider cultural, ideological and economic considerations, and (3) embraces the creative aspects of language in use, I hope to go some way towards countering the view that linguistics is solely concerned with an abstract, autonomous, and prescriptively determined language system.

To be fair to Venuti, he has already acknowledged the usefulness of corpus linguistic techniques in investigating the specificity of translation (2000:335-336),[20] and in supporting historical studies, "confirming or questioning hypotheses about translation in specific periods and locales" (ibid:336). He is also largely sympathetic to Keith Harvey's application of ideas from critical linguistics and politeness theory in his study of translated camp talk in French and English-language fiction, claiming that Harvey advances linguistic approaches to translation because he makes textual effects intelligible by referring to "specific cultural and political differences" between the countries involved (ibid:340). But Venuti is still clearly sceptical of universalizing tendencies in "certain types of linguistics" (ibid).

So this is where things stand now. Postmodern critics of linguistics tend to see non-essentialist, non-universalizing approaches as the exception rather than the rule in linguistically-oriented translation studies, but at least they acknowledge their existence. They also concede that certain linguistically-oriented theorists are aware of the ideological import of translations, but object that the same theorists remain unaware of, or unwilling to address, their own ideological bias in promoting certain values (rigour, coherence, objectivity) over others (ideological engagement, heterogeneity, subjectivity) in translation research.[21]

It is against the background of this uneasy truce that my study of lexical creativity in GEPCOLT is presented. I am mindful of the fact that my work has its roots in (a certain kind of) linguistic theory, and of the (justified or unjustified) prejudices that this might arouse. I am also aware of the sobering lessons that (some) linguists have learned from postmodern philosophy,[22] and will studiously avoid any sugges-

---

[20] Venuti (2000:5, 335) actually refers to the "autonomy" rather than the "specificity" of translation, but I have used the latter term here, to avoid confusion with autonomy as it has been understood in this Chapter so far.

[21] See here Arrojo's (1998) comments on Baker (1992), and Venuti's (1997) comments on Toury (1995), whom he considers as subscribing to "a linguistics-based orientation that aims to construct an empirical science of translation" (Venuti 1997:360).

[22] Graddol *et al.* (1994), an introductory textbook in descriptive linguistics, contains a particularly clear expression of how postmodernism has brought with it a number of serious challenges

tion that mine is a definitive, exhaustive or completely objective treatment of my research question. But I remain convinced that their Firthian pedigree makes many ideas from contemporary corpus linguistics eminently suitable for application in translation studies, and I am greatly enthusiastic about the possibilities that computers open up for linguistic research. These are issues I will expand upon in Chapter Two. Suffice it to say for the moment that I do not offer a grand theory of anything, but I do wish to suggest new ways of investigating translation that may be acceptable to both linguists and those working in cultural studies.

Conclusion

In this Chapter I have described the role of linguistics in much twentieth-century translation scholarship, focusing in particular on the work of Noam Chomsky and J.R. Firth. I have argued that although Firth would appear to escape many of the criticisms levelled at linguists in translation studies, his contribution has been consistently overlooked by critics, who have tended instead to view linguistics as a monolith fashioned along Chomskyan lines. Finally, I suggested that the Firthian approach, and its latter-day incarnation in corpus linguistics, might bear fruit in studies of translation. This is already happening to a certain extent in the area that has become known as corpus-based translation studies.

---

to assumptions traditionally made in linguistics (ibid:25-27). Chapters Six and Seven provide many examples of how linguists are attempting to rise to these challenges in their analyses of language use. This work shows how a large number of linguists have not been immune to postmodern currents in contemporary thought, even if Noam Chomsky remains "a devoted eighteenth-century rationalist" (Olson and Faigley 1991:64).

2. The Soft Option: Corpus Linguistics

> The most important skill is not to be able to program a computer or even to manipulate available software ... Rather, it is to be able to ask insightful questions which address real issues and problems in theoretical, descriptive and applied language studies.
>
> Graeme Kennedy (1998:3)

Introduction

A corpus is a body of texts assembled in some principled way. When we use the word corpus, there is usually also the expectation that the texts thus assembled are to be subjected to some kind of scholarly analysis. Shakespeare's collected works are his oeuvre, but when I study them they become my corpus. As such, corpora have been around for a very long time, but they have been around in hard copy, usually in the form of texts printed on paper. When Ria Vanderauwera (1985) put together a collection of Dutch novels translated into English in order to conduct her seminal research in descriptive translation studies, she was assembling a corpus. She did so according to very specific criteria related to genre, date of publication, and source and target language. But hers was a hard-copy corpus, the detailed analysis of which became a "laborious and tiresome business" (ibid:6). More recent corpus-based translation studies have taken the soft option: they have used computers to manipulate large quantities of linguistic data sourced in electronic or 'machine-readable' texts. Many such studies have drawn on the techniques and methodologies of corpus linguistics in order to investigate hypotheses that have emerged from work in descriptive translation studies. Computerized corpus-based translation studies viewed in this light stems from a union between corpus linguistics and descriptive translation studies.[1] In this and the next Chapter, I introduce the parent disciplines before going on to trace the development of their offspring. While much of the discussion in this Chapter will be concerned with methodological, institutional and technical issues in contemporary corpus linguistics, I will also attempt to show how much work in the area continues in the linguistic tradition of J. R. Firth, as described in Chapter One. But the discussion will look forwards as well as backwards, preparing the ground for a treatment of my own corpus-based methodology in Chapter Five.

---

[1] Not all uses of corpora in translation studies can trace their lineage to descriptive translation studies (DTS) as understood here however. Certain pedagogical approaches, in particular, use corpora in ways that owe little allegiance to DTS (see, for example, Bowker 1998; Zanettin 1998).

Corpus linguistics

Corpus linguistics is the branch of linguistics that studies language on the basis of corpora. It has become normal for the texts that constitute such corpora to be stored and processed in electronic form, so that for many commentators (for example, Renouf 1987a:1; Baker 1995:226), a corpus is by definition held on some kind of computer-storage medium and analyzable automatically or semi-automatically. But a corpus is not just any collection of electronic text: the fact that texts are assembled 'in a principled way' presupposes a set of criteria governing the compilation of a corpus, criteria presumably settled upon in order to make the corpus representative of some language or subset of a language. Much effort has been devoted to the vexed question of representativeness in corpora, as well as to wider issues of corpus design, and I will return to these issues in Chapter Five. For the moment it is sufficient to note that a corpus consists of real texts, ones that have occurred naturally, without the intervention of the linguist (Stubbs 1996:4). The requirement that corpora consist of naturally occurring texts means that the sets of unconnected and sometimes invented sentences used in Natural Language Processing, and especially in speech processing (Leech and Fligelstone 1992:115,119), cannot be considered 'corpora' for current purposes; nor can the kind of data elicited from native speakers by American structural linguists in the first half of the twentieth century (Sebba and Fligelstone 1994:770). The texts contained in a corpus can, of course, be records of written or spoken communicative events. But given that the focus of this book is on the translation of written texts, spoken language will be mentioned only in passing.[2] Finally, Johansson (1995:19) points out that corpus linguistics differs from other sub-disciplines in linguistics, for example sociolinguistics and psycholinguistics, in that "it is not defined by the object of study ... the object of corpus linguistics is *not* the study of corpora. It is rather the study of language through corpora". Leech (1992:105) likewise stresses that corpus linguistics refers "not to a domain of study, but rather to a methodological basis for pursuing linguistic research". Corpora thus provide data for the study of language; and corpus linguistics the methodological apparatus and analytical tools. In corpus-based translation studies, an attempt is made to study *translation* through corpora, using, and if necessary adapting, the methodologies and tools of corpus linguistics.

Corpora: a brief history

Francis (1992) gives an account of corpora before the advent of the computer, starting with Dr. Johnson's use of citations held on paper slips in the compilation of

---

[2] For a discussion of how corpora of written and transcribed spoken language may impact on the area of Interpreting Studies, see Shlesinger (1998).

his 1755 dictionary. Other lexicographers followed in Johnson's footsteps, and records of attested use were also exploited in dialect studies and grammatology in the nineteenth and early twentieth centuries. The major difficulty with such undertakings in the field of grammar was that they were inevitably skewed in the direction of "the unusual and interesting constructions that the readers encounter", and away from "the normal core of language" (Francis ibid:28-29). A similar problem occurred in lexicography, where the compilers of both the *Oxford English Dictionary* and the *Webster's Dictionary* found that they did not have enough citations to exemplify the use of frequent, simple words like prepositions, articles and pronouns (ibid:22). A further limitation of early pre-computer corpus work was that it was based predominantly on the written language. Such shortcomings led Sir Randolph Quirk to initiate the Survey of English Usage in 1959. The Survey was to cover both written and spoken English, comprise 200 samples from a variety of registers, and be reasonably representative of the English used by educated people. In short, it was to contain material on which could be based a grammar of 'standard' English (ibid:29). At the time of its inception there were no plans to computerize the Survey of English Usage. The spoken part of the Survey was, however, later computerized yielding the London-Lund Corpus (Svartvik 1990). The honour of being the first corpus of English to be held on computer, however, goes to the Brown Corpus (Kučera and Francis 1967). It was compiled between 1961 and 1964 at Brown University in the USA by Nelson Francis and Henry Kučera and consists of one million words of American English, published in 1961, and distributed across 500 text samples each of 2,000 words. The texts fall into fifteen predetermined categories, including informative and imaginative writing, and were randomly sampled within those categories. The Lancaster-Oslo-Bergen (LOB) Corpus (Johansson 1980), which was compiled between 1970 and 1978, was designed to parallel the Brown Corpus in every way but one: the LOB Corpus contains samples from British English texts published in 1961.

The Brown and LOB Corpora are still in use, more than thirty years after the former first became available. Value has been added to the corpora through part-of-speech tagging and they have proved useful in general linguistic (Stubbs 1996) and computational linguistic (see Garside *et al.*. 1987) research. By today's standards, however, these first-generation corpora are very small: recent general-purpose corpora like the British National Corpus (BNC), made available in 1995, and the Cobuild Bank of English, under continuous development at the University of Birmingham since 1980, run to 100 million and 320 million words respectively.[3] The Brown and LOB Corpora are notable for another reason: following the example of their pred-

[3] Information on the Bank of English is available at the Cobuild website, URL: http://titania.cobuild.collins.co.uk/boe_info.html. For details of the BNC see Chapter Five, this volume, or visit http://info.ox.ac.uk/bnc/.

ecessor, the Survey of English Usage, they demonstrate an attempt to represent (written) English as a whole through the judicious use of samples from a variety of text categories. Contemporary corpora like the BNC also attempt to be representative of an entire variety of English, although the BNC is more democratic than some of its predecessors, in that it seeks to represent not just the standard language as exemplified by the speech of 'educated' speakers, but that of speakers in a range of socioeconomic classes, ages, etc. Yet other recent endeavours have taken a different approach, aiming to cover a restricted subject area like the petroleum industry (Zhu 1989), or assembling a corpus for a 'special purpose', such as the extraction of definition statements from its constituent texts (Pearson 1998:48; see also Kennedy 1998:33-45). 'Monitor' corpora (Clear 1988; Sinclair 1991:24-26, 1992a:382), finally, differ from static corpora of text samples in that they attempt to use the vast potential of modern computing to extract linguistic information from a steady through-flow of unrestricted electronic text: once a text has been filtered by the computer system, the results of any analysis carried out are directed to an on-line database and the text itself is dumped or stored temporarily in a "sump" (Clear ibid:384).

As the above discussion suggests, the 1980s and 1990s saw a proliferation of new corpora of various types. They also saw a number of initiatives aimed at collecting and disseminating textual material among the international research community. Leech and Fligelstone (1992) and Aijmer and Altenberg (1991:Appendix) provide useful summaries of the English-language corpora available in the early 1990s, often from international bodies such as the International Computer Archive of Modern and Medieval English (ICAME) in Norway. McEnery and Wilson (1996:Appendix A) provide a more up-to-date list that also includes bilingual and multilingual corpora. Armstrong-Warwick (1994), Kennedy (1998), and Hockey (1998) all report on national and international projects aimed at creating and disseminating corpus resources, often for a fee. Armstrong-Warwick describes the American-oriented Data Collection Initiative (started in 1989) and the European Corpus Initiative (1991) as early largely volunteer efforts in the area. These initiatives were succeeded by more official projects like the US government-sponsored Linguistic Data Consortium, founded in 1992, and the Network for European Corpora, and later the RELATOR project, both supported by the Commission of the European Communities. These official projects demonstrate what is now perceived to be the strategic importance of corpora in the development of human language technologies on the one hand, and language planning and maintenance on the other.

The last two decades of the twentieth century were also characterized by a growth in individual researchers' capacities to process corpora. Thanks to increasing computer power and storage capacity and improved techniques for manipulating textual data, individual researchers can now hold a multi-million word corpus on the hard disk of their personal computers. This means that corpus-based studies of language are no longer restricted to large research teams sharing a mainframe computer, the scenario described by Sampson (1987) and Clear (1987). Technological advances have also meant that there is more electronic text to be had these days. Some commentators write of corpora that have "grown up for reasons totally unconnected with research" (Leech and Fligelstone 1992:118), such as the corpus of the American Printing House for the Blind, developed for the automatic conversion of written text into Braille. And corpora like the Associated Press Corpus are described as 'spin-offs' from modern computerized communications (Fillmore 1992:40). Atkins *et al.* (1994:26-27) stress the importance of phototypesetting in book publishing, which has meant the creation of an electronic version on printer's tape of every text to be printed, although others warn that typesetting tapes can be unwieldy, and often do not correspond to the final printed version of a work (Hockey 1998:107). Computerized reporting techniques have also meant that researchers can now avail themselves of huge electronic corpora of parliamentary proceedings, the Canadian Hansards (see Chapter Three), for instance, and newspaper texts: many newspapers and journals are now published in full on CD-ROM.[4] But just because a work is/was once available somewhere in electronic form, this does not mean that small-scale researchers who have succeeded in getting permission to use that work will necessarily be able to get their hands on an electronic copy. Publishers may not have the time or may simply be unable to trace electronic copies of their publications. Sometimes they may even find it cheaper to throw away typesetting tapes and disks rather than incur costs in keeping them (Hockey ibid). In such cases corpus compilers may have to re-convert desired texts to electronic form either by keyboarding or scanning, a process that is not without its difficulties (see Chapter Five). Finally, access to corpora, and information about corpora, has also been greatly enhanced by the expansion of the world wide web in recent years. Groups like the Linguistic Data Consortium and the European Corpus Initiative make information about their holdings available over the web.[5] Other concerns, such as Cobuild, allow restricted web access to the corpora themselves.[6]

The corpora and text archives mentioned so far, with few exceptions, contain text only in English. There is no doubt that English is the most computerized language in the world, and corpora of English are the best documented (Leech and Fligelstone 1992:117). This is due in part to the importance of English in world terms as a mother tongue, but also to its importance as a second language. But Sebba and Fligelstone (1994:772) suggest that even in countries where English is neither a first nor a second language (for example, Norway) research may be con-

---

[4] When purchasing electronic newspapers, however, researchers check that what they are ordering is electronic *text*, which is automatically searchable and editable, etc, and not digitized *images*, which are not (see Hockey 1998:107).

[5] See http://www.ldc.upenn.edu/ and http://www.cogsci.ed.ac.uk/elsnet/eci.html, respectively.

[6] Cobuild*Direct* (http://titania.cobuild.collins.co.uk/direct_info.html) offers access to a 56 million word subset of the Bank of English for a fee, although free trials are available.

centrated on English-language corpora at the expense of the local language. There are, however, corpora of languages other than English. Atkins *et al.*. (1994:25) mention corpora of another fifteen modern European languages, and Burnard (1992:5) adds to this list a handful of corpora of medieval and classical languages. (See also Kennedy 1998:57-60). Lesser-used languages such as Irish have also received a boost through the creation of a substantial corpus (Ó Cróinín 1999). Of particular importance to the research outlined in this book, however, are the German-language corpora of the *Institut für deutsche Sprache* (IDS), which are described in detail in Chapter Five.

Corpora: users and uses

I have concentrated so far on corpus resources, their availability and basic structure, but have said little about who uses corpora and for what. There is, in fact, surprising variety both among the people interested in corpora and in the uses to which corpora are put. Kennedy (1998:8-12) identifies four main categories of corpus-based activity – which I follow loosely in the next few paragraphs – but adds that scholars working in corpus linguistics may be identified with more than one of these areas. The first is concerned with the design, compilation, storage, and annotation of corpora for use by the wider research community. Scholars working on these issues are typically concerned with questions of corpus representativeness and classification (e.g. Atkins *et al.* 1992; Biber 1994; Nakamura and Sinclair 1995; Sinclair 1991), mark-up schemes (Burnard 1995a), and the use of computing resources (Clear 1987).

A second area in which corpora are central is descriptive linguistics. Descriptive linguists use corpora to help them describe reliably aspects of the lexicon and/or grammar of their object language.[7] Svartvik (1992b:10) points to the particular importance of corpora to linguists who are non-native speakers of an object language, and for whom introspection is strictly speaking ruled out and elicitation awkward to perform. Kennedy (ibid:88-203) gives an overview of some existing corpus-based studies of English, which cover a wide range of topics from modal verbs to referential pronouns, to studies of regional variation and language change. He notes however, that despite the range of these studies, taken as a whole, their coverage of aspects of English is "rather unsystematic" (ibid:88). Stubbs (1996:47) likewise suggests that despite initial efforts by Francis (1991, 1993), Halliday (1991, 1992), and Sinclair

[7] The label 'descriptive linguistics' as used here is not intended to suggest that its proponents focus on description to the exclusion of theory. This would not be a tenable position, as all descriptions of language are guided by some theory of language. In linguistics as elsewhere, there is no such thing as hypothesis-free investigation (Firth 1957:1, 29; Lyons 1981:40; Stubbs 1996:47). What is more, many linguists have made important, often radical contributions to linguistic theory on foot of their descriptive work. See, for example, my comments on neo-Firthian corpus linguistics below.

(1990), the production of a comprehensive, corpus-based, probabilistic grammar of English is still "uncharted territory". Significant progress has, however, been made in corpus-based descriptions of the English lexicon. The first Cobuild dictionary (Sinclair 1987a) set new standards in lexicography, and in Kennedy's words, "it is now almost inconceivable that worthwhile and comprehensive lexical descriptions can be undertaken without a corpus" (1998:91). With mention of lexicography we have drifted into the area of applications of corpus-based descriptive linguistics. Other applications include the development of pedagogical grammars, and lexical reference works that focus on multi-word units – phrasal verbs, collocations, etc – rather than traditional single headwords. In the case of English, many corpus-based publications were initially aimed at foreign learners of the language, although this is changing with increased use of corpora across the board.

One characteristic feature of corpus-based descriptive linguistics is its interest in what is probable in a language, according to the available evidence, rather than what is possible, according to a set of Chomsky-like *a priori* rules. Statements about probabilities are made on the basis of observed frequencies of linguistic features (word forms, grammatical structures, etc) in corpora, so many descriptive linguists who use corpora also have a keen interest in quantitative methods in linguistics. Quantitative methods may involve simply counting the number of instances of a particular feature in a given corpus, and perhaps expressing this number as a proportion of the overall corpus size. They may also involve the use of descriptive statistics to compute average scores for certain measures, for example, sentence length, in a given corpus. Finally, methods of statistical inference can be used to work out whether some finding (for example that two words co-occur a certain number of times in a given corpus, or that a word in one source is much more frequent than the same word in another source) is really significant or merely due to chance. The use of quantitative methods in descriptive corpus linguistics is not unproblematic however, a point I will return to in this and subsequent Chapters. But as long as due caution is exercized, it appears that researchers can benefit from combining the "richness and precision" (McEnery and Wilson 1996:63) offered by qualitative methods, with the ability to summarize and generalize offered by quantitative approaches.

Statistical methods have become particularly important in a third area of corpus activity, that of 'corpus-based computational linguistics' (Bayer *et al.* 1998). Computational linguists may use corpora merely to assess the coverage of rule-based grammars they have designed *a priori*. They are increasingly likely, however, to rely on the frequency data supplied by corpora to develop probabilistic techniques for analyzing and processing further collections of text. Probabilistic techniques have become particularly important in areas such as automatic tagging, which involves the assignment of a part-of-speech label (verb, noun, etc) to each running word in a text or corpus, on the basis of known transition probabilities between competing labels. Thus 'rain' would be assigned the label <noun> in the string 'the rain', simply because experience shows that <determiner> <noun> is a much more likely tag sequence than <determiner> <verb> in English. Probabilistic techniques are also used in automatic parsing – the analysis (normally) of sentences in a corpus into formal or functional constituents (noun phrase, verb phrase, or subject, verb, object, etc) – and in working out likely translations for certain words or strings of words, given prior knowledge of how they were translated in a previously analyzed bilingual corpus. This is the basis of statistical machine translation. Lexicographers have also made liberal use of statistical inference in the automatic extraction of habitual collocations from corpora. The statistical techniques that have come to dominate corpus-based computational linguistics over the last two decades have thus had a huge impact on a variety of areas, but they have received only the shallowest of treatments here. For a more complete treatment of statistical techniques in Natural Language Processing (NLP) see Charniak (1993) and Armstrong (1994).[8]

The fourth area of corpus work identified by Kennedy is that of applications. I have already touched on many of these, including lexicography, language teaching and learning, the development of NLP tools, and statistical machine translation. To this list could be added translation teaching and learning. Since the mid 1990s, applications of corpus research have become the focus of a number of dedicated, often biennial, international conferences, known by a variety of acronyms such as TALC (Teaching Applications of Language Corpora), CULT (Corpus Use and Learning to Translate), and PALC (Practical Applications of Language Corpora). Published proceedings of these conferences (Wilson and McEnery 1994; Botley *et al.* 1996; Lewandowska-Tomaszczyk and Melia 1997) provide a valuable snapshot of much contemporary applied work in corpus linguistics.

The sheer volume and diversity of basic and applied research currently being conducted under the rubric of corpus linguistics is obvious from bibliographies (e.g. Altenberg 1991) and other publications in the area. Journals of interest include *Computers in the Humanities*, *Literary and Linguistic Computing*, *Computational Linguistics*, and the *International Journal of Corpus Linguistics*.[9] Some publishers, most notably Rodopi in Amsterdam, have brought out entire series of edited volumes in corpus linguistics, and Edinburgh University Press has more recently launched a series of corpus-related textbooks, of which McEnery and Wilson (1996) was the first. It is clear that corpus linguists have now consolidated their position in the academy, with articles from the 1990s carrying such bold titles as 'Corpus linguistics comes of age' (Svartvik 1992) and 'Corpora are becoming mainstream' (Svartvik 1996). It is also clear that corpus linguistics has become so vast that it encompasses work by very different researchers, often with different needs and

---

[8] Garside *et al.* (1987) is a standard reference in probabilistic tagging and parsing. Brown *et al.* (1990, 1993) discuss statistical machine translation, and statistical approaches to the lexicon are addressed in Church *et al.* (1991).

[9] For details, see Kennedy (1998:86-87).

aims, and differing levels of commitment to corpus data. The "expanding universe" (Leech 1991:25) of contemporary corpus linguistics has meant that linguists are increasingly concerned to position themselves within the area, a development that has led to much insightful meta-theoretical reflection in recent years, especially amongst a group of linguists whom we may loosely label 'neo-Firthian'.

Corpora and neo-Firthian linguistics

I apply the label 'neo-Firthian' here to linguists like Gill Francis, M.A.K. Halliday, Patrick Hanks, Bill Louw, John Sinclair, Michael Stubbs, and Elena Tognini-Bonelli, because they adopt in their work, albeit to varying degrees and at different moments, a number of positions that were identified as characteristically Firthian in Chapter One of this book. These positions involve: a commitment to the social nature of language and the centrality of text in linguistic inquiry; an interest in how texts function in their contexts of situation, and how linguistic routine maintains cultural values; and a rejection of the kind of linguistic dualism that separates meaning from form, and language system from language use.

A commitment to the social nature of language, to Firth's (1957:190) "speaking person in the social process", and to the role of context of situation in interpreting text, has been a theme in much of Halliday's work in language as social semiotic (1978). It has also informed Sinclair and Coulthard's (1975) investigations into teacher-pupil interaction in the classroom, and Stubbs's (1996:101-124) work on the language used in courts of law. The latter two references exemplify studies in which features of texts, in both cases transcripts of spoken language, are related to the wider context in which they function.[10] Stubbs's work also relates linguistic features in one text, a judge's summing up, to evidence about the language in general, as extracted from a substantial electronic corpus of English. One important use of corpora in neo-Firthian linguistics is thus as sources of comparative data. In other cases, linguists focus not on individual texts, but on selected words or constructions as they are distributed across whole corpora. (Examples are legion here. For an appetizer, see Stubbs's (1995a) discussion of CAUSE and PROVIDE,[11] and Renouf and Sinclair (1991) on constructions based around 'frameworks' like *a* __ *of* in English.) In such cases, the linguist is concerned with ascertaining facts about the typical use of a word or construction on the basis of multiple fragments of co-text. Such

---

[10] From now on, I use the term 'context' as roughly synonymous with Firth's 'context of situation'. Context, as understood here, is thus a broader concept than 'co-text', which refers to the immediate textual environment of a particular linguistic item (Halliday 1978:133), or "the other words on either side of it" (Sinclair 1991:172).

[11] Here, and elsewhere, I follow standard practice by using SMALL CAPITALS to represent lemmas (see below).

fragments are usually viewed in concordance lines of the type described below. Concordance lines often reveal repeated patterns of usage that translate themselves into conventional attitudes about culturally significant concepts like work and nationality (see Stubbs 1996:157-195). This is how, Stubbs argues, linguistic patterns become vehicles for cultural transmission.

Whether the linguists I have mentioned relate features of whole texts to their contexts of situation, or track the behaviour of individual lexical and grammatical items in corpora, they still insist on the primacy of text in the study of language. But this does not make theirs a linguistics of *parole* or 'performance'. Language in use (text) is not viewed simply as the realization of potential offered by an abstract system, conceptualized as *langue*, competence, or anything else. As Sinclair points out, "we do not end up with anything like text by 'generating' word strings from grammars" (1991:102). Rather, linguists like Halliday, Sinclair and Tognini-Bonelli (1996a) insist that when we look at individual instances of language in use, we are simultaneously looking at the language system. In Halliday's (1992:66) words:

> the "system" and the "instance" are not two distinct phenomena. There is only one phenomenon here, the phenomenon of language: what we have are two different observers, looking at this phenomenon from different depths in time.

It is the power of computers that has given linguists new vantage points from which to observe both instance and system. It is not uncommon for the computer to be likened to the telescope, or the microscope, in this respect. Computers are said to have "liberated" the study of language (Clear 1987:61), allowing linguists to "see phenomena and discover patterns that were not previously suspected" (Stubbs 1996:232). Not only do neo-Firthian corpus linguists reject the foremost dichotomy in modern linguistics (that of *langue* vs *parole* or competence vs performance), they also distrust other familiar linguistic dualisms such as those that decouple lexis from syntax, and meaning from form (see, especially, Sinclair 1991). Distrust of these dualisms can also be partly put down to the use of computers in linguistic analysis. It has arisen on foot of linguists' exposure to masses of text, the kind of exposure that can only be achieved with the help of computers. And as it is particularly characteristic of studies of language that have taken lexis as their point of departure, it will be taken up again in Chapter Four.

As has already been suggested, neo-Firthian corpus linguists have made much of the ability of computer processing to reveal recurrent patterns in corpora, and it is generally agreed that one of the main uses of contemporary, multi-million word corpora is to help linguists identify what is 'central' and 'typical' in the language under investigation (Stubbs 1996:32). But in a study that focuses on creativity, as the present one does, this aspect of corpus linguistics requires greater attention. For if a corpus is to provide evidence of what is central and typical in a language, then the implications for corpus composition are clear: in Sinclair's words (1991:17):

> If we are to approach a realistic view of the way in which language is used, we must record the usage of the mass of ordinary writers, and not the stray genius or the astute journalist.

The linguist's concern with what is typical, or normal, for 'the mass of ordinary writers' might thus be thought to be at odds with any intent to study creative aspects of language use. But corpus linguistics has also given us insights into the nature of creativity in language, as well as powerful tools with which to investigate such creativity. Corpus linguists have had such insights precisely because creative uses of language are brought into greater relief when one sees them against a backdrop of what is typical for a language. The formulation of norms is not dissonant with the investigation of creativity. In Hanks's words, "we need to say precisely what the conventions of use are before we can say how they are used and exploited to create meanings" (1996:85). Innovation, and even subversion, may be characteristic of literature, for example, but one can establish that norms have been flouted only if one has evidence of what is normal in the first place – for the language in general, or for literary language in particular. Evidence regarding the language in general can be provided by a suitably large and, in theory at least, 'representative' general corpus. And norms for literary language at a given moment in history, in a given culture, should emerge from the study of a suitably designed specialized corpus. This line of reasoning is not, however, intended to mask the practical difficulties involved in fixing the limits and deciding on the composition of a corpus of either general language or literary texts, an issue addressed in Chapter Five.

Finally, some neo-Firthian corpus linguists have been particularly associated with what Tognini-Bonelli (1996a) has called the 'corpus-driven' approach to linguistic study.[12] It has already been stated that corpus linguists study language on the basis of attested use, as recorded in various corpora. They thus adopt an empirical approach that tends towards induction, rather than Chomsky-like deduction, although few corpus linguists today would hold that linguistic analysis can be based on observation alone, with no intuitive input from the analyst (see Footnote 7 and the discussion in Chapter Five). Nevertheless, Tognini-Bonelli is critical of corpus-based approaches in which the data seem to take a back seat, where the corpus is used "in order to validate or exemplify a pre-existing theory, or to build up a statistical extension to it" (1996a:3). In such cases, the evidence of the corpus is not accepted wholeheartedly, and there is a tendency either to discount data that do not conform to preconceived theories, or to standardize the data, again according to some preconceived grammatical scheme (ibid:54-65). Tognini-Bonelli argues that the corpus-*driven* approach, on the other hand, "uses a corpus beyond the selection of examples to support linguistic argument or to validate a theoretical statement"

---

[12] I say 'some' neo-Firthian corpus linguists here, as M.A.K. Halliday is one of the neo-Firthian linguists whom Tognini-Bonelli (1996a) claims does not take a corpus-driven approach.

(ibid:69). It involves a much greater commitment on behalf of the linguist to "the integrity of the data as a whole", even when it transpires that the data do not support the linguist's hypotheses. In the words of Gill Francis (1993:139), a corpus may be used as the testing-ground for theories "only if we are ready to abandon our theories at any moment and posit something new on the basis of the evidence". The corpus-driven approach, exemplified by the work of Francis (1993), Sinclair (1991, 1996, 1997), and Tognini-Bonelli (1996a), rejects the idea that linguistic theory can have a separate existence from linguistic data. Theory is built up step-by-step and in constant contact with the data.

By approaching corpus data with an open mind, allowing the data to 'speak for itself' as it were, advocates of corpus-driven linguistics have gained insights into language that challenge much of linguistic orthodoxy. They deny the distinction between form and meaning, and stress (1) the organizational role in language of syntagmatic rather than paradigmatic relations, (2) the co-selection of lexis and syntax, and (3) even the priority of lexis over syntax. The contribution to the study of lexis of John Sinclair, in particular, has been enormous, and will be treated in depth in Chapter Four. Initial efforts have already been made to relate his findings to the study of translation (Tognini-Bonelli 1996a, 1996b), but this research has not drawn on actual translations. One of the principal aims of this study is to apply Sinclair's ideas on lexis to the study of translated text, specifically in the investigation of lexical normalization.

Corpus processing

Corpora are invaluable resources in contemporary linguistics, but without techniques to search, sort, count, and display the vast quantities of data they contain, they would be of little practical use. In this section I give an overview of some of the basic processing techniques used in corpus linguistics (see also Sinclair 1991:27-36 and Barnbrook 1996). I focus on techniques that can be used with 'raw' corpora, that is corpora that are neither tagged nor parsed and but may contain minimal annotation, usually serving to indicate major structural divisions such as text, paragraph, or sentence boundaries. The techniques involved are exemplified using the WordSmith suite of tools, written by Mike Scott and marketed by Oxford University Press (Scott 1997). These tools are used to manipulate data from GEPCOLT, the corpus under investigation in this book.

Global statistics

At a very basic level, and ignoring any structural divisions or added annotation for the moment, written text can be viewed as sequences of characters delimited by spaces. Each such sequence corresponds to a running word or 'token'. When we claim to have a one million word corpus, this usually means that we have a corpus containing one million tokens. One very basic type of calculation that we might expect any corpus analysis software to carry out is a token count for individual texts in a corpus, and for the corpus as a whole. In fact, we do not even need dedicated corpus tools to get a token count for individual texts; the word count facility in most word processors will suffice. If we wish to know how many *different* words, or 'types', there are in a text or corpus, however, then we need access to a tool that will take in all the tokens in the text or corpus, eliminate any duplicates, and count each word form just once. Thus a standard tool should be able to tell us that the text fragment 'to be or not to be' contains six tokens, but only four types, as there are two tokens each of the types 'to' and 'be'.

The ratio of types to tokens in a corpus tells us something about the variety of the word forms used in that corpus. Where there is a lot of repetition, we can expect the type/token ratio to be lower than in cases where writers avoid re-using the same words. But caution must be exercized with type/token ratios for a number of reasons. Firstly, they are extremely sensitive to text or corpus length. The longer a text, the more likely it is that words will be repeated, thus lowering the ratio. For this reason, type/token ratios are normally standardized to allow comparisons between texts of different length. Standardization is usually performed by calculating the ratio for successive chunks of say 1,000 tokens in a text, and then taking an average count at the end.

Another problem with type/token ratios, and all sorts of other automated quantitative techniques in corpus linguistics, is that they may not take homographs and lemmas into account. Homographs are different words with the same spelling, for example 'bat' the animal and 'bat' as used in cricket. The problem with such homographs is that they will be counted as a single type by a piece of software that knows about the appearance of word forms, but nothing about their meanings. The solution to this problem is either to change the data, by introducing some sort of semantic annotation to the corpus, or to change the processing by making it somehow sensitive to such problems, although each of these options is fraught with difficulties, and will not be pursued here (see Sinclair 1966:419 and Barnbrook 1996:60).

A lemma is a label under which all the inflected forms of a word can be gathered, where inflections are understood as minor and predictable changes in the shape of a word that coincide with changes in the grammatical function of that word. Thus *write*, *writes*, *writing*, *written*, and *wrote* are inflected forms of the lemma WRITE, which reflect differences in values for attributes such as person, finiteness, tense, etc.[13] The problem with lemmas for corpus processing is that the software may regard different forms of the same lemma as belonging to different types, even

[13] As indicated in Footnote 11, SMALL CAPITALS are traditionally used when referring to lemmas or lexemes (see Chapter Four). Likewise, *italics* are conventionally used when referring specifically to forms of a lemma.

though the human analyst would prefer them to be counted as a single type. Unless the corpus under scrutiny has been specifically marked up to show what lemma each form belongs to, or automatic lemmatization can be carried out on the fly, then this will not be possible. There is no doubt that lemmatization allows for greater generalization in statements about the lexical make-up of a corpus, but it is not a straightforward process, and such generalization may obscure interesting distinctions: Sinclair contends that different forms of the same lemma can reflect different senses of that lemma (1991:53-65), and by conflating forms like *dying* with *die*, for example, we run the risk of losing a useful criterion for identifying what we may want to consider as a separate lexical item, that is the multi-word unit BE DYING TO, as in 'I'm dying to see the show' (Sinclair 1966:419). Nevertheless, in certain projects, notably those where researchers are confronted with vast quantities of lexical data, lemmatization is often seen as a useful step in the analysis, despite the problems involved (see, for example, Lawson 1997:231-232).

A further problem is posed by spelling variants and case differences: should the forms *criticize*, *criticise*, *Criticize*, and *CRITICISE*, for example, be normalized so that they can be treated as tokens of the same type? The problem of spelling variation is discussed in several places by Barnbrook (1996), and the issue of case is taken up by Barnbrook (ibid:7, 70) and Church *et al.* (1991:155-157). It is enough for the moment to note that, when a human analyst initiates an electronic search in a corpus, it is a simple matter to look for instances of, for example, *criticize* and *criticise* at the same time: the penultimate character just needs to be replaced by a wildcard character. But in fully automated type counts or calculations of type/token ratios, spelling variants will probably be regarded as different types (see, for example, Kucera and Francis 1967:xxi). Problems of case differences are easier to solve, namely by automatically 'folding' upper and lower case characters into a single format, although even this simple process can lead to undesired effects, such as the obscuring in English of the difference between 'Polish', the nationality, and 'polish' for shining shoes. While there are techniques for dealing with these problems, including providing non-sentence initial capitals with special mark-up (Kucera and Francis ibid:4), ideally the human analyst should be able to specify whether or not automatic processes are to be case sensitive.

Other quantitative techniques used in corpus linguistics involve the computing of average word and sentence lengths for individual texts or whole corpora, and detailed statistics on how many words there are of each length (one-letter words, two-letter words, etc). But even these apparently simple measures are not as straightforward as one might expect. For one, there is no foolproof way of automatically identifying sentence boundaries. One might assume, as do many computer programs, that a sentence ends with an ending punctuation mark (full-stop, question-mark, exclamation-mark, etc) immediately followed by a white space or other 'separator' (tab, paragraph break, etc) and then a capital letter, number or currency symbol. But without further refinement any program making these assumptions will wrongly see a sentence boundary in the string 'Mrs. Jones'. What is more, if such a program is run, for example, on an 'experimental' text that does not use upper case in any context, then it will not be able to recognize many genuine sentence boundaries. Recognizing word boundaries is not trivial either. Thus far I have made the simplistic assumption that words are coterminous with orthographic words, that is, that a word is a string of characters, which, when printed, has a space on either side.[14] This assumption, of course, ignores the fact that many linguists would prefer to treat some multi-word strings, for example, 'give up' or 'give in', as single words, and some single-word strings, for example 'cannot', as two words. And hyphens too present problems. Should 'multi-word' in 'multi-word unit', for example, be treated as one word or two? Faced with these very practical difficulties, the onus is on linguists using corpus processing tools to take into account in their analyses the assumptions made by the software, and to be aware of any settings they can change in the software in order to get something approximating their desired output. An example may help here.

Table 1 contains statistics produced for the German texts in the GEPCOLT corpus using the WordList program in WordSmith Tools. The second column (labelled A) gives overall statistics for the German texts. Subsequent columns show counts for individual texts. For ease of display, I have included statistics for only six of the seventeen individual texts in the German subcorpus. The first row of data (labelled 1) shows the number of bytes taken up by the corpus as a whole (column A), and each of the texts individually (subsequent columns). This is an indication of how much computer storage space is required to hold the corpus and/or individual files. Row 2 shows the token count for the corpus as a whole (just under one million running words), and each of the texts. This count is based on orthographic words, with hyphenated forms like *Abba-Film* counted as one word, not two. Row 3 shows the type count for the whole corpus and selected texts. This count is based again on orthographic words, unlemmatized, with no semantic disambiguation.[15]

Row 4 shows how type/token ratios are sensitive to text length. The greater the number of tokens in a text (Row 2), the lower the type/token ratio tends to be. But there is a surprise finding here. The last text listed, Gert Hofmann's *Unsere Eroberung*, labelled G, is not the longest text, but it does have the lowest type/token ratio at 8.24. When type/token ratios are standardized in Row 5, using chunks of 1,000 tokens as described above, this trend is confirmed. Hofmann's text would

---

[14] Such assumptions are not only simplistic, they are also conditioned by exposure to the written form of certain languages. Thai, for instance, uses neither punctuation nor spaces to indicate word boundaries (see Kano 1995:238-247).

[15] Note also that WordList computes the number of types separately for each text. For this reason, even if I had included all seventeen of the texts that make up the German subcorpus of GEPCOLT in this table, summing the number of types for each text would not give the same total as indicated in column A for the number of types over the whole corpus.

appear to have more repetition of types, even when its overall length is taken into account, than do the other texts considered. Its average word length at 4.81 characters is also below the mean for the corpus as evidenced in Row 6. These statistics would suggest that Hofmann's text is lexically more repetitive and uses, on average, shorter words than do the other texts. But they tell us nothing about which words are being repeated. To find this out we need access to other information, which WordList can provide, and which is discussed below (see Table 3). Keeping our attention on Table 1 for the moment, however, we see that should we wish to pursue the hypothesis that Hofmann's text is somehow 'simpler' than the others in the subcorpus – if this is what we take lexical repetition and relatively short words to indicate – then we still have to explain the finding that Hofmann uses longer than average sentences (Row 8), and exceptionally long paragraphs (Row 10), both measured in number of words. These findings may have something to do with the fact that Hofmann's novel is narrated at the breathless pace of a child, with information relayed in sustained bursts with little formal internal structuring. To be more confident about such an explanation, we would have to look at the text in detail, and relate its linguistic features to its fictional context of situation. But this example nevertheless makes the point that even crude quantitative information such as that given in Table 1 can lead to interesting hypotheses, and that in most linguistic studies, qualitative analyses soon follow on the heels of quantitative forays.

Another text represented in Table 1, Gerhard Roth's *die autobiographie des albert einstein*, labelled D, has some questionable vital statistics. The software counts only 139 sentences (Row 7) in this text, and although the average sentence length is high at 34.76 words, this cannot account for all 24,662 tokens in the text. Something has gone wrong. The explanation here is that the text does not conform to the assumptions made by the software. The author does not use capital letters at the beginning of sentences and so the software spots new sentences only when they begin with a digit (where case is not an issue) or at a new paragraph. Some of the quantitative data supplied for this text are thus unreliable, and they may even make some of the statistics supplied for the overall corpus unreliable. As sentence length does not impinge in any significant way on the study presented in this book, this shortcoming is not considered fatal here.[16] But the point is made that corpus analysts should know their software, and it is often useful to have more than a nodding acquaintance with the texts in one's corpus too.

[16] As it happens, discounting the text in question in calculations of overall corpus statistics changes very little. The average sentence length without it, for example, is 15.68 words, as opposed to 15.73 with it.

		A	...	B	C	D	...	E	F	G	...
		OVERALL		DEWELLER .TXT	DEROTH2 .TXT	DEROTH1 .TXT		DEJELIN2.TXT	DEJELIN1 .TXT	DEHOFMAN. TXT	
1	Bytes	6,243,878		945,653	204,156	175,230		455,579	401,956	572,826	
2	Tokens	970,270		146,534	31,399	24,662		71,612	63,983	94,529	
3	Types	73,137		18,263	6,845	7,954		11,844	10,576	7,785	
4	Type/Token Ratio	7.54		12.46	21.80	32.25		16.54	16.53	8.24	
5	Standardized Type/Token	49.23		48.58	49.18	56.77		49.38	50.37	38.35	
6	Ave. Word Length	5.17		5.18	5.25	5.79		5.13	5.07	4.81	
7	Sentences	55,391		8,590	1,888	139		4,267	3,827	5,542	
8	Ave. Sent. length	15.73		14.43	15.77	34.76		16.75	16.68	17.02	
9	sd. Sent. Length	14.59		11.68	9.86	106.22		11.16	9.76	12.26	
10	Paragraphs	12,808		3,215	369	381		777	281	43	
11	Ave. Para. length	72.00		45.07	83.36	58.05		90.68	220.13	1455.12	
12	sd. Para. Length	141.02		58.07	156.22	101.14		96.57	136.52	1155.70	
13	1-letter words	1,879		68	52	239		60	38	13	
14	2-letter words	83,289		14,905	2,922	1,860		6,005	5,184	8,579	
15	3-letter words	283,542		41,794	9,523	6,605		20,131	18,461	29,088	
16	....										
17	10-letter words	28,288		4,579	1,000	1,062		1,931	1,637	1,870	
18	....										
19	25(+)-letter words	43		7	8	1		4	0	0	

Table 1: Statistics for the German subcorpus of GEPCOLT and selected constituent files
sd (Rows 9 and 12) = standard deviation

Word lists

The WordList program can also give a list of all the types in a corpus or text, arranged alphabetically or in order of frequency. Table 2 shows the top twenty types (out of a total 73,137) in the German subcorpus of GEPCOLT, ranked according to frequency. As is normally the case, the most common types in the corpus are 'function' words: conjunctions like *und* 'and'; determiners (or less commonly relative pronouns) like *der*, *die*, and *das*; pronouns like *sie/Sie* 'she/they/you polite' and *er* 'he', with forms of the verb SEIN 'to be' featuring at ranks nineteen and twenty.[17] The third column in Table 2 shows the type's absolute frequency in the corpus; the fourth its relative frequency. There are thus 31,700 instances (its absolute frequency) of the type *und* in the subcorpus, which means it accounts for 3.27% (its relative frequency) of all the tokens in the subcorpus.

N	Word	Freq.	%
1	UND	31,700	3.27
2	DIE	27,598	2.84
3	DER	22,204	2.29
4	SIE	17,831	1.84
5	ER	16,858	1.74
6	IN	15,294	1.58
7	DAS	13,053	1.35
8	DEN	12,067	1.24
9	ICH	10,590	1.09
10	SICH	10,526	1.08
11	ZU	10,502	1.08
12	NICHT	10,147	1.05
13	EIN	9,093	0.94
14	AUF	9,028	0.93
15	MIT	8,906	0.92
16	ES	8,813	0.91
17	VON	7,236	0.75
18	DEM	6,832	0.70
19	IST	6,726	0.69
20	WAR	6,692	0.69

Table 2: Top twenty frequency-ranked types in the German subcorpus of GEPCOLT

[17] Function words (also known as 'grammatical words' or 'closed-class items') are distinguished from 'content' words (also known as 'lexical words' and 'open-class items') in many lexical analyses. The former include most determiners, pronouns, conjunctions, etc, the stock of which cannot be readily added to, hence the designation 'closed-class items'. The latter include most nouns, verbs, adjectives and adverbs, and their number can be increased through the formation of new words, hence the designation 'open-class items'.

When discussing Table 1, I noted a relatively low type/token ratio in the Hofmann text, and wondered which types were being repeated and might account for this finding. A look at a frequency-ranked type list for Hofmann's text on its own might go some way towards answering this question. Table 3 contains the 'head' of this list.

N	Word	Freq.	%
1	UND	3,701	3.92
2	WIR	3,111	3.29
3	DER	2,121	2.24
4	DIE	2,116	2.24
5	NICHT	1,666	1.76
6	ER	1,545	1.63
7	UNS	1,410	1.49
8	IN	1,277	1.35
9	SIE	1,260	1.33
10	SAGT	1,154	1.22
11	DEN	1,102	1.17
12	DAS	1,098	1.16
13	IST	1,043	1.10
14	AUCH	854	0.90
15	ZU	808	0.85
16	AUF	796	0.84
17	ES	790	0.84
18	SAGEN	763	0.81
19	EDGAR	732	0.77
20	JA	723	0.76

Table 3: Top twenty frequency-ranked types in *Unsere Eroberung*

It is clear from Table 3 that function words also feature prominently in the most common types in *Unsere Eroberung*, but they are not the same function words as dominate the corpus as a whole. *Wir* 'we', for example, is ranked second in the Hofmann text, and only twenty-fourth in the corpus as a whole (and if we leave out Hofmann's text when generating a frequency-ranked type list for the whole corpus, then *wir* falls to number 51 in the ranking). This finding is explained by the fact that *Unsere Eroberung* is narrated in the first person plural. Interestingly, some content words make it into Hofmann's top twenty: two forms of the verb SAGEN 'to say' (ranked tenth and eigtheenth) and the proper name Edgar, an omnipresent figure in the narrative.

Keyword lists

It would be possible to continue down the frequency ranked list for Hofmann's text and manually compare each type's position with its ranking in the corpus as a whole, but there is an easier, more systematic way of comparing word lists. Using the 'comparison' feature in WordList, users can request that a word list whose properties they are interested in be compared to a longer one, which acts as a kind of reference. The software outputs a list of types it thinks are 'key' in the smaller list, because they appear to be unusually frequent in that list, compared with their frequency in the reference. Keywords are then ranked according to their 'keyness' score.[18] Table 4 gives the top twenty keywords identified in this way in *Unserse Eroberung*. In this case, Dunning's (1993) log likelihood score was used to compute keyness, and a risk of error of one in one million, or p=0.000001, was allowed. The reference list used was that generated for all the German texts in GEPCOLT, including *Unsere Eroberung*.[19]

In Table 4, the Word column contains the type considered 'key'. Subsequent columns (Freq. and Dehofman.txt %) show the type's absolute and relative frequency in Hofmann's text. The columns labelled Corpus and Corpus % show the

	WORD	FREQ.	DEHOFMAN .TXT %	CORPUS FREQ.	CORPUS %	KEYNESS
1	WIR	3,111	3.29	5,536	0.57	4863.5
2	UNS	1,410	1.49	2,530	0.26	2173.4
3	SAGT	1,154	1.22	1,717	0.18	2048.9
4	EDGAR	732	0.77	732	0.08	1656.1
5	UNSER	713	0.75	890	0.09	1419.9
6	SAGEN	763	0.81	1,219	0.13	1284.3
7	FRAGEN	466	0.49	644	0.07	868.2
8	FRAGT	432	0.46	536	0.06	862.6
9	SCHAUSPIELER	354	0.37	366	0.04	785.6
10	JA	723	0.76	2,110	0.22	678.4
11	NUN	504	0.53	1,105	0.11	647.5
12	RUFT	291	0.31	337	0.03	605.5
13	HERR	331	0.35	569	0.06	525.7
14	ACH	284	0.30	414	0.04	509.8
15	UNSERE	291	0.31	492	0.05	468.2
16	RUFEN	225	0.24	273	0.03	455.1
17	SCHLACHTHOFDIREKTOR	190	0.20	190	0.02	429.0
18	UNSEREN	198	0.21	270	0.03	371.8
19	ANZUG	177	0.19	207	0.02	366.0
20	NICHT	1,666	1.76	10,147	1.05	348.3

Table 4: Top twenty keywords in *Unsere Eroberung*

[18] For information on the computations and the statistical tests used to arrive at a keyness score, see Scott (1997). Note that it is possible for a type to be assigned a negative score, thus making it an unusually infrequent type in a given list.

[19] Leaving out *Unsere Eroberung* when generating the reference list would have the effect of increasing the keyness scores for the keywords identified in this text, in other words, it would make them even more 'key', but it would have only a minor effect of their relative ranking in the range shown in Table 4.

type's absolute and relative frequency in the corpus as a whole. The final column contains the type's keyness score.

Table 4 shows that first person plural pronouns (*wir* 'we' and *uns* 'us') and inflected forms of the corresponding possessive determiner (*unser*, *unsere*, *unseren* 'our') are key in *Unsere Eroberung*. So are a number of reporting verbs, including SAGEN (already identified as accounting for two of the most frequent types in the text in Table 3, now identified as accounting for the third and sixth most 'key' types in the text), FRAGEN 'to ask' (forms of which are ranked seventh and eighth) and RUFEN 'to call' or 'exclaim' (twelfth and sixteenth).[20] A picture begins to emerge of a text in which the narrative follows a child-like pattern of quoted speech built up around repetitive phrases like 'we say/ask/exclaim' and 'he says/asks/exclaims'. Again, my aim here is not to give an exhaustive analysis of the lexical characteristics of any single text in GEPCOLT. Rather I wish to show how quantitative techniques, including techniques of statistical inference, can launch wider, more qualitative studies of texts and corpora.

Another measure that relies on the comparison of word lists is that of lexical density. Put simply, lexical density refers to the proportion of content or 'lexical' words in a corpus or text. It is computed by dividing the number of content tokens in a corpus by the total number of tokens in the corpus, and multiplying by 100 to express the result as a percentage.

For instance, in the paragraph immediately preceding this one there are 66 tokens. If we mark off the following as function words – that, the, of, or, a, it, by, and, to, as – then we are left with 40 tokens accounted for by content words.[21] The lexical density of the paragraph would thus be:

$$\frac{40}{66} \times 100 = 60.1\%$$

As this example illustrates, computing lexical densities requires us to have a workable list of function words to compare against our corpus, as it is easier to say what the function words of a language are and eliminate these from the token count than it is to predict all the possible content words that may appear in a corpus. But, like most things in linguistics, even listing function words is not unproblematic. For example, should 'is' be considered a function word in English? (When it is a full

[20] Other notable content words are *Schauspieler* (9) 'actor', *Schlachthofdirektor* (17) 'slaughterhouse director', and *Anzug* (19) 'suit'.

[21] This process can be emulated using WordList by 'matching' a file of function words against the wordlist for a given text or corpus, and eliminating any types found in both lists. Note that this is not the same as using a stop list (a list of types to be ignored) when generating word lists in the first place.

verb? When it is an auxiliary?) And what do we do with prepositions, which appear to be closed-class items, but also appear, in some cases, to have 'content'. Despite problems such as these, lexical density has been found to be a useful measure in corpus linguistics, because it can help distinguish between different genres, with certain types of spoken texts, for example, exhibiting characteristically low lexical densities and thus high redundancy (see Stubbs 1996:73-74).

Clusters

All the word listing and counting techniques we have encountered so far have been based on single orthographic words, that is, one-word types. It is also possible to get lists of repeated 'clusters' of orthographic words using the WordList program. Two-word clusters may or may not be very revealing of the patterns of repetition in texts, with sequences like 'in the' likely to feature prominently in English-language texts, but three-word clusters are often interesting. Table 5 contains the twenty five most frequent three-word clusters in Hofmann's *Unsere Eroberung*. Table 6 gives equivalent data for Christopher Middleton's translation of the novel.

N	Cluster	Freq.	%
1	SAGT UNSER EDGAR	312	0.33
2	DER HERR SCHLACHTHOFDIREKTOR	177	0.19
3	SAGT DER SCHAUSPIELER	150	0.16
4	SAGT DER HERR	93	0.10
5	SAGEN WIR UND	90	0.10
6	DER HERR PFARRER	79	0.08
7	FRAGT DER SCHAUSPIELER	67	0.07
8	FRAGT DER HERR	65	0.07
9	FRAGT UNSER EDGAR	62	0.07
10	DER SCHAUSPIELER UND	60	0.06
11	SAGT DIE MUTTER	57	0.06
12	UNSER EDGAR UND	53	0.06
13	FRAGEN WIR UND	52	0.06
14	RUFT DER SCHAUSPIELER	52	0.06
15	HERR SCHLACHTHOFDIREKTOR UND	48	0.05
16	RUFEN WIR UND	46	0.05
17	RUFT DER HERR	41	0.04
18	HIN UND HER	39	0.04
19	AUF DER BÜHNE	37	0.04
20	SAGT ER UND	36	0.04
21	SAGT DIE WITWE	35	0.04
22	NACH UNSERER EROBERUNG	31	0.03
23	SAGT DER SCHLÄCHTER	31	0.03
24	SAGT FRAU KOHLHUND	29	0.03
25	WIR UND ZEIGEN	29	0.03

Table 5: Top twenty five most frequent three-word clusters in *Unsere Eroberung*

Although the Tables differ in some respects, they both reveal more evidence of the repetitive narrative patterns suggested by other quantitative lexical analyses of Hofmann's text. In particular, we see a proliferation of 'so-and-so says/asks/exclaims' type clusters that can be said to characterize both source and translation.

N	Cluster	Freq.	%
1	OUR EDGAR SAYS	312	0.32
2	THE ACTOR SAYS	153	0.16
3	WE SAY AND	74	0.08
4	OUR EDGAR ASKS	72	0.07
5	THE ACTOR ASKS	68	0.07
6	THE DIRECTOR SAYS	66	0.07
7	A LONG TIME	63	0.06
8	FOR A LONG	49	0.05
9	THE DIRECTOR ASKS	45	0.05
10	THE ACTOR EXCLAIMS	44	0.05
11	ON THE STAGE	41	0.04
12	WE ASK AND	38	0.04
13	ALL THE SAME	37	0.04
14	HE SAYS AND	35	0.04
15	WE DON'T KNOW	35	0.04
16	THE WIDOW SAYS	33	0.03
17	OUT OF THE	32	0.03
18	TO THE SLAUGHTERHOUSE	32	0.03
19	AFTER OUR CONQUEST	31	0.03
20	SO AS TO	31	0.03
21	THE BUTCHER SAYS	31	0.03
22	THE PASTOR SAYS	31	0.03
23	IN ANY CASE	30	0.03
24	FRAU KOHLHUND SAYS	29	0.03
25	FOR A MOMENT	28	0.03

Table 6: Top twenty five most frequent three-word clusters in *Our Conquest*

Concordancing

Perhaps the most familiar corpus processing technique is that of concordancing. A concordance is a listing of all occurrences of a selected item, or 'node', in a text or corpus. These occurrences are conventionally displayed in KWIC (key word in context) format, where the software outputs a series of concordance lines, each displaying a single occurrence of the node, along with the words immediately to its left and right in the text or corpus. Figure 1 shows a concordance of the node 'conscience' in the English subcorpus of GEPCOLT. It was produced using the Concord program in WordSmith Tools.

The concordance, Sinclair has claimed, is at the centre of corpus linguistics, "because it gives access to many important language patterns in texts" (1991:170). Examples of such patterning are visible in Figure 1. It is clear, for instance, that

```
1. day that you developed a  conscience. Nothing would have pleased m
2.  ischarge me with a clear conscience. Although he is always lying
3.  ns victory.... With good conscience I now follow the path to whic
4.     She had both a guilty conscience and urgent news. The guilty c
5.  ter off to have a guilty conscience. But you really showed him wh
6.  o jutta now had a guilty conscience although she was still furiou
7.  ling a mixture of guilty conscience and relief. Walking along the
8.   urgent news. The guilty conscience was stronger. Not a cop after
9.  nd Flores in a daze. His conscience was clear: the little book wa
10. had a human life on his  conscience - four or five of them, he co
11. have a good deal on its  conscience. Especially when someone stil
12.  under the weight of my  conscience, but rather under a curious c
13. re than a total lack of  conscience on your part. What do I mean
14. decision on a matter of  conscience. Was I to show Knight's Cross
15. s we now have a pang of  conscience about not being a better repl
16.  apprehension, pangs of  conscience and a sense of sin, but they
17. Jenner felt no pangs of  conscience. He considered that he had de
18.  we were alone with our  conscience. That would be t
19. n the shoulders and the  conscience. His worries carry the day an
20. ed, and appealed to the  conscience of the jury. He had not prepa
21. ve a human life on your  conscience, Mr Kurt? I hope not." Horgan
22. order you revoked. Your  conscience was the worst thing that coul
```

Figure 1: Concordance of the node 'conscience' in the English subcorpus of GEPCOLT

'conscience', in this corpus at least, repeatedly occurs with 'guilty' and 'pang(s) of' to its left, and in constructions like 'on his/its/your conscience'. Such patterns are easily spotted thanks to sorting routines that allow concordance lines to be displayed, for example, in alphabetical order of the first or second word to the left of the node. They are essentially lexical and lexico-grammatical patterns in that they reveal repeated combinations of lexical words, eg 'guilty conscience', and repeated occurrences of certain words in certain grammatical constructions, or with certain parts of speech, eg 'HAVE + Nominal Group + on + possessive determiner + conscience'. Kennedy (1998:8) suggests that using KWIC concordances actually predisposes linguists towards studies of lexis and lexical grammar, because the amount of co-text available in concordance lines is too limited to allow the analysis of syntax or discourse. There may be some truth in this, but it is also the case that some linguists are convinced that even syntactic studies should start by focusing on lexis, as "syntax is driven by lexis: lexis is communicatively prior" (Francis 1993:142). It is also true that even though concordance lines, once committed to hard copy as in Figure 1, may be shorter than the analyst would like, it is usually possible to view expanded co-text on line. This is a standard feature of tools like Concord.

Lexical and lexico-grammatical patterning are discussed in greater detail in Chapter Four. For now it is enough to note that concordancing is subject to the same constraints as affect type counts, calculations of type/token ratios, etc. Unless the corpus is marked up to differentiate between competing meanings of homographs, or to associate forms with their lemmas, for example, or the concordancing software is somehow modified to take such details into account, then we will not be able to get a concordance for animal senses of 'bat' to the exclusion of sporting senses, nor will we be able to get a concordance of a lemma like SAY, as opposed to its forms.[22] This is not to say that standard concordancers offer no flexibility. Indeed, searches can be made more flexible with tools like Concord, simply by using wildcards.

Wildcards are characters that can stand in for other characters. Wildcards that can stand in for any single character are useful in searches for words where there is likely to be spelling variation. Using the '?' wildcard, for example, we can form a search term '?nquiry' that will uncover all instances of *enquiry* and *inquiry* in a given corpus. Another common wildcard, the Kleene star *, can be used to replace any number (including zero) of other characters in a search term. By searching the English subcorpus of GEPCOLT, for example, for instances of 'translat*', we retrieve 66 concordance lines with *translate*, *translated*, *translates*, *translating*, *translation*, *translations*, and *translator* at their centre. Different wildcards can be combined in a single search. Thus the search term '?nquir*' uncovers a total of fifty instances in the English subcorpus of GEPCOLT of *enquire*, *enquirers*, *enquiries*, *inquire*, *inquired*, *inquiringly*, etc. Wildcards can also be used in 'phrase' searches. Using 'on * conscience' as the search term in Concord will thus retrieve the following lines (numbered 10, 11 and 21 in Figure 1) from the same corpus:[23]

```
1. had a human life on his conscience - four or five of them, he co
2. have a good deal on its conscience. Especially when someone stil
3. ve a human life on your conscience, Mr Kurt? I hope not." Horgan
```

Figure 2: Concordance of the node 'on * conscience' in the English subcorpus of GEPCOLT

Conclusion

In this Chapter the notion of 'corpus' was introduced and a brief overview was given of the historical development of corpora and the uses to which corpora are currently put. Some comments were then made about how neo-Firthian corpus lin-

---

[22] These need not be considered problems if, following Sinclair (1991), researchers rely on the co-text itself to disambiguate homographs, on the one hand, and subscribe to the point of view that merging forms into an overarching lemma serves only to obscure useful linguistic distinctions, on the other. Having said this, some corpus processing tools do allow searches by lemma. See, for example, the discussion of COSMAS in Chapter Five.

[23] Information on other possible wildcards in Concord is available under 'search word syntax' in the program's help files.

guists approach questions concerning the nature and study of language. I hope to have shown that these linguists adopt a holistic view of language, in which there is no discontinuity between text and context, and in which each instance of language use "both maintains and perturbs the system" (Halliday 1991:33). The relevance of this position to descriptive translation studies – where individual translations are ideally situated in their contexts of production and/or reception, and are seen to either maintain or subvert prevailing norms, while at once contributing to shifts in those norms over time – will, it is hoped, become clear in the next Chapter. Finally, I discussed basic corpus processing techniques and attempted to show how quantitative and qualitative analyses can proceed hand in hand. Thus far the discussion has focused on common words and repeated lexical patterning in texts and corpora. In later Chapters I will attempt to show how knowledge of typical or repeated patterns in corpora can form the backdrop against which lexical creativity is recognized and evaluated.

3. Turning Corpus Linguistics on its Head Corpus-Based Translation Studies

> Translation studies is, in a sense, turning corpus linguistics on its head... Translation scholars are ultimately not interested in the words or syntactic structures themselves. What they are interested in are abstract, global notions such as explicitation and simplification, which are independent of specific languages and have various manifestations on the surface.
>
> Mona Baker (1996b:185)

Introduction

In Chapter One I discussed the often controversial role of linguistics in translation scholarship and suggested that while some criticisms of linguistic approaches are justified, others are based on too narrow a view of linguistics and its application to translation studies. In particular, critics of linguistics often overlook non-Chomskyan approaches to the study of language, including the work of Firth and his successors. This is an unfortunate blind spot, because neo-Firthian corpus linguists share much common ground with scholars working in the area of descriptive translation studies in particular. Both groups insist on the primacy of authentic data – actually occurring text in corpus linguistics, and actually occurring translated text in descriptive translation studies – and both are concerned to identify recurring patterns in texts, and to relate these patterns, and deviations from them, to features of the wider context of situation. Given the common ground they share, it is not surprising that the two are beginning to converge in what has been dubbed 'corpus-based translation studies' (Baker 1996b). In this Chapter I trace the development of corpus-based translation studies starting with the impetus it received from descriptive translation studies. My discussion of the latter will be short and of necessity selective.[1] Its main purpose will be to highlight the provenance of ideas that have been particularly influential in computerized studies of translation. These ideas relate to the hypothesized tendency of translators to simplify texts, make implicit meaning explicit, and normalize linguistic usage. I ask to what extent these tendencies can be, and have been investigated in computerized studies, and suggest possible ways of exploring the issue of lexical normalization. The Chapter ends with a critical appraisal of the role of computerized corpora in translation studies, pointing in particular to some of the dangers that lurk in current scholarship.

---

[1] For a more comprehensive treatment see Hermans (1999).

Descriptive translation studies

Descriptive translation studies (DTS) is a convenient label for an approach to translation scholarship that began to emerge in the 1970s and flourished in particular in the Netherlands, Belgium, and Israel, although it was by no means limited to these countries (see Hermans 1999:7-9). DTS marked a self-conscious departure from much previous scholarship in the area, which had been highly speculative and prescriptive in its orientation, concerned as it was with determining what an ideal translation should strive to be "in order to minimise its inevitable distortion of the message, the spirit, and the elegance of the original" (Baker 1993:236). Proponents of DTS sought instead to engage with real translation phenomena, to describe translations as they actually occur, and to account for observed features of translations with reference to the literary, cultural and historical contexts in which they were produced. Such an agenda helped effect a shift to the target pole in translation scholarship. Whereas previously the key to determining the 'ideal' translation had lain in the source text, scholars like Gideon Toury (1980:82, 1985:19, 1995:12-14) now argued that translations were facts of the target textual tradition only, and the most appropriate way to investigate them was thus from the point of view of the target culture. Although DTS scholars are not the only ones to have turned their attention to the target pole – the same kind of shift is evident in early *skopos* theory (Vermeer 1978) – and DTS in no way ignores source texts and cultures, the 'target-orientedness' of DTS remains one of its best-known characteristics. This target-orientedness was legitimized in part with reference to Itamar Even-Zohar's 'polysystem' theory.

Drawing on Russian Formalism, Even-Zohar (1978, 1979) developed the idea of literature as a heterogeneous conglomerate of individual literary systems, each with modelling principles of its own, but all jostling for position in the wider polysystem. According to Even-Zohar (1978:118-119), the body of translated literature in any single culture constitutes a system of its own, and thus takes part in the dynamic interaction between systems in the polysystem. Because polysystems are in a constant state of flux, no single system occupies its position as of right, for all time. Thus while other approaches have tended to see translated literature as "not only second-hand, but also generally second-rate, and hence not worthy of too much serious attention" (Hermans 1985a:8), Even-Zohar stresses that translated literature, like all literary systems, is not inherently peripheral or conservative, rather it *becomes* either central or peripheral, primary or secondary, etc, depending on the overall state of the polysystem (1978:120ff). Polysystem theory has been important in the recent development of translation studies, and corpus-based translation studies, for a number of reasons. Firstly, it reinstates translated literature as a system worthy of study in its own right. Secondly, it imputes a certain specificity to translated texts (Even-Zohar ibid:118) that warrants their investigation as a coherent body of texts, in other words, as a corpus. And thirdly, given that translated literature functions as a system in the target culture polysystem, it validates the study of such translated literature against the backdrop of non-translated literature in the same, target language.

If target-orientedness is a feature of DTS, then so too is a strong emphasis on empirical data. Of all the scholars linked to DTS, it is Gideon Toury who has become most associated with empiricism. Central to Toury's approach is the conviction that translation studies can be and should be pursued as an empirical science, with real translation phenomena, and not some idealized version of them, as its object of enquiry. As an empirical discipline, translation studies should aim to describe, explain and predict phenomena pertaining to its object level (1995:1).[2] Descriptive statements and explanatory hypotheses are thus handled by the descriptive branch of translation studies, in which regularities in observed behaviour are explained by the operation of hypothesized 'norms'. The theoretical branch, in turn, takes care of predictions relating to as yet unencountered instances of translation. Such predictions are cast as probabilistic 'laws', effectively the translation of statements about observed regularities of behaviour and their conditioning factors into statements regarding the "*likelihood* that a kind of behaviour, or surface realization, would occur under one set of specifiable conditions or another" (ibid:16). Neither notion is unproblematic, as we shall see.

Norms, universals, and laws of translation

For Toury (1995:54), translation as a culturally significant activity is subject to constraints that extend far beyond those imposed by the source text, the systemic differences between the languages and textual traditions involved, or even the cognitive apparatus of the translator. Socio-cultural constraints are imposed by more or less binding intersubjective norms that represent, in sociological terms:

> the translation of general values or ideas shared by a community – as to what is right and wrong, adequate and inadequate – into performance instructions appropriate for and applicable to particular situations, specifying what is prescribed and forbidden as well as what is tolerated and permitted in a certain behavioural dimension. (Toury 1995:54-55).

Norms are thus of an abstract nature; they are not themselves observable. Their

---

[2] The foundations of Toury's approach to the study of translation were set in a series of articles published in the 1970s and gathered together in a single volume in 1980 (Toury 1980). This volume has, however, been largely superseded by Toury's 1995 book *Descriptive Translation Studies and beyond* in which he incorporates more recent research findings and answers some of the criticisms levelled against his earlier work. It is to this 1995 publication therefore that I will refer for the most part in the following discussion, although reference will be made to earlier publications where appropriate.

operation is, however, observable in regularities of behaviour "in recurrent situations of the same type" (ibid:55). A further crucial point about norms is that they are not immutable. They differ from culture to culture and between groups within a culture, and they change over time. Norms serve as the backdrop against which behaviour is evaluated and positively or negatively sanctioned. They thus exert a kind of regulatory force on translators' activities, but they are also reinforced by translators, or other agents in the translation process, by virtue of their tendency to conform to prevailing norms. It is possible to deviate from norms, but there is often a price to pay if one does so, and not everyone is equally well placed to do so. Deviation can, of course, only be recognized if the norms governing a particular type of behaviour have already been recognized. In this way, even creative translation solutions, like creative uses of language in general, can be interpreted only in the light of behaviour that tends to conform to the relevant prevailing norms.

Subsequent commentators, including Nord (1991), Chesterman (1993), and Hermans (1996), have sought to define a more differentiated approach to sociocultural constraints in translation. Their sometimes conflicting contributions are summarized in Baker (1998a). For the sake of clarity, however, we restrict ourselves here to Toury's approach. There is another reason to adopt Toury's version of norms: Toury makes a distinction between norms themselves – 'performance instructions' that are acquired by individuals in the course of their socialization – and the realization of such norms. Other commentators allow the term 'norm' to be homonymous, referring to both an observable regularity in behaviour and the unobservable, underlying mechanism that accounts for this regularity (see Hermans 1999:80). This position, while reflecting a common-sense understanding of the term, might suggest that an observed regularity, for example, repeated use in a text of a full nominal group where a pro-form might suffice, reflects unambiguously an underlying norm – in this case, one that predisposes translators to make explicit in the target text information that is only implicit in the source text (Toury 1978:95; Baker 1996b:180). Practice shows however, that it is very difficult to associate unambiguously many observable patterns with a unique underlying norm,[3] suggesting that the two ought to be kept separate. We will return to this point below.

Toury goes on to list various specific norms that may operate in any translation activity. The 'initial norm' is that which informs the basic choice between subjecting oneself "to the original text, with the norms it has realized, or to the norms active in the target culture, or in that section of it which would host the end product" (1995:56). The first option reflects the pursuit of what Toury terms "adequate" translation; the second the pursuit of "acceptable" translation (ibid:56-57). The initial norm, he stresses, should not be over-interpreted. Its use is more as an explanatory tool that may serve to elucidate either macro or micro-level decisions. Toury also

[3] See Newman (1987:79-80) and Baker (1996b:180) on this point.

posits "preliminary" and "operational" norms (ibid:58-59). Preliminary norms are those that relate to (a) translation policy, for example what texts are selected by a culture for translation in the first place, and (b) the directness of translation: is translation via a third language permitted, prohibited, tolerated or preferred and in what circumstances? Operational norms are either (a) matricial, that is, governing the very existence of target text material and its distribution in the target text (matricial norms thus govern features such as omissions, additions, and text segmentation) or (b) textual-linguistic, governing the actual linguistic formulation of the target text.

Despite Toury's seemingly neat typology of norms, he is aware that norms interact in complex ways and that they are inherently variable and unstable (ibid:59-62). The ensuing difficulties in tracking their operation, Toury claims, should not be taken to imply that there is no such thing as norms active in translation. Rather they suggest that "real-life situations tend to be complex; and this complexity had better be noted rather than ignored if one is to draw any justifiable conclusions" (ibid:63). This complexity has indeed been noted by several commentators who have pursued the notion of norms in descriptive studies of translation. One observation is that, when studying translations, we may expect to find "a variety of competing, conflicting and overlapping norms and models which pertain to a whole array of other social domains" (Hermans 1996:39). Another obvious difficulty is that, as indicated above, norms are not directly observable. Rather we observe repeated patterns, for example, in the choice of texts translated into a particular language, or in the linguistic formulations used in translated texts, and then we interpret these patterns as evidence of the operation of hypothesized preliminary and operational norms respectively. Corpus linguistic techniques can point up repeated linguistic patterns in texts, and instances that appear to be deviations from these patterns, but it is still up to the analyst to decide whether or not these patterns are norm induced, and if so, what norm, or group of norms, applies. The scenario described here is clearly a data-driven one. In practice, repeated observations of recurring patterns, and even non-empirically validated hunches, can lead to strong expectations among researchers that a particular norm will be operating at a particular time. Researchers then undertake hypothesis-driven studies of corpora and look for evidence of putative norms in translated texts. Notwithstanding the comments made above, if we make the simplistic assumption that a particular textual-linguistic phenomenon indicates the operation of a particular norm, then we can assume, as does Toury, a distributional basis for the study of norms. The more frequent a phenomenon – Toury's interest is in phenomena that constitute shifts from 'adequate' translation – the more likely it is to represent "a more permitted (tolerated) activity, a stronger tendency, a more basic (obligatory) norm" (Toury 1995:68-69).

In his earlier work, Toury (1978:95) suggests that phenomena that occur with a high frequency should not be automatically assumed to have been caused by translation norms. Rather, they may be evidence of "universals of translation behaviour". While norms are socially and culturally determined, and change over time, universals represent general tendencies, and are observed irrespective of the translator, language, genre, or period. The distinction between shifts in translation due to the operation of norms and those that represent translation universals is not at all clear, although Toury suggests that it might be made on the basis of a combination of 'theoretical speculation' and the findings of empirical studies "carried out along similar lines and relating to different languages/literatures and to various periods in history" (ibid:95-96). But despite the fact that a number of studies have been carried out on textual features that point to explicitation in translation (Blum-Kulka 1986; Olohan and Baker 2000; Weissbrod 1992; Øverås 1998), for example, there seems to be no agreement yet on whether it is a universal of translation or merely norm-induced.[4]

Other details pertaining to norms and universals have still to be ironed out. Mona Baker (personal communication), for example, points out that if universals, by definition, cannot be accounted for in terms of the socio-cultural, historical constraints that fashion norms, then there must be cognitive factors involved, ones that have not yet been investigated within translation studies. Thus while the *description* of the textual-linguistic features that constitute realizations of norms, on the one hand, and universals, on the other, may proceed along broadly the same lines, with researchers expecting differences in the degrees to which norms and universals are manifest, *explanations* of norm-induced regularities and those due to universals of translation behaviour will differ in kind, and not just degree. In other words, universals are not just norms that allow no deviation. They are relatable to cognitive factors rather than social ones.

Despite the problems involved in their investigation, linguistic manifestations of hypothesized norms and universals of translation have become the focus of much work in DTS in general, and in corpus-based studies in particular (for an overview of such work see Baker 1993, 1996b; Laviosa-Braithwaite 1998). As already indicated, explicitation is one tendency that has received attention in the literature. Others include the translator's supposed tendency to simplify, and to normalize linguistic usage in target texts. All three tendencies, and studies that have sought to uncover evidence for them, are discussed in greater detail below. It has also been suggested that translators tend to steer a middle course between poles such as those of orality and literacy (Shlesinger 1989) – a tendency Baker (1996b:184) has dubbed "levelling out" – and that they avoid mirroring repetitions that occur in source texts (Shlesinger 1991; Toury 1991). Neither of these tendencies is discussed in detail here, although one might say that they point to a desire or need (conscious or otherwise) to ensure target textual conventionality that is consistent with a tendency to normalize linguistic usage. Finally, translations are said to exhibit a

---

[4] Weissbrod (1992) and Øverås (1998) consider explicitation to be norm-governed. Toury (1978) is confident that explicitation is a universal tendency, as is Blum-Kulka (1986). And Olohan and Baker (forthcoming) pursue the study of explicitation as a 'potential' universal.

distribution of lexical items that distinguishes them from original texts in the same language (Gellerstam 1986; Laviosa 1998b; Shamaa 1978:161-173; Toury 1989, 1995:206-220). Such a distinctive distribution of lexical items could be a symptom of one or all of the tendencies already mentioned – explicitation, simplification, normalization, levelling out and avoidance of repetitions must all have an effect on the lexical profile of texts – although in the relevant research, the influence of the source language and text(s) is usually acknowledged.

It has already being stated that norms and universals are in some ways the staples of the descriptive branch of translation studies. They represent explanations for patterns repeatedly observed in translated texts. But universals also have the power of prediction: if we accept that some type of behaviour – explicitation, for instance – is a universal of translation, this means that we predict explicitation will occur in instances of translation that we have not yet encountered. This predictive power of universals is what makes them look quite like Toury's (1995) 'laws' of translation (see also Chesterman 1993:4, who sees the two as largely synonymous). The difference is that Toury's laws are probabilistic and more nuanced than most articulations of universal tendencies in translation. They are cast in the form:

> if X, then the greater/the lesser the likelihood that Y (Toury 1995:265)

where X is some kind of conditioning factor, and Y an (aspect of an) observed instance of behaviour.

Repeated cycles of description, ensuing formulation of hypotheses cast as probabilistic laws, and testing of these hypotheses on larger bodies of data, would lead, according to Toury, to increasingly refined hypotheses and more and more elaborate studies. Given a more refined theory, researchers could aim towards multi-conditional laws of the type:

> if X_1 and Z_1, then the likelihood that Y is greater than if X_1 and Z_2, and even greater than if X_1 and Z_3 (ibid:266).

As the above paragraph suggests, Toury's 'laws' can be regarded as *hypotheses* to be tested and refined on the basis of more and more elaborate studies (see also Chesterman 1997:71-72; Shreve 1996:82, 1997:53; and Hermans 1999:92-93). In fact, 'law' is an unfortunate choice of term in this case. For many people 'laws' are prescriptive, which Toury's probabilistic laws are clearly not meant to be. For others, 'laws', understood as descriptive statements of general principles, are associated primarily with the natural sciences, and Toury's use of the term can be interpreted as a mere ploy to buoy up his "claim of scientificity" (Venuti 1997:361).

Terminological debates aside, many commentators are sceptical about any quest for laws of translation. For Toury, the ultimate aim of translation laws is to state "the inherent relations between all the variables found to be relevant to translation"

(1995:16). As Hermans (1999:92) points out, this project relies on the assumption that *all* the variables relevant to translation, as well as the relations between them, can be known. It also raises – but does not answer – the question of who decides what is relevant to translation. Toury's approach seems to suggest that natural laws of translation are discoverable from translation data, and that the theorist's subjectivity need not encroach upon a properly, that is scientifically, conducted study of translation. This kind of objectivism, prevalent in much of Toury's work, and in some projects in corpus-based translation studies (Tymoczko 1998:653), has been criticized by Venuti (1997:361-363) and Tymoczko (ibid:653-654). Venuti finds it particularly damaging, as it stands in the way of fruitful interaction between Toury's scholarship and other developments in translation studies, namely those inspired by varieties of psychoanalysis, feminism, Marxism, and poststructuralism, "all discourses that insist on the difficulty of separating fact from value in humanistic interpretation" (Venuti ibid:363).

Herman's, Tymoczko's and Venuti's objections to 'laws' of translation are accepted here. It seems unlikely that any researcher could ever monitor all the variables relevant to any particular act of translation, or that any formulation of laws, or norms for that matter, could ever be made wholly objectively (see Venuti ibid:362). These objections notwithstanding, I have a particular interest in the substance of the first of two 'laws' proposed at the end of Toury's 1995 book. The law of growing standardization states that:

> textual relations obtaining in the original are often modified, sometimes to the point of being totally ignored, in favour of [more] habitual options offered by a target repertoire. (ibid: 268)[5]

What this means is that the linguistic choices translators make are, for some reason, more conventional from the target language point of view, than are those made by original writers from the source language point of view. Whereas original writers may create dense networks of links in their texts, building up text-specific or 'instantial' meanings (Halliday and Hasan 1976:289), translators are thought to undo

[5] Toury's law of growing standardization was formerly known as the 'law of conversion' (Toury 1980, 1993). 'Conversion' here refers to the conversion in translation of textemes ("any element, at any level, participating in textual relationships and carrying textual functions", Toury 1980:96) to repertoremes ("any sign, irrespective of rank and scope, which forms part of an institutionalized repertoire", Toury 1995:268). Toury's alternative formulation of the law of standardization runs: "in translation, source-text textemes tend to be converted into target-language (or target-culture) repertoremes" (1995:268). Hermans finds this formulation most unhelpful, as "any language is an institutionalized repertoire of signs, and any word in a sentence a texteme" (1999:93). I follow Hermans here in preferring the formulation that stresses the replacement of elements in the source text that have special status in that text by more mundane or habitual items in the target text.

these links, and replace them with something more run-of-the-mill in the target language. Toury's law of standardization would thus seem to have much in common with the hypothesized norm/universal of normalization in translation. The principal conditioning factor that Toury mentions in the case of growing standardization concerns the position of translated literature within the literary polysystem. Basically, Toury suggests that the more peripheral translation is, the more it will accommodate itself to established models and repertoires in the target polysystem (1995:271).[6]

Toury uses an example from *The Great Gatsby* to illustrate standardization in translation: F. Scott Fitzgerald describes Gatsby's lawn as running towards the front door, jumping over sundials, and drifting up the side of the house in bright vines. As 'drifting up' would not normally collocate with either 'lawn' or 'vines', their co-selection is not a routine use of English; rather it marks an *ad hoc* use which assumes special 'textemic' status. Toury shows that in translation into German, French and Hebrew, the special effect of the English text is jettisoned as the translations make use of "items of their respective linguistic repertoires whose collocability with the replacements of 'lawn' and/or 'vines' ... **is much more habitual**" (1995:269, Toury's emphasis).

Toury's second example of standardization draws on an experiment conducted by Kurt Kohn using a short English text that can be interpreted as referring to the fact that the protagonist is being held either in prison or in a wrestling hold. Kohn shows how the text is translated into German by advanced students of translation in such a way as to rule out one of the readings. Toury maintains that in such cases where the ambiguity in the source text may itself count as functional, any disambiguation "would involve an irreparable dissolution of more, and more intricate textual relations" (ibid:270). In this case, while intricate source-textual relations – those between potentially ambiguous lexical items whose co-occurrence reinforces and eventually actualizes such ambiguities – are undoubtedly undone in translation, one would not necessarily claim that the lexical choices made in the target text are somehow more 'habitual', 'standard', or 'normal' than those made in the source text; they simply do not give rise to the same confluence of ambiguity. I would like to suggest therefore, that what is described as lexical normalization below can be a concomitant of 'growing standardization' as discussed by Toury, but that the two do not necessarily go together. Toury's law of growing standardization is particularly interesting in the present context however, because it provides insight into how lexical meaning can be text-specific, rather than predictable on the basis of conventional meanings attached to words in their host repertoires. This is one aspect of Toury's work that links him to corpus linguists like John Sinclair, a point that is taken up again in Chapter Four.

Toury's second law, the law of interference, in its most basic formulation

---

[6] For a critique of this position, see Hermans (1999:93-94).

states that:

> in translation, phenomena pertaining to the make-up of the source text tend to be transferred to the target text (1995:275)

and may be conditioned by factors such as text type, linguistic level, and the relative prestige or power of the languages and cultures involved in the act of translation (ibid:278-279). It is interesting in the present context because it seems to run counter to Toury's first law: items pertaining to the make-up of the source text would not normally be expected to represent habitual choices in the target text.

So far I have introduced a number of tendencies that are thought to be characteristic of translation, whether they are described as norms, universals, or laws, but have said little about where the evidence for these tendencies has come from. Some evidence comes from studies conducted within the DTS framework outlined above and using hard copy corpora. But electronic corpora are becoming increasingly popular in studies of translation norms and universals. Below I describe a number of corpus-based projects in translation studies, paying particular attention to the different types of electronic corpus currently in use, and the methodological implications of using them. Some of these studies are hypothesis-driven, that is, they set out to find textual evidence for abstract notions like 'simplification' or 'explicitation'. Others are data-driven in that they aim to describe low-level linguistic features of texts, which may or may not be later explained in terms of these same abstract notions of simplification, explicitation, etc. Most are exploratory in nature, designed, to a greater or lesser extent, to show what can be done with electronic corpora.

Corpora in translation studies

Theorists like Gideon Toury stress the need to observe regularities – and provide explanatory hypotheses for those regularities – on the basis of ever-expanding corpora of texts, claiming that explanations of features observed even in a single translation must rely on the study of bigger corpora, compiled "according to some principle: translator, school of translators, period, text-type, text-linguistic phenomenon, or any other principle which could be given a justification" (Toury 1995:38). Toury thus gives an indication of the kind of design criteria that may guide corpus construction in translation studies. More elaborate typologies of corpora in use in translation studies have been established by Baker (1995) and Laviosa (1997). Central to such typologies are three basic questions:

> How many languages are represented in the corpus in question?
> In the case of monolingual corpora, do all texts originate in the language of the corpus, or are some, or all of them, translations?
> In the case of bilingual and multilingual corpora, is there a relationship of translation between the different language sections of the corpus?

Monolingual single and comparable corpora

A corpus that contains texts in one language only is, quite obviously, a monolingual corpus. If all the texts in a monolingual corpus have the same kind of provenance, for example if they are all translations into that language, or if they were all originally written in that language, then we can talk of a 'single' monolingual corpus (Laviosa 1997:292-3). As this definition suggests, a single monolingual corpus can either be translational or non-translational. From the point of view of the translation scholar, familiar corpora such as the British National Corpus (BNC) and the Brown Corpus, introduced in Chapter Two, are single non-translational corpora. Single non-translational corpora, especially those containing specialized texts, can be used: in translation pedagogy, to reinforce students' knowledge of normal target language patterns and improve translation quality (Bowker 1998; Pearson 1996, 1999); as an aid in translation quality assessment (Bowker 1999); and in terminology extraction (Pearson 1998). Major reference corpora like the BNC and the Cobuild Bank of English can also be used as 'controls' in descriptive studies of translation, allowing patterns observed in a source or target text to be set off against what is known about the language in general (Kenny 1998b; Munday 1998).

Single translational corpora, on the other hand, are used by scholars interested in studying translated text in and for itself. Such studies are motivated by a belief in the specificity of translation, by a conviction that there are features that occur in translated text but not in original text (or at least not to the same extent), and that can be explained not with reference to 'interference' from a source language, but rather in terms of the nature and pressures of the translation process itself. Single translational corpora may also be used to home in on the style of individual translators, although there are still very few examples of such work (see Baker in press, 2000). The best known translational corpus, and a pioneering development in the field, is the Translational English Corpus or TEC (Baker 1999:283-287; Laviosa 1997:296-309; Olohan and Baker 2000). The TEC is held at UMIST in Manchester, and contains texts translated into English from a wide variety of languages – thus allowing the influence of any one particular source language to be more easily isolated – and distributed across genres such as fiction, biography, news and inflight magazines. At the time of writing it contains 6 million words, although its compilers intend to increase this to between 20 and 30 million words by 2003 (Olohan and Baker ibid). Most notably, the TEC can be accessed freely by researchers worldwide through the project's web site.[7]

In order to ascertain that some pattern is specific to, or particularly characteristic of translated text, researchers using single translational corpora typically cross-check their findings against a corpus of texts originally produced in the target language. Thus a corpus like the BNC can act as a control for English in general, as suggested

---

[7] The project's URL is http://ubatuba.ccl.umist.ac.uk/tec/.

above. Some translation researchers go one step further, however, and construct their own control corpus of original texts. This results in a monolingual 'comparable' corpus, so called because the two sets of texts are comparable by virtue of their having been created in similar circumstances, to fulfil similar roles. Thus a monolingual comparable corpus might consist of a set of newspaper articles written in English for publication in a specific section of a national newspaper, alongside a set of articles translated into English for publication in the same section of the same newspaper. Such a collection actually exists as a subcorpus of the English Comparable Corpus (ECC), a sister project of TEC (Laviosa-Braithwaite 1996; Laviosa 1997, 1998a, 1998b). Another notable monolingual comparable corpus is reported on by Gellerstam (1986). It is held at the University of Gothenburg and consists of 75 novels published in Swedish in 1976, half (sic) of them originally written in Swedish, the other half translated into Swedish, mostly from English. More recently, the Savonlinna School of Translation Studies in Joensuu, Finland has started to construct a monolingual comparable corpus of original Finnish writing and translations into Finnish from English, German and Russian (Baker 1999:284, 296 n.3).

As suggested above, monolingual comparable corpora are useful in the investigation of features that are particularly characteristic of translated texts as opposed to originals. They offer the considerable advantage that they allow comparisons between sets of texts to be made on the basis of global quantitative measures. Measures such as type-token ratios, lexical densities and mean sentence lengths (see Chapter Two) can be meaningfully compared across texts or corpora in the same language in order to ascertain whether, for example, translated texts typically contain less varied vocabulary, or shorter sentences than originals, features that might be expected if translation really does involve simplification, as suggested by some writers. By way of contrast, the same measures cannot be as easily used in bilingual comparisons of source texts and target texts. This is because such measures are highly language dependent. If a language is morphologically 'rich', we might expect relatively high (unlemmatized) type-token ratios for texts in that language, simply because they will contain a greater variety of forms than texts in a morphologically 'poorer' language. Compare the number of forms for any regular verb in Spanish to the number of forms for an equivalent verb in English, for example. Lemmatization can help overcome this problem, but problems related to orthographic conventions and homonyms will still remain (see Chapter Two and Munday 1998 on these issues). Similar problems occur with lexical densities: languages use function words in different ways. If we compare something as apparently simple as definite and indefinite across languages, we find that English has the articles 'the' and 'a' or 'an', Irish has a definite article but not an indefinite one (the absence of a determiner implies indefiniteness) and Norwegian has an indefinite article but no free-standing definite article (a suffix on the noun in question indicates definiteness). Translation scholars who wish to make comparisons of lexical densities in source and target texts may have to factor into their calculations the cumulative effect of such systemic differences, in order to distinguish between effects of translation, and those due simply to the grammars of the two languages involved. Likewise, average sentence lengths vary according to language. Thus Arabic typically has much longer sentences than English, if sentence boundaries are identified at full stops and other conventional sentence-ending punctuation marks (Baker 1992:193, 215). Translation scholars therefore have to ask themselves what, if any, are the implications of an Arabic translation having a higher mean sentence length than its English source text.

Fortunately, these problems do not arise with monolingual corpora. Global measures like those mentioned above have been applied by Sara Laviosa in an analysis of translated and original newspaper articles in English (Laviosa 1998a). Laviosa hypothesizes that the translated texts will have a lower type-token ratio, lexical density and mean sentence length than the originals. These observable textual features, she proposes, would be consistent with an underlying (universal) tendency of translators to simplify. Her hypotheses are borne out on two counts, those of lexical density and mean sentence length, but she finds no significant difference in type-token ratios between translated and original texts.[8] Lexical density is also lower in translated narrative prose than in comparable originals, according to a second study conducted by Laviosa (1998b). But this time mean sentence length turns out to be higher in the translated texts than in the originals.[9] In this second study, Laviosa identifies what she calls 'core patterns of lexical use' in translated text, so called because they are confirmed for both newspaper articles and narrative prose. Thus, compared to original texts, translated texts are found to display: lower lexical densities; higher proportions of high frequency word forms; more repetition of high frequency word forms; and less variety (in terms of the number of different lemmas accounted for) in the most frequently used word forms.[10] Laviosa's work, although not conclusive, is important because it demonstrates how computerized quantitative studies, conducted entirely in the target language environment and on raw corpora, can reveal potentially interesting facts about the global distribution of lexical items in translated text. The earlier paper cited here (Laviosa 1998a) is also an example of how one can attempt to make operational in computerized corpus analysis, abstract

---

[8] Al-Shabab (1996:101-112), on the other hand, finds that radio news broadcasts translated from Arabic into English do have a lower type-token ratio than comparable original English broadcasts (no test of statistical significance is used), but his findings are based on a very small corpus (22,772 running words in all) and are complicated by the fact the Arabic texts were not translated by English native speakers.

[9] Mean sentence length may not be a good indicator of simplification anyway. As Puurtinen (1998:525) points out, keeping sentences short may require writers to use concise complex syntactic structures that actually render texts more difficult to understand.

[10] Laviosa does not make explicit her criterion for identifying a word form as 'high frequency', but it appears from the statistics she gives that she is concerned with forms that account for at least 0.1% of the tokens in their respective corpora.

notions like 'simplification'. Laviosa is more circumspect in the second paper however. Rather than attribute the core patterns of lexical use she discovers to translators' tendency to simplify,[11] she suggests that possible explanations would have to be sought in the relevant source texts, thus reintroducing a bilingual dimension (1998b:565).

Like Laviosa, Gellerstam (1986) uses a comparable corpus to study the distribution of lexical items in translated text. Looking specifically at vocabulary used much more often in novels translated into Swedish than in comparable Swedish originals – but ignoring those lexical differences that can be explained in terms of differences in material culture – Gellerstam finds that the translations contain more loan words and fewer colloquialisms than the originals, and that certain Swedish words are used in translation in ways that differ from their use in original Swedish. Gellerstam's study is limited by the fact that only translations from English are considered, making generalizations about non-language pair specific translation behaviour impossible. Indeed, Gellerstam makes no attempt to explain his findings in terms of general translation tendencies, socially, cognitively or otherwise determined. Rather they are seen as reflecting the influence of the English source texts (ibid:88).[12] Nevertheless, it remains a good example of how quantitative analyses can become qualitative (See Chapter Two on this point). The software helps make quantitative distinctions (frequent vs infrequent forms), leaving the human analyst to make qualitative ones (loan words vs indigenous ones; neutral vs colloquial words; etc).

Olohan and Baker's (2000) study of reporting structures in translated and original English differs from those already mentioned in two respects. Firstly, they are interested in a single word – the complementizer 'that' – rather than global patterns of lexical distribution. And secondly, whereas studies like Laviosa's (1998a, 1998b) make heavy use of word listing tools to compute global statistics for corpora, Olohan and Baker rely on the power of a concordancer to reveal patterns of omission and inclusion of optional 'that' with the reporting verbs SAY and TELL in the Translational English Corpus and a comparable subcorpus of the BNC. They find that optional 'that' is used far more frequently by translators than other writers of English, and suggest that this indicates a tendency towards syntactic explicitation in translation. Interestingly, they emphasize that this process must be 'inherent' and 'subliminal', as "Translators clearly do not adopt a conscious strategy of spelling out optional syntactic elements such as *that* in reporting clauses more often than writers producing original texts in the same language" (Olohan and Baker 2000).

In a separate study based on TEC, but making only limited use of comparable

---

[11] By contrast, Al-Shabab (1996:110) sees similar patterns uncovered in his limited study (see Footnote 8) as indicators of simplification.

[12] Gellerstam's findings may thus be interpretable in the light of Touryan 'interference' (see above), which may have cognitive explanations, but is also socio-culturally determined in the sense that different cultures show different levels of tolerance for interference (Toury 1995:275).

original English language data, Baker (in press, 2000) analyzes the individual styles of two translators – Peter Bush and Peter Clark. Clark's output is found to have a lower type-token ratio and mean sentence length than that of Bush, leading Baker to speculate that Clark makes a greater, though probably largely subconscious attempt to mediate his (Arabic) source texts by making them "less challenging linguistically". Again she homes in on the verb SAY in order to monitor the use by the two translators of reporting structures in their narratives. A concordance of the node SAY in each translator's output reveals interesting differences in their preferences for direct vs indirect speech, historic present vs past tense, etc. In a very Firthian move, Baker then attempts to relate her description of Bush's and Clark's respective 'linguistic habits' to what is known about their social and cultural experience and positioning. The latter information is either accessible in the header files of the TEC, or is elicited specially from the translators involved. Baker is aware, however, that the situational and cultural context in which translators operate is just one source of explanations for the linguistic patterns observed in their work. Other sources are, of course, the source texts and original authors involved. But while the headers in the TEC do include much valuable information about source texts and authors, the user does not have access to the source texts themselves. Thus while monolingual translational corpora have been invaluable in attempts to describe the specific nature of translated text and to pinpoint aspects of the styles of individual translators (and not just original authors), some researchers (Laviosa 1998b:565; Puurtinen 1998:529) have argued that studies based on them may sometimes need to be supplemented by an analysis of the relevant source texts.

Parallel corpora

A body of texts in one language along with their translations into another is known as a 'parallel' corpus. Most parallel corpora are bilingual, but parallel corpora can contain translations into several target languages of the same source-language texts: multilingual parallel corpora have been compiled, for example, by the Multiconc consortium (King 1997) and the Oslo Multilingual Corpus project.[13] Two of the best known bilingual parallel corpora are the Canadian Hansards – the bilingual proceedings of the Canadian Parliament (Brown *et al.* 1990:82) – and the English-Norwegian Parallel Corpus or ENPC (Johansson and Hofland 1994; Johansson *et al.* 1996; Johansson 1998). Both are bidirectional: the former contains French originals and their translations into English, and English originals and their translations into French; the latter translations (of mostly fiction) into Norwegian from English, and into English from Norwegian.

Alignment techniques (see Chapter Five) are used to provide explicit links

[13] The URL of the Oslo Multilingual Corpus project is http://www.hf.uio.no/iba/prosjekt/.

between words or sentences that are judged to be translations of each other in a parallel corpus. Corpora aligned in this way can furnish ready-made translations for use in Machine(-aided) Translation. Thus Brown *et al.* (1990, 1993) use the Canadian Hansards as a data source in their statistical approach to Machine Translation. Aligned parallel corpora are also used as sources of empirical data in contrastive linguistics. One recent collection edited by Johansson and Oksefjell (1998) contains numerous examples of contrastive studies of words and structures in two, or sometimes three, languages. These studies rarely provide any insights into translation *per se* however, and some contrastive linguists are even uneasy about using translated text to exemplify the patterns of an object language in the first place. So far there seems to be little overlap in the interests of contrastive linguists and translation scholars when it comes to using parallel corpora (see Baker 1999:282-283 on this point).

One scholar who has used a parallel corpus to conduct research within the framework of descriptive translation studies is Linn Øverås (1996, 1998). Øverås uses data from the ENPC to look for evidence of explicitation in translation. Drawing on previous work by Blum-Kulka (1986) and Weissbrod (1992), she describes shifts in cohesion that affect the level of explicitness in target texts vis-à-vis their source texts. Thus the insertion into an English target text of conjunctions such as 'and', 'then', or 'but', can make inter-clausal relations that were implicit in the source text, explicit in the target text. Øverås evaluates a number of 'explicitating' and 'implicitating' shifts in both English-Norwegian and Norwegian-English translation. She confirms that the former are far more common than the latter and concludes that explicitation can be considered a feature of the translations in her corpus.

A significant feature of Øverås's analysis is that it is manual. It is not the software that uncovers instances of shifts, but the human analyst. This is probably what allows Øverås to recognize an impressive variety of shifts, the surface realizations of which are not always predictable, making them difficult to access automatically in a corpus with only minimal mark-up. Øverås uses the Translation Corpus Explorer, a browser designed for use with parallel corpora (Ebeling 1998), to facilitate the initial collection and presentation of data, but once she has isolated her subcorpus – the first fifty sentences from forty novels in the ENPC and their translations – she proceeds in a traditional, sequential fashion, working her way through the aligned pairs of source and target sentences to see what she finds. This contrasts with the direct access approach adopted in studies that use a concordancer to pinpoint occurrences of words or constructions specified in advance by the linguist (examples include Baker in press, 2000; Munday 1998; Olohan and Baker 2000). Øverås's approach has the advantage that she is not likely to miss any relevant shifts in the subcorpus she focuses on, but it is easier to ensure depth rather than breadth of coverage given such detailed manual analysis.

Jeremy Munday (1998) arguably gets more mileage out of the computer in his analysis of shifts in the English translation by Edith Grossman of Gabriel García

Márquez's short story *Diesiciete ingleses envenenados*, although his 'corpus' is very small (roughly 4,500 running words in each language). He uses basic statistics and frequency lists (generated by WordSmith Tools) to get an idea of which lexical items might be worth investigating in the translation, and then homes in on selected items using a concordancer. The concordancer (the Concord program in WordSmith) is used not just to reveal all instances of words like *su/sus* and 'her', but also to show features of word order in the two texts: Munday marks up his texts, making sentence boundaries explicit by the insertion of the start-of-sentence tags <s> (in the Spanish originals) and <se> (in the English translations). He then uses these tags as search terms in order to reveal all elements in sentence-initial position in each text. The microstructural shifts (Leuven-Zwart 1989, 1990) that Munday discovers in the use of pronouns and the positioning of adjuncts in the two texts contribute, he argues, to an overall change in narrative viewpoint, with the translation losing some of the immediacy and cinematic quality of the original. Munday goes on to suggest that some of these shifts may be explained in terms of the translator's idiolect, and others in terms of her conforming to target language norms, as evidenced in the BNC and the Associated Press Corpus, used by Munday as control corpora. The idea that translators may have a particular tendency to conform to target language norms, in other words, to normalize, is one that comes up again and again in the literature. It is also central to the study reported on in this book, and is discussed in detail below.

Another example of a computerized study using a small (non-aligned) parallel corpus and conducted within a descriptive translation studies framework is provided by Opas and Kujamäki (1995). Opas and Kujamäki use the Text Analysis Computing Tools (TACT) available from the University of Toronto (see Kennedy 1998:86, 262-263) to study stream of consciousness techniques in the Finnish and German translations of Samuel Beckett's prose text *How it is*. They track the translation of items like 'I' and 'yes', which are constantly repeated in the source text, and conclude that the German translation manages better than the Finnish one to emulate the effect these repetitions have on the overall narrative viewpoint of the original piece. In order to check whether this finding is due to the individual translators' preferences or is a reflection of the fact that English and German are closely related, whereas English and Finnish are not, they look at a second Beckett text *All Strange Away* in translation into another language that is closely related to English-Swedish. Here they find that microstructural shifts in translation such as the nominalization of verbal constructions, the addition of explicitating pronouns, and the conversion of non-finite constructions involving the English verbal suffix '-ing' to finite constructions in Swedish, all contribute to a target text that is more concrete, more explicit, and less timeless than the original. Their ultimate conclusion is that the micro- and macrostructural shifts they discover in their modest corpus – *How it is* contains around 36,000 running words; *All Strange Away* fewer than 5,000 – are due not to systemic differences between the languages involved, but to the initial norm followed by the translator. Whereas the German translator "seems to subject himself more to the original text", the Finnish and Swedish translators are thought to "commit themselves to the target language readers" (Opas and Kujamäki 1995:291). Opas and Kujamäki (ibid) note that the unnamed German translator has translated all of Beckett's oeuvre, whereas the Finnish and Swedish translators have translated only single texts by him. There is thus an implied link between the German translator's commitment to Beckett as an author and his close paralleling, in translation, of selected features of one of Beckett's texts.

The survey given here of research in descriptive translation studies conducted using computerized parallel corpora is short and draws on relatively small-scale studies. Although larger studies have been conducted using hard copy corpora – Vanderauwera (1985), introduced at the beginning of Chapter Two, remains one of the best examples – they have not yet been emulated, to my knowledge at least, in computer-assisted studies. This may have something to do with the not inconsiderable practical difficulties that face scholars who wish to compile a parallel corpus in electronic form. These difficulties, which have to do with copyright problems, issues of 'balance' in corpus composition, and corpus alignment, are discussed in detail in Chapter Five. For the moment it is enough to say that GEPCOLT, the two-million word parallel corpus constructed especially for the study reported on in the latter half of this book, appears quite substantial in comparison to other parallel corpora used so far in translation studies.

Bilingual and multilingual comparable corpora

Bilingual and multilingual corpora need not necessarily contain texts related to each other through translation. Rather their component texts may be comparable on the basis of similarity of their content, domain and communicative function (Zanettin 1998:617). Such bilingual and multilingual comparable corpora have been used in contrastive linguistics (Aijmer *et al.* 1996) and lexicography (Teubert 1996), but their use in descriptive translation studies is limited by the fact that they tell us nothing about actual translations, and so this category of corpus will not be further elaborated upon here. For a discussion of how bilingual comparable corpora may be of real assistance in translator training however, see Zanettin (1998).

Normalization in translation

Normalization – described above as the exaggerated use in translated texts of features that are typical of the target language – is one tendency that has been observed in both monolingual comparable and bilingual parallel corpora. From the point of view of the user of a monolingual comparable corpus, normalization can be said to have occurred when translations contain more (or a higher proportion of) instances of some feature deemed typical of conservative target language writing, than do comparable originals. Thus Toury (1980:130, 1995:105) describes how binomials – the simultaneous use of near-synonyms like 'law and order' in English – were used to a greater extent in Hebrew translations in the second quarter of the twentieth century than they were in original Hebrew composition at that time. In a sense translators sought to enhance the Hebraity of their texts by using a device that was characteristic of canonical texts in that language.

From the point of view of the user of a parallel corpus, normalization may be said to occur when translators opt for conventional target language solutions to problems posed by creative or unusual source text features. Another way to say this is that normalization occurs when translations contain fewer instances of abnormal or creative target language features than would be expected on the basis of their respective source texts alone. Lexical normalization, that is normalization at the level of individual words and collocations, has been observed in a number of sources. Vanderauwera, for example, observes that translators of Dutch fiction into English exhibit "reserve in rendering unusual and mannered imagery and word choice in the target text"(1985:108). Øverås (1996, 1998) too finds examples where unusual collocations in both English and Norwegian originals are translated by more conventional ones. And Malmkjær (1998) demonstrates how, in multiple translations into English of Hans Christian Andersen's *The steadfast tin soldier*, seven out of eight translators use a conventional target language collocation to translate a Danish collocation that in fact contravenes norms for that language. Such comments on lexical normalization have, however, been made either in passing or on the basis of very small samples: Vanderauwera's (1985) comments come as part of a broad ranging study of Dutch novels in English translation; as already mentioned, Øverås (1996, 1998) is primarily concerned with describing explicitating shifts in her corpus of 2,000 source language sentences and their translations; and Malmkjær (1998) is more concerned with making a methodological point about the use of parallel corpora in translation studies than with lexical normalization *per se*. A single example thus suffices for her purposes. Toury's (1995:102-112) study of binomials in original and translated Hebrew, on the other hand, is presumably based on a substantial corpus, but he gives few details of its size, except to say that it is being extended "incessantly" (ibid:110). To my knowledge, no large-scale, systematic study has yet been conducted on the issue of lexical normalization in translation, and the topic has barely been broached within the framework of computerized, corpus-based translation studies. The corpus-based study reported on in the latter half of this book is thus intended as much to test the methodological waters as it is to uncover hard evidence, if there is any, of lexical normalization.

We have been concerned so far with lexical normalization, but normalization can also apply to other linguistic levels. Baker (1996b:183) suggests that it is also evident in the use in translated text of conventional grammatical structures and punctuation, an assertion that is backed up by several studies based on comparisons of source and target texts: Vanderauwera (ibid:93ff) provides several examples of 'textual conventionality' in her Dutch-English translation corpus, and normalizing strategies have also been observed in the work of simultaneous and consecutive interpreters (Shlesinger 1991). Malmkjær (1997) and May (1997) focus on the tendency of translators to normalize unconventional source text punctuation. According to May, "the changes that translators impose on punctuation have a regular, even predictable quality that suggests an overall 'editorial' rather than interpretive or creative approach to this aspect of language" (ibid:10).

If normalization is as prevalent as these studies suggest, the question arises as to whether translators are somehow inherently more conservative, or less creative, than other writers, or is there some cognitive constraint operative in the translation process that makes translators fall back on the routine of the target language? This type of analysis might be expected if one were to treat normalization as a universal feature of translation. Normalization may, however, be more easily explained in terms of socio-cultural, or even economic constraints. In cultures where the initial norm that seems to inform most translation decisions biases translations towards target language and culture acceptability, translated texts that deviate from such target acceptability may run the risk of being ignored, criticized, or ultimately rejected by their intended audiences, and so involve higher financial risks for publishers. Given the already precarious position of translated literature in English-language markets (Pym 2000; Rectanus 1990:3; Vanderauwera 1985:20ff; Venuti 1995:12), translators may be put under pressure to produce 'normal' target language texts by editors, or other agents in the publishing world (Kenny 1998b). The dynamics of the literary marketplace may affect linguistic choices in English-language translations in another way: translation rights for foreign literary works are often sold simultaneously to US and British publishers who then share translation costs (Rectanus 1990:32). In order to ensure that translations are maximally acceptable to audiences on both sides of the Atlantic,[14] publishers may insist on a kind of 'international' English that avoids vocabulary specific to a certain region (Pym 2000). This could result in lexically conventional target texts, although the phenomenon is still largely unexplored.[15] Finally, translators may even internalize certain markets' preference for 'fluent' (Venuti 1995) translations, and attempt, consciously or subconsciously, to pre-empt any criticism of their work by conforming to target language norms.

This is one side of the story, in which literary translators' creativity would seem

---

[14] Rectanus (1990) does not discuss how licensing arrangements impact on other English-speaking areas, Australia and New Zealand, for example, but presumably these areas are not unaffected by such arrangements.

[15] A related issue is raised by Sager (1997) who points to the need to use geographically and temporally neutral vocabulary when translating literature intended to be of universal significance. In such cases the use of non-culture specific terms is a literary device, rather than an economic expedient.

to be constrained by markets, publishers, editors, and perhaps even their own desire to have their work accepted. But it is not the full story. There are also publishers and translators who are less concerned with commercial success than others, and thus more willing to take risks on experimental translations of experimental source texts. Some translators delight in translating unconventional source texts in unconventional ways. Malcolm Green, translator and co-founder of Atlas Press, for example, is described in the British Centre for Literary Translation's *Directory of Literary Translators* as devoted to "excavating the obscure, translating the impossible and relieving German letters of its stodgy image". Lawrence Venuti is another translator who prefers the marginal to the mainstream (1996:92), and who seeks to subvert rather than reproduce the dominant discourse of the target culture (see Venuti 1995, 1996). If normalization is a real trend in German-English translation, for example, we might expect it to be bucked in translations completed by Malcolm Green and like-minded translators. At the very least, experimental source texts should provide examples of creative formulations – which can be reconstructed or normalized by their translators – and thus data for an investigation of source and target text creativity. In any study of normalization and creativity in translation it would thus seem appropriate to include works, as does the present study (see Chapter Five), brought out by publishers and/or translators whose stated aim is to bring marginal and experimental works to the attention of new audiences.

The ideas expressed here are, in the absence of appropriate research, necessarily tentative. They do indicate, however, one interesting way in which the linguistic features of texts may vary according to extralinguistic factors such as publishing strategies and literary goals, and thus how textual patterns might somehow be related to the wider context of situation as suggested by Firth. As we have seen, Toury (1980, 1993, 1995) has already attempted to build extralinguistic factors into his theoretical apparatus, notably in the guise of conditioning factors in his 'laws' of translation, but this line of inquiry has received much criticism and has not been pursued by others in DTS (Hermans 1999:36). Other, though not all, polysystems-inspired projects in translation studies have been described as "intricate" and "ingenious", but ultimately "bloodless" (Hermans ibid:117), with the struggles inherent in literary polysystems being waged by competing norms and models, rather than "individuals or collectives who stand to gain or lose something by the outcome" (ibid:118). In corpus-based translation studies, Mona Baker (1999, in press 2000) has been particularly concerned to relate textual patterns in translations to the personal histories and cultural agendas of the people who produce them. Corpus-based translation studies thus has the potential to personalize findings where at least one of its predecessors depersonalized them. At the same time corpus techniques can give researchers a bird's eye view of patterns found in the collective output of translators at a particular juncture, allowing generalizations to be based on hard evidence. As indicated in Chapter Two, this ability to zoom in and out from the general to the particular and back again is one that is particularly associated with the use of computers in the study of language. It is also regarded as one of the greatest strengths of corpus-based translation studies (Tymoczko 1998:652-653). Other strengths, and potential weaknesses, of corpus-based translation studies are discussed in the next section.

Advantages and limitations of corpora in translation studies

One of the greatest advantages offered by contemporary corpora in translation studies stems from the fact that they consist of texts in electronic form, and can thus be stored, distributed, and manipulated in ways that enhance their usefulness vis-à-vis hard copy corpora. Because data can be retrieved very quickly, studies involving electronic corpora can be supplemented, replicated, or even replaced by what emerge as more appropriate studies, with an ease that does not apply to non-electronic corpora. Where a corpus is available to the wider research community, subsequent researchers can corroborate, or repudiate, the findings of an initial study based on that corpus, or they can refine the hypotheses on which earlier studies were based – all desirable developments if one believes in the possibility of cumulative knowledge in a subject area. Different processing techniques – word listing, concordancing, etc – allow the same data to be viewed from a variety of angles, stimulating multiple analyses and inviting researchers to constantly rethink their positions. Likewise, the ease with which comparative data can be taken into account also encourages researchers to look at their data with fresh eyes. All of these factors suggest that corpus-based translation studies has the potential to be a decentering, dynamic force in translation studies as a whole (see Tymoczko 1998:652).

But while electronic corpora offer many advantages in the study of translation, some theorists have sounded a note of caution about their use. There is a danger, for example, that instead of realizing their potential to help translation studies "remain vital and move forward" (Tymoczko ibid), corpora could actually become a source of stasis and conservatism in translation practice, pedagogy, and theory. This could happen if commentators confuse what is 'normal' in a target-language corpus, for example, with what the translator ought to write, or if (trainee) translators feel obliged to reproduce translation solutions that have already proved their worth and have subsequently become institutionalized in some parallel corpus. Even in DTS, description can quickly fall into prescription; some commentators would even say that it inevitably does so (Newman 1987:71-71). Thus when translations do not reflect the norms of other target language production, they are sometimes described as *failing* to conform to such norms (see Puurtinen 1997:327, who goes on, however, to suggest that different norms may prevail in the case of translated text anyway). A related danger is recognized by Tymoczko (1998), namely that researchers may not be able to see past current constitutive norms of translation and may thus exclude from translation corpora examples of what has been considered as translation in other periods or cultures. Norms may start out as mere explanations for regularly observed patterns in translation behaviour, but there is a risk that they can start to restrict the potential of translation studies in general, and corpus-based translation studies in particular.

Similar problems can arise once we start to quantify phenomena in translated texts. Solutions that are in the majority may begin to take on a kind of special status, exceptions or indeterminate cases being relegated to the ranks of the unanalyzed. The temptation to disregard marginal or problematic cases is related to the universalizing impulse in some corpus-based translation studies. But, as Tymoczko (1998:657) argues, corpus-based translation studies is likely to remain "open to difference, differentiation, and particularity" precisely because it embraces natural language in all its variety, and this is what will save corpus-based translation studies from universalist programs of research and universalist conclusions. It has already been argued (in Chapter Two) that the particular, the unusual instance, can stand out starkly against the background of what is more general, more normal, in a corpus. It should also be pointed out that although corpus-based translation studies lends itself to the investigation of global patterns, allowing generalizations over entire corpora to the apparent detriment of individual texts or parts of texts,[16] the statistical basis of corpus linguistics can counter this tendency using, for example, measures of variance, which indicate the extent to which individual components deviate from the average score. Corpus linguistics is self-correcting in another way: studies using subsequent corpora can show how findings for an initial corpus or sub-corpus are indicative of the data it contains rather than translation in general. This is especially the case where researchers have carefully recorded their procedures and assumptions, thus allowing results from different, but compatible, studies to be compared.[17]

Tymoczko (1998:654) stresses that just as the value of corpora in translation studies cannot rest on their ability to furnish evidence of universals of translation, nor can it rest on any claims to objectivity – even corpus compilation relies on intuition and value judgement. Malmkjær also argues that the selection of translated texts for inclusion in a parallel corpus inevitably affects what the observer will notice and that conventional parallel corpora still only provide, for each instance, "the result of one individual's introspection, albeit contextually and cotextually informed" (1998:539). Not only can the choice of text included in a corpus be a limiting factor in some studies, the very presentation of the data can be restrictive too.

[16] Type-token ratio, lexical density, and mean sentence length, are good examples of measures that can be applied globally: every text has a type-token ratio and a lexical density; every sentence a length.

[17] The findings for mean sentence length in two studies conducted by Laviosa (1998a, 1998b) and reported on above provide a good example of the case in point.

Malmkjær (1998:539) argues that "in order to be able to provide any kinds of *explanation* of the data provided by the corpus, rather than mere statistics, analysts really need substantially more context than computers tend to search and display". And Øverås (1996:52, 88) complains about the lack of co-text available to her when investigating translation norms on the basis of aligned sentences from the English-Norwegian Parallel Corpus. But this objection is one that relates to particular software or working methods rather than to corpus linguistics or corpus-based translation studies in general: corpus-processing tools like those included in the WordSmith suite (see Chapter Two) allow very generous chunks of co-text to be viewed at any time. Researchers analyzing their texts on their own PCs, for example, can expand and contract the amount of co-text viewed as they desire.[18]

In summary, researchers who use corpora and the techniques of corpus linguistics in the investigation of translation should clearly be aware then that they have not found the key to a completely objective treatment of their object of enquiry. Nor are their investigations likely to yield incontrovertible universals of translation. Even the seemingly less ambitious search for norms of translation is fraught with difficulties: corpora can reveal quantifiable textual and extratextual regularities, but quantification can never be an end in itself. Regularities have to be interpreted, and their interpretation as evidence of the operation of norms is by no means straightforward, as repeated studies have shown. What is more, the computer-aided analysis of corpora is highly dependent on the software in use. Researchers should know when to use what tool, and when the tools themselves become the limiting factor. If we approach corpora with realistic goals, however, there is much to be harvested from them. The challenge for contemporary scholars is to work out how this potential can best be realized.

Conclusion

Mona Baker (1999:287) has said that corpus-based translation studies has as many agendas as there are researchers working in the area. In this Chapter I hope to have given some idea of what these agendas are, and who is pursuing them. Many scholars in corpus-based translation studies are interested in finding evidence for the DTS-inspired norms, universals, or laws of translation, discussed at the beginning of this Chapter. How they go about their research depends to a large extent on their aims, but also on the type of corpora they have at their disposal. I hope to have shown in this Chapter, how monolingual and bilingual, comparable and parallel, and general reference or control corpora all have their part to play in the research programmes of corpus-based translation studies. Some consideration has also been

---

[18] All corpora and corpus-processing tools have their strengths and weaknesses. For an overview of some of the weaknesses see Facchinetti (1998).

given here to the idea that translators tend to normalize linguistic usage in translation. In later Chapters I pursue this idea in a corpus-based study of lexis in original and translated text, bearing in mind always the limitations of corpora and corpus-processing tools outlined at the end of this Chapter. But first we look at how lexical issues have been treated in general and corpus linguistics.

4. A Word about Words

We're tired of trees.

Gilles Deleuze and Félix Guattari (1987:15)

Introduction

'Lexis' is often used simply to refer to "the vocabulary of a particular language" (Trask 1993:160). The study of lexis thus construed may involve listing the vocabulary items – the 'words' or 'lexical items' – of a language, observing diachronic change and synchronic variation in their use, studying their internal structure, or mapping out the relationships between them. In neo-Firthian linguistics, on the other hand, 'lexis' is understood in more abstract terms: it refers specifically to a level of linguistic organization that relates lexical items to the patterns in which they occur, in much the same way as the grammatical level is said to organize grammatical categories such as word class or phrase into higher structural units.[1] Lexical items, in this scheme of things, are seen first and foremost as subject to collocational patterning, that is, they are characterized by their tendency to co-occur with certain other lexical items.

The present research, which aims to track the translation into English of lexically creative points in German source texts with a view to establishing whether or not normalization typically takes place, draws on both traditions in the study of lexis. In general, lexical creativity is seen here as residing either in the creation of new words, or in the novel collocation of existing words.[2] The study of new word formation draws on traditional categories of morphology, the internal structure of new words being described in terms of the processes of derivation and compounding underlying them. Newly created words are analyzable not just from the point of view of their internal structure: they can also be related to words already existing in the same language, by virtue of the sense relations they contract with those words. Such sense relations have been studied extensively in the area known as 'structural semantics'. While structural semantics has characterized words in terms of both the syntagmatic and paradigmatic relations that hold between them and other words in the same language, the emphasis has arguably been on paradigmatic relations, that is, those said to hold between words that can substitute for each other in a given construction. Syntagmatic relations, on the other hand – those holding between

---

[1] It is important to point out, however, that while grammatical organization can be said to rely on fairly hard-and-fast 'rules' for combining grammatical categories, lexical patterning is probabilistic in nature. See, for example, Halliday's comments (1966:153, repeated below) on grammatical systems and lexical sets.

[2] Lexical creativity may also reside in the novel presentation of an existing word, see Chapter Six, examples (1a) and (2a).

items that are found with each other rather than instead of each other – have been studied in particular detail by neo-Firthian corpus linguists, with the syntagmatic relation of collocation receiving most attention in the literature. In this Chapter I survey these three complementary approaches to the study of lexis – morphological treatments of word formation, the structural semanticist's treatment of sense relations, and the neo-Firthian approach to collocation. Where appropriate, I exemplify word formation patterns, sense relations, and collocations using either familiar English words, or data from the German subcorpus of GEPCOLT. I take a special interest in the study of collocation, and show how the neo-Firthian study of syntagmatic relations at the lexical level, and abstractions based on those syntagmatic relations, have given rise to many new insights that challenge linguistic orthodoxy. Finally I suggest that because the study of syntagmatic relations is necessarily text based, it has much to offer other fields concerned first and foremost with the creation and interpretation of texts, most notably the field of translation studies.

Before moving on to a discussion of new word formation, or of paradigmatic and syntagmatic sense relations between words, however, it is wise to indicate just what is meant by the word 'word'.

The word 'word'

Thus far the word 'word' has been used in a familiar, common-sense way, but it is clear that the notion requires further specification. As Sinclair (1991:176) points out, a 'word' is usually understood as an orthographic word:[3]

> a word in the Roman alphabet is based on a string of letters including hyphen and sometimes apostrophe – bounded on each side by a word space or another punctuation mark

As we saw in Chapter Two, however, the orthographic view of the word does not take into account a number of phenomena that pervade the vocabulary of languages like English: it ignores multi-word units, and it does not allow us to distinguish between homographs, or to recognize inflected forms of the same lemma as belonging somehow to the same 'word'. The notion of lemma, like the notion of multi-word unit, is an abstraction away from word forms, which are co-terminous with orthographic words. Some writers (see Carter 1987; Lyons 1977; Russ 1994) use the term 'lexeme' to designate the more abstract notion of a word that embraces the

[3] The category of 'orthographic word' refers only to the written word. Definitions of 'word' that pertain solely to the spoken medium have also been put forward, in particular spoken words have been described as having no more than one stressed syllable. Such definitions are not unproblematic (see Carter 1987:6), but the definition of the spoken word need not detain us here, the emphasis of the present research being on written corpora.

concepts labelled here by the terms 'multi-word unit' and 'lemma', as well as capturing the idea that different words have different meanings and so homographic forms have to be interpreted semantically before we can say which 'word' they realize. This use of the term lexeme is followed here. The term 'word form' is reserved for uninterpreted orthographic words. The label 'lexical item' will continue to prove useful as "a fairly neutral hold-all term which captures, and to some extent, helps to overcome instabilities of the term *word*" (Russ 1994:7). Having said this, there are many occasions on which a common-sense understanding of 'word' is sufficient, and the word 'word' is perfectly serviceable, in particular when it is used in standard compounds such as 'word formation' below.

Word formation

Compounding and derivation are the two principal ways of forming new words in both German and English.[4] The distinction between the two processes relies on another distinction, that between free and bound morphemes. Free morphemes are minimal meaning units that can stand alone as independent words. Bound morphemes are minimal meaning units that must be combined with other morphemes (which may be free or bound) to form free-standing words.

Compounding

Compounding is the combination of two or more free morphemes in a single lexical item. In English, compounds thus formed may be written as two or more orthographically separate words, as in *post box*, a single hyphenated word *post-box*, or a single unhyphenated word *postbox*, to use an example from Carter (1987:4). Compounds that are written as orthograpically separate words – Smadja and McKeown (1990:253) call them "open compounds" – abound in English and require special treatment in processes like automatic tokenization, that is, the identification of the boundaries of linguistic items, in this case lexical items. In German, on the other hand, compounds are written as single orthographic words. In some cases, notably in technical German, hyphens are inserted between the components of complex compounds to aid comprehension, and especially if there is a danger of ambiguity. Russ (1994:236) gives the example of the compound *Druckerzeugnis*, which can be read as *Druck-Erzeugnis*, 'printed product', or *Drucker-Zeugnis*, 'printer's report'. While (unambiguous) familiar compounds, and *ad hoc* compounds whose internal structure is made explicit by the use of hyphens, should pose no real

---

[4] There are other, 'minor' word formation processes including blending, clipping, reduplication, the formation of acronyms, and borrowing. See Russ (1994:232-233, 248-260) for a description of the operation of these processes in German.

difficulties for automatic processing in German, other *ad hoc* German compounds may be problematic (see Lehr 1996:84, 139), a point I will return to below. For the moment it is enough to note that familiar and *ad hoc* compounds alike pervade the German language, the ease with which they can be formed being considered a "distinctive and characteristic feature" (Durrell 1991:486) of that language. Whether or not new words created by compounding are accepted by the linguistic community and are eventually entered into dictionaries depends upon a number of factors, including how long the community expects a new coinage to be relevant (Aitchison 1994:157-168), but highly idiosyncratic literary coinages like those in GEPCOLT – Gerhard Roth's (1986) *Mundnase*, which consists of the free morphemes *Mund*, 'mouth', and *Nase*, 'nose', is a good example – might be expected to remain limited to the text for which they were created.

Compound lexical items can be classified in a number of ways, for example according to the parts of speech of their component morphemes, or the syntactic or semantic relationship between those components. Russ (1994:221-225) provides an overview of how such classifications are usually applied to German compounds. In Chapter Six, these classifications will prove useful in the case-by-case analysis of creative *ad hoc* compounds in GEPCOLT, and their discussion is deferred until then.

Derivation

Derivation is the process whereby new words are formed by adding affixes, which are by definition bound morphemes, to stem morphemes, which may be either free or bound. [5] Affixes are normally either prefixes, placed before stems, or suffixes, placed after stems,[6] although the latter are more common in both German and English. Certain affixes typically occur with nouns, others with adjectives, and still others with verbs. Durrell (1991:487-508) and Russ (1994:226-228) give detailed lists of the affixes that occur with the major parts of speech in German, some of which feature in the analysis in Chapter Six of derived forms in GEPCOLT. The addition of a suffix to a stem often changes the part of speech of the stem, although this is not always the case: the addition of the suffix *-in* to a noun in German, for example, makes that noun feminine, without changing its part of speech. And in a

---

[5] The morphological process of inflection, introduced in Chapter Two, also involves the addition of an affix to a stem or 'root'. In the case of inflection, however, we say that the addition of such an affix provides information about the grammatical function of the lexical item in question. It does not mean the creation of a new lexical item. The addition of a derivational affix to a stem, on the other hand, creates a new lexical item.

[6] The categories of 'infix' (for German and English) and 'circumfix' (for German, see Russ 1994:227), are also identified in the literature, but they are of only marginal interest here.

special case, known as 'zero derivation' or 'conversion', a word can change part of speech without the explicit addition of a suffix. In German, the conversion of infinitival verbal forms to nouns – known as verbal nouns because they are derived from verbs – is a very productive process. The German subcorpus in GEPCOLT abounds in examples: a familiar one is the conversion of the verb *rauchen*, 'to smoke', to the noun *das Rauchen*, 'smoking'. Once a verb has undergone conversion, the resulting noun becomes subject to the usual nominal inflections, and it can also form compounds with free stems that would have constituted complements in a verbal structure. A single example will suffice to show how productive the conversion + compounding chain can be: the German for 'to pull a sled', used several times in Christoph Ransmayr's *Die Schrecken des Eises und der Finsternis*, is *einen Schlitten ziehen*. The verb ZIEHEN can be converted into the verbal noun *das Ziehen*, which can be combined with its object *Schlitten*, 'sled', to yield *das Schlittenziehen*, which appears three times in the novel. Its genitive form is *des Schlittenziehens*, which also appears three times. An example of each is given in (1a) and (2a) respectively. As (1b) and (2b) show, such forms are usually translated into English using gerunds, and complements and gerunds written as orthographically separate words. Forms like *Schlittenziehen* are called 'complex verbal nouns' in this book, thus distinguishing them from complex words formed solely through derivation *or* compounding.

(1a)	(1b)
ransmayr.de P706 Mit solchen Füßen, sagt Klotz, sei schon das eigene Gewicht ein großer Schmerz, jede andere Last aber und auch das <u>Schlittenziehen</u> jetzt unerträglich.	ransmayr.en P706 With feet like these, Klotz says, his own weight is pain enough – any other burden, however, even <u>pulling the sled</u>, is unbearable.
(2a)	(2b)
Mit unbeschreiblicher Freude begannen wir das harte Automatentagewerk des <u>Schlittenziehens</u>.	ransmayr.en P653 With indescribable joy we began the hard mechanical work of <u>pulling the sled</u>.

The intention here is not to give a comprehensive overview of word formation patterns in German, a task that has already been undertaken by writers such as Durrell (1991:485-508) and Russ (1994:217-241). Rather, the aim is to stress that compounding pervades the German language, and that certain derivational processes such as the addition of the suffix *-in*, and conversion, are highly productive, that is, they can give rise to a large number of new forms, in contemporary German. Such ubiquitous and productive patterns pose a particular problem for analysts studying lexical creativity in a small corpus: analysts have to decide whether a derived/compound form that occurs only once is merely a routine application of a derivational/

compounding rule, or whether the form has some special significance. Recourse to comparative data can be a great help in such cases. By checking standard lexicographical sources, and the written components of corpora like the Mannheim Corpora (see Chapter Five), for example, researchers can ascertain whether a form is already fully lexicalized, and/or used by other writers. If a form that occurs only once in the small corpus under consideration turns out not to occur at all, or only very rarely, in such reference sources, then we can be more confident of its special status and that it merits further analysis.

Structural semantics

The discussion so far has centred on the internal structure of words, their morphology, and on how minimal units of meaning, morphemes, can be combined to create new words. Another way of analyzing new lexical creations is by relating them to lexical items already in existence in the language under investigation. As indicated above, the area of linguistic scholarship known as structural semantics provides us with an apparatus for describing the relations between the lexical items of (a subset of) a language's vocabulary. It will be possible here to give a only a very brief account of the scholarship in this area; for a more comprehensive treatment see Lyons (1977:230-335).

Structural semantics draws on the linguistic theory of Ferdinand de Saussure, who held that linguistic signs have semantic value by virtue of their differential positions in systems of mutually defining signs. Applying this fundamental idea to the more specific area of vocabulary we can say that the lexemes of a language do not exist in isolation: their meanings are defined by the sense relations they share with other lexemes in the language in question, or in some relevant subset of that language. A lexeme *a*, for example, might have more or less the same sense as a lexeme *b*, a relation of synonymy thus existing between the two. Absolute synonymy is, of course, rare: few synonyms are completely interchangeable in every context. But even if synonyms *a* and *b* differ stylistically, for example, we can still say that by substituting *a* for *b* in a particular sentence, we do not change the propositional meaning of that sentence (Carter 1987:19). By indicating that synonyms can be substituted for one another, we make it clear that synonymy is a paradigmatic relation between lexemes.

Another paradigmatic relation that has received much attention in structural semantics is that of antonymy: if a lexeme *a* is substituted for its antonym *b* in a particular structure, then the propositional meaning of any sentence containing that structure changes, because *a* and *b* are somehow opposite, or otherwise incompatible, in meaning. Various subtypes of antonymy have been proposed in the literature (see Carter 1987:19-20; Cruse 1986:197-264; Lyons 1977:270-290). These include the relations of:

complementarity, which holds between lexemes expressing binary opposites, each of which excludes the other: a familiar example of complementaries is the pair MALE-FEMALE;
conversenesss, where there is a measure of logical reciprocity between lexemes, as in the pair BUY-SELL;
antonymy in the more restricted sense of gradable opposites, for example HOT-COLD;
incompatibility, the relation between contrasting lexemes in a many-member lexical set such as SUNDAY-MONDAY-TUESDAY ... SATURDAY; and
reversiveness, the relation between two lexemes, one of which denotes a change from a state *A* to a state *B*, and the other of which denotes a change from a state *B* to a state *A*, where *A* and *B* can represent more or less determinate states as denoted by the reversive pair DRESS and UNDRESS, or relative states, as in SHORTEN and LENGTHEN.

The paradigmatic relation of hyponymy holds between a more general lexeme, known as the 'superordinate', and a more specific lexeme, its 'subordinate' or 'hyponym'. This relation is exemplified by the pair ANIMAL-DOG. This sense relation is clearly hierarchical, the concept expressed by the more specific lexeme being a 'type of' whatever is expressed by the more general lexeme. Another hierarchical sense relation identified in the literature is that of meronymy (see Cruse 1986:157-165), the relation between parts and their wholes, for example BRANCH and TREE.

All the sense relations discussed so far involve some kind of relatedness of meaning. Even the relations of opposition and contrast are based on "contrast within similarity" (Lyons 1977:288); the lexemes in question differ along some relatively easily identified dimension. Thus BUY and SELL represent different roles in the same transaction, and SUNDAY and MONDAY are both days of the week, albeit different days. It is, of course, also possible to posit a relation of unrelatedness of meaning, but one would normally identify such a relation between two lexemes if there were some other way in which those lexemes were related. Thus the lexemes BAT_1 (animal sense) and BAT_2 (sports sense), used as examples of homographs in Chapter Two, share the same form but have unrelated meanings. The fact that formally similar or identical lexical items can have different meanings is exploited in the rhetorical device of the pun. As many instances of lexical creativity in GEPCOLT coincide with puns, it is worth expanding on the ways that lexemes can be formally similar or identical: homonyms, as exemplified by BAT_1 and BAT_2, have identical sounds and spelling; homographs have different sounds but identical spelling; homophones have the same sound but different spelling; and paronyms display slight differences in both sound and spelling. The lexical relations of homonymy, homography, homophony, and paronymy are, strictly speaking, relations of form rather than sense. But when a suitable textual or situational context is created, the presence of a particular homonymic, homographic, or homophonic word form can invoke both lexemes that share that form, and thus their respective unrelated senses.[7] An example from Delabastita (1996a:128) may serve to clarify this point: in the pun *Wedding belles* the lexeme BELLE is present in the text, but its homophone BELL is also invoked by the co-text, by virtue of a syntagmatic relation one of its forms *bells* habitually contracts with *wedding*.

In the above example, the form *belles* appears to substitute for *bells* in the structure in question, and so the two forms can be said to be in a paradigmatic relation.[8] But Delabastita's example also demonstrates the importance of syntagmatic relations at the lexical level, relations that have also been the focus of some research in structural semantics. Lyons (1977:261-266) points to the importance of the work of W. Porzig in this regard. Central to Porzig's thesis is the idea that the meaning of certain collocationally restricted lexemes cannot be adequately described without reference to the lexemes with which they are syntagmatically related, "whether explicitly in texts or implicitly in the language system" (Lyons ibid:262). Porzig's ideas were developed at much the same time as Firth was developing the notion of collocation, but it was Firth who was to have the greater influence on the subsequent investigation of collocation within the framework of corpus linguistics. This may be due to Firth's insistence on the use of actually occurring text in the study of collocation, a principle which also lies at the heart of corpus linguistics. Whatever the case, it is worth pointing out that syntagmatic relations had already been given some consideration in structural semantics, even if the emphasis in the area was primarily on the kind of paradigmatic relation more favoured by theorists such as Trier (see Lyons ibid:250-261). Two of the main achievements of corpus linguists, however, have been to place the study of syntagmatic lexical relations on an empirical footing, and to move such relations, starting with the category of collocation, to the centre-stage of at least one branch of linguistics. These developments are discussed in detail in the rest of this Chapter. Two final points are made here first regarding the treatment of paradigmatic relations in corpus linguistics: firstly, corpus linguists have been able to supplement largely intuitive knowledge of lexical paradigms with quantitative information, for example about the distribution of complementaries like MAN-WOMAN; and secondly, even though the study of collocation begins with syntagmatic relations, the contrastive study of several collocations involving a given lexical item inevitably involves taking paradigmatic relations into consideration. This second point is taken up again below.

---

[7] In the case of paronymy, the presence of one form may invoke the sense of a lexeme of similar form as well, given an appropriately contrived context or co-text.

[8] It is also possible to say that both lexemes realized by the single phonological form [belz] are "co-present in the same portion of text" (Delabastita 1996a:128), rather than one substituting for the other.

Collocation

John Rupert Firth was an early champion of the study of lexis. As indicated in Chapter One, Firth held that the main concern of linguistics was to make statements of meaning, and to do so in linguistic terms. Aware that such statements of meaning could not be achieved in one fell swoop, Firth proposed that the linguist make a first abstraction by isolating a piece of actually occurring language. The meaning of such a piece of language would then be dealt with by dispersing it into a series of levels. In his earlier work, Firth identified five such levels, namely, the phonetic, morphological, lexical, syntactic and semantic levels.[9] These levels provided the context in which a particular form could assume a function and thus be said to have meaning at that level. By the time Firth published his 1951 paper 'Modes of Meaning',[10] these levels had been refined somewhat: the morphological level is dropped, and the collocational level replaces the lexical level.[11] Collocation has since become central to the study of lexis and constitutes the main focus of the rest of this Chapter. Put simply, it refers to "the occurrence of two or more words within a short space of each other in a text" (Sinclair 1991:170). Before discussing collocation in detail however, some preliminary remarks are called for, which, it is hoped, will pre-empt any confusion caused by conflicting uses of the term 'collocation' in the literature.

Conflicting definitions of collocation

Firth was originally concerned to show that the lexical company a word keeps in a text contributes to the (collocational) meaning of that word. Using what is now a rather dated example, he claimed, that "one of the meanings of *ass* is its habitual collocation with an immediately preceding *you silly*, and with other phrases of address or of personal reference" (Firth 1957:195). This type of meaning can be stated purely in terms of the formal items encountered together in texts; it is "an abstraction at the syntagmatic level and is not directly concerned with the conceptual or idea approach to the meaning of words" (ibid:196). This distinction has been overlooked by some critics of the Firthian approach to collocation: Herbst (1996) and Packalén (1994), for instance, prefer to consider as collocations only those

---

[9] See 'The Technique of Semantics,' originally published in 1935 and reprinted in Firth (1957:7-33).

[10] Reprinted as Firth (1957:190-215).

[11] Some commentators prefer to stick to Firth's original term 'lexical level', as it suggests "greater generality and parallelism with the grammatical level" (Halliday 1966:161). As indicated in the introduction to this Chapter, lexis is considered here as the more general concept, and collocation a particular type of lexical patterning.

co-occurrences that do not seem to be motivated by extralinguistic reality, thus applying a kind of dualist logic that Firth himself eschewed.[12] Nor is Firth's notion of collocation linked to the 'selectional restrictions' posited in transformational grammar, despite the fact that some commentators, for example, Van Brederode (1980), treat the two terms as practically synonymous. Trask's (1993) *Dictionary of Grammatical Terms in Linguistics* does not even have a separate entry for 'collocation.' Rather we are led directly to the headword 'collocational restriction' which is defined as:

> A **selectional restriction**, particularly one which is unusually idiosyncratic or language-specific: *grill* (US *broil*) collocates with *meat* but not with *bread*, while the reverse is true for *toast*. (Trask 1993:49)

Trask (ibid) even gives Firth's 1951 paper as an appropriate reference for this term, but this is surely a misrepresentation of Firth's idea of collocation. Selectional restrictions refer to a concept in the semantic theory of mentalist linguistics, according to which certain word combinations are described as ill-formed on the basis of a mismatch between values for semantic attributes said to be shared by the words concerned, attributes which are arrived at intuitively by the linguist. Thus the German verb FRESSEN 'to eat' is often described as requiring a subject with the features *+animal -human* (see, for example, Packalén 1994:226) and this restriction is said to prevent it from combining with human subjects in stretches of language produced by people or, when they have been programmed to perform appropriately, machines. Thus selectional restrictions are not only arrived at deductively, they deal with negative evidence by proscribing co-occurrence (Hanks 1996:79; Lehr 1996:52).[13] In much of the literature on collocation that has emanated from non-Firthian quarters, a similar tendency towards prescriptivism can be discerned. Smadja (1993:144), for example, writes of violations of "purely lexical rules" (as opposed to syntactic or semantic rules) and claims that certain word combinations are "invalid" "simply because they do not exist", while others are 'correct' because they do exist. Likewise, Benson *et al.* (1986a:Introduction, 1986b) list word combinations that are not allowed, alongside those that are. Collocations in the Firthian sense, however, represent an empirical category. They are arrived at by induction,

---

[12] Herbst (1996:384), for example, asks "wouldn't it be true to say that the fact that certain words tend to co-occur must be attributed to certain facts of the world – together with the way the world is conceptualised in language?" Compare Sinclair's observation that it would be surprising if "patterns of social and natural organization" were not reflected in language, "but we try not to inflate this expectation into preconception" (1966:410).

[13] Although certain theorists who draw on the category of selectional restrictions admit that they can be contravened for stylistic effect, descriptions of such possible contraventions are often as limited as the restrictions themselves (see, for example, Packalén 1994:226).

through the observation of actually occurring language. This is one point that Firth is quite clear on: "An approach to the meaning of words, pieces, and sentences by the statement of collocation", he says, "ensures that the isolate word or piece as such is attested in established text" (1957:xi). But even if a particular collocation has not been attested in a corpus, even a very large one, this does not indicate that it could not exist. In Sinclair's words, "there are virtually no impossible collocations, but some are much more likely than others" (1966:411). Given that one of the central concerns of the present research is to investigate lexical creativity in translation, it makes sense to follow Sinclair's line: an approach to language that views instances of linguistic behaviour in terms of their probability, rather than their possibility, is more amenable to the concept of creativity.

Another tendency in the literature on collocation, and one that is evident in Trask's definition given above, is to consider as collocations those lexical combinations that are not predictable either with reference to *a priori* syntactic or semantic categories, or from the standpoint of a second language. Packalén (1994:224), for instance, gives the example of the German collocation *fliessendes Wasser*, which is used to describe what English speakers call 'running water', and suggests that the German preference for this lexical combination over, say, *rinnendes Wasser*,[14] is unmotivated, given that the two combinations are grammatically equally well-formed and equally interpretable with regard to some extralinguistic context. The fact that German speakers simply do not say *rinnendes Wasser* seems all the more inexplicable to Packalén given the existence of the cognate collocations *rinnande vatten* and *running water* in Swedish and English respectively. The paradox implicit in the assertion that familiar collocations can somehow be described as 'unpredictable' or 'idiosyncratic' has been spotted by Lehr (1996:86). She points out that those collocations described as unpredictable, for example, by Smadja and McKeown (1990),[15] are thought of as usual and highly predictable within neo-Firthian linguistics, precisely because they occur with a noticeably high frequency in the corpora investigated by linguists. Smadja *et al.* come very close to acknowledging the chink in their theoretical armour when they admit that "while collocations are not predictable on the basis of syntactic or semantic rules, they can be observed in language and thus must be learned through repeated usage" (1996:5). But the realization that there is a level of linguistic organization that cannot be accounted for by the rule bases of much of modern linguistics does not lead Smadja *et al.* to abandon those rule bases. Rather collocation picks up where syntax and semantics left off. Lexis is again assigned the role of "picking up the scraps from the tables of syntax" (Jones

---

[14] For Packalén (ibid), this is a 'starred' example, and thus ill-formed.

[15] See also Smadja (1989:163, 1993:143) and Benson *et al.* (1986a:xxv, 1986b:258), the latter of whom describe certain collocations as 'arbitrary and non-predictable'.

and Sinclair 1974:15).[16]

Lehr (1996:86) is also critical of the use of contrastive linguistic data in the identification of collocations. Such data are commonly used in foreign language teaching where collocations are often considered as lexical combinations that language learners would not produce merely on the basis of knowledge of their own language.[17] For Lehr (ibid:61), this approach is unsatisfactory as it cannot be used for the lexical description of a single language on its own terms. Likewise, if one of the main aims of the present study is to see what happens to unusual collocations in German source texts when those texts are translated into English,the focus cannot be on German collocations considered remarkable from an English-language point of view (this would include some of the most mundane collocations in German), but rather must be on source-language collocations considered remarkable from a source-language point of view.

For the purposes of the present study then, collocation refers to the co-occurrence of semantically uninterpreted lexical items within a specified distance of each other in naturally occurring text.[18] It is not related to the transformational grammarian's notion of selectional restrictions; nor can the identification of collocational patterns in one language be based on contrasts between it and a second language. Adopting this essentially Firthian position, however, by no means resolves all the questions raised by the positing of a collocational level of organization in language. Since the 1960s, theorists associated with the Firthian School have been variously concerned with issues such as: what are the 'lexical items' whose behaviour we wish to specify? How can lexical organization be best observed and reported on? And, in the early days at least: do we need to posit a separate lexical level in the first place? And while there are still no definitive answers to many of these questions, the research they have engendered over the last thirty or so years has yielded an impressive body of knowledge on the methodology of lexical research, on the one hand, and the nature of language itself, on the other.

Beginning the study of lexis: the groundwork

As already indicated, the term collocation gained currency in linguistics following

---

[16] Jones and Sinclair actually make this claim about the work of fellow neo-Firthian M.A.K. Halliday (1961).

[17] Smadja *et al.* also appeal to cross-linguistic difficulties as motivation for their *Champollion* program, which extracts collocations and their translations from bilingual corpora. "Collocations", they claim, "are notoriously difficult for non-native speakers to translate, primarily because they are opaque and cannot be translated on a word-by-word basis" (1996:1). See also Benson *et al.* (1986b:259) who include differences between American and British English in their discussion.

[18] 'Semantically uninterpreted' here means that the lexical items in questions are considered without any reference to their meaning.

its use in Firth's 1951 paper 'Modes of Meaning' (1957:190-215).[19] But as Lehr (1996:28) points out, Firth's discussion of the lexical level of language was of a programmatic nature, and it was left to his students to justify and refine many of Firth's categories, and to develop systematic methodologies for studying lexis.[20] One of the earliest papers on the subject, M.A.K. Halliday's 'Lexis as a Linguistic Level' (1966), is devoted to defending the setting up of lexis as a part of language form. Halliday (ibid:148) suggests that lexis can be seen as within language form, but outside grammar, "lexical patterns thus being treated as different in kind, and not merely in delicacy, from grammatical patterns". Halliday justifies this position by claiming that the classes set up to account for lexical patterns cut across those posited in grammatical description (ibid:153), and although both lexical and grammatical patterning "are referable in the first place to the two basic axes, the syntagmatic and the paradigmatic"(ibid:152), the theoretical categories required on either axis differ from grammar to lexis. Thus Halliday (ibid) claims that, on the syntagmatic axis,

> in place of the highly abstract [grammatical] relation of structure, in which the value of an element depends on complex factors in no sense reducible to simple sequence, lexis seems to require the recognition merely of linear co-occurrence together with some measure of significant proximity, either a scale or at least a cut-off point. It is this syntagmatic relationship which is referred to as 'collocation'.

Likewise, whereas grammar organizes classes of items into 'systems' on the paradigmatic axis, with their 'known and stated set of terms in choice relation', such systems lending themselves to a deterministic model, lexis requires that formal items be grouped into open-ended paradigmatic 'sets', "assignment to which is best regarded as probabilistic" (ibid:153). Or, as Sinclair puts it, "one lexical item is not chosen *rather than* another, lexical items do not contrast with each other in the same sense as grammatical classes contrast" (1966:411).

The discussion of Halliday's 1966 paper is brought to a close here with a reiteration

---

[19] Mitchell (1975:134) points out that the term 'collocation' was not actually coined by Firth. Nevertheless, Firth's use of the term was so influential that it marks an appropriate starting point for any discussion of the subject.

[20] Even Firth's use of the term 'collocation' lacks precision: he used it to refer variously to "the habitual company a key-word keeps" (1968:113), "the study of key-words, pivotal words, leading words, by presenting them in the company they usually keep" (ibid:107), and as "an order of *mutual expectancy*" (ibid:181). Collocation is at once an empirical phenomenon, the study of this phenomenon, or an expectation arising from it. As the definition provided by Sinclair (1991:170) and repeated above suggests, however, the present study sees collocation as an empirical phenomenon related to observed co-occurrences in real text.

of his point that positing separate grammatical and lexical levels of linguistic organization in no way implies that there is no interrelation between the two. If, according to Halliday, one speaks of a lexical level, "there is no question of asserting the 'independence' of such a level, whatever this might mean; what is implied is the internal consistency of the statements and their referability to a stated model" (ibid:152). Here Halliday is echoing Firth's (1957:199, 1968:192) insistence on the interconnectedness of the levels of linguistic description,[21] an aspect of Firthian linguistics that was to take on particular significance in the work of John Sinclair (1991, 1996, 1997), Gill Francis (1993) and Elena Tognini-Bonelli (1996a), and which is described in more detail below.

While Halliday was defending the positing of lexis as a distinctive organizational level in language, Sinclair (1966), in the same volume, set about laying the methodological groundwork for the study of lexis. One of the first problems encountered in the study of lexis is, according to Sinclair, the definition of the basic unit of description, that is, the lexical item. Attempting to characterize the lexical item in terms of its distribution among items of the same level of abstraction leads to the kind of circularity inherent in the definition proffered by Sinclair (ibid:412), where a lexical item is defined as:

> a formal item (at least one morpheme long) whose pattern of occurrence can be described in terms of a uniquely ordered series of other lexical items occurring in its environment.

The problem is that the item is defined in terms of its environment, which is not actually given in the theory, but is itself defined in terms of the item. The only way out of this bind seems to be to claim that the 'environment' refers to "that extent of the text which is relevant in the description of an item" (Sinclair 1966:412) and then to admit that the environment considered relevant will vary from case to case (see Sinclair ibid:414, 415; Lehr 1996:38-39, 79). But despite the problems that Sinclair uncovers in his effort to begin the study of lexis, he does manage to make a

---

[21] Although Firth refers to 'lower' and 'higher' levels and their arrangement in ascending order from phonetics to the context of culture (1957:198-199), he still maintains that "the total complex, including what may be called the higher levels in the context of situation, is a first postulate" (ibid:199). The interconnectedness of each level of analysis with any other level, and not merely the level immediately 'above' or 'below' it, can be seen, for example, in Firth's assertion that the 'phonaesthetic' mode (his term for 'the association of sounds and personal social attitudes') "correlates more closely than the phonetic mode with features of contexts of situation in which the personal and social attitudes are more easily apprehended in the light of ordinary experience" (ibid). Elsewhere, Firth makes the point even more strongly by insisting that "studies at one level must take into account findings at other levels" (1968:192) and that grammatical and collocational meaning are useful if not necessary when making statements of meaning at the phonological level.

start: giving us definitions of key concepts such as 'node', 'span', and 'collocate'; distinguishing between contiguity of lexical items and their mere co-presence in a given stretch of text, on the one hand, and casual and significant co-occurrences of lexical items, on the other; and outlining how the identification of collocation can be refined through procedures such as sense disambiguation, lemmatization, and morphological processing. Most significantly, he stresses that the problems involved in studying lexis "are not likely to yield to anything less imposing than a very large computer" (ibid:410), thus anticipating the technological developments that were to revolutionize the study of lexis. The issues addressed by Sinclair in his 1966 paper have been taken up again and again by various commentators, including Sinclair himself, with much subsequent comment informed by access to large quantities of text and computational routines for processing such text, resources that were not available to scholars in the early days of the study of lexis. Below, these issues are discussed thematically. It is not the intention to suggest, by presenting issues separately, that they represent discrete problems; rather each question is taken in turn for expository convenience.

Nodes and collocates

Collocation was described above as "the occurrence of two or more words within a short space of each other in a text" (Sinclair 1991:170). A collocation is thus a syntagmatic relationship between at least two lexical items, though these lexical items are not usually thought of as having equal status. Collocations are generally seen as structured internally, being made up of 'nodes' and their 'collocates'.[22] The node is the item whose lexical behaviour is under investigation; the collocates those items that occur in its environment. Each collocate can itself function as a node in a subsequent investigation, but at any particular moment, only one item (the node) can occupy the centre-stage. Indeed, in computerized studies it is customary to present the node at the centre of a KWIC (Key Word in Context) concordance line, with a specified amount of co-text on either side, as illustrated in Figure 1 in Chapter Two.

Depending on the definition of collocation adopted in a particular project, the co-text given in a concordance line – the standard length is eighty characters – may or may not contain collocates of the node. For example, some commentators suggest that only those lexical combinations that display some kind of dependency relation, or "structural consistency" (Smadja 1993:157), should be considered as collocations. Thus, in concordance lines in Figure 1, Chapter Two, as the forms

---

[22] Lehr (1996:31) points out that there is often disagreement in the literature as to whether the node is part of the collocation. Catford, for example, implies that it is not, when he says that a collocation "is the 'lexical company' that a particular item keeps" (1965:10). For present purposes, the node is considered part of the collocation.

guilty and *conscience* stand in a modifier-head relation to each other, and are consistently part of the same noun phrase, they would be considered by Smadja as meeting one of his criteria for designation as a collocation.[23] In projects where nodes are manually selected, and concordance lines analyzed directly by researchers, there is arguably little need to make explicit syntactic criteria for the identification of collocations; human judgement should suffice. This does not tie the analysis to one person's intuitive judgement for all time: as long as the data on which the analysis is based are publicly accessible, the initial analyst's judgements can be confirmed, supplemented or challenged in subsequent inquiries (see Stubbs 1996: 46 on this point). In the kind of fully automatic collocation extraction envisaged by Smadja (1993), however, the imposition of syntactic restrictions can reduce to more tractable levels the vast number of collocations that would be extracted from a large corpus on the basis of co-occurrence criteria alone. But as Lehr points out in her discussion of Greenbaum's (1970, 1974) attempt to incorporate part-of-speech and syntactic information into neo-Firthian investigations of collocation, such approaches require a tagged and parsed corpus as input, and thus make demands on resources that at the time were more easily met for English than for German (Lehr 1996:51). And Sinclair is wary of any approach that seeks to impose *a priori* categories on corpus data, even categories as seemingly innocuous as part-of-speech labels. In his opinion, "we are in danger of having problematic analytical systems imposed on us, derived from traditions of language analysis which have, in the past, specifically rejected corpus evidence" (1991:22). Likewise, for grammarians who consider lexis to be prior to syntax (see Francis 1993:142, quoted in Chapter Two), it makes little sense to impose syntactic categories on corpus data prior to the investigation of lexical patterns. For these reasons, and because we are dealing with a relatively small body of data and so do not risk being inundated with collocations, a "clean-text" policy (Sinclair ibid:21) is applied in the present research. Lexical items are investigated in and for themselves rather than as exponents of any particular word class or because they have any particular syntactic function.

It was noted above that lexical items are not necessarily co-terminous with orthographic words. Once we have conceded this however, we still have to decide, when studying collocations, whether, given a case like *in order to*, we should treat *order*, for example, as a node, and *in* and *to* as its collocates, or whether the whole multi-word unit *in order to* should function as the node. Likewise, if these three orthographic words appear contiguously in the environment of another node, are

---

[23] Smadja's (1993:146-147) other conditions are that collocations are "arbitrary", by which he means unpredictable on the basis of syntactic and semantic rule bases, or contrastive linguistic knowledge, "domain-dependent", "recurrent", and that they represent "cohesive lexical clusters", which means that the words involved in a collocation cannot be seen as independent variables. Smadja (1991, 1993) also factors into his analysis the number of times a particular collocate occurs in each position relative to the node.

they to be treated as three separate collocates or one single collocate? Most people would probably find it more satisfactory to respect the integrity of the multi-word unit, but lexical tokenization is most easily carried out by computer on the basis of white spaces and ending punctuation marks such as full-stops, commas, etc. This makes the orthographic word more amenable to computational processing than the theoretically more sound lexeme, and explains why it is often the focus of collocational analysis (see Jones and Sinclair 1974:16). But this is more of a problem for English than it is for German, where compounds are written as single orthographic words rather than as multi-word units. German does have a class of lexemes that may be discontinuous however. These are separable verbs, where prefixes are either attached to the main verb (in subordinate clauses and in non-finite constructions) or separated from it (in main clauses) by any amount of intervening text. In the latter case the lexeme is clearly not co-terminous with the orthographic word, and any automatic analysis of the collocational patterns of such separable lexemes will have to take this into account.[24]

Other problems associated with the use of orthographic words in collocation analysis have been addressed in the section on concordancing in Chapter Two. One final point is made here about the role of function words in collocation analysis. It is often thought that function words contribute less than content words to the collocational meaning of words they occur with (Lehr ibid:32). For this reason, function words are often excluded from collocational analyses (Haskel 1971; Smadja 1989, 1991). In computational processing, function words are easily excluded by means of stop-lists. Jones and Sinclair (1974), however, have shown that function words are not neutral with regard to their environment: the grammatical classes of words at various positions relative to function words are highly predictable, even if the particular lexical exponents of such classes are not. This kind of relationship, that between a lexical item and the grammatical classes of the items in its environment, is subsumed by Firth's category of 'colligation' (Firth 1968:23).[25] The description of colligation requires that the linguist make abstractions on the basis of the collocations given in a text. As Firth put it, a word in a collocation "stares you in the face just as it is" (ibid:182-183), but the identification of colligation requires another level of processing, which can either be done automatically or on an *ad hoc* basis by the linguist (Tognini-Bonelli 1996a:75). Recent developments in corpus linguistics, where the emphasis is on spotting repeated patterns, suggest that the extra effort is worth it. According to Elena Tognini-Bonelli (ibid):

---

[24] The investigation of all orthographic variants of separable lexemes is possible, for example, with *COSMAS*, the software developed for use with the Mannheim Corpora at the *Institut für deutsche Sprache* (see al-Wadi 1994; and Chapter Five).

[25] Firth also used 'colligation' to describe syntagmatic relationships between one grammatical class and another (1968:111). Sinclair (1996:85) calls this "full colligation".

> Collocational and colligational patterns will, together, form the basis of the formalisation of repeated events. Only a descriptive statement that identifies their interconnections will yield insight into meaning.

The discussion of colligation is taken up again below. For the moment it is enough to say that if collocational and colligational patterns are as interrelated as Tognini-Bonelli suggests, then it may not be wise to exclude function words, which have special powers of colligational prediction, from lexical analyses.[26]

Spans

If the node is the lexical item (or orthographic word) whose lexical behaviour is under investigation and its collocates the lexical items (or orthographic words) that appear in the environment of the node, then the specification of that environment takes on particular importance. The theoretical difficulty inherent in mutually defining items and environments has already been alluded to above. The pragmatic solution is to define an arbitrary environment, conventionally referred to as a 'span', whose boundaries are delimited either by some kind of structural unit (for example, a phrase, sentence or entire text or discourse), or by distance from the node, which is usually measured in words, a special case being adjacency to the node. Firth tended towards structural boundaries, though he allowed for spans to cross speaker turns in conversation (1968:197). Jones and Sinclair, on the other hand, base their spans on "a standard number of orthographic words, disregarding the grammatical structures of which they form a part" (1974:21),[27] while Haskel (1971) and Smadja (1991, 1993) use both structural boundaries and distance in words to delimit spans in their studies of collocation. Jones and Sinclair (ibid) arrive at an optimum span length of four words to the left and four words to the right of the node word by measuring the influence of each unique word form, or 'type' (see Chapter Two), on the types around it, in each of ten 5,000-word texts. This span length still holds sway in Sinclair (1991). Martin *et al.* (1983:84) prefer a span of five words to the left and five to the right (disregarding punctuation), but Lehr (1996:78-79) suggests that fixed span lengths, especially such short ones, make more sense for English than they do for German, where there is no upper limit on the number of tokens that

---

[26] Several studies have already made interesting observations about the collocational patterning of function words. See for example Renouf and Sinclair (1991). Other studies, focusing on the computational analysis of collocation, do not exclude function words, but assign them different status to that assigned to content words. Smadja and McKeown (1990) and Smadja (1993) describe such work.

[27] Jones and Sinclair (1974:2), following Firth (1968:107), allow spans to extend beyond the boundaries of speaker turns in conversation.

can intervene between the two parts of a separable verb in a single clause. She prefers a flexible approach to span length, gradually expanding spans on a case-by-case basis, while at the same time introducing restrictions on the relative frequency of co-occurrence of node and collocate (see below) in order to limit the number of collocations derived from a corpus (ibid:39, 186ff). Likewise, although Haskel uses the same fixed span lengths as Jones and Sinclair (1974) for computational processing, she notes that "a span of two is adequate in most sentences to collect the words that have a direct structural or semantic relationship; in other cases a span of eight may be required to get all the related words" (1971:166). Mason (1997) is more critical of Jones and Sinclair's approach to spans. In particular he takes issue with the assumption, also made by Berry-Rogghe (1973, 1974), that spans are symmetrical around the node. Mason's experimental findings suggest that the area of influence of a node, its 'lexical gravity', is not symmetrical.[28] Mason (ibid:374) also suggests that "different words, and even different forms of a word, have different patterns", thus presenting an argument against lemmatization in collocation analysis (see also Sinclair 1991:53-65, quoted in Chapter Two above). He also notes that certain grammatical words "increase the variability of words in their immediate environment", which is consistent with Jones and Sinclair's (1974) finding, also reported above, that function words are not colligationally neutral. Mason acknowledges that research into lexical gravity is still in its initial stages, but there is no doubt that this work will become increasingly important, especially in the computerized studies of collocation, as span size affects not only the number of collocates of a node that are taken into account in collocational analysis, but also the computational cost of processing such nodes (Mason ibid:362-363). Other issues that have assumed particular significance in the computational processing of collocations include the absolute and relative frequencies of nodes, collocates, and their co-occurrences in a corpus, and measures of statistical significance assigned to such co-occurrences. These issues are addressed in the next section.

Frequency

Thus far collocation has been described as the mere co-occurrence of lexical items within a given span. For many commentators however, it is only *recurring* co-occurrences that merit the designation 'collocation'. Firth himself was equivocal on this point. In his initial assertion that "one of the meanings of *ass* is its habitual collocation with an immediately preceding *you silly*" (1957:195, quoted above), 'collocation' could mean simple co-occurrence; the fact that the term is qualified by the word 'habitual' in this case suggesting that some collocations are not habits,

---

[28] Sinclair (1991:106) also alludes to ongoing experiments with symmetrical and asymmetrical spans, although no findings are reported.

and that in the most extreme case a once-off juxtaposition of two words could also be called a collocation. But later Firth claims that collocation "states the *habitual* company a key-word keeps" (1968:113, emphasis mine). If collocations are "habitual word accompaniments" (Firth 1968:107), then they are word combinations that occur with at least a certain threshold frequency that separates 'habits' from other linguistic events. Firth, however, does not explore the notion of frequency, although many of his successors do seek to establish absolute or relative threshold frequencies for the identification of collocations. Kjellmer (1982, 1984, 1987, 1990), for example, considers as potential collocations only those sequences that occur more than once in identical form in the Brown Corpus (see Chapter Two), thus setting a threshold of two co-occurrences for the identification of a collocation.[29] There are a number of problems associated with this approach: for one it requires that items in collocation be contiguous, secondly because it relies on absolute frequencies of co-occurrence, it is highly dependent on the length of the corpus,[30] and thirdly, it tends to foreground very common words like 'the', 'and', and 'of'. Such words are so common that their frequent presence within a specified distance of a node word is only to be expected. For this reason, researchers like Berry-Rogghe (1973, 1974), Jones and Sinclair (1974) and Church and Hanks (1990) relate the number of co-occurrences of node and collocate to the frequency of each item in the corpus as a whole. The number of co-occurrences of node and collocate states their *observed* frequency of co-occurrence. This figure is conventionally compared to the *expected* frequency of co-occurrence for the two items in question. In order to calculate an expected frequency of co-occurrence of node and collocate, however, researchers need some kind of theoretical linguistic model that allows them to predict how these items would be distributed if there were no particular attraction between them. The simplest model is that of random distribution, which Barnbrook (1996:92) summarizes as follows:

> [random distribution] says in effect that in the absence of any significant collocation between the node and the other words in the text, those other words will occur around it at random in the same proportions as they occur throughout the text as a whole.[31]

---

[29] Kjellmer imposes a second condition – that collocations be grammatically well-formed – and is thus forced to manually remove sequences that do not meet this condition from a list of potential collocates produced automatically on the basis of recurrence of sequences of orthographic words in the Brown corpus (Kjellmer 1982:25-28). Kjellmer's automatic generation of lists of recurring sequences does not require him to differentiate between nodes and collocates. His understanding of the term 'collocation' is therefore more like Scott's (1997) notion of 'cluster' (see Chapter Two, especially Tables 5 and 6) than other conceptions of collocation covered here.

[30] See also comments by Smadja (1993:150) on a similar approach taken by Choueka (1988).

[31] Although Barnbrook refers here to the 'text', it is of course possible, and perhaps more usual, to rely on an entire corpus for distribution data (see Barnbrook 1996:93).

But the random distribution hypothesis is unsatisfactory as a linguistic model, as it fails to take into account the constraints imposed by the grammar of a language. As Stubbs (1995a:31) puts it:

> Standard statistical procedures assume proper random samples in which values are independent observations, but since textual data are never in this form, this calls into question whether such statistics can reasonably be used on language data.

Another drawback of calculating the expected frequency of co-occurrence of two forms *n* (the node) and *c* (the collocate) on the basis of the random distribution hypothesis, that is, by multiplying the probabilities of occurrence of *n* and *c* as if they were independent events, is that their expected frequency of co-occurrence will be artificially low, and so their observed frequency of co-occurrence will appear huge in comparison. According to Stubbs (ibid:33), given this calculation "almost any observed co-occurrence is hundreds of times more likely than by chance".

Despite the problems associated with the random distribution hypothesis that underlies their use, observed vs. expected frequencies of co-occurrence form the basis of many statistical measures used in corpus linguistics. Typically, the difference between the two figures is noted, and a measure of statistical significance is then applied to that difference. Measures of statistical significance are used to rank the collocates of a particular node according to the strength of the bond between node and collocate. For high scoring collocates, the implication is that the researcher can be relatively confident that the difference between the observed and the expected frequency of co-occurrence with the node is unlikely to be due to chance. The use of such statistical significance measures is also controversial however. Some objections to their use in the identification of collocations (see Herbst 1996) are based on a confusion of statistical significance with something approximating psychological salience: if one says that a collocation is statistically significant (given a particular quantity of text, in a particular corpus, and using a particular measure of and cut-off point for significance), this is not to make a claim about the psychological plausibility of such a collocation for native speakers of a language. Nevertheless, the use of statistical significance scores is not straightforward. Familiar measures such as Mutual Information (*MI*) and *z*-scores are said to artificially inflate the importance of collocates that have a low frequency in the corpus from which distribution information is drawn; while *t*-scores tend to draw attention to high-frequency collocates. The relative merits of different scores are discussed in Barnbrook (1996:100-101), Church *et al.* (1991), Clear (1993), and Stubbs (1995a). Barnbrook's conclusion is that "it is probably better to use as much information as possible in exploring collocation, and to take advantage of the different perspectives provided by the use of more than one measure" (ibid:101), though Stubbs advises that "linguists should certainly keep an eye on the original raw frequencies of collocations"

(1995a:40). Some software developers interested in automating collocation analysis allow for such flexibility. The *CUE* system (Mason 1996), for example, allows collocates for a chosen node to be ranked according to: their absolute frequency as collocates; the ratio of their observed to expected frequency of co-occurrence with the node; their *t*-score; or their *MI*-score. Other systems like the Sara software used in conjunction with the British National Corpus (see Chapter Five) provide information on the raw frequencies of occurrence of two word forms and their raw frequency of co-occurrence, allowing users to calculate *MI*-scores, etc, themselves.

Whether one uses absolute or relative frequencies of co-occurrence to identify collocations, it is still quite normal to omit from the analysis any lexical items for which one has only scanty evidence. Jones and Sinclair (1974:18), for example, claim that:

> to describe the collocational activity of a word reliably, at least one, probably several, hundred occurrences are required.[32] Furthermore, to establish accurately the significance of its co-occurrence with other words, these collocates themselves should have appeared in the text a reasonable number of times.

In their study of the collocation patterns of lexical words in a 135,000-word corpus, they thus impose minimum frequencies of occurrence on both nodes and collocates, as well as on the number of co-occurrences on which each collocation is based: nodes are selected from words that occur in the frequency range 90-290; collocates must have occurred at least ten times, otherwise the measure of statistical significance used would be 'rather unreliable' (ibid:33);[33] and each collocation is based on at least three co-occurrences of suitably frequent nodes and collocates.[34] Finally an arbitrarily defined (ibid:32) threshold level of significance is applied to each collocation.

The problem with rejecting low-frequency words in collocation analysis is that it usually means ignoring most of the words in a corpus. Half of the 100 million tokens of the British National Corpus, for example, are hapax legomena, that is, they represent types that occur only once (Aston and Burnard 1998:40). An even more extreme distribution pattern is evident in GEPCOLT. The German subcorpus contains 970,270 tokens and 73,137 types. Of the 73,137 types, 42,101, or 57.56%,

---

[32] See also Smadja (1989:166).

[33] Sinclair (1991:106) also imposes a minimum frequency of occurrence on collocates that are taken into consideration by specifying that collocates that do not occur at least 10% as frequently as the node be excluded from the analysis.

[34] See also Church and Hanks (1990:24) who only consider collocations that occur more than five times on the grounds that the "association ratio" (an *MI*-like measure) "becomes unstable when the counts are very small".

occur only once.[35] Types that occur ten times or more account for a mere 9.4% of the total running words. And although Renouf has claimed that the type count can be assumed to decrease proportionately as a corpus grows in size, until a point is reached in corpus development "where all the word forms in which there is a lexicological interest are sufficiently exemplified" (1987b:130), such a situation is likely to arise only with corpora containing several hundred million, if not several billion, words. Confining analysis in GEPCOLT to those types that occur, say, ten times or more, would mean drastically restricting the scope of the current project. It would also militate against the chances of discovering instances of lexical creativity, which lies at the heart of this research.[36] Lexicographers such as John Sinclair and Patrick Hanks are, in the first instance, interested in describing the recurring patterns of language.[37] They thus share with computational linguists such as Frank Smadja and Andrea Lehr a concern with developing tools and methodologies for automatically extracting non-idiosyncratic linguistic information from very large bodies of data. In corpus-based lexicography the aim is typically to describe tens, if not hundreds, of thousands of lexemes, and their typical (collocational) behaviour, on the basis of corpora that now run to hundreds of millions of tokens. The project undertaken by Lehr (1996) involves building lexical networks on the basis of syntagmatic lexical relations in corpora (and paradigmatic relations arrived at by abstraction from those syntagmatic relations), where every single token in a corpus is potentially a node in a collocation. In cases such as these, measures of statistical significance have their advantages. They represent an impartial way of ranking the collocates of a particular node in terms of the strength of their attachment to the node, and they allow the amount of data that linguists have to consider when describing a node to be cut down to practicable levels: for huge quantities of data, the manual analysis of concordance lines can be labour-intensive and prone to error. According to Church *et al.*, "the unaided human mind simply cannot discover all the significant patterns, let alone group them and rank them in order of importance" (1991:116). In such cases the kind of collocational analysis that uses absolute and relative frequency information and optional measures of statistical significance seems to offer a workable solution (see also Stubbs 1996:174-175).[38] The main

---

[35] Note that the figures given here, computed using the *WordList* program in *WordSmith Tools*, are for unlemmatized types.

[36] This is not to suggest that all 42,101 types that occur only once in the German subcorpus of GEPCOLT are creative uses of language. Only a handful of them are, and these are spotted using an approach outlined in Chapter Five.

[37] This does not mean that exceptional or creative uses of language do not interest lexicographers. See, for example, Hanks's (1988, 1996) work on lexical 'exploitations', and Sinclair (1997) on 'semantic reversal'. Rather, as indicated in Chapter Two, they see the description of conventions as prior to the description of exploitations of those conventions.

[38] It is, of course, possible to work on a selection of concordance lines, but Sinclair points out that it is the exhaustiveness of concordances that makes them attractive to linguists in the first

disadvantage of these significance tests from the point of view of the current project is that their application makes little sense with types that occur only once in a corpus (Collier 1993:292).[39] If we wish to include collocates that occur only once in the study of any particular node in GEPCOLT, then we must forego use of the kind of significance measures mentioned above. This is not a serious drawback, however, as unlike in the projects just described, the concern here is not with establishing the collocational behaviour of as many types as is practicable in a given corpus. Rather the focus is on a single, manually selected node (see Chapter Five), so fully automatic collocational analysis of the entire corpus is not necessary. In the monolingual phases of the current research[40] the computer will be used rather to provide:

> word lists, including lists of keywords and clusters in individual texts (see Chapter Two)
> information on the frequency distribution of types across the whole corpus or in individual texts;
> information on the frequency of co-occurrence of selected types; and
> the kind of display functions offered by concordance software and illustrated in Chapter Two, Figure 1.

German *ad hoc* compounds

For the purposes of the current research then, no lower limit is set on the frequency of co-occurrence of nodes and collocates said to be in a relationship of collocation, or on the independent frequency of occurrence of either node or collocate. Hapax legomena are thus included in the analysis, where they can be considered as either nodes or collocates. In some treatments of collocation in German, certain hapax forms, namely *ad hoc* compounds, are treated as collocations in themselves.[41] This is the approach taken by Lehr (1996:139-140), who describes a routine whereby *ad hoc* compounds, as well as other compounds that are not found in the particular dictionary being used as a control, are split into their component parts for the pur-

---

place, and so they should be trimmed only "when the number of instances becomes quite unmanageable otherwise", and when the selection criteria have been chosen "very carefully" (1991:43).

[39] There is, however, at least one class of test that can be validly applied to rare linguistic events: likelihood ratio tests (Dunning 1993) can be used to identify significant collocations in corpora, even when there are only sparse data available. But these tests do not seem to have been embraced by lexicographers, perhaps because the latter are interested primarily in repeated, and thus well-attested, co-occurrences.

[40] Software designed specifically for bilingual applications and used in this research project is discussed in Chapter Five.

[41] Other theorists have argued that even common compounds should be considered collocations. See, for example, van der Wouden's comments on Dutch (1992:452-454).

poses of automatic collocation analysis. An example from GEPCOLT is used here by way of illustration: the form *Eintagebärte*,[42] literally 'one-day beards', would be split into the components *ein* + *tag(e)*[43] + *bärte*, or perhaps *eintag(e)* + *bärte*, depending on the contents of the hypothetical control dictionary. In Lehr's scheme *eintag(e)* would then be considered as collocating with *bärte*, or vice versa, depending on which form is considered the node.[44] A further level of analysis, one that takes into consideration the relative frequencies of each form in the corpus as a whole, would then be used to indicate whether the collocation *eintag(e)* + *bärte* occurs with greater than expected frequency, and/or whether it is statistically significant or not (Lehr ibid:207-246). In the current research however, and for reasons already outlined above, we are more interested in absolute frequencies of co-occurrence than in relative ones, and we have eschewed the use of measures of statistical significance. There is therefore no methodological need to automatically split compounds such as *Eintagebärte* into their component parts in order to arrive at adequate statistical information on *eintag(e)* and *bärte* as separate forms. This is not to say that such forms are not split into their component parts when analyzed manually. Indeed in Chapter Six, it is clear that the form *Eintagebärte* is split up in order to ascertain in what, if any, kind of compounds or collocations *eintag(e)* and *bärte* (or the more abstract lemma BART) normally participate. Such decomposition of *ad hoc* compounds is, however, carried out only on a case-by-case basis and is not an automatic part of the analysis. The fact that Lehr associates *ad hoc* German compounds with collocations is, however, theoretically interesting. It shows that these compounds are not considered as having the same stability or applicability as fully lexicalized (compound and non-compound) words in German. And this is undoubtedly the case. Yet the view is taken here that *ad hoc* compounds have a status that is different to that of collocations. It is argued in Chapter Six, that creative writers attempt to confer a more universal status upon singular events or situations by providing a 'word' for those events or situations, and although unusual collocations are startling in themselves, they are startling in a different way to unusual, *ad hoc* compounds. For these reasons, and for ease of analysis and exposition, *ad*

---

[42] This form is used by Pieke Biermann in her novel *Violetta* and is deemed to be an *ad hoc* compound on the basis that it is not found in any of the lexicographical sources consulted, it does not occur in nearly 63 million words of the written Mannheim Corpora, and it is recognized as a novel and humorous creation by native German speakers (by analogy with *Dreitagebart*, literally 'three-day beard', which an unshaven man is commonly said to possess).

[43] The *e* is put between parentheses here as, in synchronic terms at least (see Russ 1994:222), it is a mere linking morpheme, a *Fugenelement*, with no inflectional meaning. Note also that a certain level of regularization of forms is implicit in the folding of all characters to lower case in this example.

[44] For Lehr (1996:38), the phrase *kollokiert mit*, 'collocates with', expresses a directional relationship: nodes are said to collocate with collocates, but not vice versa.

hoc compounds are dealt with separately from unusual collocations in the study presented in this book.

Lexis and linguistic theory

Thus far we have been concerned with mainly methodological issues in lexical research, and in particular in collocational research. Given that corpus linguistics has been described as "a methodological basis for pursuing linguistic research" (Leech 1992:105, quoted in Chapter Two), it should come as no surprise that questions of methodology are constantly to the fore in the area. But the concern with methodology has not prevented linguists from getting on with the job of linguistic description, and from gaining new insights into language on foot of their descriptive work. The accumulation of such insights has meant that what started out as a "methodological change and *quantitative* explosion" is now described by some linguists as a "theoretical and *qualitative* revolution" (Tognini-Bonelli 1996a:40).[45] As Tognini-Bonelli's use of the word 'revolution' suggests, many of these insights present a challenge to linguistic orthodoxy, representing a move away from the kind of autonomous rule-driven linguistics that is so unpalatable to some translation theorists (see Chapter One), towards a more 'humanist' and 'social' linguistics (Stubbs 1996:237), that, I would like to argue, will be more adequate to the task of describing and explaining the complexities of translation. The broad lines of this challenge to linguistic orthodoxy were introduced in Chapter Two. We turn now to the details.

Several commentators have described the general thrust of the theory that dominated linguistics during the mid to late twentieth century along the following lines:[46] under the influence of Chomsky's Generative-Transformational Grammar, linguistic theory "has been massively biased in favour of the *paradigmatic* rather than the *syntagmatic* dimension" (Sinclair 1997) and thus has been concerned with systems of competing choices in the grammar. Lexis comes into play only to fill structural slots left open by the grammar, to put 'leaves' on trees generated by the rules of syntax. Even in Halliday's competing systemic functional grammar, 'word statements' have been seen merely as "instantiations of class statements" (Tognini-Bonelli 1996a:39). The dominant position of rule-driven syntax in linguistic theory has meant that text has been perceived "as a series of relatively independent choices of one item after another, and the patterns of combination have been seriously undervalued" (Sinclair ibid). One of the most important contributions of corpus-driven linguistics has been the redirecting of attention towards syntagmatic patterning in

---

[45] See also Leech (1992:106) and Clear (1993:274).

[46] See, for example, Francis (1993:139-140), Francis and Sinclair (1994:199), Sinclair (1997), Stubbs (1996:Chapter Two), and Tognini-Bonelli (1996a:25-26).

language. The study of habitual collocations, for example, provides evidence that lexical items are selected more than one at a time. Colligational patterns too emphasize the fact that lexical items can have typical grammatical environments: lexis is not isolated from grammar. The co-selection of lexical items, as well as the co-selection of lexis and grammar are two of the early insights afforded by corpus-driven linguistics. Collocation has already been discussed in detail above. We turn now to the interaction of lexis and grammar. As is consistent with the holistic approach to linguistic description advocated by Sinclair (1996:95) and Tognini-Bonelli (1996a:34, 72), the discussion of the alignment of lexis and grammar will inevitably lead us into a discussion of the alignment of sense and structure, and ultimately the intentions of speakers and writers.

The interaction of lexis and grammar

One simple but powerful illustration of the interaction of lexis and grammar comes in the form of the observation that individual lemmas have characteristic grammatical environments. Sinclair (1991:73-74) points out, for example, that the phrasal verb SET IN tends to occur in the small or minor part of sentences, typically in subordinate clauses and in sentence-final position. Repeated observations of this kind have led Francis to claim that "particular syntactic structures tend to co-occur with particular lexical items, and – the other side of the coin – lexical items seem to occur in a limited range of structures" (1993:143). Not only do individual lemmas have characteristic grammatical environments, the patterns of distribution of forms of a single lemma differ too. Thus there is almost no overlap between the collocations in which the singular and plural forms of the lemma EYE participate (Sinclair 1996:84). The collocates associated with *eye* include *caught* and *mind*, while *eyes* tends to collocate with adjectives such as *blue* and *brown*. The different patterns of collocation and colligation of the singular and plural forms of EYE point to different senses of the lemma. The singular form, unlike the plural, "hardly ever refers to the anatomical object, except when talking about injury or handicap" (Stubbs 1996:38). Sinclair (1991:42ff) also finds that different senses of the lemmas DECLINE and YIELD are associated with different forms of those lemmas, and the different structures in which those forms participate. It is observations such as these that have led Sinclair to the conclusion that differences in form and structural environment indicate differences in meaning and to the very strong claim that "there is ultimately no distinction between form and meaning" (ibid:7). The consequences for theories of text interpretation are far-reaching. One is that ambiguity in natural language texts has been grossly exaggerated, especially by those concerned with Natural Language Processing (Sinclair 1997): the form and collocational and colligational environments of a word in a text indicate how that word is to be interpreted, regardless of how many meanings are attached to it in the dictionary.

The idiom principle and the open-choice principle

Investigations of syntagmatic patterning in texts have also shown that "the co-selection of syntax and lexis often involves not just one word but a series of them" (Francis 1993:143). The tendency of words to "go together and make meanings by their combinations" (Sinclair 1996:82) has been called the 'phraseological tendency' (Sinclair 1996) or 'idiom principle' (Sinclair 1987b, 1991). The idiom principle, whereby "a language user has available to him or her a large number of semi-preconstructed phrases that constitute single choices, even though they might appear to be analysable into segments" (Sinclair 1987b: 320), is capitalized upon when language users create texts. Likewise, it becomes the default mode of interpretation of texts. It contrasts with Sinclair's 'open-choice principle', which reflects the view that text is built up and interpreted using a 'slot-and-filler' approach: "At each point where a unit is completed (a word or a phrase or a clause), a large range of choice opens up, and the only restraint is grammaticalness" (ibid: 319-20). While the idiom principle is dominant in text creation and interpretation, the open-choice principle becomes operative at what Sinclair (ibid:324) calls "switch points". These are points in texts where readers or listeners are forced to abandon one mode of interpretation in favour of another. Sinclair (ibid) holds that lexical choices "which are unexpected in their environment" presumably occasion such switches. Habitual collocations are one important manifestation of the idiom principle, but unusual collocations occasion switches. They represent points at which default interpretations cannot apply. They thus exhibit a special type of markedness that translators may or may not seek to recreate.[47]

Semantic preference and semantic prosody

Sinclair's idiom principle/phraseological tendency was first identified on the basis of evidence provided by routine patterns of collocation. By considering the part-of-speech categories of the words occurring with the node, the identification of recurrent colligational patterns becomes possible. If an element of semantic interpretation is introduced into the analysis of recurring syntagmatic patterns, collocates can be grouped in such a way as to suggest that nodes have a 'semantic preference' for certain types of collocates.[48] By integrating pragmatic information into the analysis, in the guise of 'semantic prosodies', which reveal speakers' attitudes, we arrive at an even more detailed description of the "rich repertoire of multi-word patterns that

[47] For a discussion of switch points applied to translation, see Kenny (1998b).

[48] Semantic preference is described by Sinclair (1997) as "the restriction of *regular* co-occurrence to items which share a semantic feature" (emphasis mine). Semantic preferences differ from 'selectional restrictions', discussed above, in that they are arrived at by induction, and do not rely on negative evidence.

make up text" (Sinclair 1991:108). Recent work by Sinclair (1996, 1997) and Tognini-Bonelli (1996a) has sought to integrate precisely such semantic and pragmatic information into the analysis of syntagmatic patterns in texts. The kind of patterning that Sinclair refers to is found to extend beyond single words (common or rare), frequent collocations and typical idioms (Sinclair 1996:83). It is illustrated here using Sinclair's example of a typical idiom, that is the expression NAKED EYE. Sinclair demonstrates first of all that, given 151 instances of the expression extracted from a 211 million word corpus, NAKED EYE occurs routinely with THE in the first position to its left (designated N-1). At position N-2 we find a preposition (usually either WITH or TO) in 90% of cases. This second observation shows a strong colligational pattern. The N-3 position is dominated by lexemes such as SEE and VISIBLE. Thus the idiom NAKED EYE is said to have a 'semantic preference' for words that have to do with 'visibility'. The criterion of semantic preference, Sinclair (ibid:86) admits, "is another stage removed from the actual words in the text, just as colligation is one step more abstract than collocation". It is useful, however, because "it captures more of the patterning than the others". It is clear though, that while collocational and even colligational patterns are computable, the latter once part-of-speech information has been incorporated into either the corpus or the procedures used to analyze the corpus, semantic preferences are less amenable to automatic recognition: there is less predictability in the form and position of the words expressing the relevant semantic feature. If this is the case for semantic preferences, it is even more true of semantic prosodies. A semantic prosody, according to Louw (1993:157) arises from a "consistent aura of meaning with which a form is imbued by its collocates". The seemingly innocuous phrasal verb SET IN, for example, becomes imbued with a negative aura because of its habitual collocation with lexemes like ROT, DECAY, and RIGOR MORTIS (Sinclair 1991:74-75). Likewise, the expression NAKED EYE has become imbued with a prosody of "difficulty" (Sinclair 1996:87). Semantic prosodies are subject to enormous variation in their linguistic realization. They are also "largely inaccessible to human intuition about language" (Louw 1993:157), and have to be spotted on the basis of copious amounts of corpus data. But despite their elusive quality, Sinclair is in no doubt as to the importance of semantic prosodies. He argues that the semantic prosody of an item is the reason why it is chosen in the first place, "over and above the semantic preferences that also characterise it" (1997). Put simply, semantic prosodies indicate how whole meaning units are supposed to function. They represent "the functional choice which links meaning to purpose" (Sinclair 1996:88). Sinclair goes as far as to suggest that the semantic prosody probably represents "the boundary of the lexical item" (ibid). This argumentation is taken up by Tognini-Bonelli when she claims that semantic prosodies "represent the outer limit of the unit of meaning where, to put it in Firthian terms, the co-text merges with the context and a certain item achieves a purpose in a certain environment" (1996a:86-87). Sinclair concludes that "so strong are the co-occurrence tendencies of words, word classes, meanings and attitudes that we must widen our horizons and expect the units of meaning to be much more extensive and varied than is seen in a single word" (1996:94).

Sinclair's approach is thus a far cry from that of traditional dictionaries where meaning is seen to reside in discrete lexical units, with all the problems of 'ambiguity' that this entails. Nor does it allow the kind of division of labour that is possible if we consider grammar and lexis as handling different types of semantics. But for all the complexity of Sinclair's approach to units of meaning, it is difficult to deny that he has put his finger on an obvious but until-now elusive aspect of the meaning of, for example, the word BUDGE, when he claims that we use this word because we wish to express our *frustration* at our inability to budge something, or at someone else's refusal to budge (Sinclair 1997). Such observations regarding how units of meaning are dispersed over larger stretches of text than was previously thought to be the case illustrate how important it is to take syntagmatic relations seriously, and to proceed to general statements of meaning on the basis of recurrent syntagmatic relations. This approach does not pre-empt any discussion of paradigms, construed as systems of competing choices: Lehr (1996), in her automatic analysis of German collocation, provides a good example of how the analyst can move from statements regarding syntagmatic co-selection to statements regarding substitution systems of collocates, on the one hand, and nodes, on the other. The former are built up by bringing together all the collocates of a single node in a particular corpus. The group of such collocates is known as the 'collocational range' of that node. Substitution systems of nodes known as 'collocational sets' are then built up by bringing together nodes that have substantially the same collocational ranges. Lehr's position is neo-Firthian in that her notion of system "is strictly related to abstractions made from observation of patterns at the syntagmatic level" (Tognini-Bonelli 1996a:34). Putting syntagmatic relations first should guarantee that linguistic description will stand the test of re-application to "similar relevant events in renewal of connection with experience" (Firth 1968:199). It also means that neo-Firthian linguistics is necessarily text based, which makes it more interesting for the study of translation than linguistic theories that are based on abstract, autonomous systems of rules. Translation involves the purposeful use and manipulation of texts. Approaches to linguistics that shed light on how texts are routinely built up and interpreted, and how such routine can be exploited to create special textual effects, must be of interest to translation theorists. I suggested above that Sinclair's (1987b, 1991) notion of switch points may provide a useful category in the study of translation. Elsewhere (Kenny 1998b) I have argued that departures from expected profiles of semantic prosodies could provide interesting cases of such switches: if one were to write, for example, that 'happiness had set in', the clash between the negative prosody of the verb SET IN, mentioned above, and the normally positive associations of the lexeme HAPPINESS might force readers to switch to another mode of interpretation. Departures from expected profiles of semantic prosodies are thus a special case of unusual collocation that may be of interest in studies of normalization in translated texts. If it were shown that such source text collocational clashes were rendered in the target text by wordings that contained no such clashes, then this could lend weight to the hypothesis that translators tend to replace unconventional source text collocations with conventional target language ones.

Semantic reversal

Switch points have recently been revisited by Sinclair (1997) in his discussion of 'semantic reversal'. Sinclair (ibid) explains this phenomenon as follows:

> Instead of expecting to understand a segment of text by accumulating the meanings of each successive meaningful unit, here is the reverse: where a number of units taken together create a meaning, and this meaning takes precedence over the 'dictionary meanings' of whatever words are chosen.

Sinclair gives the sentence 'The ambience borders on the holy...' as an example of semantic reversal. Here *holy* has to be interpreted as an abnormal mental state, simply because the phrasal verb BORDER ON has picked up a prosody of abnormality from its usual collocates. But the evaluative feature of abnormality would not be assigned to the lexeme HOLY by any dictionary. Rather this meaning flows from the text to the lexical item, instead of the other way round. This is the essence of semantic reversal.

Semantic reversal is introduced here as a final example of how meanings are created in texts, and how these meanings can fall anywhere on a cline from the wholly routine to the extremely creative. Routine meanings are created and interpreted on the basis of recurrent patterns in language – patterns of collocation, which determine the semantic preferences and prosodies of lexical items, and patterns of colligation. And creativity can reside in deviations from such established patterns. Semantic reversals are also examples *par excellence* of purely textual meaning. They point up the fact that "a text is a unique deployment of meaningful units, and its particular meaning is not adequately accounted for by any concatenation of the fixed meanings of each unit" (Sinclair 1997). Languages and cultures may have established repertoires of meaning units, but each text will use those repertoires in its own way. Some texts create completely new meanings that could not have been predicted on the basis of the relevant linguistic and cultural repertoires, although they are relatable to those repertoires and thus interpretable by text receivers. Sinclair recognizes the "intricate patterns that knit a text together" (1991:8) and the uniqueness of the meaning relations established in each text. He also points to the tradition in linguistics of falling back on descriptions of repertoires of words and grammatical structures, divorced from their use in real text, and thus the inability of such traditional approaches to engage with the complexities of real texts. These are aspects of Sinclair's work that make it most amenable to application in translation studies. What Sinclair argues about language and linguistic description is paralleled closely by what Toury (1993, 1995) argues about source texts and the process of translation. As we saw in Chapter Three, according to Toury's (1993:28, 1995:268) law of growing standardization, the web of intratextual relations exhibited by a source text is dissolved upon translation, never to be fully reconstituted in the target text. The textual meanings unique to a source text are replaced by habitual options from target language/culture repertoires. The net result is that target texts are often more 'normal' for the target language and culture than the source text is in its linguistic and cultural home. I would like to suggest here that Sinclair, and other linguists working in the neo-Firthian tradition, have developed an approach to linguistic description that takes full cognisance of the intricacies of intratextual ties, and that this approach can be applied to the study of such ties in original and translated texts, and thus to the hypothesized process of normalization.

Conclusion

In this Chapter I have attempted to describe a number of ways in which linguists have approached the study of words, and the relations between words. The emphasis in the first part of the Chapter was on ways of forming new words, by means of the familiar morphological processes of compounding and derivation. It was suggested here that new formations are interpreted by language users in the light of what they know to be routine in the language in question, and that standard lexicographical sources, and, more importantly, corpora, can provide useful evidence of such linguistic routine. Relations between words were then viewed in terms of the kind of paradigmatic sense relations posited in structural semantics, and it was suggested that formal lexical relations, such as homography and paronymy, may also be of interest in the analysis of novel lexical items in GEPCOLT. I then discussed the syntagmatic relation of collocation, putting particular emphasis on approaches that view collocation as an organizing principle in language, and not merely a catch-all for semantic or cross-linguistic anomalies. The initial discussion of collocation addressed mainly theoretical and methodological issues, such as the definition of collocation, and procedures for identifying various categories of collocation, including statistically significant collocations. In the latter part of the discussion I attempted to show how recent work on collocation, and the more abstract but related categories of colligation, semantic preference, and semantic prosody, has contributed to a new understanding of how text is created and interpreted, and most notably, how instances of lexical creativity can be discerned against the background of the usual patterns of language use. At the end of the Chapter, I suggested that many insights from the corpus-based study of syntagmatic relations could be brought to bear on the study of translation, and in particular, on the putative phenomenon of normalization in translation. Just how this might be done is the subject of the next Chapter.

5. The How of it
Creating and Using a Parallel Corpus

> The computer is incurably and pedantically data oriented. For a linguist, there are no short cuts to his or her abstractions. The first stage of adaptation is to resign oneself to plodding through the detail.
>
> John Sinclair (1991:27)

Introduction

At the beginning of Chapter Two we noted that corpus linguistics is, above all, a way of studying language: corpora provide the data for linguistic study; and corpus linguistics the tools and methodologies. We now turn our attention to the specific corpora used in the project in hand, and the tools and methodologies used to extract and evaluate useful data from these corpora. The principal data source consulted is the purpose-built German-English Parallel Corpus of Literary Texts, or GEPCOLT. Comparative data for English and German are supplied by the British National Corpus (BNC), and the group of corpora known here as the Mannheim Corpora. All three are described below, along with the software used to access them. Given that one of the aims of the study described in this book is to investigate whether or not lexical normalization is a feature of translation in GEPCOLT, we need a method of pinpointing instances of lexical creativity in the German texts under investigation, and tracking and evaluating – from the point of view of target language creativity – their translations into English. A number of ways of doing this, all of which rely on the ability of corpus processing tools to produce concordances and word lists of various types, are introduced and assessed below. We start, however, with a discussion of the general issues that face corpus compilers.

Issues in corpus compilation

> The beginning of any corpus study is the creation of the corpus itself. The decisions that are taken about what is to be in the corpus, and how the selection is to be organized, control almost everything that happens subsequently. The results are only as good as the corpus. (Sinclair 1991:13)

As Sinclair's comments make clear, corpus compilation is the vital first step in any corpus-based study of language, and decisions taken at this first stage have ramifications throughout the whole study. In this section I outline the main considerations in corpus design and text selection for general language corpora. Later we will see how findings from research into areas such as representativeness and sampling strategies are brought to bear on the design of GEPCOLT.

Representativeness

The design of a corpus, and the selection of individual texts for inclusion in that corpus, are determined principally by its envisaged purpose (Biber 1994:381; Engwall 1994:50; Gellerstam 1992:154; Sinclair 1991:13-14). In general linguistic research, corpora have traditionally been designed with the aim of presenting a representative sample of the language at large at a specific point in time. The Brown and LOB corpora, as well as the BNC, all introduced in Chapter Two, provide good examples of attempts to produce 'representative' corpora of contemporary English. But such endeavours are by no means straightforward. For one, it is not obvious how one can apply the notion of representativeness, as borrowed from the theory of statistical sampling, to examples of natural language. Sampling theory is concerned with how we can infer knowledge of a whole, the target population, from knowledge of a part, or sample, of such a target population. The difficulty for linguists arises because, in statistical terms, populations are always understood as the set of all possible (numeric) values for a particular variable (see Woods *et al.* 1986:49). A sample is considered 'representative' of a particular target population if its mean value for the variable in question can be said to approximate the mean value for that variable in the entire population, a scenario that becomes more likely as sample size increases. But while some linguistic studies may focus on populations of numeric values, many linguists are more interested in general terms in the *data* from which such statistical populations are drawn.[1] Such a data set can be used to derive values for many different variables and hence to construct many different sample populations. But regardless of what variable is under investigation, the strictly statistical notion of representativeness can be applied only to samples of values for a given variable and not to the data collection itself. In corpus linguistics, however, representativeness is typically imputed to data collections themselves, and there is generally no single variable on the basis of which the target population can be defined. The definition of the target population supposedly represented by a particular corpus of general language is further complicated by the fact that natural language is by its very nature heterogeneous, and almost impossible to quantify: there is no foolproof way of fixing boundaries to what can be considered texts in a given natural language, or of deciding in what proportions the speech and writing of different individuals or groups within a language community should be present in a given corpus. Difficulties such as these have led some commentators to reject altogether the notion of representativeness in relation to natural language corpora. Sinclair (1991:13), for example, eschews any discussion of representativeness, claiming instead that:

---

[1] An example from Woods *et al.* (1986:3-5, 78ff) might help here. In a study of children's language, we might be interested in voice-onset times for the alveolar stops /d/ and /t/. These would constitute a population of numeric values. The corpus of children's utterances from which a sample of such values could be drawn, on the other hand, would constitute the 'data'.

> Until we know a lot more about the effects of our design strategies, we must rely on publishing a list of exactly what is in a corpus ... Users and critics can then consider the constitution and balance of the corpus as a separate matter from the reporting of the linguistic evidence of the corpus.

Woods *et al.* (1986:55) are similarly pragmatic in their solution to the natural language sampling problem. They propose that:

> ...a sensible way to proceed is to accept the results of each study, in the first place, as though any sampling had been carried out in a theoretically 'correct' fashion. If these results are interesting ... then is time enough to question how the sample was obtained and *whether this is likely to have a bearing on the validity of the conclusions reached.*

Like Sinclair, Woods *et al.* suggest that such an approach calls for complete transparency in the reporting of research. In particular it imposes upon researchers "the inescapable duty of describing carefully how their experimental material – including subjects – was actually obtained" (ibid:56). In the current research, an attempt is made to be as explicit as possible in the reporting of text selection criteria (see below), and works included in GEPCOLT are listed in full in Appendix 1.

Sampling strategies

Random sampling vs stratified approaches

While commentators acknowledge that it is impossible to ensure a sample is representative of a particular population (Woods *et al.* ibid:52; Atkins *et al.* 1992:5), there is still agreement that one should at least try to minimize the effects of known sources of bias. One standard way to minimize experimenter bias is to use random sampling, a statistical procedure that "allows every element in the population a known probability of being selected in the sample" (Woods *et al.* ibid:52).[2] The problem with this approach is, however, that if one were to select randomly a sample of texts from the universe of all texts, one would have to have a very large sample before one could purport to have accounted for anything like the range of variability in natural language (Biber 1994:379). In most cases researchers instead identify subgroups or 'strata' in the populations they wish to investigate, and then select a specified proportion of texts to fit each stratum. This approach is, according to Biber, "more conservative, in that it insures representativeness in the desired proportions for each of these text categories, and at the same time it enables smaller sample

---

[2] The term 'random' is used here in its statistical sense. Compare Van Doorslaer (1995) for whom 'random' selection implies absence of procedure.

sizes" (ibid:383). Strata are usually considered hierarchical (Biber 1994; Halverson 1998), with distinctions such as spoken vs written text being made at the highest level in the hierarchy, and subsequent distinctions like published vs unpublished (for written texts) being made at lower levels. In cases where corpora are not intended for the investigation of a language in its entirety, but rather some subset of that language, the highest level in the hierarchy will be suitably restricted, for example to French novels in Engwall (1994).

Internal vs external criteria

For general language corpora, the universe of natural language utterances is usually stratified on the basis of 'external' criteria, that is those related to situational factors such as:

- the *domains* individual texts supposedly belong to – chemistry, linguistics, etc, although imaginative texts are often considered a class apart, regardless of what they are 'about';
- the *situations* in which texts are produced and received – among friends, in parliament, at publishing houses, etc;
- the *people* who produce and receive texts – adults or children, males or females, etc;
- the *time period* in which texts are produced – ranging from a single year for synchronic corpora such as Brown and LOB to several centuries for diachronic corpora like the Helsinki Diachronic Corpus (McEnery and Wilson 1996:183); and
- the *medium* of dissemination – print, broadcast, etc.

Situational and demographic criteria are used, for example, as selection criteria in the spoken part of the British National Corpus (Burnard 1995b). For the written component of the BNC, texts were selected to fit certain domains (imaginative or informative, the latter category being divided into several subdomains), and according to their date (1960-1993 for imaginative texts; 1975-1993 for informative texts) and medium of publication (book, periodical, unpublished, etc). Texts included in the Brown and LOB corpora were selected on the basis of their belonging to particular domains and having been published in 1961.

The alternative to the use of external criteria in corpus design is to use 'internal' criteria, that is those related to the formal linguistic characteristics of texts.[3] As such formal characteristics cannot be known in advance of analysis of texts, however, corpus design is normally based on external criteria. But corpora designed according-

[3] The internal features of texts are not independent of features of the external context of situation; in fact the interrelationship between the two is one of the areas of study in corpus linguistics (Atkins *et al.* 1992:5).

ing to external criteria alone are "liable to miss significant variation among texts since its categories are not motivated by textual (but contextual) features" (Atkins *et al.* 1992:5). One proposed solution to this problem is to proceed in a cyclical fashion (Biber 1994), designing a corpus on the basis of external features and then, through empirical investigation of the texts ultimately selected to exemplify different strata, refining text selection so as to attain a more adequate balance of linguistic features internal to selected texts.

Text selection

Thus far we have seen that compilers of general language corpora usually reject random sampling of texts from the entire universe of natural language utterances in favour of a stratified approach. This effectively means deciding on a kind of taxonomy of text categories whose 'slots' still have to be filled with appropriate texts, or text extracts. There are two basic approaches to filling these slots. The first (used by the compilers of the Brown and LOB corpora and the BNC) uses random sampling within each text category to select exemplars that fit that category. The second 'hand-picks' texts somehow identified as optimally fitting the category in question. Engwall's (1994) selection of 25 novels for inclusion in a corpus of French best-sellers published between 1962 and 1968 exemplifies the second approach.[4] Whichever approach is opted for, researchers still require an adequate sampling frame as a starting point for the selection of texts in a particular category. The most common type of sampling frame is, according to Woods *et al.*, "a list (actual or notional) of all the subjects in the group to which generalization is intended" (1986:52-53). Such lists exist in convenient form for many types of published written texts (although the same cannot be said for spoken, or unpublished written texts). They include catalogues of books published each year (for example, *Livres de l'année* for French) and lists of books in print (*Whitaker's Bookbank* for British publications, *Global Books in Print* for American and British publications combined, and the *Verzeichnis Liefbarer Bücher* for German-speaking countries). These sources ideally give researchers exhaustive accounts of book *production* in the various geographical areas covered. Should corpus compilers also wish to consider the *reception* these books get in their respective cultures, in terms of their dissemination or critical appraisal, they can refer to best-seller lists, and library lending statistics, on the one hand, and critical reviews and lists of prize-winning works on the other.[5]

---

[4] Engwall (1994:62-63) manages to narrow down the number of suitable texts by refining the selection procedure so as to include only works (1) written by authors born in France, (2) set in post-1945 France, and (3) written by authors in the youngest age-group represented. A final consideration is that the corpus should include only one novel per author.

[5] For a detailed description of the use of information sources on the production and reception of published works in the compilation of the British National Corpus, see Burnard (1995b).

As we will see below, however, these sources are not always reliable when it comes to unearthing information about translated works, and compilers of translation corpora may have to turn to other, dedicated, sources.

Full texts vs text extracts

Once an adequate sampling frame has been identified for each text category to be included in a corpus, and a strategy for selecting individual texts has been decided upon, researchers have to make a final decision as to whether the corpus is going to consist of full texts or text extracts. The arguments in favour of text extracts – which are often randomly selected from their respective texts (Burnard 1995b; Engwall 1994) – are that: they allow corpus builders to get better coverage of a language variety by including extracts from more works than would be the case if whole works were included; having extracts of equal length makes for easier statistical comparisons between texts; and it is easier to secure permission to hold extracts as opposed to complete works in electronic form (Aston and Burnard 1998:22, 39). The principal arguments against the use of extracts (see Baker 1995:240; Biber 1994:389; Sinclair 1991:19) are that linguistic features are rarely distributed evenly throughout texts and an extract can thus misrepresent the overall text;[6] short extracts also make the study of larger text patterns, for example those that extend beyond paragraphs or even chapters, impossible. Using text extracts is considered particularly problematic in cases where researchers are interested in rare linguistic features. Biber (ibid:390), for example, has shown that:

> frequency counts for common linguistic features are relatively stable across 1,000 word samples, while frequency counts for rare features ... are less stable and require longer text samples to be reliably represented.

As the present study focuses on the translation of rare lexical features it is clear that short text extracts would constitute an inadequate basis for the research. And as special emphasis is to be placed on hapax legomena, statements about the uniqueness of particular words or collocations have got to be based on full knowledge of all the texts in the corpus. The corpus constructed for the present research therefore consists of full texts. While this means a loss in terms of coverage of a wider selection of works, it also means a gain in terms of the confidence with which we can say

---

[6] Engwall (1994:63) attempts to overcome this difficulty by selecting one 2,000 word extract from each of ten sections into which each novel in her corpus of French novels is divided, the idea being that ten extracts from a single novel give a more representative picture of that novel than a single 20,000 word extract taken from the beginning, middle, or end of the novel. In contrast, the compilers of the English-Norwegian Parallel Corpus selected extracts of 10,000-15,000 words from the beginning of a number of works of fiction and non-fiction (ENPC 1997).

that an instance of a particular feature is unique. The inclusion of full texts also has implications for future uses of the corpus, as corpora that include full documents are "open to a wider range of linguistic studies than a collection of short samples" (Sinclair 1991:19).

The German-English Parallel Corpus of Literary Texts (GEPCOLT)

Having considered general issues regarding corpus design and text sampling above, as well as issues that apply specifically to translation-oriented corpora, addressed in Chapter Three, we can now describe GEPCOLT in some detail. As is the case with all corpora, the single most important determining factor in the design of GEPCOLT is its intended purpose. GEPCOLT was designed for use in the investigation of normalization and creativity in translation. The specific question that the corpus is intended to shed light upon is whether or not translators typically draw on more conventional target language resources to replace unconventional, or text-specific, lexical features in source language texts, as suggested by much of the research reported on in Chapter Three. In order to pursue this question it is clear that we must have access to a collection of source language texts and their translations into a target language, in other words the data to be analyzed will have to be drawn from some kind of parallel corpus. As the name GEPCOLT suggests, the parallel corpus duly constructed consists of German source language texts and their translations into English. This particular language pair and direction was selected for a number of reasons. The first, and most obvious, relates to the linguistic competence of the researcher. A second reason is that given the relatively limited size of the corpus to be constructed, it was clear from the start that supporting data for any findings would have to be gleaned from external sources, and reference corpora for English and German were readily available in the form of the British National Corpus and the Mannheim Corpora respectively. A third reason relates to perceptions of German literature in the English-speaking world: although more nuanced accounts exist in specialized publications (see, for example, Rectanus 1990:117-126), popular sources tend to perpetuate the perception that German fiction, in the wake of literary giants like Heinrich Böll and Günter Grass, has been marred by "over-introspection or pedantry" (*The Economist* 11 November 1995, p.7). The huge success enjoyed by the English translations of Michael Ende's *Die Unendliche Geschichte* and Patrick Süskind's *Das Parfum* in the early to mid-1980s did little to change this perception. Neither text is particularly associated with Germany, characterized as they are by elements of fantasy and fairy tale. And, according to Rectanus, both exhibit "characteristics which US publishers and agents frequently find lacking in contemporary German literature: strong central characters and plot development" (1990:151). The expectation that contemporary German literature is somehow dull,[7] although the same perception does not exist, for example, for contemporary Austrian literature, may affect how German literature is translated into English, and how easy it is to market in the English-speaking world, but it may also have an affect on the linguistic make-up of works that are translated. The author and translator Pieke Biermann (personal communication) has suggested, for example, that "British publishers and maybe even translators do not expect ... a German author and/or the German language to be funny", and that much of the wit in her 1990 novel *Violetta* was simply overlooked in translation into English, as it was not expected to be there in the first place. Given that the German language seems most amenable to lexical creativity, allowing as it does "infinite possibilities of composing words" (Biermann ibid), it was expected at the outset that German novels would supply interesting data for a study of lexical creativity. But a study of German literature in English translation also offered the intriguing prospect of investigating whether perceptions related to the source literature spilled over into the linguistic make-up of target texts. [8]

Thus far we have seen that GEPCOLT is designed as a bilingual, parallel, unidirectional corpus. It has also become clear that it is made up of literary texts. The decision to focus on literary texts was made because it was thought that they may contain more instances of lexical creativity than other texts. This assumption is consistent with claims, made by scholars such as Snell-Hornby (1988a:51-52) and Venuti (1995:41), that literary texts give full rein to the creative potential of language while other text categories draw on a reduced linguistic potential, but it still remains only an assumption. An extensive contrastive textological investigation, which lies beyond the scope of the present book, would be required before we could say with confidence that this is actually the case. Having identified the category of literary text as of interest in the current research, the target population was further narrowed down to works of narrative fiction, and specifically to novels. The selection of novels was motivated by a number of factors. Firstly, a suitable sampling frame was available for German novels in translation in English. This is related to the fact that novels are in some respects "prototypical texts" (Atkins *et al.* 1992:2). Although

---

[7] This is a perception shared by some Germans. The author Pieke Biermann (personal communication), for example, puts limited interest in German literature in the English-speaking world down not just to "British or US-American lackings", but rather to shortcomings in the source literature itself: "It is, I'm afraid, due to the fact that the literature written in the two Germanies after 1945 rarely offers anything interesting to anybody outside them". Prominent critics such as Marcel Reich-Ranicki have also been vociferous in their criticisms of contemporary German literature (see *The Economist* 11 November 1995, p.7).

[8] The situation of translated literature in English-speaking countries is, of course, a complex one, with domestic conditions dictating how well translated literature fares as much as any inherent features (perceived or real) of source texts themselves. See Rectanus (1990:52-55) and Vanderauwera (1985:20-24) for more detailed discussions of such conditions prevailing in the American, and American and British literary marketplaces, respectively.

the characteristics ascribed to them by Atkins *et al.* (ibid) have been challenged,[9] in particular by writing practices informed by postmodern views of authorship and intertextuality, and hybrid forms do exist, published novels are still imminently recognizable as such. There is thus broad consensus – as evidenced by their inclusion in familiar catalogues – on what constitutes a novel, and a novel in translation, and this makes it much easier to fix the boundaries to the target population than would be the case if one were to set about studying translation in general, an object Toury (1995:31) describes as characterized "by its very **variability**: *difference* across cultures, *variation* within a culture and *change* over time" (see also Halverson 1998; Tymoczko 1998). Secondly, interesting data regarding normalization (and other features of translation) have been gleaned in the past from studies of translated novels. Vanderauwera, for example, suggests that while "idiosyncratic imagery and formulation are usually rendered by equally idiosyncratic imagery and formulation in translations of poetry", tolerance for the unusual in prose fiction "would seem to be rather low" (1985:109-110). If we wish then to uncover evidence of normalization, the translation of narrative prose would seem a good place to start.

The population of German novels in translation in English is still too large for a single researcher to sample adequately. For the purposes of this project, the population was narrowed down further by specifying that source language works should have been published in the 1980s and 1990s, in order to allow statements to be made about the translation of contemporary German literature. Three exceptions were made to this rule however, although their translations into English were completed well after 1960, which means that there is a level of comparability (at least on the temporal axis) between them and the imaginative texts in the BNC.[10] The three works in question were included in GEPCOLT on the recommendation of the translator Malcolm Green, who considered them to be particularly good examples of experimental German-language literature, and thus likely to yield interesting data for a study of lexical creativity.

A final point is made here about corpus size. It was envisaged at the outset that GEPCOLT would contain two million words: approximately one million words in each language. While this makes the corpus very small by current general language

[9] The characteristics of works of narrative fiction, and especially of novels, identified by Atkins *et al.* are that they are "discursive and typically at least several pages long", "integral", "the conscious product of a unified authorial effort", and "stylistically homogeneous" (1992:2).

[10] Konrad Bayer's *der kopf des vitus bering* was originally published posthumously in 1965, having been completed in 1960, although a foreword was added by Bayer in 1963 (Green 1994:59). It was translated into English in 1979. Unica Zürn's *Der Mann im Jasmin* was completed in 1966. It was first published – again posthumously – in translation into French in 1971 (Henry 1992:176), and in the original German only in 1977. It appeared in English translation in 1994. Gerhard Roth's *die autobiographie des albert einstein* was first published in 1972, and appeared in English translation in 1992.

monolingual standards, with corpora like the Bank of English (see Chapter Two) running to some 320 million words, GEPCOLT still compares favourably with other translation-oriented corpora, even those produced through collaborative efforts.[11] The German subcorpus in GEPCOLT currently contains 970,270 tokens; the English subcorpus 1,055,021 tokens.[12]

Sampling frame and text selection

Having defined the target population as German novels published mainly in the 1980s and 1990s and available in English translation, the next step was to identify a suitable sampling frame for the selection of individual texts. The original approach taken to this task in early 1996 involved consulting standard catalogues of books in print in English in an effort to identify translations from German. The intention was then to consult similar reference materials in German in order to gather relevant information about source texts and weed out any texts that did not meet the project's selection criteria. This approach soon ran into problems however, because the usual sources of information on book publishing in the English-speaking world are inconsistent in their treatment of translations. While on-line resources such as *Whitaker's Bookbank* can be searched automatically for translations from German (see Kenny 1996), not all translations are marked as such, and an automatic search of *Bookbank* will not uncover even well-known translations of works by authors such as Doris Dörrie, Günter Grass, or Patrick Süskind. It soon became clear that use of such sources would have to be supplemented by time-consuming searches through publishers' current and back catalogues, library holdings, etc, if something

---

[11] The exception is the much-fêted parallel Canadian Hansards corpus (see Chapter Three), a large sample of which, containing approximately 90 million words (in French and English), is available in aligned form from the Data Collection Initiative of the Association for Computational Linguistics (Gale and Church 1993:78). The bidirectional, German-English parallel corpus reported on in Schmied and Schäffler (1996) has a more modest target of 1.5 million words, although at the time of writing of their article, only half a million words had been computerized. As far as multilingual comparable corpora are concerned, examples such as the Aarhus Corpus of Contract Law contain one million words in each of Danish, English and French, to which one million words of German are to be added (Nielsen and Wichmann 1994:146).

[12] The difference in the number of running words between the two subcorpora is to be expected. For one, German and English have different word formation patterns: compounding is more common in German, and what is written as a single compound word in German may be translated as two or more orthographic words in English (for similar observations regarding Norwegian and English, see Johansson and Hofland 1994:31). The higher word count in English could also be due to expansion induced by processes like explicitation (see Chapter Three) thought to be typical of translation as a mediated linguistic event, although this hypothesis would have to be verified through empirical investigation of the data.

approximating a reliable sampling frame were to be ensured. Fortunately, *Boulevard Books*, the London publishing house that brings out the *Babel Guides* to literature in English translation, had just started working on a guide to German-language fiction published in English in the U.K. since 1945. An early working version of their database became the list from which texts were selected for inclusion in GEPCOLT.[13]

An initial automatic search of the *Babel* database uncovered some 76 titles originally published in German in the 1980s and 1990s. Given the relatively small size of the corpus to be built, and the rather specific question that was to be asked of the corpus, it was considered necessary to pursue in particular works that were deemed to be somehow 'experimental', and thus likely to yield interesting data for a study of lexical creativity. Advice was sought on this issue from a number of experts (acknowledged at the beginning of this book), and works by Konrad Bayer, Pieke Biermann, Elfriede Jelinek, Gerhard Roth were eventually singled out as linguistically experimental (all but Biermann are Austrians), and permission requested to use their work. [14] In all, permission was sought to use about 36 of the titles sourced in the *Babel Guide*. The initial selection of works was informed by a desire to include as many different authors, translators, and publishers as possible, but it soon transpired that copyright holders introduced an element of self-selection into the corpus. It proved impossible, for example, to get permission to use works by best-selling authors such as Doris Dörrie, Günter Grass, and Patrick Süskind, and certain publishers seem to apply a blanket policy of refusing permission for material published by them to be used in electronic form. Other copyright holders simply did not reply to (repeated) requests for permissions, thereby forcing the exclusion from the corpus of certain authors. In the end permissions were granted by copyright holders of both the original and the translation for fourteen works, which make up

---

[13] An updated database was delivered in September 1997, along with the published guide (Keenoy *et al.* 1997).

[14] The designation 'experimental' is, admittedly, a vague one. *Die Schrecken des Eises und der Finsternis* by the Austrian Christoph Ransmayr could also be described as 'experimental' in its narrative technique, intertwining as it does factual and fictional accounts of two journeys in a way that is reminiscent of Konrad Bayer's use of pastiche in *der kopf des vitus bering*. *Der Mann im Jasmin* by the German Unica Zürn also contains formally experimental elements, in particular a number of anagrams. The startling quality of much of her work though is largely due to the nature of the mental illness (her own) that Zürn describes. Experimentalism may be associated with particular publishers as well as authors. The catalogues of Atlas Press (publishers of Konrad Bayer and Gerhard Roth in translation), and Serpent's Tail (Pieke Biermann and Elfriede Jelinek), for example, are avowedly non-mainstream. As is stressed in the back matter of works in its Printed Head series, Atlas Press specializes in "the avant-garde prose "anti-tradition" of the last 100 years". Serpent's Tail similarly indicate that they seek to publish "the innovative and the challenging".

GEPCOLT as it now stands.[15] Permissions were granted for either the original only or the translation only for a further eight works, which therefore could not be included in the corpus.

As indicated above, the contents of GEPCOLT are listed in full in Appendix 1. A number of points will be made here, however, about the composition of the corpus. Firstly, GEPCOLT contains no more than two works by the same author, and only two authors (Elfriede Jelinek and Gerhard Roth) are actually represented more than once. In both cases the author's work was particularly sought after because of its reported experimental or creative quality. In relative terms, Jelinek accounts for 13.97% of the word tokens in the German subcorpus, which is roughly the same as Bodo Kirchhoff (13.94%) and still less than Dieter Wellershoff (15.10%), writer of the longest novel in the corpus. Gerhard Roth accounts for only 5.77% of the tokens in the German subcorpus. The shortest work, that by Konrad Bayer, accounts for a mere 1.36% of the German word count. In the English subcorpus, one translator, Malcolm Green, is represented three times (or four times, depending on whether the translation of Unica Zürn's work is counted once or twice – see Footnote 15), but his translation production still only accounts for 11.13% of the English tokens. Two translators are represented twice: Michael Hulse, who translated both of the Jelinek novels, accounts for 14.28% of the English tokens, still less than Paul Knight (14.90%), translator of Wellershoff's *Der Sieger nimmt alles*; and John Brownjohn, translator of Wodin's *Die gläserne Stadt* and Kirchhoff's *Infanta*. Brownjohn is perhaps over-represented with 22.56% of the English word count to his name. Walter Billeter, translator of Bayer's *der kopf des vitus bering*, at the other end of the scale, accounts for a mere 1.33% of the English subcorpus. These imbalances are an inevitable consequence of using full texts rather than text extracts, on the one hand, and of literary production in general, on the other: realist texts tend to be longer than experimental ones, although there are exceptions, and writers/translators of realist texts may thus end up producing greater quantities of text than their colleagues working on more experimental texts. The issue of imbalances is also raised here to underline a second point: the construction of translation-oriented corpora inevitably involves a second set of variables that builders of monolingual corpora do not have to contend with. If monolingual corpus builders choose to strike a balance between the output of various authors represented, for example, in a written corpus, builders of bilingual parallel corpora have to consider the composition of both source and target components and balancing one side may not necessarily mean balancing the other. If demographic factors such as author sex and nationality, or

---

[15] Fourteen original German works translate into fifteen works in English as Unica Zürn's *Der Mann im Jasmin*, actually a collection of short novels, was published in two separate books in English – *The Man of Jasmine and other texts* and *The House of Illnesses* (both translated by Malcolm Green and published by Atlas).

age of intended audience, etc, are also used as selection criteria in a parallel corpus, the situation becomes even more complex. The German subcorpus in GEPCOLT, for example, contains five works by four women authors, but only one of the works in the English subcorpus is translated by a woman,[16] and this despite the fact that women such as Lene Vennewitz (noted for her translations of Heinrich Böll) and Helen Lowe-Porter (translator of Thomas Mann) are among the best known translators into English of twentieth century German fiction. Because of such complexities, it is more convenient to limit the *selection* criteria for texts in GEPCOLT to the ones outlined above: texts should be novels originally published in the 1980s and 1990s (although exceptions can be made on this count) and some at least should be identified as 'experimental'; finally there should be a reasonable balance, in quantitative terms, between the contributions of different authors and translators. Other situational and demographic information is, of course, vital for an in-depth analysis of the texts included in the corpus, and if we wish to nuance any findings against the backdrop of the author's or translator's sex, age, country of birth, etc. But this kind of information can be encoded as *descriptive* attributes attached to each text, often in the form of a header. In other words, some attributes of texts become criteria for their inclusion in a corpus, while other attributes are descriptive and are articulated once the texts have already been selected.[17]

Data capture, editing and mark-up

Texts, once selected, have to be acquired and converted to electronic form, if not already available in that form. Four of the texts in GEPCOLT were supplied in electronic form, one (Bayer's *der kopf des vitus bering*) by the German publisher, the other three (the two Roth texts and Zürn's *The Man of Jasmine*) by the English translator Malcolm Green. This left nearly 99% of the German texts and 91% of the English texts to be converted from hard copy using optical character recognition (OCR) software. Using a Hewlett Packard scanner and the Omnipage Professional OCR program (version 4.0) produced by Caere, all remaining texts (more than 957,000 words in each of German and English) were converted to electronic form and saved as Rich Text Format (.rtf) files for later proof-reading and editing in Word for Windows. Although files are ultimately saved as simple text files for processing by programs such as Multiconcord and WordSmith Tools, it is useful to save them in the first instance as .rtf files (or in some specific word-processing format) as this format preserves features present in the printed text, such as bolding

[16] The translation of Pieke Biermann's *Violetta* is, in fact, a collaborative effort between two women: Jill Hannum and Ines Rieder.

[17] For a discussion of the application of selection and descriptive features in a monolingual general language corpus, see Burnard (1995b:10-15).

and italics. If desired, these features can then be automatically replaced by TEI-conformant tags indicating how such highlighting is rendered in the printed version (see Johansson *et al.* 1996:88).[18] Omnipage Professional was used firstly because it can handle different character sets without the user having to reinstall a new version of the program each time, and secondly because the user can view a digitized image of the document just scanned (usually facing pages) before the system starts to convert that image to editable text. If something has gone wrong at the first stage (for example, if two facing pages have been merged into one), the user can intervene and re-scan the page(s) there and then, thus saving much time when it comes to editing the text.[19] Running Omnipage Professional on a Pentium PC, it was possible to scan and OCR approximately 50,000 words an hour, giving an estimated total of thirty eight hours to convert some 1.9 million words of hard copy into electronic text in optimum conditions.

Once texts had been converted to electronic form, they were then proof-read and edited using Word for Windows. Standard edits included removing manual page breaks and 'stray' page numbers and replacing them with a tag of the form <pb n=*n*>, where pb stands for 'page break', n stands for 'number' and its value *n* is some integer. The only other mark-up tag inserted in texts indicates the presence of a footnote or endnote. The start of such notes is indicated by the opening tag <note place=*p* resp=*r*> where *p* can have the value 'end' or 'foot', and *r*, which indicates who is responsible for the note, can have the value 'author', 'translator', 'editor', etc. The tag </note> marks the end of each note. Diagrams, figures, tables and illustrations were also removed from electronic versions of the texts. None of these was replaced with a tag, although it would be relatively easy to insert a suitable 'omit' tag, along the lines described by Laviosa (1997:301) and Johansson *et al.* (1996:93), simply by referring to their respective hard copies. Illustrations play an important role in Zürn's *Das Haus der Krankheiten* and Roth's *Am Abgrund*, for example, and so cannot be completely ignored in the electronic corpus. They are, however, not vital for the kind of lexical analysis envisaged in the current research and so can be omitted for the time being. Front and back matter was scanned and edited for each novel but is stored separately from the main body of the text for the time being.

---

[18] The TEI, or Text Encoding Initiative (see Burnard 1995a), provides a set of guidelines for the interchange of machine readable text. The guidelines are concerned with both *what* should be made explicit in an electronic text (for example, structural features like headings and body text), and *how* such features should be encoded (using 'tags' like <head> and </head> to indicate the start and end of such features). The encoding system proposed by the guidelines is based on the Standard Generalized Mark-up Language (SGML) of the International Standards Organization (ISO 8897), another application of which is HTML, familiar to many as the mark-up scheme used to create web pages.

[19] Neither of theses facilities was available, for example, with Caere's 'light-weight' Omnipage Lite.

Finally, running heads and soft hyphens (the latter are particularly common in German texts) were removed from the electronic texts. In some cases the global deletion of soft hyphens was erroneous, but these errors were usually picked up in proof-reading.

Proof-reading consisted essentially of two operations: spell checking using standard facilities in Word; and the global searching and replacing of known scanning errors. Thus ‘e’ was often mistaken for ‘c’, so un-German strings like *scin* had to be globally replaced by the correct *sein*. The time taken to proof-read a text depends naturally enough on its length, but also critically on the quality of the scan and OCR performed on the text. In cases where characters on a printed page have ‘bled’, the quality of the OCR might be very low. Texts where this has happened can take more than twice as long to edit as better quality texts of comparable length. It is estimated that some 320 hours were spent editing and proof-reading texts included in GEPCOLT. Even with the most careful editing, however, mistakes inevitably remain in the electronic versions of texts. It is hoped that most of these will be uncovered (and corrected) as the texts are used in electronic analyses.

I have already indicated that there is only minimal mark-up within the running text of the electronic version of novels included in GEPCOLT. The corpus has been designed, however to allow for a substantial amount of extra-textual information to be added to each file in the form of a header. Laviosa (1997:303) points to a number of reasons why such information is important. Firstly, in the case of general language corpora, full documentation of extra-textual features allows lexicographers and descriptive linguists to make associations between textual patterns and elements of the context of situation. Secondly, the recording of demographic and situational features relevant to particular texts is vital where such features are referred to in order to achieve some kind of representativeness of a corpus vis-à-vis a target population. Thirdly, these features can function as “variables that can be manipulated in order to create tailor-made subcorpora and to test theory- and/or data-driven hypotheses”. Finally, extra-textual features are valuable “as objects of study in themselves”. In the case of translational corpora, they may be able to tell us something about the preliminary norms operating at a particular time and in a particular place. Laviosa (ibid:304-308) provides an extensive list of the kind of attributes and possible values that could be recorded for both original and translated texts in a monolingual comparable corpus, although these attributes are equally applicable to parallel corpora. It is clear that the recording of such attributes takes on greater importance as a corpus grows and especially as the number of users of a corpus grows: while compilers of small corpora are probably aware of the nationality, sex, age, etc, of the authors and translators included, this information will need to be made available in a systematic way to newcomers to such corpora. As all but one of the English translations contained in GEPCOLT have been made available to the research community over the internet as part of the Translational English Corpus (see Chapter Three),[20] they have already been annotated with appropriate headers. An example header is provided in Appendix 2. While information on original works and their authors can be easily gleaned from the dust jackets and front and back matter of individual publications, the same cannot be said for translations and translators. Information about translators and the translation process (for example, who commissioned the translation, whether it was edited after completion, etc) had to be elicited directly from translators using a questionnaire designed by Sara Laviosa for use with the TEC.[21]

Corpus alignment and bilingual concordancing

GEPCOLT has been designed to enable research, in the first instance, into the translation of lexically creative stretches of language. Once lexically creative points have been identified in source texts, a quick and efficient way is required of locating their translations in the relevant target texts. One way to approach this task is to say that we need, firstly, some way of matching up, or 'aligning', translation problem-solution pairs, possibly across the entire corpus, and, secondly, a way of accessing such aligned pairs on the basis of some query, most likely a search word of the kind familiar from monolingual concordancing (see Figure 1, Chapter Two, where the node *conscience* is the search word). Ideally the user would use some kind of query system to input a search word in one of the languages of the corpus, and the system would output all the lines (or sentences, or paragraphs) in the corpus containing that word, along with their matching lines, sentences, or paragraphs, in the other language of the corpus. In other words it would output a bilingual concordance.

There are a number of approaches to the alignment of parallel corpora. One is based on the assumption that alignment can be carried out on a sentence-by-sentence basis. The most basic approach is to posit a relationship of equivalence between the first sentence of a given source text and the first sentence of its respective target text, the second sentence of the source text and the second sentence of the target text, and so on. This is the approach used, for example, by the *Aligner* program in the WordSmith suite of tools (Scott 1997). Aligner takes as input two texts in which sentences have already been numbered consecutively by another program in the suite, *Viewer*,[22] and interleaves the texts on a sentence-by-sentence basis. This approach runs into difficulties the moment a source text sentence is translated

[20] The exception is Natascha Wodin's *The Interpreter*, which has not been included in the TEC for copyright reasons.

[21] In a minority of cases, translators could not be contacted, either through their publishers, the British Centre for Literary Translation, or the Translators' Association in the UK. Efforts continue to contact them.

[22] Viewer recognizes sentences using fairly standard procedures: the program assumes that sentence boundaries consist of a sentence-ending punctuation mark (.!?) followed by one or more

by two target sentences (or vice versa), or is not translated at all. Radical redistribution of information in target texts will also cause misalignments.[23] A more sophisticated type of alignment takes into account the length of a source sentence and its assumed target sentence, whereby sentence length is measured either in words (Brown *et al.* 1991) or in characters (Gale and Church 1993). Yet another approach uses either probabilistic pairings between source and target words (arrived at by induction from the texts under consideration) or a bilingual dictionary of a priori lexical equivalents, as an aid to sentence alignment (Catizone *et al.* 1991).

Researchers at the *Consiglio Nazionale delle Ricerche* in Pisa have opted for an exclusively lexical approach to 'linking' source and target text segments (Peters and Picchi 1998). They use a machine-readable lexicon to create links between source and target text words occurring within a specified search zone in each text. If a direct link cannot be found for the search word, the Pisa system then creates links for words found in the immediate environment of the search word in order to ultimately identify a central point around which an equivalent stretch of target language co-text can be constructed. The Pisa approach offers one considerable advantage over competing sentence-based approaches: it does not rely on assumptions made about the linear progression of source and target sentences, or their respective lengths, and is therefore not subject to the kind of misalignments that these assumptions can bring about (see Johansson and Hofland 1994:34-35). The Pisa system was developed for Italian and English, and although the developers are confident that it could be adapted for German and English (Carol Peters, personal communication), this would require the availability of machine-readable bilingual German-English dictionary, a demand that could not be met for the present research.

A hybrid approach to sentence alignment has been developed by Knut Hofland of the University of Bergen (Johansson and Hofland 1994; Johansson *et al.* 1996; Hofland and Johansson 1998). Hofland's *Translation Corpus Aligner* uses both sentence length and a bilingual list of 'anchor' words to establish correspondences at sentence level.[24] It was originally designed to operate on pairs of texts in English and Norwegian, but has since been adapted for other language pairs, including

---

word separators (for example a white space or a tab character), and a capital letter, number or currency symbol (Scott 1997).

[23] Such misalignments can be rectified by the user from within WordSmith's Viewer and Aligner simply by using the mouse to drag displaced sentences back to their proper positions. It is clear though that such manual intervention is impractical for entire corpora of texts. Given this difficulty as well as the fact that WordSmith Tools has no facility for producing bilingual concordances, its use in the current research is limited to the monolingual analysis of each of the subcorpora in GEPCOLT.

[24] Hofland's aligner measures sentence length in characters rather than words. One advantage of this approach is that it is not prone to error caused by cross-linguistic differences in word counts (Johansson and Hofland 1994:30). See also Footnote 12.

German-English. Alignment involves numbering consecutively each sentence, or, more properly, 's-unit', in the source and target texts. For each source sentence a cross-reference to the corresponding sentence in the target text is then inserted, and vice versa. Source and target sentences are then held in a database with explicit links between them. While a source sentence may have exactly the same position in the linear progression of the source text as its translation has in the target text, this is not necessarily the case. The following example from Unica Zürn's *Der Mann im Jasmin*, aligned using Hofland's program, illustrates the second case:

> <s id=UZ1.s142 corresp=UZ1T.s139>Er drückt einen Kuß auf ihre **Hand**, und diese Hand wird schwarz.</s>
> <s id=UZ1T.s139 corresp=UZ1.s142>He presses a kiss on her hand and the hand turns black.</s>

Here the 142nd sentence in the source text (called 'UZ1') corresponds to the 139th sentence in the translation ('UZ1T'). This example was extracted from the relevant database using the *Translation Corpus Explorer*, a browser for parallel text developed by Jarle Ebeling of the University of Oslo for use with the English-Norwegian Parallel Corpus (Johansson and Hofland 1994; Johansson *et al.* 1996; Ebeling 1998). The search word was *Hand* and the search language German. As Hofland's aligner does not rely solely on positional information – it does not even require paragraph progression to be the same in source and target texts – but can link sentences on the basis of equivalences between anchor words, it offers impressive output: error rates of only 2-3% are reported for English and Norwegian (Johansson *et al.* 1996:101). The Translation Corpus Aligner and the Translation Corpus Explorer are not commercially available, however, and their use is not as straightforward as competing, although arguably less sophisticated, products like Multiconcord.

Multiconcord

Multiconcord is a multilingual[25] concordancer developed by David Woolls and a consortium of European universities as part of the Lingua programme (Woolls 1997). It allows standard searches for single words or for multi-word phrases. It also allows the use of the * wildcard (see Chapter Four), at the beginning and/or end, or in the middle of words or phrases. Searches can be refined so as to specify a context word that must appear within a specified distance (up to six words to the left and/or right) of the search word. Results of searches can be viewed in either sentence or paragraph mode. They can be filtered by assigning each hit to one of four *ad hoc* categories, and then displaying or deleting whole categories at will. Multiconcord's

[25] Even though only two languages can be displayed at any one time, Multiconcord is considered multilingual as the user can search on a source language text and its translation, or on two different translations of a single source text in a third language.

'test' facility can be used to save results to a file, which can later be opened in Word, and converted very easily to a table allowing parallel display of search and target language hits. Alternatively results can be saved to a standard text file and arranged in interleaved pairs.

Multiconcord is notable because it does not work with pre-aligned text pairs. Rather it aligns on the fly, making certain assumptions about the relationship between source and target language texts. The first assumption is that there is the same number of paragraphs in the source text and its translation, and that paragraph progression is the same in source and target texts. If paragraphs have been omitted, inserted, or transposed in translation, Multiconcord's search algorithm will fail. This means that researchers may have to 'doctor' texts before submitting them to analysis using Multiconcord. This might mean inserting dummy paragraphs where omissions have occurred in the target text, for instance, or conflating target language paragraphs where translators have split a single source language paragraph. Many translation researchers will feel a certain unease at tampering with their object of inquiry in this way, but the effects of such interventions can be tempered by recording them in the corpus itself. And the insertion, for example, of tags to mark omitted or split paragraphs, makes it easy to retrieve instances of such manipulations, which may themselves be of interest, for instance, in a study of matricial norms in translation (see Chapter Three). In the present research, the focus is anyway less on the integrity of paragraph progression and more on finding convenient ways of pinpointing in target texts, translations of unusual lexical choices, which are usually, though not always, observable below sentence level. A second assumption made by Multiconcord is that the progression of sentences within target paragraphs more or less mirrors that of the source text. The program can handle cases where two short sentences are merged in translation, or a long sentence is split in two, but not cases where source and target sentences appear in completely different places in their respective paragraphs. Again, radical redistribution of sentences within paragraphs does not seem to be a feature of any of the texts in GEPCOLT, so Multiconcord's second assumption does not appear particularly problematic. Multiconcord further assumes that long sentences are generally translated by long sentences, and short sentences by short ones. The search algorithm is designed to cope with some variation in sentence length, but experience has shown that, particularly with longer paragraphs, Multiconcord sometimes returns the sentence adjacent to the one desired in the target text. Because the user can switch easily from sentence to paragraph view, however, this does not cause serious problems. Even if results (in the form of source and target sentences) have already been saved to file, it is a simple matter to go back to the data and view in paragraph mode those hits for which sentence mode gives unreliable results.

In general, Multiconcord is a very user-friendly program. It requires little previous knowledge of computing to use and comes with excellent on-line help. It is very flexible because it does not have to be tailored to the languages of the texts being searched. It is also widely available at a reasonable price to researchers, and the Multiconcord consortium can even supply a multilingual corpus that has been hand-crafted to work with the program. In order to perform bilingual searches, Multiconcord requires texts to contain minimal SGML mark-up, namely a <body> start and </body> end tag, and a tag at the beginning of each paragraph <p> and the beginning of each sentence <s>. Multiconcord is conveniently supplied with an ancillary program called 'Minmark' that performs such tagging on text files, so users, once they have ascertained that target paragraph progression matches that of the source language texts, have very little pre-processing to do.

There are a number of real difficulties associated with Multiconcord however. One is that Multiconcord cannot cope with extremely long paragraphs. One of the novels in GEPCOLT, Gert Hofmann's *Unsere Eroberung*, for example, contains more than 94,000 words, but only forty three paragraphs. Unless source and target paragraphs are split up into more manageable segments Multiconcord will simply fail as it assumes a maximum of 99 sentences in a paragraph, and can read no more than 32,000 characters in one go (David Woolls, personal communication).[26] Secondly, Minmark, the mark-up program supplied with Multiconcord, assumes, like many such programs (see Chapter Two, and Footnote 22 this Chapter), that all sentences start with capital letters. This, unfortunately, is not the case with two of the more experimental texts contained in GEPCOLT: Gerhard Roth's *die autobiographie des albert einstein* (already mentioned in this regard in Chapter Two) and Konrad Bayer's *der kopf des vitus bering*, both of which hardly use capital letters at all, breaking not only the rule that sentences should begin with capital letters, but also the rule that all German nouns should begin with capitals. Minmark recognizes paragraphs reliably for these texts; the trouble is that it sees each paragraph as containing one long sentence. In this case it is possible to insert sentence tags manually, or automatically – using the global search and replace facility in Word, for example – after sentence-ending punctuation marks that are followed by a white space. This solution quickly runs into a problem familiar to computational linguists, however, and already raised in Chapter Two: sentence ends cannot be identified reliably on the basis of full stops. Full stops are also used in abbreviations, dates, after ordinal numbers in German, etc. There are, of course, ways to overcome these difficulties, but ultimately there is a trade-off between the time required to correct faulty sentence tokenization, and the benefit gained in so doing. Thirdly, tags other than those inserted by the Minmark program may severely reduce the reliability of Multiconcord. Finally Multiconcord has an upper limit of 250 on the number of hits it will return for any one search. In order to overcome this constraint, researchers may have to conduct more than one search using, in each case, different texts in the search lan-

[26] There is a further limitation on the number of characters (the maximum is 6,000) that Multiconcord can output to the display screen (David Woolls, personal communication).

guage. As Multiconcord provides helpful messages as to the number of hits encountered in each file as it goes along, the researcher will know which text Multiconcord stopped searching in, and can then initiate a second search from that file on. If there are more than 250 hits for a particular search term in one file, however, the researcher will only see the first 250 using Multiconcord. This is obviously a greater problem for researchers interested in seeing all instances of very frequent items than it is for researchers interested in rare items.

Comparative data

The need for comparative data in corpus-based studies of language is well known (see Stubbs 1996:69-70). Comparative data may be required to help isolate features peculiar to a particular text or text category, or because the corpus under investigation is too small to supply reliable frequency data for a selected phenomenon. In this section I describe the two main sources of comparative data used in the current research, along with the software used to access them. These sources are the holdings of the *Institut für deutsche Sprache* in Mannheim, known here as the Mannheim Corpora, and the British National Corpus.

The Mannheim Corpora

The corpus holdings of the *Institut für deutsche Sprache* (IDS) in Mannheim are constantly evolving.[27] The bulk of the research reported on in this book draws on a group of the IDS's written corpora as they stood in late 1998, and which contained just under 63 million running words in total. Constituent corpora included: the LIMAS corpus, a one-million word sample corpus of texts included in the 1971/72 *Nationalbibliographie* and constructed along the lines of the Brown and LOB corpora (see Chapter Two); *Mannheimer Korpus I* and *II*, together accounting for around 2.5 million words, and made up of texts from a variety of categories and published between 1950 and 1967, and 1949 and 1974, respectively; the *Mannheimer Morgen* corpus (32.5 million words in September 1998; over 67.5 million in June 2000), made up of articles from the daily newspaper from which it takes its name; the *Bonner Zeitungskorpus* (three million words), likewise consisting entirely of newspaper texts; four *Handbuchkorpora* (eleven million words in all), mostly made up of journalistic texts; the *Grammatik-Korpus* containing 200,000 words of literary texts; and the *Wendekorpus* consisting of texts produced during the period of German political upheaval from 1989 to 1990 (3.3. million words). Other corpora are made up entirely of works by Goethe, the Brothers Grimm, Thomas Mann, and Karl

[27] For up-to-date information on the Institute's current holdings, visit http://www.ids-mannheim.de/kt/corpora.html.

Marx and Friedrich Engels. It is clear that many of these corpora are either very specialized or heavily biased in favour of newspaper texts. Researchers can, however, tailor corpora to their needs, either by creating user-defined corpora on the basis of existing ones, or by selecting or deselecting texts contained in a pre-defined corpus. The pre-defined *Public* corpus, which contains all the publically accessible written corpora held by the IDS, was used in its entirety in the current research.[28] Although it contains some material dating from the eighteenth and nineteenth centuries whose comparability with contemporary German texts may be limited, hits from this material are clearly marked as such, and so can be evaluated appropriately on a case-by-case basis.

The Mannheim Corpora are accessed using dedicated software known as COSMAS (al-Wadi 1994), short for COrpus Storage, Maintenance and Access System. COSMAS allows sophisticated searches using standard wildcards and logical operators, and users can specify a maximum distance in words, lines, sentences, or paragraphs, between two elements in a query. COSMAS thus allows users to search for discontinuous elements that extend beyond a predetermined number of words, a feature that is vital in the study of German lexis (see Lehr 1996:78-79; and Chapter Four this volume). COSMAS is optimized for the study of German in other ways. It allows searches to be conducted, for example, by word form or by lemma. In the latter case, users can specify whether they wish to see all compounds and/or derived words formed from the lemma in question, as well as all instances of its inflected forms, in selected corpora or texts. This facility is of particular interest in the present research: given that lexical creativity may reside in the creation of new words by either derivation or compounding (see Chapter Four) and that creative uses of language are put into sharp relief against the backdrop of what is typical in a language, access is required to the derived and compound words in which a stem typically participates, in order to evaluate the novelty of a candidate 'creative' form. Finally, COSMAS can display hits as KWIC concordances, allowing single line or expanded displays, and offers facilities for automatic collocation analysis.

At the time of writing, the IDS corpus holdings that can be accessed using COSMAS amount to some 450 million running words of written and spoken German, of which 117 million words are publically accessible over the internet. Access is free, and users can stay logged on to the IDS for up to one hour in each session. COSMAS has also been rendered considerably easier to use by the provision of a web interface.

The British National Corpus

The British National Corpus (BNC) has already been mentioned in several places

---

[28] In this and subsequent Chapters, the IDS's *Public Corpus* is usually designated by the more transparent label 'written Mannheim Corpora'.

in this book (see, for example, Chapter Two and above). In this section I make some general comments about the genesis and composition of the BNC, and about SARA, the dedicated software used to access the corpus. These are described in detail elsewhere, notably in Burnard (1995b) and Aston and Burnard (1998).

The BNC is a 100-million word corpus of contemporary British English compiled by a consortium of publishers, university research centres and the British Library for use in areas such as linguistic research, Natural Language Processing, and lexicography. 90% of the BNC is made up of written English (produced between 1960 and 1993). The remaining 10% is made up of transcripts of spoken British English, recorded mainly in 1993. The BNC consists of 4,000 samples of British English "selected so as to reflect the widest possible variety of users and uses of the language" (Aston and Burnard ibid:Preface). For written English, the various text categories are filled by extracts (not usually longer than 40,000 to 50,000 words) from randomly selected texts. BNC texts contain extensive TEI-conformant mark-up: each text is preceded by a header, in which many external features (for example, the author, date of publication, age of intended readership, etc.) of the text are recorded, and which also contains information on editorial decisions made when converting the text to electronic form. Internal features of texts, such as major structural divisions and the part of speech of all running words, are also explicitly marked up.

The SARA client program allows users to query and browse BNC texts held on a networked SARA server. In query mode, users can search for instances of particular orthographic words or phrases, and check on the frequency of the former in the corpus. Using the syntax of Unix regular expressions (see Lawler 1998), users can search for word forms or phrases that match a pre-defined pattern. Instances of word forms or phrases are most commonly displayed in KWIC concordance format, with the usual sort options available. If users wish to investigate collocation specifically, they have to refer to these concordance lines to see what word forms co-occur with the current node word. Having selected a collocate in this manner, they may then request information on the number of co-occurrences of collocate and node, given a user-defined span. In browse mode, SARA allows users to scroll through selected texts in their entirety.

Extracting instances of lexical creativity from GEPCOLT

Thus far we have concentrated on the three main data sources used in the current research: GEPCOLT, the Mannheim Corpora, and the BNC, as well as the various software programs used to extract information from these sources. We turn now to the step-by-step procedure adopted to investigate the translation of lexical creativity in GEPCOLT. An obvious prerequisite in this investigation is a way of identifying lexically creative points in the German source texts. Once such points have been isolated, we then need a way of assessing the creativity of their respective English translations.

One concern informs every stage in the procedure adopted, namely that it should make real use of the fact that the texts under analysis are in electronic form and thus amenable to computational processing. In the first stage, we want to be able to use the computer – or rather the relevant software – to retrieve as many instances as possible of lexical creativity in the source texts. Just how well the software performs this task can be judged according to two criteria, those of precision and recall. Let us imagine that some standard exists according to which a finite set of word forms and collocations in the German source texts in GEPCOLT is deemed 'creative'.[29] If the software were to retrieve *all* such creative word forms and collocations, we would say that recall was perfect. If the software were to retrieve *only* those creative word forms and collocations, and no others, we would say that precision was perfect.[30] In short, we want the software to retrieve all and only the right answers to the question: which word forms and collocations in the German texts in GEPCOLT are creative? But this is clearly not the kind of question one can ask of corpus-processing software, and we are forced to recast the question in more tractable terms. We do this, in the first instance, by assuming a quantitative or distributional basis for creativity.

First, if we assume that creative word forms are ones that occur with a very low frequency in a given corpus, and we equate 'very low frequency' in this case with one occurrence, it becomes a simple matter to retrieve all the hapax legomena (word forms that occur only once), in a given corpus. Second, if we assume also that creative word forms are ones that occur in the writing of one author only – thus allowing for cases where a writer invents a creative form and then reuses it, perhaps several times – we can spot and retrieve such writer-specific forms by automatically comparing word lists for individual texts or authors against some reference word list. These methods have already been introduced in the discussion in Chapter Two of word lists and keyword lists. Their application to selected texts in GEPCOLT is described below.

A quantitative basis can also be assumed for collocational creativity. Basically, it could be assumed that creative collocations are ones that occur rarely, perhaps just once, in a given corpus. The automatic retrieval of such creative collocations is not straightforward however. As we have already seen in Chapter Four, the thrust of automatic collocation analysis is towards identifying common collocations, and the

---

[29] I use the word 'imagine' here as no such standard exists. Although quantitative information can give strong clues as to the relative creativity of a linguistic form, I take it for granted that the perception of creativity is subjective in the final analysis.

[30] More formal definitions of precision and recall can be found in Lawler and Aristar Dry (1998:267).

measures of significance typically used are valid, according to Dunning (1993:71), only if "either enormous corpora are used, or the analysis is restricted to only the very most common words (that is, the ones least likely to be of interest)". Given the difficulties involved in automatically extracting collocations when data are sparse,[31] two compromise approaches are adopted below. The first involves: selecting a node that is relatively common in the corpus under investigation – and well distributed across its component texts – and then examining an automatically generated concordance of this node to see if it contains any creative collocations. This approach ensures broad coverage of collocations from across the whole corpus, but the collocations concerned involve only a single node. The second approach is based on the assumption that collocations used by one author only, or in one text only, could be creative. As was the case with writer-specific word forms above, this allows for cases where a writer invents a creative collocation and then reuses it, even repeatedly. One simple, though crude, way of extracting repeated collocations from selected texts is to look for repeated 'clusters' of three or more orthographic words in those texts (see Chapter Two). This approach suffers from the same weaknesses as were identified earlier in Kjellmer's (1982, 1984, 1987, 1990) treatment of collocation (see Chapter Four), namely: it relies on contiguity of items; it is highly dependent on text length; and it tends to foreground common words. It is, nevertheless, an easy way of surveying an individual writer's habits of lexical combination, and is too tempting to ignore in the current research.

Whichever technique is used to retrieve potentially creative forms or collocations from the German subcorpus in GEPCOLT, the creativity of candidate forms still has to be evaluated by the human analyst. In this study, words or collocations observed to occur only once, or in the writing of only one author, are considered as potentially creative. A search is then made first in standard lexicographical sources, and then in the written Mannheim Corpora, in order to ascertain whether patterns that are unique in GEPCOLT are recorded or occur naturally elsewhere. If so, they are usually eliminated from the analysis.[32] As a final check, native German speakers are consulted to ensure that the remaining word forms and collocations are creative, or at least highly marked, in their eyes.

Hapax legomena

In order to find out which word forms occur only once in the German subcorpus of

---

[31] Although, as in Chapter Four, Footnote 40, we note the potential of the statistical analyses discussed in Dunning (1993).

[32] Exceptions are made for *Einbeinigkeit* (see (4a) in Chapter Six), and the collocations *sämtliche Augen zudrücken* and *das Schrillen des Telefons* (see examples (3a) and (24a) to (31a) in Chapter Seven).

GEPCOLT, the *WordList* program was run on all the German texts in the corpus.[33] As indicated in Chapter Two, WordList performs a number of basic tasks. Firstly, it computes a variety of global statistics for the corpus as a whole and each of its constituent texts. Secondly, it creates an (unlemmatized) alphabetical listing of all the word forms in the corpus. And thirdly, it creates a frequency-ranked listing of those word forms, again unlemmatized. As the focus here is on word forms characterized by their low frequency of occurrence, it is the third function that is of greatest interest. As already indicated in Chapter Four, the output of the WordList program showed that the German subcorpus of GEPCOLT contains 970,270 running words (tokens) and 73,137 different word forms (types). The frequency-ranked word form listing showed that of these 73,137 different word forms, 42,101, or 57.56%, occur only once. This meant that a huge tail of hapax legomena had to be somehow pruned in order to arrive at an interesting and manageable set of data for further analysis. The pruning process is greatly facilitated by the fact that, within the frequency-ranked word form list, forms occurring with the same frequency are listed alphabetically. This usually means that different forms of the same lemma that happen to occur only once are listed one after the other, and the researcher can eliminate all of them from the analysis in one fell swoop if appropriate.[34] Alphabetic listing of forms occurring with the same frequency also means that verbal forms belonging to different lemmas but sharing the same prefix are listed consecutively. There are, for example, forty hapax verbal forms in the German subcorpus of GEPCOLT that begin with the prefix *auseinander*, which means roughly 'apart', or 'from one another'. Such complex separable prefixes combine with so many stems that their co-occurrence with a particular stem is unlikely to be significant. Their elimination

---

[33] The following settings were specified before the program was run:
minimum word length in characters: 1
maximum word length in characters: 35
minimum frequency of occurrence of form: 1 (default)
maximum frequency of occurrence of form: 50,000
stop list selected: no
hyphen breaks word: set to 'no'
tags to ignore <*>: set to 'yes'
numbers included: set to 'no'
It was decided to set the 'hyphen breaks word' option to 'no', as this allows creative forms like *Zwei-fel* (see Chapter Six) to be captured as a single word in the analysis, rather than as two separate forms *Zwei* and the rather dubious *fel*. This setting did not result in any undue 'noise' in the list output by *WordList* as most soft hyphens had already been removed from the corpus in the editing phase.

[34] It is, of course, possible that individual forms of a lemma will be highly significant, possibly because those forms do not usually exist, as is the case for certain 'defective' verbs. No such cases caught the analyst's eye in the current research, although creative derived, as opposed to inflected, forms were spotted. The latter are discussed in detail in Chapter Six.

from the analysis is another crude though useful way to prune the data. Other hapax forms can be eliminated on the basis that they are non-standard orthographic variants that are not intended as creative lexical forms, but rather as textual indicators of the region or social class to which a speaker belongs. Yet other forms occur only once partly because they belong to the terminology of highly specialized fields and are therefore of limited general interest. This applies to many of the medical and scientific terms found in Gerhard Roth's *die autobiographie des albert einstein* and the nautical terms in Christoph Ransmayr's *Die Schrecken des Eises und der Finsternis*. Once word forms have been eliminated from the analysis using the heuristics outlined so far, the analyst is faced with a still extensive list of forms that require closer attention. In the present research the approach taken to the remaining forms was to first consult standard lexicographical works in order to make certain that the forms in question were not already fully lexicalized, although unknown to the researcher.[35] A further check involved consulting the written Mannheim Corpora, to see whether forms had been used by other writers, even if they were not recorded in standard lexicographical sources. Thus the form *Kriegswolle*, literally 'war wool', used once by Elfriede Jelinek in *Die Ausgesperrten*, was found to occur once in Günter Grass's *Die Blechtrommel*. As a final check a Germanist and native German speaker was consulted, who recommended that a handful of remaining unremarkable forms be eliminated from the analysis. This left a total of 117 hapax forms, listed in Appendix 3, forty six of which are discussed in detail in Chapter Six.[36]

Thus far we have seen that a list of 42,101 hapax forms in the German subcorpus of GEPCOLT yielded 117 forms that were ultimately deemed creative on the basis of comparative empirical evidence and native-speaker intuition. In this case, we can say that the recall of creative hapax forms by the software is perfect, although given that the set of creative hapax legomena in a corpus is a proper subset of all the hapax legomena in that corpus, this is something of a trivial achievement. Precision, on the other hand, turned out to be very low: fewer than 0.0028% of the hapax

[35] The expression 'fully lexicalized' is used here to mean generally recognized as a word and recorded in standard lexicographical sources. The lexicographical sources used in the current research were the *Collins German Dictionary* (Terrell *et al.* 1997), *Langenscheidts Großwörterbuch Deutsch als Fremdsprache* (Götz *et al.* 1997), and Wahrig's *Deutsches Wörterbuch* (Wahrig 1986). 'Lexicalized' is used to mean assigned a lexical label, even if this label is used by a single writer only.

[36] The 117 forms referred to here are distributed between four Tables in Appendix 3. Six forms are included in Table18: Orthographically Creative Forms; eight in Table 19: Creative Derived Forms; six in Table 20: Creative Complex Verbal Nouns; and the remaining ninety seven in Table 21: Other Creative Compounds. There are only eighty eight matching source and target segments in Table 21, however, as some segments contain more that one instance of creative compounds. The segments in question are numbers 4, 39, 57, 62 and 85, all of which contain two instances of creative compounds, and number 12, which contains five such instances.

forms identified by the software turned out to be creative. But although the human analyst had to "plod through the detail" (Sinclair 1991:27) to eliminate a huge amount of noise, this process, though time-consuming, was not as tedious as it might have been without an alphabetically sorted, electronic word list. Moreover, there is a certain pleasure in finding 117 needles in a haystack.

Writer-specific forms

In Chapter Two, we saw that the comparison option in WordList can be used to output a list of keywords in a selected file. These are word forms whose frequency in the selected file appears to be unusually high or low compared to their frequency in some larger reference list. This reference list can be the word list generated for an entire corpus, including the individual file under investigation. If a word form appears exclusively – and often enough – in the selected file, then it will be considered key. The operation of WordList's comparison feature was illustrated in Chapter Two, Table 4, using Gert Hofmann's *Unsere Eroberung*. Table 7 shows the keyword list generated for Unica Zürn's *Das Haus der Krankheiten* using the same settings, and omitting four 'negative' keywords.[37] Whereas all of the keywords computed in this way for Hofmann's text were conventional forms, the form ranked fifteenth in the keywords for Zürn's text, *Augenherzen,* literally 'eye-hearts', appears to be a creative form coined by the writer.

If we allow a greater risk of error in the output of the word list comparison program, then we get more word forms listed as 'key'. By increasing the risk of error to one in one hundred thousand, or p=0.00001, the list of keywords for Zürn's text rises to forty five forms, and another of Zürn's creative coinages is revealed. This second coinage, *Busenstube*, 'bosom room', appears three times in *Das Haus der Krankheiten* and is ranked thirty ninth in the keyword list. In this case, increasing the value for p has improved both precision and recall of creative forms – we now have two creative forms out of forty five, as opposed to one out of thirty in Table 7 – but increasing p any further reveals no interesting new data. The keywords facility in WordList thus has the potential to uncover interesting data for studies of lexical creativity, but it may not be practical to apply it to every text individually in a very large corpus, adjusting the settings accordingly each time. As it happens, only three writer-specific creative forms were unearthed this way in GEPCOLT (with p lowered to 0.0001): the two already mentioned, and *Irrenwäscher*,

[37] Keyness is computed using Dunning's log likelihood scores, and a risk of error of one in one million, or p=0.000001 is allowed. Finally word forms must occur at least twice in the text in question in order to be considered key. This last condition does not raise any problems for the current study of lexical creativity, as creative hapax legomena are considered separately.

N	WORD	FREQ.	DEZUERN4 .TXT %	CORPUS FREQ.	CORPUS %	KEYNESS
1	ICH	293	4.34	10,590	1.09	373.1
2	MORTIMER	32	0.47	34		227.6
3	DOKTOR	33	0.49	88		187.9
4	MICH	95	1.41	2,330	0.24	176.7
5	AUGEN	50	0.74	1,017	0.10	108.2
6	KRANKHEITEN	16	0.24	30		100.2
7	MIR	72	1.07	2,488	0.26	95.1
8	TODFEIND	11	0.16	11		79.1
9	MEINE	38	0.56	968	0.10	68.1
10	HERZEN	14	0.21	71		64.3
11	FEINDE	9	0.13	25		50.6
12	SONNENGEFLECHTE	7	0.10	7		50.3
13	KABINETT	8	0.12	16		49.3
14	BÄUCHE	6	0.09	11		37.8
15	AUGENHERZEN	5	0.07	5		36.0
16	WEIßHAARIGE	5	0.07	7		33.5
17	ZIMMER	17	0.25	397	0.04	32.8
18	LINKE	7	0.10	37		31.6
19	MEINER	18	0.27	473	0.05	31.3
20	HAUS	19	0.28	543	0.06	30.6
21	UNKAS	4	0.06	4		28.8
22	WEIßHAARIGEN	4	0.06	4		28.8
23	FALLENSTELLER	4	0.06	4		28.8
24	HERZFÖRMIGER	4	0.06	4		28.8
25	AUGENKRANKHEIT	4	0.06	4		28.8
26	MEISTERSCHUß	4	0.06	4		28.8
27	HABE	29	0.43	1,283	0.13	27.9
28	LINKS	9	0.13	117	0.01	26.3
29	GENESUNG	4	0.06	7		25.5
30	ADLER	5	0.07	19		25.5

Table 7: Positive keywords in *Das Haus der Krankheiten*

literally 'lunatic washer', from Gerhard Roth's *Am Abgrund* (ranked 92nd in the relevant keyword list). Whether or not this is good recall of creative writer-specific forms in the source texts, we cannot say, because we do not know how many such forms there are, in other words, we have no answer key. What can safely be said, however, is that the precision of the technique is not high, with the researcher having to scan through a few hundred keywords for the longer texts, without necessarily finding any particularly creative ones.[38]

[38] The number of words identified as key can vary according to the length of the text involved, all other things being equal. In general, there tends to be more repetition of word forms in longer texts, which means that there is more evidence on which to base keyness scores, and longer keyword lists are thus output.

Unusual collocations

There is an element of serendipity involved when linguists uncover instances of unusual collocations in corpora: lexicographers, for instance, commonly scan through many hundreds of concordance lines when preparing a lexicographical description of a particular node. As they do this, they begin to discern (with the help of standard sorting routines) norms of usage of the node, and, against this backdrop, what have been dubbed 'exploitations' of these norms (Hanks 1988:40-41). Exploitations, that is, non-typical uses of a node, whose rhetorical effectiveness relies on the fact that they deliberately flout some convention of the node's normal use, are considered irrelevant to lexicography (Hanks ibid:42), where the concern must be with describing typical lexical behaviour. They have, however, been instrumental in the development of certain strands of thought in theoretical linguistics. For a start, it is often only when we recognize exploitations that we become aware of the existence of underlying norms of usage of a given node. This is an insight that emerges, for example, from Louw's (1993, 1997) treatment of irony (and insincerity) in literary and non-literary texts alike. And, as they represent lexical choices that are unexpected in their environment (Sinclair 1987a:324), lexical exploitations occasion switch points, which in turn draw attention to the operation of the idiom and open-choice principles in textual interpretation. Sinclair's (1997) example of 'semantic reversal' also relies on his recognizing the usual collocational patterns of the node *borders on*, as well as the text-specific effects created by a writer's departing from such normal patterns. But despite the obvious importance of unusual collocations in pointing up habits of linguistic usage and the effects of departing from such habits, writers on the subject rarely make explicit the process by which they choose, or perhaps 'come across' the examples they comment on at length.

In many cases nodes are clearly selected by linguists to exemplify a particular linguistic category: a typical idiom, frequent collocation, or rare word in Sinclair (1996); words that bear particular ideological loads in Tognini-Bonelli (1996a:96-99) and Stubbs (1995b); or words that have positive or negative semantic prosody in Stubbs (1995a); etc, but there is usually no indication of why, for instance, BROOK (Sinclair ibid) is considered a better example of a rare word than any of the other possible candidates in English. In some cases, linguists describe the behaviour of nodes whose collocational interest has been pointed out by other, acknowledged sources (Stubbs 1995a, 1995b, 1995c), thus shifting the burden of node selection further back along the chain. In yet other cases, linguists investigate nodes about which prior claims have been made in the absence of corpus data. Partington's (1995:105-109) discussion of the supposedly unproblematic translation pair 'correct' and Italian *corretto* is a good example of this latter category. Nakamura and Sinclair (1995) give a rare account of exactly how they select a single node, in this case *woman*, in research that aims at ascertaining whether the distribution of collocates of a chosen node across the Bank of English can say anything about the internal structure of the corpus. *Woman* is selected for investigation on the basis that it is neither very common nor very rare, and is well distributed across the corpus (it is ranked somewhere between the 200th and the 2,000th most frequent word in each of the subsections of the Bank of English). It is also a non-homographic content word, which makes it amenable to the kind of analysis Nakamura and Sinclair are interested in. Despite their use of a "simple statistical criterion" in selecting this node, Nakamura and Sinclair (ibid:100) concede that "personal preference" ultimately plays a role in selecting *woman* from a number of competing candidate nodes, all of which meet the more 'objective' criteria already mentioned.

The above overview of how linguists typically select nodes for investigation in collocation-oriented research suggests that there is an inevitable role for intuition (one's own, or that of other linguists), and even good fortune, in the selection of nodes considered worth analyzing in corpus linguistics. This is not denied by corpus linguists; what is important for many of them is that they remain accountable to the facts the corpus reveals about their chosen nodes. The challenge of selecting *particular* nodes for analysis is, of course, not one that is faced by linguists who aim to extract collocational information about *all* the nodes in a corpus. But, as was pointed out in Chapter Four, even these endeavours usually involve arbitrary cut-off points for levels of statistical significance of the co-occurrence of node and collocate, as well as the dismissal of nodes and/or collocates whose independent frequencies of occurrence do not reach a certain minimum threshold. Given this kind of statistics-based automatic collocation extraction, much evidence is discarded on the basis that the statistics cannot handle it. There are thus problems associated with both the 'hand-picking' of nodes for collocation analysis and existing methods of automatic collocation extraction from electronic corpora. Given the difficulties associated with the latter when corpora are small and lexical evidence is sparse, and given that one of the aims of the present research is to investigate the potential of corpus linguistic techniques in studying normalization in translation, rather than to supply as near an exhaustive account as possible of all the collocations in any particular corpus, I have opted to hand-pick a single node for analysis, with a view to establishing whether or not unusual collocations involving that node in GEPCOLT are normalized in translation. The node I have selected is the lemma AUGE, 'EYE'.

The node AUGE

The node AUGE was selected for analysis in the present research for a number of reasons. Firstly, it occurs frequently enough – and in all texts – in GEPCOLT to allow generalizations to be made about its typical use. The WordList program shows that AUGE occurs some 1,159 times in the German subcorpus of GEPCOLT, with individual forms of the lemma distributed as indicated in Table 8.

The most common form *Augen*, 'eyes', occurs over one thousand times, making it the 110th most common form in the German subcorpus; the second most common form *Auge*, 'eye', occurs 129 times, making it the 689th most frequent form; and

FORM	RANK	NO. OF OCCURRENCES
Augen	110	1,017
Auge	689	129
Auges	5138	13

Table 8: Distribution of forms of the lemma AUGE in the German Subcorpus of GEPCOLT

even the least common form, the genitive *Auges*, occurs often enough (thirteen times) for some knowledge to be gleaned about its typical use in GEPCOLT. The lemma AUGE is also sufficiently common in the language at large (it occurs over 12,000 times in the written Mannheim Corpora) to enable reliable comparisons to be made between its use in GEPCOLT and other, literary and non-literary texts.

A second reason for selecting AUGE as a node in the present research is that interesting observations have already been made about its usual English-language equivalent EYE. Sinclair's (1996:84) observation that the singular and plural forms of EYE display different collocational tendencies and tend to reflect different senses of the lemma has already been noted in Chapter Four. Other linguists have highlighted creative collocations involving the node EYE in the work of Sylvia Plath (Louw 1997:248) on the one hand, and Ruth Rendell (Lynne Bowker, personal communication) on the other. It seems plausible that German-language writers may use AUGE in similarly creative ways. Finally, given that the lemma AUGE participates in numerous fixed and semi-fixed phrases, as illustrated by corpus data and most monolingual German dictionaries, it was hoped that creative collocations involving this node would stand out reasonably well against this background of more-or-less predictable lexical behaviour. Figure 3, which contains just twenty five lines from the concordance for AUGE in GEPCOLT (sorted by the first and second words to the left of the node), reveals a number of such fixed expressions or typical collocations including *mit eigenen Augen*, 'with (one's) own eyes', *eingesunkene(n) Augen*, 'sunken eyes', and *entzündete(n) Augen*, 'inflamed eyes'. The full concordance, which is too long to reproduce here, contains many more.

Having singled out AUGE for analysis, the next step is to identify unusual collocations in GEPCOLT involving this node. One way to approach this task is to eliminate concordance lines that are obviously conventional uses of AUGE, because they recur often and in the work of more than one writer.[39] Most of the uses of AUGE in GEPCOLT are eliminated in this way. But if repeated patterns are deemed to be evidence of lexical conventions, it does not follow that a pattern that occurs only once in a corpus, especially a small corpus, is lexically unconventional. As was the

[39] Although source file names for the various lines in Figure 3 are not listed here, in order to save space, the Concord program, like most good concordancers, does output the exact source of each occurrence of the node.

```
1.  Bilder, ohne Erinnerung vor den eigenen Augen, nur noch vor Schmerz rudernde Gli
2.  vorwärts, indem er sie in ihren eigenen Augen erhob und ihr zeigte, wessen der m
3.  l käme. Menschen, die mit ihren eigenen Augen und Ohren isoliert waren vom Rest
4.  en sagen, ehe Sie die Dinge mit eigenen Augen sehen und falsche Schlüsse ziehen.
5.   den Jungen auch. Ich hab's mit eigenen Augen gesehen-grün und blau. Alle beid
6.   Liste, so konnte ich heute mit eigenen Augen sehen, scheint er täglich neu anzu
7.  einheit(o gegen das, was ich mit eigenen Augen gesehen und gelesen hatte und was
8.  r sein möge, was sie im Ort mit eigenen Augen gesehen hatten. Dann gedachten sie
9.  ar auf Deck geeilt, um sich mit eigenen Augen Gewißheit darüber zu verschaffen,
10. t erinnerten die Augen an seine eigenen Augen, aber vorherrschend waren die Unte
11. lächter, dem er mehr als seinen eigenen Augen zu trauen scheint. Ach, leider nic
12.  starrte mich an ... die türe besaß ein auge, dessen blick ich ausgesetzt war. I
13.  wahrgenommenwerdens. ich betrachte ein auge. Seltsames sonnenbällchen. die inne
14. ein Mann mit einem runden Glas in einem Auge, zu seinen Füßen ein kleiner Junge
15. reundlich heraus und zwinkert mit einem Auge. Die oft umgenähten und mit Schonba
16. nem die Hände herunter, es schloß einem Augen und Mund, war eine Verhöhnung des
17. die leuchtendblaue Regenbogenhaut eines Auges in der Finsternis.        »
18. in heimliches Zeichen. Das Zucken eines Auges oder die verstohlene Bewegung eine
19. in den Rest davon, den ihre einfältigen Augen erblicken sollen. Schwer denken si
20. ägt. Er erhascht mit seinen einfältigen Augen gerade noch die leidenden Körper,
21. e, hervorragende Nasen und eingesunkene Augen... (Julius Payer)  Ich habe bedeut
22. gekommen. Nur die dunklen eingesunkenen Augen verrieten ihre Überanstrengung. Si
23. Sofa und hatte vor Müdigkeit entzündete Augen. Als sie vor ihm auftauchten und D
24. chechen wieder da sind. Mit entzündeten Augen ziehen sie auf nachgiebigen Beinen
25. d döste aus verschwollenen, entzündeten Augen vor sich hin. Es war kein abwesend
```

Figure 3: Selected lines from the concordance of AUGE in GEPCOLT

case with hapax legomena, the uniqueness of a pattern may be a mere accident of corpus composition. Again the onus is on the researcher to compare findings for his/her corpus against other sources. Some collocations will be confirmed as conventional by their inclusion in standard lexicographical sources, others will be attested in larger corpora.

In evaluating concordance lines, a distinction must be made between patterns that are repeated across texts written by different authors, and those that are repeated only within the writing of a single author. As Hanks (1988:41) puts it, "repeated evidence from the same source is still not evidence for a convention, but only evidence for the repetitive nature of idiosyncrasy". But while lexicographers interested in recording the conventions of lexical use will reject repeated idiosyncrasies, the latter can provide useful data for the literary critic (see Louw 1997:248)

```
1.  gen. Meine Neugier zieht das Zimmer der Augen natürlich vor, denn wie es um mein
2.  anderen ersparen möchte. Das Zimmer der Augen im Haus der Krankheiten wird für m
3.  n Raum der Herzen und um das Zimmer der Augen. Meine Neugier zieht das Zimmer de
4.  ich bereits. An der Türe zum Zimmer der Augen blieb ich heute stehen und hätte s
5.  t für immer. Auf dem Weg zum Zimmer der Augen dachte ich an einen Satz, den ich
6.  ut, die             Tür zum Zimmer der Augen zu öffnen. Auch hier war Mondlicht
7.  te ich heimlich die Tür zum "Zimmer der Augen".  Da stürzte sich der rote Skorpi
```

Figure 4: Lines from the AUGE concordance that contain *Zimmer der Augen*

or the analyst interested in the translation of unusual collocations, including those used habitually by an author. The concordance of AUGE in GEPCOLT reveals such repetitive idiosyncrasies, in particular in the work of Unica Zürn. The lemmas ZIMMER, 'room', and HERZ, 'heart', collocate repeatedly, but idiosyncratically, with the node

AUGE in Zürn's writing. Figure 4 shows a group of seven lines in the AUGE concordance that contain the nominal group *Zimmer der Augen*, 'room of the eyes'. These and other examples of unusual collocations are discussed in Chapter Seven.

In conclusion, the full concordance of the node AUGE, containing 1,159 lines, gives full recall of the approximately thirty examples of AUGE deemed creative in GEPCOLT, although, as the ratio 30:1,159 suggests, a lot of noise has to be filtered out before we get at the creative collocations. This last task is greatly facilitated, however, by the ability of the concordancer to display repeated patterns. The real problem with the treatment of creative collocations outlined here is that it is limited to a single node: we know a lot about how AUGE is used creatively in GEPCOLT, but little about the creative use of other nodes.

N	Word	Frequency
1	HAUS DER KRANKHEITEN	14
2	SAGTE DOKTOR MORTIMER	9
3	DAS HAUS DER	7
4	KABINETT DER SONNENGEFLECHTE	6
5	ZIMMER DER AUGEN	6
6	DER WEIßHAARIGE HERR	5
7	IN DIE AUGEN	5
8	SAAL DER BÄUCHE	5
9	DER WEIßE ADLER	4
10	IM HAUS DER	4

Table 9: Top ten most frequent three-word clusters in *Das Haus der Krankheiten*

Clusters

One way of uncovering creative collocations that are not tied to a particular node is to look for indicative 'clusters' in individual texts, as indicated above (see also Chapter Two). If an idiosyncratic collocation occurs often enough and with no formal variation, then we might expect it to appear in the list of repeated clusters generated by WordList for the text in question.[40] Table 9 shows the ten most frequent three-word clusters in Zürn's *Das Haus der Krankheiten.* Not surprisingly, *Zimmer der Augen* turns up in the top five most frequent clusters.[41]

The most frequent cluster in Table 9 is the title of the book 'The House of Ill-

[40] The condition that collocations appear with no formal variation in order to be picked up as clusters by WordList, is dictated by the fact that clusters are identified on the basis of strings of orthographic words that recur in the same order each time.

[41] Note here that one instance, namely the one where *Zimmer der Augen* is enclosed in inverted commas (Figure 4, line 7), is not included in Table 9, as it occurs in a different, though related text – *Der Mann im Jasmin*, also by Zürn.

nesses', which is an unusual collocation in itself. Other unusual clusters – apart from *Zimmer der Augen* – are *Kabinett der Sonnengeflechte*, 'cabinet of the solar plexuses'(ranked fourth), and *Saal der Bäuche*, 'hall of the bellies' (eighth). Further down the list, at position twenty six, is the cluster *Kammern der Hände*, 'chambers of the hands', which occurs three times.[42] These recurring clusters are clearly semantically related to each other, and to the writer-specific forms *Augenherzen*, 'eye-hearts', and *Busenstube*, 'bosom room', already identified as keywords in the same text in Table 7. They, along with other forms and collocations in the text, including *Kopfgewölbe*, 'vaults of the head', and *Raum der Herzen*, 'suite of the heart', point to an extended metaphor in the source text in which the body is seen as a house. They are undoubtedly creative, and they pervade Zürn's short text – *Das Haus der Krankheiten* contains only 6,750 running words – and so are of obvious interest in the current study. They may have been discovered just as easily by glancing at the published volume, however. Most of them occur in the table of contents of the work. Most of them also occur in Zürn's illustrations, which are reproduced in Malcolm Green's translation of *Das Haus der Krankheiten*, although they do not appear in the published original.

Indicative clusters are not always so easily spotted without the help of the computer, however. Consider, for example, the top ten frequency-ranked four-word clusters in Natascha Wodin's *Die gläserne Stadt*, reproduced in Table 10.

N	Word	Frequency
1	IN DEM ICH MICH	8
2	VON SCHWESTER MARIE-JOSEPH	7
3	DAS SCHRILLEN DES TELEFONS	6
4	AM ANDEREN ENDE DER	5
5	DAS ALLES NICHT MEHR	5
6	ICH KANN ES NICHT	5
7	IN EIN PAAR TAGEN	5
8	ZWISCHEN OST UND WEST	5
9	ABER ICH KANN ES	4
10	AUF DER SUCHE NACH	4

Table 10: Top ten most frequent four-word clusters in *Die gläserne Stadt*

Some of these clusters reflect more or less fixed expressions like *auf der Such nach*, 'in search of', and *in ein paar Tagen*, 'in a couple of days', or completely conventional statements like *Ich kann es nicht*, 'I can't'. One contains a proper name *Schwester* (Sister) *Marie-Joseph*. The interesting cluster here, from our point of view, is *das Schrillen des Telefons*, literally 'the shrilling of the telephone'. The

[42] All translations given here are by Malcolm Green.

collocation of SCHRILLEN with TELEFON actually occurs seven times in Wodin's text, the seventh instance coming in the modified form *das drängende Schrillen des Telefons*, literally 'the urgent shrilling of the telephone'. It appears to be a favoured, although not completely idiosyncratic collocation for Wodin: it is not listed in any of the lexicographical sources consulted, but it does occur five times in 110 million words of the enlarged Public Corpus accessible over the internet from the *Institut für deutsche Sprache* (see above). This collocation is worthy of our attention, however, because it is highly emotive and distributionally marked vis-à-vis more normal collocations like KLINGELN or LÄUTEN (both meaning 'to ring') + TELEFON in German, and because Wodin seems to make repeated use of it in one particular form, namely as a verbal noun. We come back to this example then, at the end of Chapter Seven.

We have seen so far that computing clusters for individual texts can reveal instances of creative collocations in GEPCOLT, but this technique is most useful in texts where exact repetition is used as a literary device, or where the nature of the fictional or – in Zürn's case – hallucinatory world described requires repeated use of unconventional multi-word units. It did not reveal any interesting collocations in the other original texts in GEPCOLT.

Evaluating the creativity of translations in GEPCOLT

Once word forms or collocations of particular interest have been identified in source texts, finding out how they are translated in their respective target texts is easy, given an aligned parallel corpus and some way of extracting bilingual concordances from that corpus. As indicated above, Multiconcord is used in the present research both to align the texts in GEPCOLT and to extract bilingual concordances in a convenient form. It is then up to the human analyst to isolate in the target segment of each bilingual concordance the translation solution adopted to the problem posed by the creative form or collocation in the source segment. In most cases this is a fairly straightforward process, although the issue of compensation (see Chapter Six) can complicate matters somewhat.

For the purposes of the present research, whether or not lexical normalization is deemed to have taken place in translation depends on whether or not the translator has matched a lexically creative form or collocation in the source text with an equally creative form or collocation in the target text. Individual lexical items and collocations are considered to be creative in the target language if they are not already known to the researcher, not attested in standard target language lexicographical sources, and/or not present in the comparative data supplied by the British National Corpus. As the discussion in Chapters Six and Seven shows, however, the treatment of creativity in both German and English extends beyond merely corroborating that a given lexical form or collocation does not occur elsewhere. Rather, creativity is evaluated against the background of the 'normal' patterns of combination – as attested by lexicographical and corpus evidence – of the morphemes and words that combine to produce creative forms and collocations, in both source and target languages.

Conclusion

As the discussion in the first part of this Chapter has shown, much thought and practical work goes into the design, compilation, and alignment of a parallel corpus. Given that building a parallel corpus can be a taxing and time-consuming business, researchers who go to the trouble of doing so need to be sure that their labours will bear fruit by enabling studies that would not have been possible otherwise. In this Chapter, I hope to have shown that a parallel corpus in electronic form, and appropriate tools for processing it, can enable analyses that would not otherwise be pursued by individual researchers, simply because they would be too impractical, and perhaps ultimately unreliable: even if a researcher did have the time to find manually all the hapax legomena, or instances of AUGE, etc, in the German texts in GEPCOLT – and their translations in the English texts – the work involved would be so tedious that it would be difficult to maintain the level of concentration required to record all such instances, or even the enthusiasm to want to. The great advantage of using an electronic corpus is that once the initial scanning, proofing, and aligning has been done, corpus-processing software can take on the burden of the donkey work in corpus analysis. The human analyst still has much work to do, but it is work that requires judgement, and not just the ability to recognise that two strings are the same, or keep running counts and remember the whereabouts of all the instances of a particular string seen so far in a corpus. And, as already suggested at the end of Chapter Three, an electronic corpus allows multiple complementary and sometimes overlapping analyses to be carried out in the same project. All of these points have been exemplified in the methodology for a corpus-based investigation of lexical creativity outlined in this Chapter.

What emerges from this Chapter then, is a methodology for investigating lexical creativity and normalization in translated literature. The methodology described relies crucially on the availability of suitable electronic corpora – both bilingual parallel, and monolingual reference corpora – and tools for processing them, and the lexical data ultimately selected for analysis depend to a large extent on both the composition of the parallel and monolingual reference corpora, and the computer-assisted procedures used to access them. The in-depth analysis of lexical data thus acquired is the focus of Chapters Six and Seven.

6. Lonely Words
Creative Hapax Legomena and Writer-Specific Forms

Lonely words are also interesting. Almost anything can happen to them.
J.R. Firth (1957:14)

Introduction

The creative word forms identified in Chapter Five are all restricted in their distribution. For the most part, they occur only once, but if they do recur, it is within the confines of a single text. In this Chapter, we look at the translation into English of these creative loners, with a view to establishing whether or not they are normalized in the target language. The hapax forms investigated here are either creative presentations of existing words, or new coinages. The former are investigated under 'creative orthography' below; the latter in the sections on derived forms, complex verbal nouns, and compound forms. Not all the creative hapax forms uncovered in GEPCOLT are discussed in detail here, however. We concentrate rather on a selection of forty six forms, singled out for commentary because of their particular usefulness in exemplifying different types of lexical creativity in German. A further seventy one creative hapax forms are included, with their translations, in the bilingual concordance in Appendix 3 (see Chapter Five, Footnote 36). In this Appendix, an indication is given of whether the highlighted German lexical items are deemed to have been normalized in translation into English. The intention here is to supply summary statistics that, although crude, will give a global overview of the translation of creative hapax forms in GEPCOLT. The global picture provided by these statistics is discussed towards the end of this Chapter, where tentative generalizations are made about the association between normalization and specific types of source text lexical creativity, on the one hand, and demographic factors such as translator and publisher of the target text, on the other. Similar generalizations are attempted in the case of the four recurring writer-specific forms discussed at the end of this Chapter, and which are all novel German compounds.

The discussion of novel German compounds in this Chapter leads us to consider how the constituents of such compounds – usually familiar words in themselves – typically combine in the language at large. The overlap here with studies of collocation as outlined in Chapter Four will be clear. Indeed, in that Chapter it was pointed out that *ad hoc* compounds in German are treated as a special case of collocation by some researchers, although it was also argued that compounds that are written as single orthographic words differ in certain respects from what are traditionally regarded as collocations, and on that basis it was decided to treat them separately. The artificial nature of the line thus drawn between collocations and *ad hoc* compounds starts to become apparent, however, in the discussion of compounding below: much of the discussion draws on concepts familiar from theoretical investigations of collocation, including those of semantic preference and semantic prosody. Nonetheless, the distinction is maintained as a methodological convenience for the time being. There is also an extent to which a further delineation drawn here is not completely watertight: although creative word formation in GEPCOLT is discussed in this Chapter under the separate headings of derivation and compounding, some coinages involve both processes and some overlap between these two categories will also be inevitable.

In cases where normalization is deemed to have taken place in GEPCOLT, reference is often made to translators' efforts to compensate for the loss of the particular source-text effect that has been normalized. The notion of compensation applied in such cases draws on Harvey (1995), who uses the term to describe cases where translators use linguistic-stylistic devices (alliteration, idiom, metaphor, neologism, rhyme, etc) to make up for the loss of an effect created by the same, or a similar or different, linguistic-stylistic device in the source text. Given the relatively short extracts treated in each case, it will not be possible to consider "displaced compensation", that is, instances of compensation occurring at a point in the target text that is "a long distance from the source text loss" (ibid:83), or "generalized compensation", which occurs where "the target text includes stylistic features that help to naturalize the text for the target reader and that aim to achieve a comparable number and quality of effects, without these being tied to any specific instances of source text loss" (ibid:84). While this would be a serious flaw in a project that aimed at an exhaustive treatment of compensation in a given translation corpus, this is not the case in the present work where the primary aim is to investigate lexical normalization independently of any parallel process of compensation. The category of compensation is, however, introduced at relevant points in the discussion in order to stress that when a translator normalizes a particular feature in a source text segment, this may not be the end of the story: translation is a complex process, and although it is sometimes helpful to single out for investigation a feature such as lexical creativity in source and target texts, it would be foolhardy to adopt an approach that admitted of no connection between the disappearance of one source text feature and the emergence of another, perhaps compensating feature, in a target text.

Hapax Legomena

Creative orthography

The novel presentation of existing words in the German subcorpus of GEPCOLT can be seen in the unconventional use of upper and lower case letters, the use of non-standard spelling, and the use of idiosyncratic hyphenation. As the emphasis here is on hapax legomena, detailed analysis will be made only of those unconventional forms that occur once in the corpus. It should be noted, however, that some hapax words form part of a larger pattern, with other hapax words, or indeed with forms that occur more than once in the corpus. This is the case, for example, with a series of twenty one hapax forms from *qacksalbereien* to *qintessen* found in GEPCOLT. All twenty one conform to a pattern also observable in forms such as *qelle* (which occurs twice in the corpus) and *qantum* (three times), in that they involve the systematic omission of the letter 'u' after 'q'.[1] All such examples stem from a single text, Gerhard Roth's *die autobiographie des albert einstein*, in which the author also avoids the use of capital letters, normally required at the beginning of sentences and all German nouns. Both Roth's non-standard spelling and exclusive use of lower case are reproduced by his translator, Malcolm Green. There is, however, an interesting difference between the source and target texts: unlike Roth, Green feels obliged to draw the reader's attention to the fact that his non-standard spelling and use of lower case are deliberate, and motivated by the formal features of the source text. It seems that while reader tolerance of experimental forms is taken for granted in the case of the source text, the translator has to explicitly defend, through a translator's note, the same features in the translated text. Green's translation appears in the 'Printed Head' series published by Atlas Press. A second book from this series is included in GEPCOLT, namely Konrad Bayer's *der kopf des vitus bering*. In this work, Bayer also eschews use of upper case letters, although he employs broadly standard orthography. The exclusive use of lower case is followed by Bayer's translator, Walter Billeter, but Billeter does not feel obliged to defend this feature of the target text, perhaps because, in the absence of accompanying non-standard spelling, the reader does not really risk being overwhelmed by the unconventional nature of word forms at this albeit superficial level.

Other general patterns in GEPCOLT include the use of non-standard spelling to depict regional dialects or the speech of foreigners,[2] to indicate abnormal acoustic circumstances,[3] and when citing sources that use archaic forms.[4] Such non-standard

---

[1] As is the case with English, which however makes exceptions for foreign names such as 'Qatar', standard German orthography requires that 'q' be followed immediately by 'u', except in abbreviations such as *qm* for *Quadratmeter*, 'square metre', or acronyms like *QWERTY-Tastatur*, 'QWERTY keyboard'.

[2] Pieke Biermann, for instance, uses non-standard spelling to depict the Berlin dialect spoken in particular by the prostitutes in her novel *Violetta*; Erich Loest uses non-standard spelling to depict the Saxon dialect and the German of a Polish couple; while Austrianisms are common in the work of both Elfriede Jelinek and Gerhard Roth.

[3] For example, the echo inside the eponymous monument in Loest's *Völkerschlachtdenkmal*, or the effect of a heavy cold on one of the characters in *Violetta*.

[4] Works by Christoph Ransmayr and Konrad Bayer, both of whom cite earlier sources, contain archaic forms.

spellings are mostly used to provide information about speakers and/or other aspects of the context of situation, but they rarely occasion switch points, where readers are forced into alternative modes of interpretation, and they will not be dealt with in any detail here.[5]

A third category of non-standard presentation of word forms mentioned above is the use of idiosyncratic hyphenation. In *Die gläserne Stadt*, Natascha Wodin uses hyphens creatively, to destabilize accepted meanings of words by remotivating them etymologically. In (1a) below, for example, she forces a re-analysis of the synchronically non-compositional word *Zweifel*, 'doubt', through the judicious insertion of a hyphen after *Zwei*. The component thus highlighted, *Zwei*, takes on the meaning it has as a free morpheme: 'two'. Wodin thus creates what Delabastita (1996:128) calls a "vertical wordplay", that is a communicatively significant confrontation of two formally similar linguistic structures,[6] co-present in the same portion of text (here in the same orthographic word). The word *Zweifel* thus contains the

(1a)	(1b)
wodin.de P474 S1 ich bin das Pendel, und es geht ja längst nicht mehr um L oder Helmut, Deutschland oder Rußland, ich löse eine Menschheitsfrage, in der ich nicht mehr bin als ein Wassertropfen im Ozean, es geht um die Zahl Zwei, die in allen Dingen enthalten ist, wie nah liegt das Wort **Zwei-fel**, der über alles herrschende Gott Zweifel,	wodin.en P474 I myself was that pendulum, and it had long ceased to oscillate between L and Helmut, Russia and Germany. I was solving a universal problem in which I represented no more than a drop in the ocean. The question at issue was the dichotomy inherent in all things, the figure **2** that formed the emblem of the Great God Doubt.

[5] Some instances of non-standard spelling may, of course, be intended to depict a regional accent, and to occasion a switch point at the same time. Example 2 in Appendix 3, Table 18: Orthographically Creative Forms, contains two such examples. Here the narrator slips from more-or-less standard German into Viennese dialect, depicted by the non-standard spelling in the source segment. In the middle of it all, he uses the forms *spannungsimpulserl* and *amblididuderl*, non-standard spellings of *Spannungsimpuls*, 'electric pulse', and *Amplitude*, 'amplitude'. These non-standard spellings are not only indicative of the pronunciation of a particular region, they also suggest diminutives, because of the final *erl*, and could therefore be considered as creative derived forms. The latter analysis might suggest, however, that it is solely the addition of the suffix *erl* that makes these examples extraordinary, when it is clear that there is more than mere suffixation going on: the use of dialect to speak about such technical concepts is noteworthy in itself. The most general solution, that of considering these forms as instances of creative orthography, is thus adopted here. As is clear from Table 18 in Appendix 3, Malcolm Green translates the source segment in question using a kind of Cockney dialect, at the same time creating a mismatch between register and subject matter, to echo that of the source segment.

[6] The formal relation between *Zweifel* and *zwei* can be said to be one of paronymy.

form *zwei*, and doubt becomes predicated upon the dichotomy inherent in all things, and not just the competing alternatives (two lovers, two countries) in the narrator's own insignificant life.

Like all puns, Wodin's creation is particularly challenging for the translator. It poses the problem of how one can reproduce in the target language an effect that relies upon formal similarities between discrete meaning units in the source-language. In some cases historical links between two languages may mean that the formal features capitalized upon in the source-language pun are actually shared by the target language (Delabastita ibid:135-136), but this does not apply in the present case. In (1b) the translator, John Brownjohn, chooses to translate Wodin's pun using related rhetorical devices, embellishing the source text metaphor of 'doubt as a God' with the addition of the figure 2 as the 'emblem' of that God, and arguably through the use of alliteration and upper case in the '**G**reat **G**od Doubt'. Brownjohn thus does not recreate Wodin's creative orthographic form: he replaces the unconventional orthographic form *Zwei-fel* with the formally conventional figure '2', but compensation may be said to have taken place in the form of the insertion of a non-conventional metaphor in the target text.

A second example from *Die gläserne Stadt* appears to embody both false analysis and false synthesis (Lecercle 1990) at the same time. It belongs somewhere between the categories of unusual orthography and the creation of new words by blending or compounding. Anticipating her Russian lover's reaction to the news that she is to arrive in his country on May 13th, the narrator makes sadistic fun of his superstitiousness. The normal German word for superstition is ABERGLAUBE, attested some 215 times in the written Mannheim Corpora. The related form *Gläubigkeit*, which appears 151 times, either as an independent form or as part of a compound, is used to mean religious devoutness or naïve trust. Wodin blends the two into the form *Aber-gläubigkeit*, but by separating components using a hyphen, she gives the first part the integrity of the free morpheme *aber*, which means 'but'. The lover's superstitiousness becomes the inevitable reason for him to balk at the narrator's plan, to say 'but ...'.

(2a)	(2b)
wodin.de P492 S7 Die wahnwitzige russische **Aber-gläubigkeit**....	wodin.en P492 Him and his crazy Russian **superstitions** ...

As in example (1b), the translator does not attempt to recreate the vertical pun of the original. Nor is there any attempt to compensate for its loss. The lexically and orthographically creative form *Aber-gläubigkeit* is simply replaced by a conventional English form, perhaps understandably so: the ease with which the German pun is created owes as much to formal similarities between semantically related lexical items and the fact that the word *aber* is orthographically contained in one of those items, as it does to the ingenuity of the writer. Such a confluence of circumstances does not hold for English, and any attempt to recreate in translation both the sense and formal characteristics of the German pun would probably be overly convoluted vis-à-vis the source text.

Creative derivation

In her novel *Lust*, Elfriede Jelinek uses the derived form *Pantoffelheldinnen*, The form is striking not just because it is unique, but also because it embodies a semantic anomaly, as the feminine suffix *-in* is added to a noun, *Pantoffelheld*, that cannot normally be feminized.[7] *Pantoffelheld* is a conventional pejorative expression for a 'hen-pecked husband', made up of two free morphemes, *Pantoffel*, 'slipper', and *Held*, 'hero', the juxtaposition of which is clearly ironic.

(3a)
jelinek1.de P99 S3 Diese Frau steht auf den Papiersohlen der **Pantoffelheldinnen** da, die stundenlang verzweifelt Nahrung in sich herumirren lassen, die von ihren Familien verschmäht wurde.

(3b)
jelinek1.en P99 There she stands on her paper-thin soles. One of the **legion of henpeckers** who spend their lives eating leftovers spurned by the family.

The feminine form of *Held* (*Heldin*) is fully lexicalized in German in much the same way as 'heroine' is fully lexicalized in English, and appears in compound forms like *Hauptheldin*, literally 'main heroine', and *Volksheldin*, 'people's heroine', in the German subcorpus of GEPCOLT. What is interesting about *Pantoffelheldinnen* though, is that the culturally defined condition that *Pantoffelheld* refers to is an exclusively male experience, an assertion backed up by all fourteen instances of the lexeme in the written Mannheim Corpora. There is no female version of a *Pantoffelheld* attested in these corpora or in any standard lexicographical source, nor is there a related German noun that contains an agentive suffix – where the agent is conventionally understood to be a woman – in the way that the English 'henpecker' does. The addition of a feminine suffix to *Pantoffelheld* then is startling. It marks a switch point in the text and calls for a special interpretation. One possible interpretation is that the irony inherent in the mock-heroic form *Pantoffelheld* also applies to the women caught up in the same situation of constant nagging: for all their attempts to control others, they remain ignored and end up carrying out their commands themselves, joylessly finishing off the food their families have refused to

---

[7] In (3a) the derived form *Pantoffelheldin* also undergoes plural inflection yielding *Pantoffelheldin**nen***.

eat. Although the translator, Michael Hulse, presents us with the lexically conventional form 'henpeckers' in English, the irony of the passage is not lost in translation. The women are described collectively as 'legions of henpeckers', but they have none of the strength of military units, nor is there strength in their numbers. And the ineffectuality of their henpecking is still clear: the juxtaposition of henpecking with eating leftovers creates an image of farmyard hens eating scraps scattered by some less than benevolent hand. The co-text allows both the literal and conventional metaphorical meanings of 'henpeck' to be activated at the same time.[8] The translator thus capitalizes upon the formal structure of the target term in a way that is analogous to the original author's capitalizing upon the potential of German morphological patterns to create semantic anomalies. While we can claim that a single lexical item has been normalized in translation in this case, we must also acknowledge compensation in the form of vertical wordplay in English.

There are several other productive nominal suffixes in German (for a more detailed treatment see Durrell 1991:487- 490 and Russ 1994:226-227). One such suffix is *-keit* which is commonly used "to form abstract nouns from adjectives denoting a quality" (Durrell ibid:487).[9] So productive is this pattern that one would not expect a hapax form thus constructed to stand out in a corpus, but one such form does stand out in GEPCOLT. It is the form *Einbeinigkeit*, from *einbeinig*, 'one-legged', as used by Jelinek in *Die Ausgesperrten.*

(4a)	(4b)
jelinek2.de P535 S3 Bei mir ist der Aktionsradius eingeschränkt, wegen **Einbeinigkeit**, aber wenn der Mensch das, was er macht, gut macht, so muß man es immer ernst nehmen.	jelinek2.en P535 In my case the field of operations is limited on account of **oneleggedness** but if a person does what he does well you always have to take it seriously.

The conspicuousness of *Einbeinigkeit* could be due to the fact that it denotes an

[8] The use here of the terms 'literal', 'conventional', and 'metaphorical' follows Kittay (1987:20). Kittay's distinction between the literal and the metaphorical draws on Lakoff and Johnson (1980:80), who suggest that literal language speaks of how "we understand our experience directly when we see it as being structured directly from interaction with and in our environment", and that "we understand experience metaphorically when we use a gestalt from one domain of experience to structure experience in another domain". What Kittay is at pains to point out is that there are conventional and unconventional ways of understanding the world metaphorically, and that 'conventional' does not equal 'literal'.

[9] The suffix *-keit* is normally described as being in complementary distribution with *-heit* and *-igkeit*. *-keit* is used when the stem adjective ends in *-bar*, *-ig*, *-lich*, and *-sam*, and, in most cases, *-el* and *-er* (see Durrell 1991:489). Although the comments made here apply to forms ending in *-keit* (including those ending in *-igkeit*), a cursory check of forms in GEPCOLT ending in *-heit* shows that they hold, on the whole, for the latter as well.

unusual state of affairs – we normally expect animate and inanimate objects to have more than one leg, if they have legs at all – but a look at all the instances of nouns thus formed in GEPCOLT reveals another anomaly. There are 1,415 such instances, with some 240 types (including *Einbeinigkeit*) represented only once, while the most frequent type *Wirklichkeit*, 'reality', appears 136 times.[10] What is striking is that the quality denoted by the stem adjective is, in the vast majority of cases, itself an abstract, an insight that is implicit in the examples of words formed with *-keit* given by both Durrell (1991) and Russ (1994). And although *einbeinig* can be used metaphorically, in its literal meaning it unequivocally refers to a concrete, physical characteristic. *Einbeinigkeit* is thus odd in the same way as its translation, 'oneleggedness', is odd. A look at nouns ending in '-ness' in the English subcorpus of GEPCOLT shows that it too is far more likely to be used with abstract adjectives (see also Aitchison 1994:164) than with ones denoting physical characteristics, although there are exceptions.[11] *Einbeinigkeit* and its translation 'oneleggedness' are therefore considered equally odd on semantic and morphological grounds. *Einbeinigkeit* is also distributionally marked: it occurs once in almost 63 million words in the written Mannheim Corpora (in the writings of Karl Marx and Friedrich Engels), and is thus far less common than the adjectival/adverbial form *einbeinig*, which occurs ten times in the same corpus. The selection of such a marked form over, for example, a subordinate clause using the unmarked *einbeinig* (*weil ich einbeinig bin*, 'because I'm one-legged' or the arguably more natural 'because I only have one leg') forces a special interpretation: while finite verbs fix an event or situation in time, nouns have no such temporal reference and an event or situation designated by a noun can thus be said to have a certain universal status. Nouns are also often more economical and easily manipulable than verb phrases or whole clauses, and their ease of use can help the concept they designate gain currency, and in some cases become institutionalized. In the case of *Einbeinigkeit* it seems that the speaker, an objectionable former Nazi who lost a leg in the War, uses this nominal form in an attempt to confer a special status on his predicament, as if it has some kind of official recognition. The use of the bare nominalization *Einbeinigkeit* after the preposition *wegen* in (4a) parodies the language of bureaucracy, as does the English translation 'on account of oneleggedness'. We can conclude that both the oddness (semantic, morphological and distributional) of the German original and the parodic tone are preserved in translation.

In the same novel, Elfriede Jelinek creates an entirely new adverbial form

---

[10] Given the high number of occurrences of this suffix in GEPCOLT, statistics from this small corpus are considered adequate here. By way of comparison, the written Mannheim Corpora contain 95,686 instances of the suffix *-(ig)keit*, distributed across 5,990 types.

[11] Exceptions include 'blackness' (*Schwärze* in German) and 'prettiness' (*Hübschheit*), both of which could be described as denoting perceptions rather than intrinsic physical characteristics, and 'nakedness' (*Nacktheit*), which denotes a (temporary) state. 'Baldness' (*Kahlheit*), however, usually denotes a more permanent characteristic.

adamsäpfelnd from the noun ADAMSAPFEL, 'Adam's apple':

(5a)	(5b)
jelinek2.de P736 S1 Hans schluckt **adamsäpfelnd**.	jelinek2.en P736 Hans swallows. **His Adam's apple bobs**.

This creation can be regarded as an indirect derivation as it takes the form of a present participle and so presupposes the existence of a verb ADAMSÄPFELN, which is not attested in any lexicographical source, or in the written Mannheim Corpora. The meaning of such a hypothetical verb, 'to adam's apple', is not obvious, but the form of *adamsäpfelnd* makes it immediately recognisable as an adverb of manner.[12] Nevertheless, this hapax legomenon is as startling in its context as 'Hans swallows adamsappling' would be in English. A more common way in German of indicating the prominence of a man's Adam's apple as he swallows is to describe the action using the verb RUCKEN, 'to jerk' or 'jolt'. RUCKEN collocates with ADAMSAPFEL four times in the written Mannheim Corpora.[13] Jelinek, however, chooses not to describe the action in question in conventional terms, but creates an arguably more graphic image by making the prominence of Hans's Adam's apple the manner of his swallowing. This time her translator opts for a normalized translation: he translates Jelinek's pithy sentence using two short sentences that describe two different actions, which are nevertheless to be understood as simultaneous. The movement of Hans's Adam's apple is described in conventional terms. It bobs, as do two Adam's apples (out of thirty five) in the British National Corpus.

(6a)	(6b)
wodin.de P573 S4 es sind die Hände eines Jünglings, die mich berühren, die Lippen eines Hermaphroditen, eines Wesens halb Mann, halb Frau, die mich küssen, einer Frau ohne Brüste und eines Mannes ohne Phallus, eines Wesens ohne die Schwüle und Wülste des Geschlechtlichen, nicht Vater und nicht Mutter, ausgeschlossen aus den Vorgängen **angstschweißiger** Körperlichkeit, den nie haltbaren Momenten der Lust, denen die grauenhafte Ernüchterung folgt,	wodin.en P573 The hands that caress me are those of a youth, the lips that kiss me those of a hermaphrodite, half man, half woman, a man without a phallus and a woman without breasts, a creature without sexual protuberances, neither father nor mother, exempt from the processes of **fearful, sweating** carnality, the fleeting moments of pleasure that give way to terrible disenchantment.

[12] Most participles used as adverbs are adverbs of manner. See Durrell (1991:134).

[13] Another verb HÜPFEN, 'to hop', is also used three times in this context, but by the same author in the same text (Erwin Strittmatter's *Ole Beinkopp*).

Other derived hapax legomena in GEPCOLT include the adjectives *angstschweißig* (6a) and *todesschweißig* (7a), both found in Natascha Wodin's *Die gläserne Stadt*. Although both the compound noun ANGSTSCHWEIß, literally, 'fear sweat', and the adjective/adverb SCHWEIßIG are fully lexicalized in German (the *Collins German Dictionary* translates the former as 'cold sweat' and the latter as 'sweaty'; and ANGSTSCHWEIß occurs nineteen times in the written Mannheim Corpora), the adjective ANGSTSCHWEIßIG is not attested in any of the corpora or lexicographical sources consulted. Its meaning seems transparent though, because of the adjective's association with its nominal stem. Syntactically, the compound ANGSTSCHWEIß is thus considered a subordinating compound, as the first component *Angst*, 'fear', modifies the second (known as the 'head') *Schweiß*, 'sweat', thus restricting the meaning of the compound to a particular type of sweat. Semantically, there is a causal relationship between the two components: the sweat in question is induced by fear. This causality seems to be inherited by the derived adjective ANGSTSCHWEIßIG, which Wodin then uses to modify the noun *Körperlichkeit*, 'carnality'. In the English translation the two meaning components of ANGSTSCHWEIßIG are expressed separately and the causal relationship between them is diluted. The unusual form *angstschweißiger* is replaced by two more conventional adjectives in juxtaposition and this normalization results in a weakening of the semantic relations that hold between linguistic units in (6b) vis-à-vis their counterparts in (6a).

A similar analysis can be applied to the form *todesschweißiger*: the causal relationship between the head *Schweiß* and modifier *Tod*, 'death', – L is perspiring because he is dying – is undone in a normalized translation that merely juxtaposes 'perspiring' and 'moribund'.

(7a)	(7b)
wodin.de P641 S10. Rußland riecht für mich nach Tod, es hat die Ausdünstung von L's vergifteter, **todesschweißiger** Haut.	wodin.en P641 To me Russia now seemed redolent of death. It carried the effluvium of L's poisoned, **perspiring, moribund** flesh.

Unlike ANGSTSCHWEIß, however, the stem TODESSCHWEIß, literally, 'death sweat', appears to be quite a rare word. It is not included in any of the dictionaries consulted, but it does appear once in the Mannheim Corpora, in Goethe's *Die Leiden des jungen Werther*. It appears to be particularly favoured by Wodin, however, who uses it twice in quick succession, in the earlier half of her novel. On these occasions, Brownjohn translates *Todesschweiß* as 'sweat' and 'sweat of death'.

In (8a) Pieke Biermann derives the form *Faustrechtlerin* from the stem FAUSTRECHT, itself a fully lexicalized compound that appears 25 times in the written Mannheim Corpora and is translated in bilingual dictionaries as 'law of the jungle'. Biermann's creation is formed by adding to the stem the agentive suffix *-ler*, followed by the feminine suffix *-in*.[14] While the formally similar lexeme FRAUENRECHTLERIN exists in German – it is listed in all the lexicographical sources consulted, and translated as 'feminist' or 'Women's Libber' by the *Collins German Dictionary* – there is, to my knowledge, no precedent for the addition of the agentive suffix to the stem *Faustrecht*. In the same way one does not normally talk of 'lawyers of the jungle', so this expression might have made a suitably creative and humorous translation of *Faustrechtlerinnen* (although it would not have the startling quality of the contrast between FAUST, 'fist', and FRAU, 'woman', implicit in Biermann's original form). Biermann's translators, Jill Hannum and Ines Rieder, however, opt for the more conventional 'women vigilantes'.

(8a)	(8b)
bier.de P102 S8 Und leise, kaum hörbar für ihre eigenen Ohren: Nimm wenigstens den letzten Rest an Aufgeräumtheit und gesteh dir ein, daß du neidisch bist auf diese –, diese –! Jawohl, diese hirnverbrannten **Faustrechtlerinnen**, die dir voraus haben, daß sie ihren Kiez kennen, verdammt noch mal.	bier.en P102 And softly, barely audible even to herself: "Just take the last little bit of your good mood and admit that you're jealous of these –, these crack-brained **women vigilantes** who have the advantage of knowing their patch. Damn it.

The form *Doppelzunge*, 'double tongue', as used by Elfriede Jelinek in (9a) from *Lust*, gives one the impression of a 'back formation'. This is the process whereby a new word is created on the assumption that an existing word is derived from it. The *Collins English Dictionary* gives the words 'edit' and 'burgle' as examples, apparently back formations from 'editor' and 'burglar'. DOPPELZÜNGIG, literally 'double-tongued' – it is translated as 'devious', 'deceitful', or 'two-faced' by the *Collins German Dictionary* – is a familiar German word, as is the noun derived from it, DOPPELZÜNGIGKEIT. They are listed in standard lexicographical sources, and DOPPELZÜNGIG appears eleven times in the written Mannheim Corpora. *Doppelzunge* however, is much rarer: it is not attested in any of the aforementioned sources, and appears to be interpretable as much in the light of the 'derived' form DOPPELZÜNGIG, as on the basis of its own constituent free morphemes.

Jelinek's use of *Doppelzunge* evokes both the sense of deceitfulness of DOPPELZÜNGIG, as well as the physical sense of ZUNGE, 'tongue', central to the sexual act described in the extract. Michael Hulse's translation of the nonce word *Doppelzunge* is 'forked tongue', which captures both the physical and abstract sense of the original. The association with the sexually loaded symbol of the snake, also conventionally linked

[14] The resulting form is then inflected for plural number in (8a) yielding *Faustrechtlerin**nen***.

with slyness, is consolidated by the use of the word 'hissing'. Hulse uses a conventional collocation to translate the isolated hapax form *Doppelzunge*, but once one looks beyond this single target-text collocation, compensation is evident in (9b): the sentence Hulse creates is inventive in its use of word-play, in particular the double entendre 'she puts a good face on things' and the parallelism in 'he buries a bad face in things'.

(9a)
jelinek1.de P195 S11 Sie leiht von oben ihr Antlitz, während er von unten aus seinem Handelskammerl heraus mit der **Doppelzunge** seines Geschlechts Versprechungen macht.

(9b)
jelinek1.en P195 Above, she puts a good face on things, while below he buries a bad face in things, hissing promises with his **forked tongue**.

In (10a) Jelinek converts an adjectival noun[15] *der Allerwerteste*, literally 'the most-worthy', a conventional euphemism for the posterior (it is listed in all lexicographical sources consulted and appears seventeen times in the written Mannheim Corpora), into an adjective, which is then used, along with the formally similar *empfehlenswert*, 'worthy of recommendation', to qualify the noun *Region.* Even though Jelinek's use of ALLERWERTEST as an adjective is idiosyncratic, its double meaning is clear: it specifies exactly which region of the director's wife's body is being referred to, as well as how highly it is prized. While this is less explicit in (10b), the referent of the expression 'high-yield region' is still obvious from the co-text. Again Hulse does not attempt to recreate the formal characteristics of one of Jelinek's word-plays, although the form *asset* might have offered some potential in this regard. Instead he replaces an unconventional form with a more conventional one, but he does manage to recreate the striking harvesting, even pillaging, metaphor of the original text.

(10a)
jelinek1.de P263 S4 Ihre empfehlenswerte **allerwerteste** Region hat er gründlich abgeerntet, da wächst so schnell kein Futter mehr.

(10b)
jelinek1.en P263 He has reaped her **high-yield** region thoroughly, it has his recommendation, and now there won't be any fodder growing there in a hurry.

---

[15] All German adjectives can be used as nouns. The adjective *alt*, 'old', for example, can be used to mean 'the old man' *der Alte*, or 'the old woman' *die Alte*, etc. The first letter of an adjective used as a noun is always written in upper case, and nouns thus formed are normally declined in exactly the same way as adjectives that precede nouns (for details see Durrell 1991:124-127). The example *der Allerwerteste* conforms to both of these criteria, but there is no corresponding adjective *allerwertest* in current usage from which it can be said to be derived.

Complex verbal nouns

If it is true, as noted in the discussion of *Pantoffelheldinnen* in (3a) above, that some hapax legomena stand out because they are semantically anomalous, then still others stand out because of their syntactic complexity. This is especially true of verbal nouns that have combined with their complements and/or accompanying adjuncts to form single orthographic words.[16] Some of the more striking once-off examples in GEPCOLT of this word formation pattern are given in (11a)-(16a).[17]

(11a)
bier.de P23 S3 Auch das nonchalante **Einfachsodasitzen** ist nicht seine Stärke.

(11b)
bier.en P23 **Just sitting there** casually does not come easy to him.

(12a)
wodin.de P147 S5 Aber es ist keine Erinnerung an Kinder, keine Gesichter, keine Stimmen, ein beständiges Abseits, ein beständiges **Dabeiseinwollen**, das nicht gelingt, bis auf das eine Mal, wo ich in der Mitte des Kreises stehe, und alle singen »flög ich zu dir« und deuten mit dem Finger auf mich.

(12b)
wodin.en P147 But even that isn't a recollection of children or faces. What I do recall is perpetual isolation, a perpetual **desire to join in** that was fulfilled only once, when I stood in the middle of the ring and everyone sang "to you" and pointed at me.

(13a)
roth2.de P233 S10 Wieder fiel Sonnenberg das Gesetz des »**Unbekannt-bleiben-Müssens**« ein, das er im Bus so stark gespürt hatte.

(13b)
roth2.en P233 Sonnenberg recalled once more the law of "**having-to-remain-unknown**" which he had felt so strongly in the bus.

(14a)
wodin.de P282 S4 Nicht nur das Es-

(14b)
wodin.en P282 **Not being allowed**

[16] The terminology used here follows Russ (1994): 'complement' is used to describe constituents that must accompany a particular verb in order to construct a grammatical sentence; 'adjunct' to describe non-obligatory accompanying constituents. The latter are called 'adverbials' by Durrell (1991).

[17] In some cases the individual components of the compound maintain a limited independence from each other through their separation by hyphens, aiding comprehension (see Russ 1994:236) and signalling perhaps the tentative nature of these new creations. In one case (13a), quotation marks additionally signal this tentativeness.

senkönnen, sondern auch das **Nicht-aufs-Klo-müssen** war eine deutsche Eigenschaft, eine Selbstverständlichkeit, die mir völlig, auf Gedeih und Verderb abging,

to go to the bathroom was as German as being able to eat – a natural condition from which I was totally debarred, for better or worse.

(15a)
gold.de P48 S5 soweit hatte er die Sprache schon verstanden: Zum **Geohrfeigtwerden** hatte man stramm zu stehen, mit den Händen an der Hosennaht ...

(15b)
gold.en P48 He had already grasped that much of the language: while **having your ears boxed** you had to stand stiffly to attention, hands held neatly against the trousers' side seams;

(16a)
wodin.de P11 S6 mein ständiges Gefühl von Illegalität in diesem Land, von **Belangtwerdenmüssen**, weil ich die Tochter von Vaterlandsverrätern bin, weil Rußland immer eine Utopie für mich geblieben ist.

(16b)
wodin.en P11 this eternal sense of illegality and **guilt**, because I'm the offspring of traitors to their country – this country – and because Russia has always remained a utopia for me.

(11a), for example, consists of the nominalized form of SITZEN, 'to sit', and the adjuncts *einfach so*, 'simply', and *da*, 'there'. The resulting form is less startling than it is amusing. The nominalization seems to transform the action of 'just sitting there' into something deliberate and self-conscious. This humorous incongruity is captured in the target text – being casual is not easy – but (11b) is lexically conventional compared to its source text.

Some of the complex verbal nouns in (11a) to (16a) have a modal as their head, and a main verb and possibly even one of its complements as their modifier. Thus *Dabeiseinwollen* (12a) consists of the nominalized form of the verb WOLLEN, 'to want', and the verb DABEISEIN, 'to be there'/ 'to be involved', and (13a) consists of the nominalized form of the verb MÜSSEN, 'to have to', the copula BLEIBEN, 'to remain', and its complement *unbekannt*, 'unknown'. In (14a) the main verb GEHEN, 'to go', is understood, although not present, and the compound consists of the nominalized form of MÜSSEN, the direction complement *aufs-Klo*, 'to the toilet', and the negative *nicht*, yielding *das Nicht-aufs-Klo-müssen*, 'not having to go to the toilet'.[18] In (15a) and (16a) the highlighted verbal nouns show the respective

[18] Note here that what is expressed in terms of necessity in the source text (14a) is translated in

narrators to be patients rather than agents of the unpleasant actions described: the nominalized verbs are in the passive voice, adding to their syntactic complexity. The compound in (15a) consists of the past participle of the verb OHRFEIGEN, 'to box (someone's ears)', and the nominalized form of the passive auxiliary WERDEN. (16a) is even more complex in that it contains the modal verb MÜSSEN, as well as a passive auxiliary WERDEN, and *belangt*, the past participle of BELANGEN, 'to prosecute'.

As has already been suggested in the discussion of example (4a) above, nominalizations may be used to confer a kind of timelessness on the event or situation they describe.[19] Such actions or situations can take on the status of a universal law or characteristic as in (13a) and (14a) respectively, or they can be understood to be habitual (15a) or constant as in (12a) and (14a). And note the collocation of the forms *Dabeiseinwollen*, 'wanting to join in', in (12a) and *Belangtwerdenmüssen*, 'having to be prosecuted', in (16a) with *beständiges* and *ständiges* respectively, both of which translate roughly as 'constant' or 'perpetual'. The habitual or constant nature of the actions and situations described in (12a) to (16a) is captured in all their translations, either through the use of gerunds in (13b) to (15b), or the use of adjectives like 'perpetual' and 'eternal' in (12b) and (16b) respectively. But, with the exception of (13b), where Malcolm Green uses hyphenation to create the form 'having-to-remain-unknown', these translations are lexically conventional, and unusual source-text lexical units can be said to have been normalized in translation.

Normalization may be understandable in these cases. Given that the source text forms in question are not so much semantically striking as syntactically complex, translators may view them simply as instances of authors doing something that can be done quite easily in German, but not in English. But there is an extent to which the forms listed in (11a) to (16a) are pushing to its limits the systemic potential of German to create complex verbal nouns, and this, I would argue, makes them somehow more mannered than other verbal nouns in GEPCOLT.

Compounds

As already indicated in Chapter Four, the formation of compounds is considered a characteristic feature of German, and we can expect compounds to abound in GEPCOLT, and to make up a substantial proportion of those word forms that occur only once in the corpus. Given the relatively small size of GEPCOLT, however, it

---

terms of permission in the target text (14b). The narrator's experience in German is one of alienation from, amongst others, her fellow inmates in the home, who don't need to go to the toilet as often as she does. In English, all the children seem to be operating under the same restrictions imposed by the authorities who run the home.

[19] This applies as well to English gerunds, which are based on non-finite verbal forms.

comes as no surprise that many of these compound hapax legomena are already fully lexicalized, and thus included in standard lexicographical sources and/or attested in the Mannheim Corpora, and/or familiar to native German speakers if not to non-natives. Such forms are eliminated from the present analysis in the manner described in Chapter Five. In what follows, a detailed commentary is given on some of the more inventive *ad hoc* compounds found in GEPCOLT. Examples are presented either in order of the text in which they appear, or so as to reflect their formal similarity, or the fact that they have some syntactic or semantic trait in common.

Examples (17a) to (19a) come from Elfriede Jelinek's *Die Ausgesperrten.* In these extracts *Anna*, the name of one of the four teenage protagonists in the novel, is used as a modifier in subordinating compounds whose heads are *Augen*, 'eyes', *Brüste*, 'breasts', and *Rock*, 'skirt'. The relation between the two components of each of the compounds would seem to be one of possession: the particular referent in each case is the eyes, breasts, or skirt, belonging to Anna. The normal way of expressing this relation in German is to append the genitive *-s* to the name of the possessor, which is then normally placed before the possessed entity as in *Annas Kopf*, 'Anna's head', but which can also come after the possessed entity as in *die Zunge Annas*, 'Anna's tongue'.[20] In German, as in English, there is normally no article in front of the genitive form of a person's name when the latter precedes the possessed noun. In the examples (17a) and (19a), however, the highlighted compounds are preceded by a determiner. In (18a) there is no determiner, but *Annabrüste* seems to have the status of a place name, following as it does *in Richtung*, 'in the direction of'. (17a) to (19a) then are highly unconventional. As unexpected linguistic choices they call for a special interpretation. One interpretation of (17a) could be that the author is suggesting that the fact that these are Anna's eyes is almost irrelevant, her eyes represent the eyes of an entire generation, one that is vulnerable to destruction brought on by the unchecked assimilation of the horrors of contemporary Austrian society. In (18a), where Anna is passively enduring sexual advances from a complete stranger, while her friends use the opportunity to steal the stranger's wallet, Anna is being treated as a sex object: Anna as a person is irrelevant; it is her breasts that count. Likewise in (19a), Anna has again engaged the attention of a stranger so that her friends can assault and rob him. Again Anna's personal dignity is diminished; she is treated like an object. Much the same interpretations can be made of the translations of these extracts in (17b) to (19b), in which Michael Hulse forces the reader to sit up and take notice by using compounds that mirror exactly those created by Jelinek. This is a case of lexical (and grammatical) unconventionality in the source text being matched in the target text.

It has already been suggested that lexicalization, the provision of a word for a

[20] The structure *Annas X* is attested twenty five times in the novel *Die Ausgesperrten*; whereas *determiner X Annas* is attested only four times.

(17a)
jelinek2.de P531 S3 aber manchmal fürchtet man sich entsetzlich, sieht man die Hoffnungslosigkeit dieser Generation in diesen **Annaaugen**, die keine Hinterwand haben, und so kann das scheußliche Außen direkt ins Gehirn wandern und dort gnadenlose Verheerungen anrichten.

(17b)
jelinek2.en P531 but sometimes you're terribly afraid when you glimpse the hopelessness of her generation in those **Annaeyes**, there is no wall behind them so the hideousness outside has free access to the brain and can cause pitiless devastation.

(18a)
jelinek2.de P215 S3 Sie tut, als gehörte sie dahin, in Richtung **Annabrüste**.

(18b)
jelinek2.en P215 As if that were where it belonged, it ventures towards the **Annabreasts**.

(19a)
jelinek2.de P558 S1 Hier ist die Einfahrt bereits, hinein und die Hand kleidunter geschoben, hier ist aber gleichzeitig auch das personifizierte Verbrechen des Diebstahls und Raubes eingetroffen, und als der Linzer unter dem **Annarock** wühlt, trifft den Linzerkopf ein harter Schlag aus einer fremden Faust, die sogar einem Arbeiter gehört: Hans.

(19b)
jelinek2.en P558 Here we are, the entry. In we go. And in goes the hand, shoved under the dress. But here comes the Crime of Robbery personified, too. And just as the fellow from Linz is rummaging about under the **Annaskirt**, his Linz-head is dealt a hard blow by an unknown fist, one that belongs to a worker at that: Hans.

concept (see Lyons 1977:236), and in particular nominalization, can have the effect of imbuing that concept with a more universal status, as well as making it easier to refer to it in a variety of linguistic structures, that is, if we concede that single words are more easily manipulable, than, for example, entire sentences. Lyons (ibid:243) points out that lexicalization can also have the effect of "transferring information from the syntagmatic to the paradigmatic dimension". A good example of such a transference of information between dimensions is found in (20a). Here Jelinek sums up in a single lexical unit, *Abwaschwassertee*, 'dishwater tea', what is commonly expressed in sentences like the invented: *Der Tee schmeckt wie Abwaschwasser*, 'This tea tastes like dishwater' (see the example given under DISHWATER in the *Collins German Dictionary*). Jelinek's new full-blown word takes on the status of paradigmatically related lexemes, for example co-hyponyms like *Kamillentee*, 'camomile tea', and *Zitronentee*, 'lemon tea', so that it seems that the tea really is made with dishwater, and that this is not a mere figure of speech.

(20a)
jelinek2.de P697 S1 Der **Abwaschwassertee** wird in Pappbecher geschöpft und für wenig Geld verkauft, das man für eine Maturareise spart.

(20b)
jelinek2.en P697 The **dishwater tea** is ladled into paper cups and sold for small sums that are being saved up for a school-leaving outing.

In (20a) Jelinek takes a clichéd collocation and creates a new compound from it, forcing the reader out of the kind of complacency that is perpetuated by clichés. The translator, Michael Hulse, has a similar cliché at his disposal in English,[21] which he condenses into a collocation, achieving much the same effect as Jelinek does.

Many of Jelinek's coinages seem to be designed to force non-complacent responses in the reader, and thus to maximize the effect of Jelinek's own criticism of Austrian society. In the same way, Pieke Biermann uses lexically creative forms to criticize the characters in her novel *Violetta*, but she does so in an arguably more light-hearted fashion than Jelinek. In (21a), for instance, she pokes fun at Erika and Alfred Henke, a neo-Nazi couple under police surveillance in the novel, calling them *Berufsteutonen*, 'professional teutons'. The joke is of course that agentive nouns modified by *Beruf* normally refer to activities that can be carried as the agent's main employment and source of income as opposed to as a hobby, on an amateur basis (in the case of sports), or as a civic duty (soldiers doing military service, for example). The written Mannheim Corpora contain well over one hundred such examples, the most common ones including *Berufsboxer*, 'professional boxer(s)', *Berufsjäger*, 'professional hunter(s)', and *Berufsoffizier*, 'regular officer(s)'. Borderline cases include illegal activities that some people can nevertheless make a living from: *Berufskiller*, 'professional killer(s)', and *Berufsverbrecher*, 'professional criminal(s)'.[22] The implication in (21a) is that being German is an activity that can be approached with the kind of casualness that befits a hobby, or else with the kind

[21] Five out of eleven instances of 'dishwater' in the British National Corpus are pejorative references to either soup or coffee.

[22] Some examples in the Mannheim Corpora that do not fit these patterns are *"Berufsurlauber"*, 'professional holiday-makers', *Berufsschlesier*, 'professional Silesians', *Berufsjammerer*, 'professional whingers', *Berufsbayer*, 'professional Bavarian', and *Berufschristen*, 'professional Christians'. The incongruity of the first of these exceptions – how can one conduct on a professional basis an activity that normally means suspension of whatever activity we call our profession? – is signalled by the use of inverted commas. The second two examples come from the same newspaper article in which the writer criticizes politicians who have made a career of whipping up public opinion on the vexed question of Silesia, and are clearly meant to portray those politicians as cynical and opportunistic. The fourth refers to an actor who has made a career out of playing Bavarians, and the fifth comes from a newspaper article that claims that lay people are becoming alienated from the Church and leaving its running to 'professional Christians'.

of thoroughness and commitment that befits a life-long career. The latter is, of course, the path the Henkes have taken, with their fetishizing of German order and their intolerance of non-Germans. Random selections of instances of the node 'professional' in the British National Corpus show that its co-occurrence with agentive nouns follows much the same pattern as that of the most common uses of *Beruf* with German agentive nouns (although fewer exploitations of the normal patterns were found in the BNC than in the written Mannheim Corpora). Jill Hannum and Ines Rieder are thus able to reproduce the ironic effect of Biermann's novel compound by juxtaposing 'professional' with 'Teutons'.

(21a)	(21b)
bier.de P1703 S5 Wahrscheinlich haben die sich wieder zusammengerauft, die beiden **Berufsteutonen**.	bier.en P1703 The two **professional Teutons** have probably made up.

In (22a) Biermann pokes fun at another German stereotype: the gentle and earnest *Alternativer*. This one, the caretaker of a building that has just been ransacked, wears his hair long, is a member of a men's discussion group, and most notably, wears *Bergauf-Sandalen*, literally 'up-hill sandals'.[23] The translators do not attempt to recreate this image in English. Rather they translate this form using a conventional superordinate, 'sandals'.

(22a)	(22b)
bier.de P1623 S5 Der Hausmeister, ein hagerer junger Mann mit langen Haaren, Shorts und **Bergauf-Sandalen**, saß umringt von Redakteuren auf einem Stuhl davor, hielt die Hände auf den Unterbauch gepreßt und blutete im Gesicht.	bier.en P1623 The caretaker, a gaunt young man with long hair, shorts and **sandals**, was sitting in front of it, with his hands pressed to his stomach, his face bleeding, and a group of editors around him.

Wordplay

At another point in *Violetta*, Biermann refers to a group of young men who scurry out of the bushes in a sudden rainstorm, observing that they run for cover even though they do not need to keep their hair dry. In fact, the young men in question do not have any hair to talk about, but rather something resembling *Eintagebärte*, literally, 'one-day beards', on their scalps.

---

[23] Although no instances of this compound could be found in either lexicographical sources or in the Mannheim Corpora, one native informant did think he had heard of *Bergauf-Sandalen* before, but could not remember where.

(23a)
bier.de P1908 S9 Sie hatten keine; bloß eine Art **Eintagebärte** auf der Kopfhaut.

(23b)
bier.en P1908 They didn't have any, just a **short one-day stubble** on the scalp.

(23a) is interesting for a number of reasons. For one, beards usually grow on men's faces, not on their scalps. Compare the English 'stubble', which refers to bristly growth on shaven legs, chins, heads, etc. More importantly, in German when a man is unshaven it is normal to say that he has a *Dreitagebart*, 'a three-day beard' not an *Eintagebart*. DREITAGEBART is used some fifteen times in the written Mannheim Corpora – all but three corpus examples come from newspaper articles describing suspects in police investigations – although it does not appear in any of the lexicographical sources consulted.[24] Biermann thus uses the 'frame' (Leppihalme 1996) provided by the already lexicalized compound *Dreitagebart* for the purposes of comic word-play.[25] Biermann's creation is comical because it is so exaggerated. If normal stubble is three day's growth to a German, then one would have to have a very closely shaven head indeed to sport only one day's growth. Neither this element of hyberbole, nor the collocational clash of 'beard' with 'scalp' has been captured in the English translation of (23a). The translators have gone for a literal rendering of *Eintage*, the first part of Biermann's compound, and have eliminated the collocational clash in the original by putting 'stubble' on their skinheads' heads. English does not have a frequent equivalent of *Dreitagebart* that could be used as a frame to be alluded to in a pun that would reflect Biermann's *Eintagebärte*. It does, however, have the expression 'five o'clock shadow', that could perhaps have been exploited by the translators in this case, who opted instead for normalization.

(24a) contains yet another wordplay. This time one of the police officers in Biermann's novel is expressing her frustration at the crowds thronging the gallery-cum-bar where she had arranged to meet her colleagues for a quiet update on their current investigation. Here the pun involves the form *Kultur*, which by itself translates as 'culture'. When it appears in the compound *Kulturbeutel*, however, the whole compound translates as 'wash bag' or 'toilet bag'. Schade disparagingly describes the event being hosted by the gallery as a *Kulturbeutelparade*, literally 'a parade of toilet bags', indicating that she is convinced neither of the sincerity of the crowds attending, nor of the artistic merit of this so-called cultural event. The same disparaging attitude is evident in the description 'culture vulture thing' in (24b). Although the translators do not try to recreate the vertical wordplay in (24a), there is an

---

[24] The *Collins German Dictionary* entry for BART does, however, include *ein drei Tage alter Bart*, which it translates as 'three day's growth (on one's chin)'.

[25] Note here that a similar analysis could have been applied in the case of example (8a) *Faustrecthlerinnen*, which is arguably a play on the lexicalized compound FRAUENRECHTLERIN.

element of compensation in the use of rhyme in (24b). 'Culture vulture' is not an original creation however. It is already fully lexicalized and listed as a headword in the *Collins English Dictionary*, for example. Thus a creative form is replaced by a more standard one, although the humour and disparaging tone of the original are reproduced in translation.[26]

(24a)	(24b)
bier.de P1428 S1 »Das kann wirklich kein Mensch ahnen, daß ausgerechnet hier jetzt eine **Kulturbeutelparade** stattfindet«, sagte Schade entschuldigend, als Lietze sich endlich zu dem Tisch im hintersten rechten Bogen der Galerie durchgezwängt hatte.	bier.en P1428 "Nobody could've guessed there'd be some **culture vulture thing** going on here of all places," Schade apologised, after Lietze had finally forced her way through to the table in the furthest away bay on the right hand side of the gallery.

Wordplay is also at the centre of the form *Schlaraffenrock* created by Elfriede Jelinek in *Lust*. The form is a blend of *Schlafrock*, 'dressing gown', and *Schlaraffenland*, 'land of milk and honey', and is based on the formal similarity between the first component of each.[27]

(25a)	(25b)
jelinek1.de P151 S1 Der **Schlaraffenrock** (im Reich der Mode der Reichen gekauft. In Wien!) schlenkert an der todmüden Frau herum.	jelinek1.en P151 The **undressing-gown** flaps about the woman. She's dead tired.

The interpretation of this form is aided by both the standard meanings of the blended components, and by the co-text: the novel describes an Austrian businessman's relentless sexual exploitation of his wife. The form *Schlaroffenrock* suggests that the woman's dressing gown contains something that offers her husband unlimited potential for self-indulgent pleasure. In English, no two formally similar lexical items with the meanings of *Schlafrock* and *Schlaraffenland* spring to mind, but Michael Hulse does manage to create a very effective pun on the word 'dressing gown', simply by adding the prefix 'un-' to it. If one of the characteristics of lexical items is their relative stability of form and meaning (Cruse 1986:24-25), then Hulse's in-

[26] Lynne Bowker (personal communication) suggests '*sub*-culture vulture thing' as a more original translation for *Kulturbeutelparade*.

[27] *Schlaf* and *Schlaraffen* can be considered paronyms here. *Schlaraffen* appears in a limited number of other compounds in the Mannheim Corpora, for example *Schlaraffenleben* and *Schlaraffentum*, both roughly equivalent to 'life of milk and honey'.

tervention has the effect of destabilizing this particular lexical item. While 'dressing gown' has become an almost non-compositional multi-word unit, in that its meaning is not unambiguously obvious from the meanings of its parts – a dressing gown is worn before dressing, or after undressing, rather than during dressing – Hulse's creation makes the related 'un-dressing gown' compositional again. The reader's attention shifts from the whole to the first part of the lexical item, which brings into focus the paradigmatically related reversive pair DRESS-UNDRESS. The contrast between what dressing gowns normally stand for – they arguably signify modesty – and what this particular dressing gown signifies to the woman's husband – unbridled carnal pleasure – finds expression in Hulse's adapted form 'un-dressing gown', and the lexical creativity of the original is reproduced in translation.

Anaphoric relations

In the examples given so far, the need to refer to the wider co-text in order to interpret novel forms was minimal. This was mainly because such forms were generally interpretable thanks to the paradigmatic relations they contract with other forms in the language system. In a number of cases in GEPCOLT, however, novel compounds are interpretable as much in the light of syntagmas that have already appeared in the same text, as in the light of paradigmatically related lexical items. (26a) from Natascha Wodin's *Die gläserne Stadt* is one such example. Here the narrator refers to L's *Apfeldieblachen*, literally, his 'apple thief's laugh', which is arguably interpretable as meaning something like the laughter of a child who is up to largely harmless mischief. This is the interpretation that the translator, John Brownjohn, seems to have given expression to in (26b).

(26a)	(26b)
wodin.de P582 S2 L mit seinem neuen, schlanken, verjüngten Körper, mit seinem alten **Apfeldieblachen** im Gesicht.	wodin.en P582 I couldn't take my eyes off L, with his new, slim, rejuvenated body and his old, **inimitable, mischievous smile**.
(27a)	(27b)
wodin.de P125 S3 Sein gebräuntes Gesicht lacht in den Falten. <u>Das Lachen eines Apfeldiebes</u>.	wodin.en P125 His tanned face was creased with laughter, <u>the laughter of a boy stealing apples</u>.

(26a), however, is clearly related anaphorically to the extract in (27a) taken from a much earlier point in the novel, where the narrator first describes L's laughing face. The novel compound *Apfeldieblachen* is a lexicalization of the syntagma *Das Lachen eines Apfeldiebes*, literally, 'the laughter of an apple thief', and despite the fact that (26a) and (27a) are separated by a substantial amount of text, there is a strong cohesive link between the two; in fact, the intervening distance serves to make the reiteration of the orchard robber image seem all the more deliberate. Three points are of interest here. Firstly, (26a) demonstrates how novel compounds can be used as a kind of shorthand for a concept already introduced in a more periphrastic way in the same text. As in other examples, lexicalization serves to help the concept in question to crystallize, to take on a certain text-specific validity. Secondly, the fact that *Lachen* co-occurs not with its usual collocates in (26a) and (27a), but with *Apfeldieb* on both occasions, points to the systematic development of a symbol in Wodin's novel. According to Louw, the systematic development of symbols (in poetry) "most frequently involves the removal from a form of its normal collocates and their replacement with a set of collocates which, within the body of a poet's work, consistently and gradually build up the new symbolic form" (1997:248). But if Wodin is deliberately associating *Lachen* with *Apfeldieb* rather than its usual collocates, Brownjohn, in (26b) at least, chooses instead to use a conventional collocation 'mischievous smile' – there are fourteen instances of 'mischievous smile', and one of 'mischievous smiles' in the British National Corpus – thus abandoning Wodin's emerging symbol, dismantling the cohesive tie with (27a), and replacing a lexically unconventional form with a conventional one. The translation in (26b) would thus seem to constitute a good example of the conversion of textemes to repertoremes (see Chapter Three) as well as an example of lexical normalization. Thirdly, the distance between (27a) and (26a) in the source text – (27a) occurs in paragraph 125; (26a) in paragraph 582 – may be part of the explanation for the normalization/conversion evident in (26b), a point taken up again below.

The hapax compound *Fragen-keine-Antwort-Rad*, literally 'questions-no-answer-wheel', used by Wodin in (28a) also forms part of a cohesive chain and helps establish the wheel as a symbol of relentless agitation and entrapment. The compound is formally similar to *Frage-und-Antwort-Spiel*, 'question and answer game' listed by the *Collins German Dictionary*, but unlike the latter, the questions in Wodin's compound are not met by answers, and there is no resolution to the spinning of a wheel to match the kind of resolution one normally expects at the end of a game.

(28a)	(28b)
wodin.de P499 S3 Ich wache auf, neben Helmut, in meinem **Fragen-keine-Antworten-Rad**.	wodin.en P499 I awoke beside Helmut in my **wheel of unanswered questions**.

The highlighted compound in (28a) points anaphorically to the sentence in (29a) and cataphorically to (30a), both of which occur very close to (28a) in the source text. Although Brownjohn recreates the wheel image in English, he stops short of creating a compound to match Wodin's in terms of formal creativity. Rather Brownjohn's relies on a novel collocation – WHEEL and QUESTION do not collocate at all in the British National Corpus, given a ten-word span – involving discrete lexical items.

(29a)
wodin.de P499 S1 Ein Rad von Fragen, in dem ich hänge, und es dreht sich Tag und Nacht.

(29b)
wodin.en P499 I was suspended inside a wheel composed of questions, and the wheel turned day and night.

(30a)
wodin.de P502 S1 Und das Rad dreht sich weiter, erbarmungslos, als könnte es nie mehr stillstehen, und irgendwelche zusammenhanglosen Sätze splittern von mir ab, Satzfetzen, Hautfetzen.

(30b)
wodin.en P502 And still the wheel continued to turn, relentlessly, as if unable to stop, and some incoherent sentences flew off me, verbal fragments, shreds of skin.

(31a) involves a novel compound *Schuhputz-Montag* that is related anaphorically to the underlined extracts in the immediately preceding sentences. In this example, the narrator is commenting on the regimented housekeeping routine of the neighbour whose balcony she faces and for whom the days of the week are defined by household chores. Shoe-cleaning becomes a symbol for this regimentation, in both the source and the target texts, with Brownjohn's translation recreating Wodin's lexical chain and culminating in the novel collocation 'shoe-cleaning Monday'.

(31a)
wodin.de P492 S3 Auf dem Balkon gegenüber putzt die Frau mit den griesgrauen Dauerwellen Schuhe. Das heißt, daß Montag ist. Mein unfehlbarer Wochenkalender vor dem Fenster, seit fünf Jahren. Schuheputzen ist Montag, Kleiderlüften ist Dienstag, Wäscheaufhängen ist Mittwoch, Fensterputzen ist Freitag. An diesem **Schuhputz-Montag** rufe ich L an und sage, daß ich komme.

(31b)
wodin.en P492 The woman with the semolina-gray perm was cleaning shoes on the balcony across the way. That meant it was Monday. My unerring guide to the day of the week for the past five years, right outside my window: Monday was shoe-cleaning, Tuesday clothes-airing, Wednesday laundry-drying, Friday window-cleaning. This particular **shoe-cleaning Monday** I put a call through to L and told him I was coming.

Other writers also use creative compounds that are interpretable in the light of previously occurring syntagmas. In (32a), for example, Gert Hofmann refers to the *Gabelfingerknochen*, literally 'the fork-finger-bones', of the slaughterhouse director in his novel *Unsere Eroberung*. The interpretation of this compound would be difficult – are the slaughterhouse director's finger bones forked? or does the compound refer to the fingers with which he picks up his fork? etc – were it not for the preceding sentence, given here as (33a), in which the children narrating the tale remark upon the director's mutilated hand (his other hand is artificial), with its two fingers jutting straight from the wrist like the prongs of a fork. Christopher Middleton's translation is interpretable equally only in the light of (33b).

(32a)
hofmann.de P72 S18 Ja, ruft er, während seine **Gabelfingerknochen** hart und weiß hervorstehen, was macht man nun mit ihnen?

(32b)
hofmann.en P72 Yes, he exclaims with his **fork fingerbones** sticking out hard and white, what are we going to do with you?

(33a)
hofmann.de P67 S2 Diese beiden Finger, wir können nicht sagen welche, ragen wie zwei Gabelzinken aus seinem Unterarm hervor.

(33b)
hofmann.en P67 These two fingers, we can't tell which they are, jut forward from his wrist like the prongs of a fork.

In the same novel, the children are forced into the pig house by the slaughterhouse director. The references to the pig house are too numerous to mention here, but they do provide an antecedent for the highlighted compounds in (34a) and (35a), translated literally by Middleton as 'pig house air' and 'pig house taste', where the 'air of/from the pig house' (or perhaps even 'smell of the pig house') and the 'taste of the pig house' might be expected.

(34a)
hofmann.de P98 S1 Draußen auf der Großen Viehstraße klopfen wir uns den Rock und die Hose von der **Schweinehausluft** gut ab.

(34b)
hofmann.en P98 Outside, on the Great Cattle Path, we brush the **pig house air** well and truly off our coat and trousers.

(35a)
hofmann.de P98 S22 Butterschmalz, sagt der Herr Schlachthofdirektor und spuckt, weil auch er den schlechten **Schweinehausgeschmack** ein für allemal loswerden will, ein paarmal kräftig auf den Boden, gibt es keins.

(35b)
hofmann.en P98 Butterschmalz, the director says, and because he too wants, once and for all, to be rid of the bad **pig house taste**, he spits on the ground vigorously a few times, there isn't any.

Middleton's translations have the same effect as Hofmann's novel compounds: the entities referred to are given more definite expression in single lexical units, be they compounds or multi-word units. They seem somehow more tangible, their tangibility being reinforced by the fact that they can be brushed off clothes and spat out, respectively.

A final example of a novel compound that is anaphorically related to an earlier syntagma comes from Pieke Biermann's *Violetta*. In (36a) one of the characters in the novel refers to the occupant of a car parked nearby as the *Körriewurschtfresser*, literally the 'curry sausage eater', where the use of *fresser* is highly pejorative. The comedy in (36a) lies in the fact that the consumption of a curry sausage has become the defining characteristic (compare familiar examples like 'beer drinker', 'meat eater', etc) of the man staking out the speaker's apartment, on the basis of an observation made in (37a). As was the case with *Apfeldieblachen* and *Das Lachen eines Apfeldiebes* in (27a) and (26a) above, there is a considerable amount of intervening text between (37a) and (36a) – some 6,000 words and several scene changes – and this may have contributed to the normalization of Biermann's novel compound in (36a). In the normalized translation in (36b), eating a curry sausage, *the* traditional popular snack in Berlin, is seen less as a defining characteristic, and more as an incidental one. The translation in (36b) does, however, manage to recreate the colloquial tone of (36a), using a topic-comment structure typical of spoken English, as well as colloquialisms like 'guy'.

(36a)	(36b)
bier.de P1398 S1 »Der Wagen mit dem **Körriewurschtfresser** is immer noch weg, wa?«	bier.en P1398 "The car with the **guy and his curry sausage**. It's still gone?"

(37a)	(37b)
bier.de P1265 S8 Die andere Stimme kam von weiter weg. »...'ssn det für'n Wagen da!... janzen Nachmittag schon... jetzt frißt der noch 'ne Körriewurscht ! «	bier.en P1265 The other voice came from farther away. "... what's that car doing! ... all afternoon ... now he's eating a curry sausage!"

Semantic preference

In (38a) Biermann uses the novel compound *stöckelschuhfreundlich*, 'high-heel-friendly'.

(38a)	(38b)
bier.de P229 S7 Und auch nicht **stöckelschuhfreundlich** genug.	bier.en P229 And it wasn't **high-heel-friendly** either.

This compound is not particularly startling: the adjective *freundlich* can, after all, be used in conjunction with a variety of nouns to create compounds of the form *X* + *-freundlich* meaning, roughly, well disposed towards, good for, or at least not damaging to, *X*. Such is the combinability of *-freundlich* with nouns, that Russ

(1994:231) describes it as a "suffixoid", a morpheme that lies somewhere between a free and a bound form. English too has developed the familiar analogous and homologous combining form '-friendly'. The suffixoid *-freundlich* is very common in German, and yet the form *stöckelschuhfreundlich* – said not to be a characteristic of a particular Berlin Underground station – in (38a) strikes the reader as somehow humorous. In order to tease out why this might be the case, it is worth looking at lexicographical descriptions of *-freundlich* and other instances of its use in naturally occurring text. *Langenscheidts Großwörterbuch Deutsch als Fremdsprache*, for example, gives the following useful information:

> **-freundlich** *im Adj, begrenzt produktiv*; **1** mit e-r positiven Einstellung zur genannten Person / Sache « -feindlich; **kinderfreundlich** <e-e Gesellschaft>, **menschenfreunlich** <e-e Gesinnung>, **regierungsfreundlich** <Truppen> **2** für die genannte Person / Sache gut « -feindlich; **arbeitnehmerfreundlich**, **familienfreundlich** <ein Gesetz>, **umweltfreundlich** <ein Produkt>

What is noticeable in this entry is that although *-freundlich* is defined as meaning well-disposed towards or good for the named person or thing, in all but one example (*umweltfreundlich*, 'environment friendly') of typical compounds containing *-freundlich*, it is persons, not things, who are the beneficiaries of whatever it is that is *freundlich*.[28] Thus the prototypical use of *-freundlich* as identified by lexicographers is in compounds that describe something as being good for humans, in one form or another.

There are just under 2,500 instances of the suffixoid *-freundlich* in the written Mannheim Corpora, including around two hundred instances of nouns derived from adjectives containing *-freundlich*, that is, of the form *X-freundlichkeit*. Just under half of the total is accounted for by the lexeme UMWELTFREUNDLICH, and there is a group of semantically related lexemes including, for example, RECYCLINGFREUNDLICH. Many of the remaining instances tend to involve groups of people on the one hand, as in FAMILIENFREUNDLICH, 'family friendly' (115 adjectival uses), and KINDERFREUNDLICH, 'child friendly' (130 adjectival uses, 30 nominal), RUSSENFREUNDLICH, 'Russian friendly', POLENFREUNDLICH, 'Pole friendly', (two each), or individuals, on the other: CHIRAC-FREUNDLICH, DE-GAULLE-FREUNDLICH, JELZIN-FREUNDLICH (one each). The suffixoid also combines with abstract nouns like INVESTITION, 'investment', and INNOVATION, 'innovation', to form compounds that indicate the thrust of some agent's policies, as well as with a group of nouns including PFLEGE, REPARATUR, and WARTUNG, to indicate that a product is easy to care for, repair, or maintain, respectively. There

---

[28] Such persons are designated by the words *Kinder*, 'children', *Menschen*, 'people', *Regierung*, 'government', *Arbeitnehmer*, 'employees', and *Familien*, 'families'.

are very few instances of non-human concrete nouns combining with *-freundlich*.[29] Data from both lexicographical sources and the corpus thus indicate that people and the environment are given pride of place when it comes to combining with the suffixoid *-freundlich*, but that the latter also tends to combine with certain other groups of semantically related, usually abstract, nouns.

Exceptions to this rule-of-thumb in the written Mannheim Corpora include BUSFREUNDLICH, 'bus friendly' (nine instances), and LKW-FREUNDLICH, 'truck friendly' (one instance), which refer either to the convenient access to local transport of certain tourist hotels, or to transport policy in general, and more notably BIERFREUNDLICH and BANANENFREUNDLICH. The former, 'beer friendly', occurs four times in the written Mannheim Corpora, each time in a newspaper text (articles and letters to the editor) from a short period in 1973, and referring to a particular women's group in Frankfurt.[30] The latter, 'banana friendly', also from a newspaper article, occurs in the segment: *Zwei Jahre ist es her, da ging die wunderbare "bananenfreundliche" Zeit zu Ende. Anfang Juli 1993 hebelte Brüssel den freien Bananen-Welthandel aus.* 'The wonderful 'banana-friendly' days came to an end two years ago when Brussels put a stop to free world trade in bananas' (my translation). The oddness of the form *bananenfreundliche* is further underlined by the fact that it appears in inverted commas. I would like to suggest here that this form is unusual for the same reason that Pieke Biermann's use of *stöckelschuhfreundlich* is unusual: it involves the combination of the suffixoid *-freundlich* with a non-human concrete noun, when *-freundlich* clearly has a semantic preference for people and the environment, and certain sets of abstract nouns. Biermann, like the creator of the lexeme BANANENFREUNDLICH, creates a comic effect by combining *-freundlich* with a far less noble partner than normal: mundane high-heeled shoes. The English combining form *-friendly* seems to have the same sort of semantic preferences as its German counterpart. The *Collins English Dictionary* entry for this form is as follows:

> **-friendly** *adj. combining form.* helpful, easy, or good for the person or thing specified: *ozone-friendly.*

Evidence from the British National Corpus suggests that this combining form is

---

[29] There is a small set of adjectives like ZAHNFREUNDLICH, RÜCKENFREUNDLICH, KREUZFREUNDLICH, AUGENFREUNDLICH, that indicate that something (for example, a product or sitting position) is good for or easy on a human being's teeth, back or eyes. These are considered here as still referring to humans, albeit a part of them.

[30] It is not clear from the contexts downloaded from the written Mannheim Corpora whether BIERFREUNDLICH indicates that the women in question are well disposed towards beer, or whether it is a play on the fully lexicalized intensifier+adjectival compound BIERERNST, literally 'beer serious', usually translated by the collocation 'deadly serious'. The question, which need not detain us here however, could be resolved by access to the full newspaper texts.

used most commonly in combinations related to the environment: out of just over 400 instances of 'X-friendly' in the BNC,[31] there are fifteen instances of 'eco-friendly', ninety nine of either 'environmentally-friendly' or 'environment-friendly', and thirty one of 'ozone-friendly'. Most other uses refer to benefits to people; the most common example being 'user-friendly', which appears some 125 times in the BNC, especially in connection with consumer goods such as computers. There is also a subset of uses in which something is described as being 'friendly' for some kind of animal, and wildlife in particular, a use that is arguably related to the environment. Even examples like 'car-friendly' (one occurrence) and 'cycle-friendly' (three occurrences) can be grouped under the environment heading. There is an interesting set of examples related to the music industry (chart-, club-, dance-, FM-, Hacienda-, indie-, MTV-, NME-, radio-, rave-, studio-friendly), many of which appear to come from popular music magazines, and a smaller set related to the media in general (lens-, media-, television-friendly). Thus the combining form '-friendly' seems to have been embraced in particular by text producers in certain areas, notably the environment, consumer goods, and music journalism. Like its German counterpart, however, it does not combine readily with non-animate concrete nouns that do not refer to the environment in some shape or form. This makes 'high-heel-friendly' as odd in English as *stöckelschuhfreundlich* is in German. Biermann's translators thus exploit the preferences of the combining form '-friendly' in much the same way as Biermann exploits the semantic preferences of the suffixoid *-freundlich*, and in doing so they avoid normalization in their translation of Biermann's creative hapax form.

Semantic prosody

As already indicated in Chapter Four, semantic prosody refers to the way certain nodes become imbued with a consistent aura of meaning by virtue of their habitual contact with certain collocates. If we accept that a free morpheme like BAJONETT can become imbued with a negative prosody by virtue of its contact with lexemes like ANGRIFF, 'attack', and LEICHE, 'corpse', not to mention its occurrence in such gruesome contexts as (39a) and (40b),[32] then its co-occurrence with the seemingly neutral *Andenken* in (41a), taken from Jelinek's *Die Ausgesperrten* can be regarded as something of an oddity.[33]

---

[31] There are 404 instances of 'X-friendly' in the BNC. A further ten instances of 'X-unfriendly' are ignored here.

[32] Examples here are taken from a concordance of the node *Bajonett* in the written Mannheim Corpora. The translations in (39b) and (40b) are my own.

[33] *Bajonett* might, of course, be considered a 'negative' word even before its collocates are considered. As a weapon it might automatically be negatively evaluated by many native speakers.

(39a)
ein blutrotes Plakat , das ein auf ein Bajonett aufgespießtes Baby ...

(39b)
a blood-red poster, with a baby speared by a bayonet ...

(40a)
die von Krüppeln, zermanschten Leichen, Bajonetten, uniformierten Sadisten ...

(40b)
by cripples, mashed corpses, bayonets, uniformed sadists ...

(41a)
jelinek2.de P543 S6 Halt, Anni, ich weiß etwas, um das klägliche Ergebnis zu verbessern, nämlich das **Andenken-bajonett** unseres Vaters, das er wiederum von seinem eigenen Vati hat, man glaubt nicht, daß dieses Ungeheuer Eltern besitzt, die es einmal geboren und gezeugt haben, er hat aber doch, Beweis: das Bajonett, welches noch aus dem Ersten Weltkrieg stammt.

(41b)
jelinek2.en P543 The result is pathetic. Hang on, Anni, I know how we can make it look less pathetic, Father's **souvenir bayonet**, which he in turn had from his Dad, you wouldn't believe this monster had parents who begat it and gave birth to it once upon a time, but he did, the bayonet is the proof, it dates back to the First World War.

If we consider compounds in the Mannheim Corpora containing the form *Andenken* in first position (there are nineteen in all), we can see that they usually pertain either to some kind of commercial activity as in *Andenkenladen*, 'souvenir shop', and *Andenkenverkäufer*, 'souvenir sellers' or to photos as in *Andenkenbilder*, 'souvenir photos'. *Andenken* can be said to have a semantic preference for 'commercial activity', on the one hand, and to combine readily with *Bilder*, on the other. The combination of *Andenken* with *Bajonett* in (41a) is unexpected given the normal behaviour of the former, and might call for a special interpretation. The association of a bayonet with the souvenir industry establishes an incongruity, a clash of prosodies that is perhaps intended to reveal a perversion in the Father's psyche. The same disturbing clash of prosodies is evident in the English translation, 'souvenir bayonet', in (41b): data from the British National Corpus would suggest that 'souvenir' usually collocates with lexemes such as SHOP and SELLER, although one instance of 'souvenir' in the BNC has the same gruesome quality as *Andenkenbajonett*, namely when it is in collocation with the form *shrapnel* in a *Daily Mirror* article.

(42a) contains another example of a clash of prosodies, this time involving the intensifier *stink-* and the adjective FREUNDLICH.

(42a)
bier.de P691 S3 Er versuchte ein **stinkfreundliches** Lächeln, aber es blieb im Schmerz stecken.

(42b)
bier.en P691 He attempted a **super-friendly** smile, but it faltered because of the pain.

In *Langenscheidts Großwörterbuch Deutsch als Fremdsprache*, Götz *et al.* (1997) summarize the use of the intensifier *stink-* as follows:

> **stink-** im Adj, begrenzt produktiv, gespr pej; verwendet, um bestimmte Adjektive zu verstärken » sehr; **stinkfaul, stinkfein** (= übertrieben vornehm), **stinklangweilig, stinknormal, stinkreich, stinkvornehm, stinkwütend**

Stink- is thus characterized by lexicographers as a morpheme of limited productivity used pejoratively in spoken language to intensify certain adjectives. The examples given translate roughly as 'bone idle', 'dead posh', 'deadly boring', 'boringly normal', 'stinking rich', and 'raging'. A concordance of the morpheme *stink-* in the written Mannheim Corpora reveals the extent to which these compounds are used: STINK(E)SAUER occurs forty three times; STINKNORMAL seventeen times; STINKLANGWEILIG eight times; STINKREICH four times; and STINKFAUL once. Three other instances of *stink-* occur in the written Mannheim Corpora, namely in the compounds STINKBOURGEOIS, STINKKONSERVATIV, and STINKREAKTIONÄR, all of which come from a single source that aims to illustrate the use of such intensifiers in political discourse. What is remarkable about the data supplied both by lexicographical sources (the *Collins German Dictionary* also lists all the *Langenscheidt* examples with the exception of STINKFEIN) and the corpus, is that many of the adjectives intensified by *stink-* already describe unpleasant attributes. Given that *stink-* regularly co-occurs with such adjectives, its association by text producers with other adjectives, describing less obviously negative attributes such as richness and poshness, inevitably reveals such text producers' negative evaluation of richness, finery, etc. Attributes thus intensified are understood to be considered somehow excessive or distasteful. This is the case as well with Biermann's description of a character's smile as STINKFREUNDLICH. While friendliness would not normally be presented as a negative characteristic, it is clear that in this case the sincerity of the attempted friendly smile is very much in doubt.

The English translation in (42b) of *ein stinkfreundliches Lächeln* is 'a super-friendly smile'. Here the translators have chosen to use the prefix 'super-' to intensify the adjective 'friendly'. The *Collins English Dictionary* describes this use of the prefix 'super-' as indicating that something is 'beyond a standard or norm', and suggests as synonyms 'exceeding' and 'exceedingly'. The character in Biermann's novel thus attempts an exceedingly friendly smile, but is it an *excessively* friendly smile? Evidence from the British National Corpus suggests that 'super-' is used to intensify predominantly positive adjectives such as 'clean', 'confident', 'efficient', 'smooth', 'snug' and 'strong'.[34] Its use in advertising texts, in

[34] 'Super-' is also used very frequently as an intensifier in sports, in particular boxing ('super lightweight', 'super middleweight', etc) and skiing ('super giant slalom'), where it further specifies the class in which athletes compete.

particular in combinations like 'super deluxe' and 'super luxury', also suggests that 'super-' is used to portray objects referred to in a very positive light. The prefix 'super-' thus carries none of the negative prosodies that the German *stink-* would appear to have. Hannum's and Rieder's translation of *stinkfreundliches Lachen* as 'super-friendly smile' thus captures the intensity, and perhaps exaggerated nature of the smile (given the circumstances in which the character smiles; he is, after all, in pain), but it does not embody a clash of prosodies like Biermann's creative compound does, and so does not represent as disruptive a switch point as the original author's invention.

Creative imagery

It is clear from many of the above examples that lexical creativity is often associated with imaginative representations of the world, and that such representations are often realized through metaphor. Some metaphors, however, become conventional. The similarities some metaphors suggest may become run-of-the-mill (see, for example, the suggested similarity between dishwater and tea in (20a) and (20b) above), and this is reflected by their inclusion in lexicographical sources, and/or frequent collocation in corpora. If writers wishes to give conventional metaphors a new lease of life, they can choose to change the formal presentation of the metaphor as, I have argued, Elfriede Jelinek does in (20a). Non-conventional metaphors, on the other hand, might be expected to be realized by unusual collocations or compounds, that is by collocations or compounds whose absolute frequency in a corpus is very low (possibly equal to one), and that are not listed in familiar dictionaries. (43a) and (44a) contain examples of such imaginative compounds in GEPCOLT. In (43a), from Georges-Arthur Goldschmidt's *Die Absonderung*, the writer presents us with the memorable image of fingers descending from the sky (*Himmelsfinger*) to pull up the earth's skin (the *Erdenhaut*) here and there, thus creating the stippled effect of small pointed mountains. James Kirkup recreates the image in English using the equally rare collocations 'heavenly fingers' and 'earth's skin'.

(43a)
gold.de P9 S4 Nach der weiten Fernen über Fernen aufdeckenden Norddeutschen Ebene fingen Berge an vorbeizuziehen, kleine spitze Berge, die ersten, die er gesehen hatte, als hätten **Himmelsfinger** die **Erdenhaut** stellenweise nach oben gezogen.

(43b)
gold.en P9 After the vast North German plain with its endless horizons, small pointed mountains drifted past, the first he had ever seen, looking as if **heavenly fingers** had hauled up the **earth's skin** here and there.

In (44a) the narrator in Natascha Wodin's *Die gläserne Stadt* describes how one of the nuns at the children's home in which she lived force-fed her using the common technique of appealing to the child's sense of familial devotion, enjoining her to consume a spoonful per family member. In the child's mind each spoonful becomes one of these imaginary relatives, and when she vomits her food up later, she vomits *graubraune Linsenonkels*, 'grey-brown lentil uncles', and *gelbe Puddingtanten*, 'yellow blancmange aunts'. The translation in (44b) is arguably normalized vis-à-vis the source text. For one, whereas the child is stuffed *with* a huge extended family in German, she is force-fed *on behalf of* the same family in English. In English the uncles and aunts she throws up have the colour of lentils and blancmange respectively, in German they are made of lentils and blancmange. These subtle changes make the English translation marginally more realistic overall than the German original. But if we focus on the translation of the hapax forms *Linsenonkels* and *Puddingtanten* alone, we see that 'lentil-grey uncles' and 'blancmange-yellow aunts' represent novel collocations in English, and so in this case normalization is not deemed to have taken place.

(44a)
wodin.de P281 S1 ich wurde gemästet, genudelt mit einer gigantischen Verwandtschaft, die nicht einmal in meiner Vorstellung vorhanden war, und später spie ich sie wieder aus in hohem Bogen, graubraune **Linsenonkels** und gelbe **Puddingtanten**, deutsche Cousinen und Cousins, deren Existenz für mich ich mir so heiß wünschte, die einem Appetit und andere glückliche Eigenschaften zu verleihen schienen.

(44b)
wodin.en P281 I was force-fed and crammed on behalf of a multitudinous family whose existence defied even my fertile imagination, only to spew them up when lunch was over: **lentil-gray uncles**, **blancmange-yellow aunts**, and a gaggle of assorted culinary cousins whose function was to impart an appetite and other desirable qualities.

Co-ordinating and copulative compounds

In (45a) *Anna* is the first component of a hapax compound noun. While the form *Annakollegin* could be interpreted as 'Anna's schoolmate', the co-text makes clear that this is a co-ordinating rather than a subordinating compound: this is not a case of a type of *Kollegin*, rather *Anna* and *Kollegin* are in apposition here. *Annakollegin* is both Anna and schoolmate; the two parts carry equal weight. The English translation of this compound makes this apposition clearer while also normalizing the unusual source text compound.

Co-ordinating compounds are much rarer than subordinating ones in German (Russ 1994:223). Nevertheless, there are a few other examples in GEPCOLT that qualify as co-ordinating compounds. The most startling of these come from Gerhard Roth's *Am Abgrund*. In (48a) one of the novel's protagonists, Alois Jenner, is contemplating his reflection without the aid of his spectacles. With his blurred vision, he sees his facial features joining up with each other. Instead of a nose and a mouth, for example, he now has a 'mouthnose' or *Mundnase*. The novel compounds in (46a) seem to present orthographically what Jenner sees, the merging of orthographic forms mirroring the merging of the facial features. The effect is reproduced in (46b) through Malcolm Green's equally novel co-ordinating compounds in English.

Yet another type of compound, a copulative compound, in which all parts are

(45a)
jelinek2.de P40 S8 Die Mädel wälzen sich auf dem Fußboden der Gastwirtschaft, die blöde **Annakollegin**, die glaubt, aus einer Wurlitzer dringen Bachklänge und nicht das, was die Jugend liebt.

(45b)
jelinek2.en P40 The girls rolled about on the café floor, their stupid **schoolmate Anna** imagined you'd get Bach on a Wurlitzer and not what youngsters love.

(46a)
roth2.de P162 S4 Ich betrachte verschwommenen Blicks mein Gesicht: eine **Mundnase**, ein **Nasenohr**, ein **Augenkinn**, ein **Lippenohr**, eine **Ohrenstirn**.

(46b)
roth2.en P162 I study my face with my blurred vision: a **mouthnose**, a **noseear**, an **earlip**, an **eyechin**, an **earbrow**.

"of equal rank, designating separate entities which together produce a new entity" (Russ 1994:224) is evident in (47a). Here Jelinek gives the teenage trio Anna, Sophie, and Rainer, an air of indignant self-importance by uniting them in a 'lobby', an effect that is maintained in translation by Hulse's equally creative copulative compound.

(47a)
jelinek2.de P144 S10 Die Lobby **Anna-Sophie-Rainer** weist derartiges zurück.

(47b)
jelinek2.en P144 The **Anna-Sophie-Rainer** lobby give stuff like this the thumbs-down.

Summary statistics and discussion

Thus far we have looked at instances of creative hapax legomena in the German subcorpus of GEPCOLT on a case-by-case basis, although instances were grouped into rough categories such as 'orthographically creative forms', 'derived forms', etc. In this section, an attempt is made to collate findings for the forty six creative lexical items discussed in this Chapter so far,[35] and to relate them to overall patterns

[35] While the numbered examples above run to forty seven, some of these numbered fragments are

of lexical creativity and normalization in GEPCOLT. Table 11 provides a summary of the findings for hapax forms covered in this Chapter, organized by kind of creative lexical process involved.

CREATIVE FEATURE	number of egs	number normalized	% normalized	number compensated	% of normalized egs compensated
creative orthography[36]	2	2	100%	1	50%
derived forms	8	7	88%	2	29%
complex verbal nouns	6	5	83%	0	0%
compounds	30	6	20%	1	17%
TOTAL	46	20	43%	4	20%

Table 11: Normalization of creative hapax legomena considered in Chapter Six, organized according to type of creative lexical process involved.[37]

Table 11 suggests that, for the small sample of examples hand-chosen from the 117 hapax forms considered lexically creative in GEPCOLT (see Appendix 3), orthographically creative forms, creative derived forms and creative complex verbal nouns are far more likely to be normalized in translation than creative compounds. These findings are, of course, to be treated with circumspection. For one, the instances covered in Table 11 were selected on the basis of their being particularly striking examples of some *ad hoc* category of analysis, rather than their being representative of the bulk of instances included in each such category. Secondly, the group of 'compounds' is treated as an undifferentiated mass, and subtler patterns of normalization may be obscured by the global figure for this category.

In order to establish just how representative the instances covered in Table 11 are of patterns of creativity and normalization in GEPCOLT at large, all 117 hapax forms included in Appendix 3 were subjected to the kind of analysis presented in this Chapter. The findings of this scaled-up analysis are presented in Table 12.

Table 12 shows that 88% of creative derived hapax forms, and 83% of creative hapax complex verbal nouns, were normalized in translation. There is no difference between the findings summarized in Tables 11 and 12 for derived forms and com-

used as background information, eg (27a), (29a), and (30a), while other fragments like (44a) and (46a) contain more than one creative hapax form. The forms highlighted in bold script in the numbered examples in this Chapter are the ones considered here.

[36] Systematic omission of 'u' after 'q' is not included here or in Table 12.

[37] Percentages are presented here and in subsequent Tables accurate to the nearest integer. This is so that figures in the Tables do not imply a level of precision that ill befits a study based on a relatively small sample of examples and involving many subjective judgements.

plex verbal nouns, as all instances of each category in GEPCOLT had already been considered in Table 11.

CREATIVE FEATURE	number of egs	number normalized	% normalized	number compensated	% of normalized egs compensated
creative orthography	6	3	50%	1	33%
derived forms	8	7	88%	2	29%
complex verbal nouns	6	5	83%	0	0%
compounds	97	37	38%	6	16%
TOTAL	117	52	44%	9	17%

Table 12: Normalization of creative hapax forms in GEPCOLT (see Appendix 3), organized according to type of creative lexical process involved.

There are striking differences between the findings for the other two categories in Tables 11 and 12 however. While 100%, that is all two, of the orthographically creative forms considered in Table 11 were normalized in translation, this figure falls to 50% for the overall corpus. The four other creative orthographic forms taken into account in Table 12 are instances of either odd spelling, or normally discrete lexical items being strung together in a single orthographic word. Two instances of the first device, and one of the second, are emulated in translation, so normalization occurs in only three out of six instances of what have been dubbed 'orthographically creative hapax forms' in GEPCOLT. Both instances of orthographically creative hapax forms presented in this Chapter (examples (1a) and (2a) above), however, involve unusual hyphenation and, simultaneously, puns. Puns are far more difficult to reproduce in translation than are simple unorthodox spellings, and so it is not surprising that both (1a) and (2a) were normalized in translation.

The difference between Tables 11 and 12 is even more striking when it comes to findings for compounds. While Table 11 suggests that only 20% of such creative hapax compounds are normalized in translation, the figure for the corpus at large given in Table 12 is actually nearer twice that at 38%. The explanation for the difference could be that Table 11 refers to hapax compounds from GEPCOLT that were particularly striking in the eyes of the researcher, because they were perceived as more humorous, evocative, or formally unusual than others. It is likely that the translators involved were also particularly struck by these examples and thus more alert to their creative nature, and the potential for creativity in their translation. If this is the case, we can conclude tentatively that around 38% of creative hapax compounds in GEPCOLT, excluding complex verbal nouns, are normalized in translation, although more striking hapax compounds are less likely to be normalized. This conclusion is not completely satisfactory, based as it is in the first instance on subjective judgements of what is and is not particularly striking. On the face of it, a less subjective conclusion might be reached on the basis of the kind of typology of compounds used in this Chapter, and applied in Table 13.

TYPE OF COMPOUND	number of egs	number normalized	% normalized	number compensated	% of normalized egs compensated
grammatical & lexical oddity[38]	3	0	0%	n/a	n/a
wordplay	3	1	33%	0	0%
anaphoric compounds	7	2	29%	1	50%
breach of semantic preference	1	0	0%	n/a	n/a
clash of semantic prosody	2	1	50%	0	0%
creative imagery	4	0	0%	n/a	n/a
co-ordinating & copulative compounds	7	1	14%	0	0%
misc.[39]	3	1	33%	0	0%
TOTAL	30	6	20%	1	17%

Table 13: Normalization of creative compound hapax forms considered in Chapter Six.

The categories used to classify compounds in Table 13 are, however, based on a blend of overlapping syntactic, semantic, pragmatic, and text-linguistic criteria. Syntactic distinctions include those between co-ordinating, copulative, and subordinating compounds, the latter of which account for most instances covered in Table 13, and between compounds that appear to be syntactically well-formed vs those that are somehow grammatically odd. Semantically motivated categories include that occupied by a single example in which a semantic preference appears to have been breached, as well as examples of wordplay. Categories that draw on readers' judgements as to what is a more or less creative image, or on the notion of semantic prosody, are essentially pragmatically motivated, and anaphoric compounds are a text-cohesive feature. The overlap between these *ad hoc* categories can be illustrated with reference to the compound *Schlaraffenrock* in (25a). It is at once an example of a subordinating compound, a play on words, and a creative image. It is

---

[38] This subcategory is used to describe the compounds *Annaaugen*, *Annabrüste*, and *Annarock* found in examples (17a), (18a) and (19a), respectively.

[39] The compounds *Abwaschwassertee* in (20a), *Berufsteutonen* (21a), and *Bergauf-Sandalen* (22a) are included under 'misc.'.

brought up in the discussion of wordplay in this Chapter because it is a particularly good example of a pun, not because this is the only category to which it could be assigned. The categories used to classify compounds in Table 13 are thus useful for describing certain aspects of individual lexical items, but they are not the kind of discrete, *a priori* categories that would be required for a definitive description of how different types of hapax compounds fare in translation, if such categories were possible in the first place.

Notwithstanding the shortcomings of the classification of compounds suggested in Table 13, interesting and largely verifiable statements can still be made about individual examples seen from a single dimension. Creative compounds that form lexical cohesive links with other elements in the co-text are a case in point. As was suggested above, whether or not such creative compounds are normalized in translation may have something to do with how much text intervenes between them and the relevant antecedent linguistic items in the co-text. When the intervening text is short, it may be easier for a translator to keep track of lexical cohesive links, and hence to reproduce them in the target text. In cases where antecedent and creative compound are very far apart, as in examples (26a) and (27a), and (36a) and (37a) above, lexical cohesive links may be undone, or at least may be realized in a less creative fashion in the target text either because the translator, who may be focusing on shorter units than the original author, has overlooked them, or because translators may be concerned that their readers will not accept creative collocations like 'apple thief laugh /orchard robber smile' – possible translations of *Apfeldieblachen* in (26a) – if such collocations are not backed up by other occurrences in the immediate environment of the same or similar image or lexical items (Mona Baker, personal communication). While it is impossible, given the present analysis, to say precisely *why* lexical normalization happens in (26b) and (36b) above, it is interesting that lexical normalization happens in GEPCOLT in precisely those cases where creative anaphoric compounds are separated from their antecedents by long tracts of intervening text, but not in cases where creative compound and antecedent are fairly close to each other in the source text, and this regardless of who the translator is.[40] It is also clear that the availability of electronic text will greatly facilitate further investigation of this phenomenon, as electronic searches can help overcome some of the difficulties involved in keeping track of lexical links established over long textual distances. For the moment, we can merely note the potential of parallel corpora in such investigations, as it is impossible to come to any firm conclusions on the basis of only two examples – in (26b) and (36b) – of normalized creative anaphoric *ad hoc* compounds discovered in GEPCOLT in the current study.

This last problem, namely that there are too few examples of a particular

---

[40] Note that John Brownjohn is deemed not to have normalized other creative anaphoric compounds in examples (28b) and (31b), although he does normalize in (26b).

phenomenon for any definitive statements to be made, is one that also applies to other categories presented in Table 13. In the case of grammatically odd hapax compounds, for example, only three instances are considered, and these all come from the same text. The fact that none is normalized in translation could have as much to do with the initial norm applied by the translator to the translation job in question as it does with the formal characteristics of the three hapax compounds concerned. A far larger set of data would be required before one could establish a link between certain formal features of source texts, on the one hand, and normalization, or its avoidance, on the other.

The problems just outlined are not necessarily solved by scaling up the analysis to include all the compound hapax forms in Appendix 3: overlapping, *ad hoc* categories remain just that, even with larger data sets; and even given three times the number of hapax compound forms taken into account in Table 13, it is still unlikely that we will have sufficient data to make definitive statements about how certain rarer compound types, for instance, grammatically odd hapax compounds, are handled in translation. For the time being then, it seems advisable to differentiate between creative hapax legomena in GEPCOLT on the basis of the formal morpho-syntactic criteria used in Tables 11 and 12. Such criteria allow for more objective and discrete categories of analysis.[41] Sticking with this analysis, it appears that while up to 50% of creative orthographic forms in GEPCOLT, 88% of creative derived forms, and 83% of creative complex verbal nouns, are normalized in translation, normalization occurs in only about 38% of cases involving creative compounds (excluding complex verbal nouns). Given that three different phenomena are included here under 'creative orthographic forms', but that there are only six instances taken into account in all, the results for orthographic creativity can hardly be considered conclusive.[42] Those for derived forms and complex verbal nouns appear more conclusive, despite the fact that we are dealing with only five and six examples of each respective category (taken from four texts by three different authors in the case of creative derived forms, and three texts by three different authors in the case of creative complex verbal nouns). A possible explanation for the high level of normalization in these categories, and one that was touched upon above, is that derivation, including the conversion process that underlies the formation of complex verbal nouns, draws on the specific systemic options available in a particular language,[43] and translators may thus see even striking uses of derivation as

[41] Within the category of 'compounds', the syntactically motivated subclasses of co-ordinating, copulative, and subordinating compounds are also relatively objectively verifiable and non-overlapping.

[42] It is worth remembering too, that systematically unorthodox orthography of the type described at the beginning of this Chapter is largely preserved in translation.

[43] Derivation, in its typical use of limited sets of known bound morphemes, some of which are in

more indicative of source-language specific relations than of source-text specific relations. Translators may therefore feel justified in drawing on the systemic resources of the target language to render even unusual derived source text forms, rather than creating novel target-text specific solutions. Compounding, on the other hand, appears to be less constrained by systemic choices in either the source or target language, and thus more susceptible to a case-by-case text-specific treatment.

Notwithstanding the apparent differences between the treatment in translation of unusual derived and compound forms, it is still significant that, viewed globally, around 44% of the instances of creative hapax forms identified in GEPCOLT according to the procedure outlined in Chapter Five, were normalized in translation. That is, the translation solutions opted for were more conventional in target language lexical terms than were the translation problems in source language lexical terms. The normalization of a substantial proportion of creative hapax legomena does appear to be a feature of translation from German into English of the literary texts included in GEPCOLT. Also, even given the admittedly superficial treatment of compensation adopted in the present research, (non-displaced, non-generalized) compensation seems to be a marginal phenomenon in the translation of creative hapax forms in GEPCOLT: as Table 12 suggests, compensation applies to only about 17% of those cases where an unusual source text lexical item in GEPCOLT has been normalized in translation.

While it has already been suggested that it is difficult to nuance these findings against a more fine-grained typology of compounds, it has also been hinted that there may be some benefit in viewing them against the background of the texts from

SOURCE TEXT FILE	**translator**	**number of egs**	**number normal-ized**	**% normal-ized**	**number com-pensated**	**% of normalized egs compensated**
bier.de	Hannum & Rieder	9	5	56%	1	20%
gold.de	Kirkup	3	1	33%	0	0%
hofmann.de	Middleton	3	0	0%	n/a	0%
jelinek1.de	Hulse	4	3	75%	2	67%
jelinek2.de	Hulse	9	2	22%	0	0%
roth2.de	Green	6	0	0%	n/a	n/a
wodin.de	Brownjohn	12	9	75%	1	11%
TOTAL		46	20	43%	4	20%

Table 14: Normalization of creative hapax forms included in Chapter Six, organized according to source text.

clear contrast to others (for example the German nominal suffix *-in* is chosen rather than no suffix, when there is a distinction to be made between female and male), is thus seen as having more in common with the notion of 'grammatical system' than does the rather more unpredictable, open-ended process of compounding.

which they are drawn, or the translators responsible for their translation. Table 14 gives an overview of normalization of lexical items discussed in this Chapter, and organized according to source file. Table 15 presents a similarly organized summary of findings for all forms included in Appendix 3. Source files are designated in both Tables using a shortened form of the original author's surname, followed by a number if there is more than one text by the same author in GEPCOLT. The *.de* extension indicates the language of the file, German. The second column in each Table contains the surname(s) of the translator(s) of the work in question. For full bibliographic details of both originals and translations, see Appendix 1.

SOURCE TEXT FILE	**translator**	**number of egs**	**number normalized**	**% normalized**	**number compensated**	**% of normalized egs compensated**
bier.de	Hannum & Rieder	12	8	66%	3	43%
gold.de	Kirkup	4	2	50%	0	0%
hofmann.de	Middleton	3	0	n/a	n/a	n/a
jelinek1.de	Hulse	18	6	33%	4	66%
jelinek2.de	Hulse	18	7	39%	0	0%
kirchhof.de	Brownjohn	3	2	67%	0	0%
loest.de	Mitchell	5	3	60%	0	0%
ransmayr.de	Woods	2	1	50%	0	0%
roth1.de	Green	7	2	29%	0	0%
roth2.de	Green	7	0	n/a	n/a	n/a
weller.de	Knight	3	0	n/a	n/a	n/a
wodin.de	Brownjohn	34	20	59%	1	5%
zuern4.de	Green	1	1	100%	1	100%
TOTAL		117	52	44%	9	17%

Table 15: Normalization of creative hapax forms in GEPCOLT (see Appendix 3), organized according to source text.[44]

The figures in Table 15 are obviously most revealing in cases where several instances of lexical creativity have been identified in a single file. Natascha Wodin's *Die gläserne Stadt* (wodin.de) provides thirty four such instances; Elfriede Jelinek's *Lust* (jelinek1.de) and *Die Ausgesperrten* (jelinek2.de) eighteen each; and Pieke Biermann's *Violetta* (bier.de) twelve. Over half of Wodin's creative uses of lexis are normalized by her translator John Brownjohn. Brownjohn is also the translator of Bodo Kirchhoff's *Infanta* (kirchhof.de), where he normalizes on two out of three relevant occasions. Given the dearth of examples of lexical creativity in the latter

[44] Note here that no creative hapax forms were identified in Konrad Bayer's *der kopf des vitus bering*, or in three of the four short works by Unica Zürn, and these files are therefore excluded from Table 15.

work, however, it is difficult to draw conclusions about Brownjohn's translational behaviour in general. All that can be safely concluded here is that, more often than not, he normalizes Wodin's creative lexis, without relying on compensation to any significant extent. Both of Jelinek's novels were translated by Michael Hulse, who normalizes in just over one third of cases, although he also introduces some kind of compensation in four out of six cases of normalization in the translation of *Lust*. Normalization is a strategy adopted twice as often in relative terms by Biermann's translators, Ines Rieder and Jill Hannum, who compensate in just under half of the relevant cases. In two cases, where the authors of relatively long works, namely Gert Hoffman's *Unsere Eroberung* (hoffman.de, approx. 97,000 words) and Dieter Wellershoff's *Der Sieger nimmt alles* (weller.de, approx. 150,000 words), use creative hapax forms on only very rare occasions, their respective translators, Christopher Middleton and Paul Knight, recreate these lexical oddities in translation. It is impossible to come to any general conclusions about the work of either translator, however, as there are no further novels translated by either of them in GEPCOLT. It seems, on the other hand, that Malcolm Green, translator of Gerhard Roth's short works *die autobiographie des albert einstein* and *Am Abgrund*, as well as of the texts by Unica Zürn, generally steers away from normalization, using this strategy in only three out of fourteen possible instances, or in approximately 21% of cases.

While very tentative conclusions can be reached about the strategies generally adopted by only a couple of translators represented in GEPCOLT, one might be more confident in suggesting that, having acknowledged, of course, that normalization can only take place if there is something to normalize in the first place, the tendency to normalize does not necessarily seem to be a function of the creativity of the source text. Lexically very creative texts like Wodin's *Die gläserne Stadt* are prone to normalization in the same way as lexically conservative works like Kirchhoff's *Infanta* are; the difference is that lexically more creative texts provide more evidence on which to base this judgement. Rather normalization is probably more a function of the translator, or the translator's brief, which may, or may not be influenced by the publisher for which he or she is working. Thus while the translations of Biermann's *Violetta*, and Jelinek's *Lust* and *Die Ausgesperrten* are all published by Serpent's Tail, the former is arguably more lexically normalized than the latter two. Again, given the small number of samples of work by each translator and publisher in GEPCOLT, it is not possible to reach any firm conclusions as to how normalization is a feature of the output of individual translators or publishing houses. What is important though, is that information about translators, publishers, etc, is recorded alongside the actual texts in a corpus, so that as the corpus grows, more and more generalizations about such connections become possible. This is why extensive extratextual information is included in the headers of each file in GEPCOLT, as already indicated in Chapter Five, and illustrated by the example header in Appendix 2.

Writer-specific forms

In Chapter Five, a number of repeated writer-specific forms were identified and deemed to be creative. They are reproduced here along with their translations in GEPCOLT, starting with the forms extracted from Unica Zürn's *Das Haus der Krankheiten* in (48a) to (56a).

(48a)
zuern4.de P11 S7 Zu einer Operation, obwohl seit gestern zwei **Augenherzen** auf Eis liegen, würde ich nicht raten, sagte Doktor Mortimer.

(48b)
zuern4.en P11 I wouldn't advise an operation," said Doctor Mortimer, "even though we've had two **eye-hearts** on ice since yesterday. .."

(49a)
zuern4.de P11 S33 Also war es doch wie eine Krankheit, wenn man keine **Augenherzen** mehr hatte.

(49b)
zuern4.en P11 So not having any **eye-hearts** was like an illness after all.

(50a)
zuern4.de P25 S25 Wenn meine **Augenherzen** auch fort sind, so haben sie bestimmt mehr getaugt als mein selbstmörderisches Herz.

(50b)
zuern4.en P25 Even if my **eye-hearts** have disappeared, they were surely more valuable than my suicidal heart.

(51a)
zuern4.de P29 S13 Mein Todfeind ist nicht wirklich im vollen Besitz meiner **Augenherzen**.

(51b)
zuern4.en P29 My mortal enemy is not really in complete control of my **eye-hearts**.

(52a)
zuern4.de P29 S17 Vielleicht hat er nur experimentiert, und nach diesem Versuch gibt er mir meine **Augenherzen** wieder langsam zurück.

(52b)
zuern4.en P29 Perhaps he had just been experimenting, and will slowly return my **eye-hearts** to me once he is finished.

(53a)
zuern4.de P28 S11 Den Saal der Bäuche und auch die **Busenstube** vermeide ich sorgfältig.

(53b)
zuern4.en P28 I avoided the hall of bellies and the **bosom-room** assiduously.

(54a)
zuern4.de P33 S1 Nicht viel anders ist es mit der **Busenstube** in diesem Hause bestellt.

(54b)
zuern4.en P33 The situation is much the same with the **bosom room** here.

(55a)
zuern4.de P33 S8 Alles hat sich schrecklich verändert, und so flößt mir die **Busenstube** nur Verzweiflung ein.

(55b)
zuern4.en P33 Everything has become terribly different, and so the **bosom room** simply fills me with despair.

(56a)
zuern4.de P28 S12 Einige Zeit im **Kopfgewölbe** zuzubringen war deswegen notwendig, weil hier sich das Fieber am fruchtbarsten entwickelt.

(56a)
zuern4.en P28 Consequently it was necessary to spend some time in the **vaults of the head** because that is where the fever really comes to fruition.

The first of these forms, *Augenherzen*, like some hapax forms already discussed, refers anaphorically to syntagmas that have already appeared in the text. These include those reproduced in (57a) to (59a).

(57a)
zuern4.de P3 S9 Die beiden **Herzen in ihren Augen** sind mitten durch die Brust geschossen.

(57b)
zuern4.en P3 "The two **hearts of your eyes** have been shot right through the chest.

(58a)
zuern4.de P10 S6 Er hat ihnen nicht das **Herz im Auge** durch die Brust geschossen, nein!

(58b)
zuern4.en P10 He didn't shoot the **hearts of your eyes** through the chest. No!

(59a)
zuern4.de P10 S7 Er hat mit seinen Schüssen die **Herzen aus ihren Augen** einfach herausgeblasen.

(59b)
zuern4.en P10 His shots simply blasted the **hearts** clean away.

The idea that eyes can have hearts may arise from a reversal of the French expression *les yeux du cœur*, in which the heart is said to have eyes.[45] Zürn spent a good deal of her adult life in France, and spoke and wrote French, so it seems reasonable to assume she was familiar with the expression. In German, *Augen* and *Herz* also collocate frequently in the context of card games, where the former refers to the points a given card may be worth, and the latter translates as the suit 'hearts'.[46]

---

[45] I am grateful to Marie-Josée Hamel for this observation. *Les yeux du cœur* is used in expressions like *regarder quelque chose avec les yeux du cœur*, literally 'to look at something with the eyes of the heart', in other words to let one's heart rule one's head.

[46] One of Zürn's accompanying illustrations to *Das Haus der Krankheiten* is of the ace of hearts.

There are thus linguistic precedents for associating hearts and eyes in German and French, and we might speculate that Zürn is exploiting these associations in a novel way. These exploitations then become lexicalized in the compound *Augenherzen*, in response to which Malcolm Green creates a concise and equally novel form 'eye-hearts'.

Busenstube and *Kopfgewölbe*, on the other hand, are paradigmatically related to a whole set of multi-word units, identified as indicative clusters in Zürn's text at the end of Chapter Five (and discussed again in Chapter Seven), and so although their translations seem relatively straightforward, they are not translated in isolation. Note also that Green manages to recreate some of the assonance of *Busenstube* in his translation 'bosom room'.

Examples (60a) to (63a) are from Gerhard Roth's *Am Abgrund*, again translated by Malcolm Green.

(60a) roth2.de P263 S4 Da kommt der Staatsbeamte herein und verlangt den Herrn **Irrenwäscher** zu sprechen.	(60b) roth2.en P263 Then the government official enters and asks to speak to the head **madmen-washer**.
(61a) roth2.de P263 S5 Der Herr **Irrenwäscher** kommt auf einem Fahrrad angeradelt und hat eine Fetten.	(61b) roth2.en P263 The head **madmen-washer** arrives by bicycle, he's as pissed as a fart.
(62a) roth2.de P265 S1 »Das weiß ich selber«, gibt der Herr **Irrenwäscher** frech zurück.	(62b) roth2.en P265 "You're telling me!" the **madmen-washer** replies impudently.
(63a) roth2.de P266 S1 Der Herr **Irrenwäscher** ist ein fülliger, behäbiger Mann.	(63b) roth2.en P266 The head **madmen-washer** is a portly, comfort-loving man.

Here the title *Der Herr Irrenwäscher*, which shows mock respect for the man charged with overseeing the laundry in a lunatic asylum, is translated as 'the head madmen-washer'. The odd form *Irrenwäscher* in the German original is explained by the fact that Roth has created a startling image whereby the clothes being washed in the machines are seen as people without bodies. The sentences immediately preceding (60a), and Green's translation thereof, read as in (64a) and (64b):

Green retains the startling image, and matches *Irrenwäscher* in English with 'mad-men washer'. He also transmits the mock respect of the original by making

(64a)
roth2.de P263 S2 In der Wäscherei geht es zu! Da werden ganze Menschen ohne Körper in die Maschinen geworfen und zerwalgt, daß alle Knochen sich abbiegen. Die Pyjamas werden eingeseift und rasiert und Haare geschnitten, usf.

(64b)
roth2.en P263 They're having a whale of a time in the laundry! Whole people without bodies are being thrown into the machines and squashed out flat as pancakes, until all their bones buckle. The pyjamas are soaped and shaved and their hair's cut etc.

his the *head* mad-men washer. Green's translation also appears morpho-syntactically marked: the modifying noun in noun-noun compounds in English is normally, though not always, in the singular, even in cases where it is clear that the modifier applies to more than one of the objects it designates – compare 'tin-opener' with the non-existent 'tins-opener'. Green bucks this trend by using 'mad-men washer' rather than 'mad-man washer'.

In none of the cases of creative writer-specific forms discussed here did normalization take place. As all examples come from the work of a single translator, however, very few conclusions can be drawn about how translators cope with repeated idiosyncrasies in general. All that can be said here is that Malcolm Green does not appear to normalize in such cases, a finding that seems largely consistent with the findings for hapax forms summarized in Table 15, and also Green's personal translation agenda of 'relieving German letters of its stodgy image' (see Chapter Three).

Conclusion

The analysis presented in this Chapter, along with that of the additional data in Appendix 3 suggests that normalization is indeed a feature of translation in GEPCOLT, occurring in 44% of cases where translators have to deal with creative hapax legomena in the source text. Compensation, albeit construed rather narrowly, does not appear to be common, occurring in only 17% of the cases where creative hapax forms are normalized. Normalization does not occur at all, on the other hand, in the handful of examples of writer-specific forms discussed, although no general trends could be discerned here, given that all examples were translated by the one person. An effort was made to nuance findings for hapax legomena against the kind of word formation patterns exemplified by creative forms in GEPCOLT. While normalization was found to be standard in the case of derived forms and complex verbal nouns, it was found that normalization of lexical items falling into the much larger category of other creative compounds occurred in only 38% of cases. A tentative explanation was offered for this finding, namely that writers' use of the former word formation processes might be seen more as them capitalizing on the systemic resources of the source language, rather than creating text-specific effects. Translators may thus feel more justified in falling back on the conventional systemic resources of the target language to render unusual derived forms and complex verbal nouns than they would be in the case of other creative source text compounds. An informal typology of creative hapax compounds in GEPCOLT was also presented in this Chapter, as were a number of factors that might motivate their creation. Even though few conclusions about normalization could be reached on the basis of this typology, it is hoped that the discussion of these creative compounds showed the usefulness in lexical studies of both structural semantics and neo-Firthian linguistics. Neo-Firthian theories of collocation proved particularly useful in the analysis of novel compounds that embody departures from the normal patterns of combination of their component parts, including those that create incongruities in the form of clashes of semantic preference or prosody. The applicability of such theories to the analysis of compounds in GEPCOLT indicates that the compound vs collocation dichotomy, upheld for methodological convenience in the present book, is perhaps a false one, a conclusion that was anticipated to a certain extent in Chapter Four. Finally, creative hapax forms were presented according to the source file from which they were extracted. It was suggested, however, that whether or not a translator tends to normalize creative lexis is not necessarily a function of how lexically creative the particular source text is, rather it may have more to do with how translators see their brief. Given that GEPCOLT contains only a limited amount of output by each translator or publisher, it is impossible to prove a clear association between normalization and either one of these variables. Nevertheless, indicative patterns of translational behaviour do begin to emerge even in a small corpus. What is important is that corpora be annotated systematically with information on variables such as source text author and publisher, target text translator and publisher, demographic information on authors and translators, etc, so that as a corpus grows, the typical behaviour of individual or groups of translators, as well as factors that may condition such behaviour, can continue to be monitored in a systematic way.

7. Two Left Eyes
Creative Collocations in GEPCOLT

> The real creativity of natural language resides in the delicate interactions among lexicogrammatical constraints during real discourse.
>
> Robert de Beaugrande (1998:788-789)

Introduction

Thus far we have viewed lexical creativity principally at the level of the orthographic word. In his treatment of creative language use, however, Partington (1998:121) observes that what is commonly known as 'wordplay' is, in general, "not simply playing with *words*", rather this rhetorical device usually draws its effects from an alteration at the level of the phrase; it is "really a play on the senses of a whole expression or idiom". In this Chapter we look at creative uses of language that extend beyond the level of the orthographic word. As was the case with the compounds treated in Chapter Six, some of the creative collocations discussed here involve exploitations of the normal patterns of combination of their components. In this respect, there is overlap between many of the compounds already discussed and some of the collocations in this Chapter, an overlap that has already been anticipated in several places in this book. On other occasions, there is no easily identifiable habitual pattern that serves as a backdrop to the unusual collocation under investigation, but the latter can nevertheless be interpreted, for example, in the light of the accompanying co-text. The Chapter starts with a discussion of unusual collocations involving the node AUGE.

Exploitations of collocational norms

As numerous studies have shown (Baker and McCarthy 1990; Hanks 1996, 1997; Leppihalme 1997; Louw 1993; Partington 1998: 121-143), the manipulation of recurring syntagmatic patterns in a language is often the basis of humour, irony, or creativity in text. It would even appear that, in English-language newspaper texts at least, manipulated forms of quotations, proverbs, and sayings, are more commonly encountered than canonical forms.[1] Such manipulations are favoured perhaps because they allow writers to demonstrate their cultural erudition and linguistic creativity, while readers who recognize the relationship between a manipulated

[1] Quotations, proverbs and sayings are three types of "preconstructed word string" discussed by Partington (1998:121-143). Partington's other preconstructed word strings include idioms, expressions and collocations, "in other words, any stretch of language which is normally used and recognised as a unit" (ibid:122).

form and the canonical form of the quotation, proverb, or saying in question can feel suitably pleased with themselves for 'getting it'. The same can be said in more general linguistic terms of exploitations of what have been described in this book as 'habitual collocations'.[2] Example (1a) illustrates this point:

(1a)	(1b)
bier.de P2 S1 **DAS GESETZ DES AUGES**	bier.en P2 **THE LAW OF THE EYE**

(1a) is the title of the 'prelude' to Pieke Biermann's *Violetta*. This short chapter, in which an eye witness gives a necessarily selective account of events surrounding an assault on a muggy day in Berlin, sets the scene for the novel. Most readers of the German text will also recognize that this title is in fact an inversion of *das Auge des Gesetzes*, 'the eye of the law', an informal, but conventional name for the police.[3] Knowledge of the canonical form of this common collocation may force the German reader to posit extra motivation for its manipulation.[4] Given that in the novel the police hunt a mysterious serial killer, who is also a photographer and hence concerned with what can be suggested to the eye, the German reader may also infer, even retrospectively, that the conflict between the forces of law and order and the photographer in question finds expression in the competition between norm and exploitation in the heading *Das Gesetz des Auges*. The English translation likewise contains a conflict between two collocations: the actually occurring one, and the norm it might be said to have displaced '(in) the eyes of the law'.

A second example from *Violetta* shows a similar manipulation of a familiar collocation. In (2a) Detective Superintendent Lang boasts of the quality of intelligence gathered by his department. Their information is better than that supplied by *die Jungs mit den zwei linken Augen*, literally 'the boys with the two left eyes'.

---

[2] Like Partington, many other writers also distinguish between different kinds of (semi-) preconstructed word strings, on the basis of the degree of syntactic frozenness, semantic transparency, etc, they display (for a useful summary of commonly applied criteria, see Baker and McCarthy 1990). Given the very general definition of 'collocation' applied in this book, that is 'the co-occurrence of semantically uninterpreted lexical items within a specified distance of each other in actually occurring text', practically all lexical-syntagmatic relationships (including idioms, sayings, etc) can be subsumed under this term. For the sake of simplicity in this book then, empirically attested idioms, etc, are considered special cases of collocation.

[3] *Das Auge des Gesetzes* is listed in all the lexicographical sources consulted, and occurs fifteen times in the written Mannheim Corpora.

[4] The kind of manipulation involved here would be dubbed 'rephrasing' by Partington (1998:127) or 'transposition' by Baker and McCarthy (1990).

(2a)
bier.de P1175 S2 »Ich sag dir doch, wir sind besser als die Jungs **mit den zwei linken Augen.**

(2b)
bier.en P1175 "I told you, we're better than the boys **with two left eyes.**

Lang's assertion is a play on the conventional collocation ZWEI LINKE HÄNDE HABEN, 'to have two left hands', a colloquial expression that means 'to be clumsy'.[5] In Partington's (1998:126) terminology, the canonical form has been manipulated through a process of 'lexical substitution' of *Augen* for *Händen*. Biermann thus exploits a common collocation used to indicate lack of dexterity to suggest that some of Lang's peers lack skill in observation. The translation in (2b) is literal, and difficult to interpret, given that the only analogous conventional collocation in English against which the reader can evaluate 'two left eyes' is the expression 'two left feet'. Although the latter is a common collocation in English,[6] it is so associated with lack of dancing skill that it does not spring to mind easily in the context of a police investigation. The translation in (2b) cannot be said to recreate the effect of the unusual source text collocation, as it is not obvious what canonical form of what collocation, if any, is being exploited, and so readers of the translation cannot share the 'smugness effect' (Partington 1998:140) enjoyed by readers of the original upon recognition of the manipulation of a familiar collocation. At the same time, the collocation 'with two left eyes' is remarkable in itself, and so it is difficult to speak of lexical normalization here.

In (3a) lexical substitution is evident once more:

(3a)
loest.de P57 S12 Ein Volksstamm mußte **sämtliche Augen zudrücken**.

(3b)
loest.en P57 A whole tribe had to **turn a collective blind eye**.

In this case, the canonical form of the collocation is EIN AUGE ZUDRÜCKEN, literally 'to close an eye', or the more emphatic BEIDE AUGEN ZUDRÜCKEN, 'to close both eyes', both conventionally translated into English as 'to turn a blind eye'.[7] In (3a) Erich Loest uses hyperbole to poke fun at the Saxons who chose to 'close *all* eyes'

[5] The German expression is listed in the *Wahrig Deutsches Wörterbuch*, and is found five times in the written Mannheim Corpora.

[6] 'Two left feet' occurs sixteen times in the BNC. On two occasions it is the name of a racehorse; on five, the name of a film. In the remaining nine cases it describes the predicament of a person who cannot dance very well.

[7] Both EIN AUGE ZUDRÜCKEN and BEIDE AUGEN ZUDRÜCKEN are listed in the *Collins German Dictionary* and *Langenscheidts Großwörterbuch Deutsch als Fremdsprache*. The former expression

(sämtliche *Augen*) to the fact that they had fought on the side of the vanquished in the Battle of the Nations, and so to the fact that they had collaborated with the Napoleonic forces. In so doing, they obviate the need for 'de-Napoleonification' of their territory. In the context of a book that follows the fortunes of Leipzig from the early 1800s through to the Nazi era and its aftermath, with its attendant concern with de-Nazification, the satirical tone is clear. It should be noted here that Loest's collocation is not completely novel: it occurs four times in the written Mannheim Corpora, twice in a single work by Heinrich Böll (*Ansichten eines Clowns*), and once in two separate newspaper articles from the 1990s. In each case, however, all three German native speakers consulted considered the use of *sämtliche Augen* to be particularly marked, given the dominance of the canonical form EIN AUGE ZUDRÜCKEN and the availability of the more emphatic BEIDE AUGEN ZUDRÜCKEN. Loest's translator, Ian Mitchell, translates *sämtliche Augen zudrücken* with a similarly marked collocation formed by inserting the modifier 'collective' into the normally fixed expression TURN A BLIND EYE.[8] The result, (3b), like (3a), emphasizes the massive scale of the collusion involved in ignoring inconvenient aspects of the recent past. Mitchell's target text collocation is as marked as the source text one; normalization does not take place in translation.

Lexical substitution is the main mechanism used to adapt a number of other familiar collocations in the German subcorpus of GEPCOLT. In (4a), for example, Natascha Wodin substitutes *Augen* for *Gliedern/Knochen* in the expression BLEI IN DEN GLIEDERN/KNOCHEN HABEN, literally 'to have lead in one's limbs/bones', a metaphor for extreme physical tiredness, variations of which are listed in several dictionaries under the headword BLEI.[9]

(4a)	(4b)
wodin.de P209 S5 Eine ständig wache, überdeutliche Müdigkeit, **Blei auf den Augen**.	wodin.en P209 Forever detectable, fatigue **lay on my eyelids like lead** ...

occurs thirty nine times and the latter eighteen times in the written Mannheim Corpora. There are also four variations on the second expression: *die Augen zugedrückt*, *zwei Augen zudrücken*, *ein Paar Augen zudrückte*, and *meine Augen zugedrückt*.

[8] There are 157 instances of turn a blind eye in the BNC, the overwhelming majority (149) of which appear in the canonical form. Of the remaining eight, two are contractions (e.g., 'UN 'will not turn blind eye to rights violations'), three demonstrate grammatical substitution (Partington 1998:126) in the replacement of 'a' by 'the' or 'that' (e.g., 'nobody here today can turn that blind eye'), one is a nominalization ('the blind eye treatment'), and two involve the insertion of modifiers ('many others turned a conveniently blind eye to their arms merchants' activities' and 'they are hoping that the authorities will turn their customary blind eye').

[9] There are three instances of *Blei in den Gliedern* in the written Mannheim Corpora but no examples of *Blei in den Knochen*.

Such is the familiarity of the canonical form of the expression that Wodin is at liberty to manipulate it in more than one way: the highlighted collocation in (4a) also involves grammatical substitution on the one hand, and ellipsis on the other.[10] Wodin's translator, John Brownjohn, carries the vehicle of the German metaphor, 'lead', over into the target text, but perhaps because he cannot rely upon readers' knowledge of any standard collocation underlying the image in English, he is forced to fill in the information left implicit in German: he inserts a predicator 'lay' into the target text and converts Wodin's metaphor to a simile using the word 'like'. This makes his syntax more standard than Wodin's: where her narrator uses two nominal groups in apposition to express her tiredness, Brownjohn prefers a full finite clause. In short, while the source text plays with syntagmatic patterning in German, the translation does not exhibit such playfulness and is more 'normal', lexically and grammatically, than the original.

In (5a), Bodo Kirchhoff describes the actions of a photographer who runs backwards with great ease, as if he had *Augen im Nacken*, literally 'eyes in the back of his neck'.

(5a)
kirchhof.de P1811 S11 Ich ging sofort auf ihn zu, und Bowles – Vollblutfotograf – lief so natürlich rückwärts, **als habe er Augen im Nacken**, und sprang dabei noch mit Aplomb über die Beete.

(5b)
kirchhof.en P1811 I made for him at once, but Bowles – a thoroughbred professional if ever there was one – retreated as nimbly **as if he had eyes in the back of his head**. He even vaulted backwards over the vegetable beds.

The collocation is odd in German, where it is more common to talk about having eyes *überall*, 'everywhere', *hinten*, 'behind', or even *hinten und vorn*, 'behind and in front'.[11] The translation into English is, however, wholly conventional.[12]

In example (6a) Wodin's narrator is described as 'drinking' brown, plague-infected foam 'with greedy eyes'. While there are a number of verbs used in German to describe intent or over-eager observation of an object in terms of the

---

[10] There is grammatical substitution of auf, 'on', for in, 'in', and ellipsis is evident in the omission of a predicator in (4a). (4a) also contains another unusual collocation: the oxymoron *wache ... Müdigkeit*, 'wakeful tiredness'.

[11] Although all three are listed in lexicographical sources such as the *Collins German Dictionary*, only the first AUGEN ÜBERALL HABEN is actually attested (three times) in the written Mannheim Corpora.

[12] The expression 'eyes in the back of one's head' occurs nine times in the BNC, and there is one clear exploitation of the canonical form ('I need another set of hands, and eyes in my backside.').

(6a)
wodin.de P536 S2 In den Buchten brodelt brauner, pestkranker Wellenschaum, den **ich trinke mit gierigen Augen**.

(6b)
wodin.en P536 **My avid eyes drank in** the brown, plague-infected foam that seethed in the bays.

consumption of that object, TRINKEN does not normally seem to be used in this way.[13] So although there is a familiar set of collocations involving the juxtaposition of verbs related to consumption and the node AUGE, Wodin's collocation of TRINKEN with AUGE in (6a) does seem to be creative, but the target text in (6b) seems less so. This is because it is quite normal to speak of observers 'drinking in' visual scenes in English. In fact, data from the BNC would suggest that DRINK IN is used to describe many sensual experiences, including those related to touch and smell.[14] On three occasions in the BNC, eyes, rather than the human possessor of those eyes, are said to 'drink in' a particular scene. Thus while the highlighted collocation in (6a) is clearly relatable to a set of conventional metaphors describing avid observation of an object, it is unusual, whereas (6b), although metaphorical, is somewhat more conventional.

Decomposed compounds

While (1a) to (6a) all involve the manipulation of the canonical form of a familiar collocation, or set of familiar collocations, (7a) involves the manipulation of the elements of a familiar compound word. The German for 'eyeball' is *Augapfel*, literally 'eye apple'. In (7a) the German compound is decomposed into its constituent parts to allow Jelinek to describe how farming co-operatives exploit their members: they take the 'apples' (*Äpfel*) from their eyes, and the dirt from under their nails (*das Schwarze unterm Nagel*).[15]

---

[13] The concordance of the node AUGE as it appears in GEPCOLT shows it collocating with verbs such as VERSCHLINGEN, 'to devour' (two occurrences – a collocation also attested twice in the written Mannheim Corpora – AUFSAUGEN, 'to soak up' (three), and ESSEN, 'to eat' (once; also attested once in the written Mannheim Corpora). There is one instance in the written Mannheim Corpora of *Das Auge trinkt mit*, 'the eye drinks with one', uttered by a wine expert commenting on the aesthetics of wine bottles.

[14] There are some fifty examples in the BNC.

[15] *Das Schwarze unterm Nagel* refers to something so meagre that it would be begrudged by only the pettiest of people. The expression *er hat nicht das Schwarze unter den Nägeln*, literally 'he doesn't have dirt under his nails', is also used to indicate extreme poverty (*Wahrig Deutsches Wörterbuch*).

(7a)
jelinek1.de P42 S16 Noch dem Kleinsten ihrer Mitglieder nehmen sie die **Äpfel aus den Augen** und das Schwarze unterm Nagel.

(7b)
jelinek1.en P42 And from the very humblest they still take **the apple of his eye**, and even his nuts as well.

English has a conventional idiom that is formally related to the highlighted collocation in (7a): the idiom THE APPLE OF ONE'S EYE is defined as 'a person or thing that is very precious or much loved' in the *Collins English Dictionary*. Michael Hulse capitalizes upon this formal similarity in (7b), where it is suggested that the co-operatives take from their members that which is most precious to them. But the literal meaning of 'apple' is also activated upon reading Hulse's translation, due to its proximity to a word denoting another foodstuff, 'nuts'.[16] 'Nuts' in turn can also refer to the testicles, and the 'body part' interpretation is reinforced by the presence nearby of 'eye'. Thus, although Hulse translates the unusual collocation *die Äpfel aus den Augen* using a conventional collocation 'the apple of his eye', once the scope of analysis is widened to take in the co-text of the target language collocation it becomes clear that Hulse is destabilizing this seemingly stable idiom. If idioms are differentiated from other collocations by their semantic opacity, that is, the fact that their meanings cannot be predicted from the meanings of their constituent words (see Baker and McCarthy 1990), then any co-text that activates certain senses of those constituent words serves to undermine the non-compositional whole. We end up with at least two interpretations: one drawing on the idiom principle; the other on the open-choice principle. Even if readers focus only on the immediate co-text of the idiom 'the apple of his eye' in (7b), there seems to be an anomaly in the latter's use as direct object complement of the verb TAKE. The evidence of thirty one instances of THE APPLE OF ONE'S EYE in the BNC suggests that this idiom occurs almost invariably as complement to copular verbs, or in apposition with another nominal group. By departing from this pattern Hulse seems to indicate that routine interpretations should be suspended. Hulse's translation not only releases a multiplicity of lexical senses in the wider co-text, it also militates against complacent readings of even the shortest stretches of language. Only the most narrowly focused analysis could conclude that there is normalization in (7b).

Lexical cohesion

In (8a) Elfriede Jelinek refers to the *Waffe des Auges*, the 'gun of the eye':

[16] This process of "replacing or coupling an idiomatic sense with a concrete one" is dubbed "relexicalisation" by Partington (1998:134).

(8a)
jelinek1.de P135 S8 Ich weiß nicht, habe ich jetzt den falschen Abzug an der **Waffe des Auges** oder die falsche Abzweigung im Reich der Sinne erwischt?

(8b)
jelinek1.en P135 I can't figure it out: is this the trigger on the **eye's rifle**, this eyeful, is this the outrigger on the ship of courting senses, this sensitive courtship?

While this original collocation does not appear to be relatable in a straightforward manner to the canonical form of any habitual collocation in German, there are links between its parts and elements in the co-text in (8a): AUGE is related semantically to *Sinne*, 'senses', the sight that the eye enables being a hyponym of 'sense'. *Abzug*, 'trigger', is related to *Waffe* through another semantic relation, namely, metonymy, and it is also related formally to *Abzweigung*, 'turn'. These connections make (8a) highly lexically cohesive, as does the device of lexical repetition seen in the repeated use of FALSCH, 'wrong'. In (8b) Hulse departs considerably from the denotational meaning of (8a) to create a text segment that is equally lexically cohesive:[17] similarities of phonic form are capitalized upon to create assonance and rhyme in 'the eye's rifle, this eyeful' and again in 'trigger' and 'outrigger'. Alternative permutations of morphemes allow 'ship of courting senses' and 'sensitive courtship' to be created from essentially the same forms. The semantic connection between EYE and SENSE evident in (8a) is maintained, and a relation of metonymy holds between 'trigger' and 'rifle', on the one hand, and 'outrigger' and 'ship', on the other. While a narrow focus on the unusual collocation *Waffe des Auges* suggests that normalization does not take place in this case, the 'eye's rifle' being equally unusual, a broader analysis shows that both source and target text exhibit intricate webs of textual relations: normalization does not apply here, and neither does Toury's law of growing standardization.

Other unusual collocations

(9a) to (18a) provide yet other examples of unusual collocations involving AUGE where there is no obvious routine collocation that is being exploited for special effect. In the first two cases the unusual collocation is confined to the nominal group within which AUGE acts as head. The remainder are divided into instances where the nominal group containing AUGE functions as subject, object, or as part of an adjunct in the clause in question.

In examples (9a) and (10a), AUGE is modified by a adjective with which it does not usually collocate:

[17] A literal translation of (8a) might read as follows: 'I don't know: do I have the wrong trigger on the gun of the eye or have I taken the wrong turn in the Empire of the Senses?'

(9a)
roth2.de P335 S8 Der Gott hat ein **dreieckiges Auge** gehabt und einen schiefen Mund, der ihm heruntergehängt ist.

(9b)
roth2.en P335 God had a **triangular eye** and a crooked mouth which hung down loosely.

(10a)
wodin.de P555 S9 ... und aus dem Spiegel trifft mich ihr strafender Blick aus **hundebraunen Augen**.

(10b)
wodin.en P555 Her **dog-brown eyes** stare back at me reprovingly from the mirror.

The unusual nature of the collocation in (9a) can be put down to the hallucinatory world inhabited by one of the narrators in Gerhard Roth's *Am Abgrund.* In (10a), however, Natascha Wodin chooses to describe a perfectly normal physical characteristic, that of brown eyes, in a mannered fashion. In both cases the translator uses a literal translation to recreate the odd collocation in the target language.

In (11a) AUGE occurs as subject of the verb BETASTEN, 'to feel':

(11a)
wodin.de P551 S3 Ich stand neben ihm in einer Tür des deutschen Hauses,in dem ich einmal Eier verkauft habe, und **Frau Dreschers Augen betasteten mich** von oben bis unten wie kleine Sonden, so, wie sie einmal meine Eier im Korb betastet hatte, und mir schien, sie müsse auch jetzt den Kopf schütteln, viel zu teuer, und entschieden vom Kauf zurücktreten.

(11b)
wodin.en P551 I stood beside him on the threshold of a German apartment where I'd once peddled eggs, and **Frau Drescher's eyes explored me** from top to toe like two little probes, just as they'd inspected my basket of eggs, and I felt sure she was going to shake her head again – "No, far too expensive"– and flatly refuse to buy.

Although it is common for AUGE to be the instrument of the action (realized as part of an adjunct) described by the related verb ABTASTEN, [18] 'to feel/frisk/sound out', or

[18] Examples in GEPCOLT include: Wodin's *Ich taste mit den Augen die Linien in seinem Gesicht ab*, translated by John Brownjohn as 'I explored the lines of his face with my eyes'. The newspaper articles in the Mannheim Corpora have *es lohnt sich, jeden Strich mit den Augen abzutasten*, 'It is worth exploring every stroke with the eyes' (said of a painting - my translation), and *dieses Stichwort meint beileibe nicht, daß der Leser mit seinen Augen Buchstabe für Buchstabe abtasten soll*, 'This heading certainly does not mean that the reader should scrutinize the text letter by letter' (my translation).

even of the verb (SICH) TASTEN (this time realized as subject), 'to grope (one's way)',[19] its co-occurrence with BETASTEN is not attested elsewhere. BETASTEN is more strongly associated with touch than are related verbs. It is used several times in the written Mannheim Corpora, for example, to describe the action of handling fruit or feeling sculptures. Wodin uses it with the subject *Frau Dreschers Augen* in (11a) to compare Frau Drescher's later scrutinizing of the narrator with her former inspection (by handling) of eggs the narrator sold as a child. Wodin uses the same verb BETASTEN in both cases: Frau Drescher's eyes 'handle' the narrator in much the same way as Frau Drescher herself once 'handled' the narrator's eggs. Although the propositional meaning of (11a) is effectively reconstructed in the target language, some of the impact of the comparison is lost as the translator opts for a more conventional rendering.

(12a) is part of Unica Zürn's dream-like record of her mental illness in *Das Haus der Krankheiten*:

(12a)	(12b)
zuern4.de P4 S3 Da hinten **legten sich meine Augen mit offenen Augen zur Ruhe**.	zuern4.en P4 There **my eyes lay down to sleep, eyes wide open**.

Here she comments on how her gaze is constantly pulled to the left, 'as far as the most distant tree, right into the white evening sky' (Malcolm Green's translation), where her eyes 'lay down to sleep'. As was the case with Roth's *dreieckiges Auge* in (9a) above, the odd collocation of AUGE with SICH LEGEN ZUR RUHE on the one hand, and *mit offenen Augen* on the other, can be explained by the surreal nature of the experience being described: eyes can have an existence independent of their 'possessors' and act purposefully; they even have their own eyes and can 'sleep' with those eyes open. In (12b), Malcolm Green depicts the same surreal scene, using similarly unusual collocations.

(13a) is from Gerhard Roth's *die autobiographie des albert einstein*, a highly experimental work also translated by Malcolm Green:

[19] Newspaper texts in the written Mannheim Corpora contain the following examples: *die Augen tasten sich vergeblich durch die Nacht*, literally 'the eyes grope their way in vain through the night', and *geräumige Podien ... machen das Darum-herumgehen und Mit-den-Augen-Tasten nicht immer leicht*, 'spacious podiums ... mean that walking round and getting a close look at [exhibits] is not always easy'(my translations). Wodin has *manchmal beginnen seine Augen durch den Raum zu schwimmen, suchend, tastend*, 'sometimes his eyes began to roam the room, groping and searching' (Brownjohn's translation).

(13a)
roth1.de P248 S6 ganz dem leidenschaftslosen duktus meiner ausführungen hingegeben, **mit ohren und augen auf aufnahme eingestellt**,

(13b)
roth1.en P248 completely absorbed in the dispassionate ductus of my observations, **ears and eyes set to record**,

The segment is part of a quote attributed to a contemporary Austrian author, Klaus Hoffer, in which Hoffer comments on his intensive observation of the furniture in his room. The odd collocation in (13a) stems from the juxtaposition of *ohren und augen*, 'eyes and ears', with *auf aufnahme eingestellt*, 'set to record'. The latter expression is normally used in the context of machines such as tape and video recorders.[20] Evidence from the BNC suggests that the same is true of the phrase 'set to record' used in (13b) by Malcolm Green.[21] The verbal group AUF AUFNAHME EINSTELLEN thus has a semantic preference for technical devices as subject. Green, like the original author, ignores this preference and instead inserts biological organs in subject position, thereby creating an unusual collocation.

In (14a) *Augen* appears as object of a verb with which it collocates commonly, AUFSPERREN.[22] (14a) is still odd, however, because of the presence of a form of GEHEN, 'to go':

(14a)
jelinek1.de P189 S17 Der junge Mann wird seine **Augen aufsperren gehen**, wenn er die neue Frisur sieht.

(14b)
jelinek1.en P189 The young man will **stare a wide open unlocked stare** when he sees the new hairdo.

GEHEN (like other verbs of motion) appears with the infinitive form of a second verb in constructions where the second verb expresses the *purpose* of going (see Durrell 1991:260), and one would expect physical displacement to be necessary to carry out the action specified by that second verb. An unextraordinary example of its use would be: *Ich gehe einkaufen*, 'I'm going shopping'. (14a) could thus be translated by something like 'The young man will go opening his eyes when he sees the new hairdo.' The source segment is odd because physical displacement is not a necessary

[20] No instances of AUFNAHME used in the sense of 'recording' were found in the written Mannheim Corpora, but the *Langenscheidts Deutsch als Fremdsprache* entry for EINSTELLEN makes clear that this verb is commonly used with technical devices.

[21] In the BNC there are two examples of 'set to record', and two of 'set up to record', where the meaning relates roughly to the adjustment of a machine for a particular purpose.

[22] The habitual collocation of AUGE with AUFSPERREN is recorded in the *Wahrig Deutsches Wörterbuch.* There are two further instances in GEPCOLT.

condition of opening one's eyes.[23] It is very effective, however, in communicating a sense of anticipation of (exaggerated) purpose and duration in the young man's staring. Hulse uses different devices to achieve much the same effect in (14b). Here the highly marked use of STARE as both transitive verb and noun functioning as direct object in the same construction,[24] coupled with the extensive pre-modification of the noun in 'a wide open unlocked stare', contributes to an exaggerated sense of revelation. Although Hulse uses different devices to Jelinek, he still manages to produce a lexically unconventional translation that produces much the same effect on the reader as does the original.

In (15a) *Augen* is again the direct object of verbs with which it does not normally collocate: AUFTAUEN, 'thaw open', and ZUKLEBEN, 'seal':[25]

(15a)
jelinek1.de P94 S8 Dieser junge Mann ist, im Gegenteil, Mitglied einer exklusiven Burschenschaft, wo der Adel den Bürgern **die Augen auftaut und gleich wieder zuklebt.**

(15b)
jelinek1.en P94 Unlike them, this man is a member of an exclusive student fraternity where the aristocracy **thaw open the eyes of the middle classes and promptly gum them shut again.**

The unconventional collocations in (15a) arise from Jelinek's use of unconventional metaphors: while it is quite common to speak metaphorically of opening another's eyes in German, the verb normally used in this context is ÖFFNEN (as in JEMANDEM DIE AUGEN ÖFFNEN, listed in all the lexicographical sources consulted). Evidence from the written Mannheim Corpora suggests that neither AUFTAUEN nor ZUKLEBEN is normally used metaphorically, and so the image created by Jelinek is all the more graphic for their presence. The graphic quality of (15a) is recreated in Michael Hulse's equally creative translation in (15b).

(16a) contains a final example of AUGE in object position in a highly unusual collocation:

(16a)
roth1.de P131 S3 **er trägt bevorzugt blaue augen.**

(16b)
roth1.en P131 **he likes to wear blue eyes.**

[23] Jelinek exploits the infinitive + GEHEN construction on at least one other occasion in the same novel: at the beginning of Lust, Heidegger's famous dictum *Die Sprache spricht*, 'language speaks', is exploited when an enigmatic voice comments *Die Sprache selbst will jetzt sprechen gehen*! The sentence is translated by Michael Hulse as 'This is language itself, wanting to get a word in.'

[24] A random selection of some three hundred instances of stare in the BNC revealed no transitive uses of this verb. Indeed, stare is recorded as an intransitive verb by lexicographical sources such as the *Collins English Dictionary*.

[25] In this case, however, it is normal for both verbs to be used transitively, so there is no grammatical anomaly as there was in (14a).

The German verb TRAGEN normally takes as object items that people *choose* to put on: clothes, glasses, etc. Its collocation with *blaue augen* in (16a) is most unusual and seems to suggest that the man in question (known as *fucks* in German and 'mista fooks' in English) can somehow choose the colour of his eyes, in the same way as he chooses to wear green trousers on the day on which he is observed by the narrator in *die autobiographie des albert einstein*. This suggestion is reinforced by the use of *bevorzugt*, 'preferably', in (16a). Malcolm Green pulls off a similar linguistic stunt in (16b): by creatively juxtaposing the verb WEAR with 'blue eyes' he seems to suggest that mista fooks's eyes are detachable, as are most objects of associated with that verb.

In (17a) and (18a) AUGE appears as part of a circumstantial adjunct. In the first example, Anna's eyes are the instrument used by her to express disapproval of Hans, to 'burn holes' into him, in Elfriede Jelinek's *Die Ausgesperrten*. The image is carried over into the translation in (17b), and the unusual collocation of AUGE with BRENNEN[26] is echoed by that of EYE with BURN:[27]

(17a)	(17b)
jelinek2.de P193 S4 Anna **brennt mit ihren Augen Löcher in Hans hinein**.	jelinek2.en P193 Anna's **eyes burn holes into Hans**.

In (18a) sleep wafts from the director's wife's eyes in Jelinek's *Lust*:

(18a)	(18b)
jelinek1.de P173 S17 **Der Schlaf weht ihr aus den Augen**.	jelinek1.en P173 **Sleep heavy in her eyes**.

On the evidence supplied by lexicographical sources, the written Mannheim Corpora, and native speaker informants, the collocation of WEHEN with SCHLAF on the one hand and AUGE on the other, appears highly creative. WEHEN is normally used to describe the blowing of the wind, or of hair in a breeze, or the drifting of a smell or sound on the air. The image of sleep becoming airborne and detaching itself from a person's eyes is more unusual than that presented in (18b), although this perception proves difficult to back up with corpus evidence. (18b) is thus recorded here as an instance of lexical normalization on the basis of introspection alone.

---

[26] AUGE and BRENNEN do collocate frequently in German, but they normally do so in cases where AUGE is subject and BRENNEN is used intransitively to denote a stinging sensation.

[27] Note though, that the grammatical function of 'eyes' changes to head of the nominal group acting as subject of the verb BURN.

Repeated idiosyncrasies

In Chapter Six, it was suggested that authors may make repeated use of an idiosyncratic collocation in order, for example, to develop symbols in their work. This section is concerned with precisely such repeated idiosyncrasies in the writing of Natascha Wodin and Unica Zürn. The discussion starts with idiosyncratic collocations involving the node AUGE. We then move on to idiosyncratic collocations that represent repeated 'clusters' (see Chapters Two and Five) in each writer's work.

Both Wodin and Zürn use AUGE in conjunction with lexical items that are not normally associated syntagmatically with that node. The cumulative effect of these repeated idiosyncratic collocations is that text- or oeuvre-specific associations start to emerge in readers' minds; the node becomes a symbol for something other than itself, but given the idiosyncratic nature of the underlying collocation, the symbol will not be a conventional one. Examples (19a) and (20a) are from Wodin's *Die gläserne Stadt*. In both examples the narrator's mother is described as having *Augen wie der Fluß*, 'eyes like the river':

(19a)
wodin.de P430 S1 Der Fluß weiß alles lang im voraus, er blubbert und weiß, daß meine Mama an der Böschung steht und lang ins Wasser schaut, und wenn sie weitergeht, bleibt sie doch wieder stehen und kriegt **Augen wie der Fluß**, einen Blick aus Blau und Schwarz, das weiß der Fluß und blubbert, das wissen wir, der Fluß und ich.

(19b)
wodin.en P430 The blue river knows what will happen long before it does. It gurgles and knows that my mother stands on its banks and stares into the water for minutes on end, and when she walks on she pauses again and **her eyes get like the river itself**, a mixture of blue and black. The gurgling river knows this, we both know it, the river and I.

(20a)
wodin.de P450 S22 Dann steht die Mutter in der Tür, mit **Augen wie der Fluß**, und sinkt vor dem Kind auf die Knie und umschlingt es…

(20b)
wodin.en P450 Then my mother appears in the doorway with **eyes like the river**, goes down on her knees before me, puts her arms around me…

In (19a) the author appears to explain what is meant by having *Augen wie der Fluß* putting as she does the expression in apposition with *einen Blick aus Blau und Schwarz*, literally 'a look of blue and black'. John Brownjohn's translation 'her eyes get like the river itself, a mixture of blue and black', is somewhat tentative compared to the original. The addition of the intensifying 'itself' in English is a self-conscious admission that the comparison being drawn is unconventional. Moreover, Brownjohn's description of the mother's eyes as 'a mixture of blue and black' could give the impression that the comparison is based solely on a superficial physical similarity. The important thing about the colour of the river, however, is that it is blue on top and black *underneath*, as is clear from the preceding paragraph in the novel, an extract of which is reproduced here as (21a) (emphasis mine):

(21a)	(21b)
wodin.de P429 S2 Da liegt der blaue Fluß, wenn man um die Kurve kommt, der blaue Fluß, der alles schon lang im voraus weiß, oben blau und unten schwarz ...	wodin.en P429 There, when you turn the corner, flows the blue river that knows everything long before it happens, blue on top and black underneath.

Blue then, is the colour of the surface; black the colour of the ineluctable depths. The two colours become associated with the river, the mother's eyes, and melancholia (in example (22a) below) in Wodin's novel.

(22a)	(22b)
wodin.de P437 S5 Er hört das Blubbern des Flusses nicht ... kennt nicht die Farbe Blau, denn mein Vater ist farbenblind, kennt nicht das Wort Melancholie, oben blau und unten schwarz	wodin.en P437 He doesn't hear the river gurgling ... doesn't know the color blue because he's colorblind, doesn't know the word "melancholia," blue on top and black underneath

The black depths of the river, and of the mother's eyes, suggest a sense of foreboding that is exacerbated by the river's apparent prescience, stressed in (19a) and (21a). The threat is not an empty one: the narrator's mother takes her own life by drowning herself in the river that knew all along what was going to happen. In this way having *Augen wie der Fluß* becomes a symbol for the mother's own death. The unusual collocation is carried over into English by Brownjohn, and the symbol maintained, although it has been argued that in the case of (19b) the effect of the symbol is attenuated somewhat by the translator's use of the words 'itself' and 'mixture'.

In Chapter Five it was mentioned that AUGE collocates commonly, but idiosyncratically with HERZ, 'heart' in GEPCOLT, and towards the end of Chapter Six we saw that some of these collocations are also associated with Unica Zürn's creative compound *Augenherzen*. Whether or not there is linguistic motivation for Zürn's imagining that eyes have hearts, as speculated in Chapter Six, there is no doubt that the image takes on a life of its own in *Das Haus der Krankheiten*. Three of the relevant instances of AUGE collocating with HERZ in Zürn's work were included in the discussion in Chapter Six. The source texts include another six such examples.

All instances of this fantastic image are reproduced in Malcolm Green's translations. Indeed it is difficult to see how he could have done otherwise, given the centrality of her eye-hearts to Zürn's tale.

It has also been observed already that ZIMMER, 'room', collocates idiosyncratically, but repeatedly, in fact eight times, with AUGE in Zürn's work. In all but one instance this is due to the presence of the multi-word unit *das Zimmer der Augen*, 'the room of eyes', of which there are six instances in *Das Haus der Krankheiten* and one in *Der Mann im Jasmin*. The exception is reproduced in (23a), along with its rather straightforward translation.

(23a)	(23b)
zuern4.de P29 S18 Auch **Augen** gehören zuweilen zu den verbotenen **Zimmern**.	zuern4.en P29 Even **eyes** belong sometimes to the forbidden **rooms**.

Das Zimmer der Augen is, of course related to a number of other multi-word units discovered in *Das Haus der Krankheiten* using WordList's cluster facility (see Chapter Five). These are: *Kabinett der Sonnengeflechte*, which occurs six times and is translated as 'cabinet of the solar plexuses'; *Saal der Bäuche* (five occurrences), translated as 'hall of (the) bellies'; *Kammern der Hände* (three occurrences), translated as 'chambers of the hands'; and *Raum der Herzen* (one occurrence), translated as 'suite of the heart'. Along with *Busenstube* and *Kopfgewölbe* seen in Chapter Six, each of these multi-word units represents a room in what appears to be the interior of Zürn's own body. Given that the whole work centres around the edifice created by Zürn's imagination, it is not surprising that these rooms, and the labels that denote them, are prominent in both the source and target text. As the translations given here suggest, the repeated idiosyncratic collocation of words denoting rooms and words denoting body parts that is evident in the source text is recreated in Malcolm Green's target text. Both the unusualness of the collocations, and the strong text cohesive links they maintain, are transferred to the target text.

A less striking collocation, but one that nonetheless points to an idiosyncrasy in Natascha Wodin's work was also discovered using the clusters facility in WordList, namely the collocation of SCHRILLEN with TELEFON. Relevant instances are reproduced in (24a) to (30a). As the paragraph numbers show, instances of *das Schrillen des Telefons* are well dispersed throughout Wodin's 92-thousand word text, although examples (28a), (29a) and (30a) occur within a short distance of each other (between paragraphs 613 and 620).

(24a)	(24b)
wodin.de P33 S10 Und plötzlich im Parterre **das Schrillen des Telefons**. Helmut. Um diese Zeit konnte nur er es sein.	wodin.en P33 Suddenly **the phone rang** – Helmut – it couldn't be anyone else at this hour.

(25a)
wodin.de P57 S10 **Das Schrillen des Telefons**. Nur zwanzig Minuten diesmal. Ihre Anmeldung Moskau. L's russisches Allo ... die rauhe Oberfläche einer Birne.

(25b)
wodin.en P57 **The phone rang.** Only a twenty-minute delay this time. Your call to Moscow, L's Russian "Allo?" – husky as only his voice could be.

(26a)
wodin.de P258 S2 **das drängende Schrillen des Telefons** riß Helmut und mich immer wieder auseinander,

(26b)
wodin.en P258 Helmut and I were continually wrenched apart by **the phone bell's insistent ringing**

(27a)
wodin.de P463 S7 Ich komme nach Hause und sehe es sofort an Helmuts Bewegungen, an den gefrorenen Muskeln in seinem Gesicht. Ein Anruf aus Moskau. **Das Schrillen des Telefons hängt noch in der Luft.** Die Stimme der russischen Telefonistin, die zwischen L und Helmut geschaltet ist.

(27b)
wodin.en P463 As soon as I walked in, I could tell from Helmut's gestures, his frigid face, that there had been a phone call from Moscow. **The air still vibrated to the sound of the bell**, to the voice of the Russian operator intermediating between Helmut and L.

(28a)
wodin.de P613 S2 Die erste Nacht in Moskau ohne ihn. **Ich warte auf das Schrillen des Telefons, da, wo es schrillen muß, an meinen Rippen**.

(28b)
wodin.en P613 My first-ever night in Moscow without him. **I waited for the telephone to ring where it had to ring, against my ribs.**

(29a)
wodin.de P616 S1 **Das Schrillen des Telefons unter der Bettdecke**. Die Vibration geht durch mich hindurch, ich reiße den Hörer von der Gabel. Ich höre, er lebt, Klara sagt mir, er lebt,

(29b)
wodin.en P616 **The telephone rang beneath the bedclothes**. Its vibrations pierced me through and through as I snatched the receiver from the cradle and learned that he was still alive—Klara told me so.

(30a)
wodin.de P620 S1 **Das Schrillen des Telefons unter der Bettdecke**. Klara sagt, er lebt. Sie sagt noch einmal das Wort »unverändert«.

(30b)
wodin.en P620 **Again the telephone rang beneath the bedclothes**. Again Klara told me he was still alive, and again she used the word "unchanged."

Wodin is not the only writer to have ever used this collocation; there is one other instance in GEPCOLT – (31a) from Dieter Wellershoff's *Der Sieger nimmt alles* – and seven instances were found in the written Mannheim Corpora.

(31a)	(31b)
weller.de P5 S1 Es gibt auch Türen, die verschlossen bleiben, an die leise, bald dringlicher geklopft wird oder hinter denen **das Telefon schrillt**, bis eine verschlafene Stimme antwortet: »Ja, was ist?	weller.en P5 There are also doors which remain locked, on which the maids knock softly, then more insistently, or behind which **a telephone shrills** until a sleepy voice answers: 'Yes, what is it?

In the written Mannheim Corpora, SCHRILLEN collocates far more often with *Alarmglocken*, 'alarm bells' – in both the literal and the figurative sense – than any other item. When it is used with TELEFON, as in (24a) to (31a), SCHRILLEN tends to be used when the ringing of a phone is unwelcome, or particularly piercing, because it comes in the middle of the night, or may be the harbinger of bad news.

Wodin's use of SCHRILLEN + TELEFON then, is not unique to her, but it is a marked, emotive use, compared to other familiar collocations in German such as KLINGELN or LÄUTEN (standard verbs meaning 'to ring') + TELEFON. The markedness of the collocation is picked up in (31b) by Wellershoff's translator, Paul Knight, who translates *schrillt* using a cognate, 'shrills', thus forming a most unusual collocation in English. But Wodin's translator, John Brownjohn, opts on six out of seven occasions in (24b) to (30b) for the more standard RING + TELEPHONE, and on the seventh occasion, (27b), also produces a translation that is more-or-less consistent with target language norms.[28] Readers of German will also note that Brownjohn normalizes other aspects of Wodin's language in the examples listed above: narrative present is translated by the more distant and apparently more rational narrative past; tenseless 'sentences' in (25a), (29a) and (30a) are matched by translations with finite verbs;[29] the description of L's voice as *die rauhe Oberfläche einer Birne*, 'the rough surface of a pear' in (25a), is normalized to 'husky as only his voice could be' in (25b); and the effect of repetition in (29a) and (30a) is attenuated by the use of a logical connector, 'again', twice in (30b). Brownjohn's normalization of the SCHRILLEN + TELEFON collocation in Wodin's writing might thus be part of a broader trend of normalization in his translation of this author, a hypothesis that seems consistent with findings in Chapter Six.

---

[28] A literal translation of the fragment highlighted in (27a) might read 'the shrilling of the telephone still hangs in the air'.

[29] The highlighted fragments would translate literally as 'the shrilling of the telephone (under the bedclothes)'.

Summary statistics and discussion

In this Chapter, a number of unusual collocations in GEPCOLT have been discussed and their translations into English evaluated from the point of view of whether or not normalization has taken place. The findings of the analysis undertaken in this Chapter are presented in summary form in Table 16:

TYPE OF UNUSUAL COLLOCATION	number of examples	number normalized	% normalized	number compensated	% of normalized egs. compensated
exploitations of common collocations	6	4	66%	0	0%
decomposed compounds	1	0	0%	n/a	n/a
lexically cohesive collocations	1	0	0%	n/a	n/a
other unusual collocations	10	2	20%	0	0%
repeated idiosyncrasies[30]	41	7	17%	0	0%
TOTAL	59	13	22%	0	0%

Table 16: Normalization of creative collocations in GEPCOLT organized according to type of creative collocation.

Table 16 indicates that thirteen out of fifty nine, or 22% of the unusual collocations discussed in this Chapter, were normalized in translation. If 'repeated idiosyncrasies' are left out of the calculations in Table 16, the percentage of unusual collocations normalized – six out of eighteen – rises to 33%. This is still lower in percentage terms than the figure for normalization of creative hapax forms presented in Table 15 in Chapter Six, where it was noted that 44% of such forms uncovered in GEPCOLT were normalized in translation into English. It should be noted, however, that whereas the concern in Chapter Six was with describing how, in theory, *all* creative German hapax forms in GEPCOLT had been dealt with in translation, the concern in the first part of this Chapter has been mainly with the

[30] Each occurrence of each repeated idiosyncratic collocation discussed in this Chapter is included in this calculation. The single occurrence of SHRILLEN + TELEFON in Wellershoff's *Der Sieger nimmt alles* (31a) is not included here, as it is not repeated within that text.

collocational behaviour of a *single* hand-picked node. The investigation of another node could, of course, yield substantially different results. And while the category of 'repeated idiosyncrasies' does open the analysis up to collocations involving other lexical items, it, too, is limited in its coverage, focusing on only a handful of unusual collocations used by just two authors.

Notwithstanding the above comments, and those made in Chapter Six on the difficulty of comparing data from *ad hoc* categories, each of which contains a different (and often low) number of examples, some cautious observations can be made on the basis of Table 16. Firstly, it appears that unusual collocations based on exploitations of habitual source language collocations are more likely to be normalized in translation than other kinds of unusual collocations. One explanation for this finding could be that, like the derived forms and complex verbal nouns discussed in Chapter Six, such exploitations might be regarded as drawing on source-language specific systemic relations, rather than source-text specific relations, and thus as more susceptible to translation solutions that draw on the systemic resources of the target language. Secondly, Table 16 suggests that (non-displaced, non-generalized) compensation is an even more marginal reflex in cases where translators normalize unusual collocations than it was in cases of normalization of creative hapax legomena: compensation is not applied in any cases of normalization referred to in Table 16. Thirdly, Table 16 indicates that repeated idiosyncrasies are less likely to be normalized in translation than other unusual collocations. But despite the relatively high number of instances (forty one) considered in this category, it must be remembered that the data on repeated idiosyncrasies referred to in Table 16 are drawn from work by only two authors, Natascha Wodin and Unica Zürn, and only two translators, John Brownjohn and Malcolm Green. It is possible that an avoidance of normalization is a feature, for instance, of the translation output of a particular translator rather than a strategy prompted by a source text phenomenon such as a repeated collocational idiosyncrasy. Having said that, it does seem likely that the sheer preponderance of instances of a single repeated idiosyncrasy, in the work of Unica Zürn in particular, would militate against routine treatment in the target language: their very prominence would draw the translator's special attention to such instances, and probably elicit special, consistently applied, translation solutions. Note though, than even with a preponderance of instances of SCHRILLEN + TELEFON, some of which occur in close proximity to each other, Brownjohn still normalizes. Finally, Table 16 also makes no distinction between unusual collocations that represent mannered ways of describing common phenomena, like a phone ringing in Wodin's novel, and quite straightforward ways of describing uncommon or fantastic phenomena, like those experienced by Unica Zürn: the content of Zürn's writing predisposes both author and translator to used unusual collocations.

The role of the translator in normalization is brought into sharper focus in Table 17, which contains a breakdown of normalization patterns of unusual collo-

SOURCE TEXT FILE	translator	number of egs	number normal-ized	% normal-ized	number com-pensated	% of normal-ized egs compensated
Bier.de	Hannum & Rieder	2	1	50%	0	0%
Jelinek1.de	Hulse	5	1	20%	0	0%
Jelinek2.de	Hulse	1	0	0%	n/a	n/a
Kirchhof.de	Brownjohn	1	1	0%	n/a	n/a
Loest.de	Mitchell	1	0	0%	n/a	n/a
Roth1.de	Green	2	0	0%	n/a	n/a
Roth2.de	Green	1	0	0%	n/a	n/a
Wodin.de	Brownjohn	13	10	77%	0	0%
Zuern1.de	Green	2	0	0%	n/a	n/a
Zuern4.de	Green	31	0	0%	n/a	n/a
TOTAL		59	13	22%	0	0%

Table 17: Normalization of creative collocations in GEPCOLT involving the node AUGE, organized according to source text.

cations in GEPCOLT, organized according to source text. The second column in the Table indicates the translator(s) responsible for the target text in each case. As was pointed out in Chapter Six, it is difficult to come to definitive conclusions about the translation strategies adopted by particular translators, publishers, etc, given only a few examples of the output of each. What Table 17 tentatively suggests, however, is that Jill Hannum and Ines Rieder, translators of Pieke Biermann's *Violetta*, and John Brownjohn, translator of Bodo Kirchhoff's *Infanta* and Natascha Wodin's *Die gläserne Stadt*, are more likely to normalize odd collocations than are other translators. The findings for Rieder and Hannum in particular are based on very sparse data (there are only two examples), but they are consistent with the finding, reported in Chapter Six, that they normalize unusual hapax legomena more often than not, in fact in 66% of cases. Likewise the findings for John Brownjohn seem consistent with his tendency to normalize creative hapax forms also observed in Chapter Six. Malcolm Green, for whom more data is available (though most of the instances referred to in Table 17 relate to repeated idiosyncrasies in Unica Zürn's *Das Haus der Krankheiten*), seems to avoid normalization as a translation strategy, a finding already suggested in Chapter Six. The finding for Malcolm Green could, of course, have something to do with the nature of the source texts he translates, and also with how his publisher sees its remit. Atlas Press specializes in the publication of texts from the avant-garde 'anti-tradition' of the last one hundred years. Print runs are small, typically around a thousand copies. Atlas is thus catering for a non-mainstream market, one populated by readers who presumably appreciate experimental writing, in original texts and in translations. John Brownjohn's translations, on the other hand, are published by far larger, and more mainstream publishers such as Harvill, HarperCollins, and Harcourt Brace. Brownjohn's substantial translation oeuvre has been widely reviewed and acclaimed for its fluent, unstilted prose,[31] and he has received several major translation prizes.[32] If Brownjohn does normalize, it is not through lack of experience or expertise. His translation strategies may, on the contrary, be explained in terms of his excelling at writing the kind of fluent prose that is valued in translations in mainstream target language circles.

Conclusion

In this Chapter, as in Chapter Six, evidence of lexical normalization has been found in GEPCOLT, although it has also been shown that normalization is far from an automatic response to lexical creativity in source texts. In fact, most of the time, creative lexis in the source texts in GEPCOLT is not normalized in translation, and some translators prove to be ingenious wordsmiths in their own right.

I have, however, been wary of generalizations in this and the last Chapter, and have tendered explanations for observed phenomena only very gingerly. There are a number of reasons for such hesitancy. The first relates to the amount of evidence on which judgements are made: for many of the tendencies tentatively observed in GEPCOLT, the available evidence was sparse; a larger parallel corpus, with greater representation of each of the writers, translators, and publishers involved, would go some way towards allowing firmer conclusions to be reached about the factors that condition normalization in translation. Along with larger parallel corpora, we would need access to larger reference corpora in both source and target languages, in order to be more confident about what is 'normal' in each. There is good reason to be optimistic here: standard monolingual corpora have grown hugely in the four decades since the Brown corpus first became available, and they are also becoming increasingly accessible. There is no reason to suppose that this trend will stop. But developing larger parallel corpora will take a special commitment from members of the translation studies community. I hope the study presented in this book has shown that such efforts will be worthwhile.

A second reason for caution stems from the ultimately subjective nature of judgements about creativity. Corpora and lexicographical sources can give us a lot to go on, but as Alan Partington (1998:148) puts it, data collection is simply a prestep to analysis in corpus research, "for there is no automatic, technological means

---

[31] Such reviews are too numerous to list here. Extracts from many of them are reproduced in Brownjohn's own *Representative list of book translations from German and French, together with screen credits and extracts from reviews.*

[32] The prizes Brownjohn has received for German-English translation, include the US-PEN Goethe House Prize (1981), the Schlegel-Tieck Prize (1993), and the Helen and Kurt Wolff Prize (1998).

to pick out occurrences of unusuality. That is the domain of the mind". It would thus be inappropriate to suggest that my findings are definitive; they are one interpretation of the data I have chosen to look at. The value of studies such as the present one, however, is that they make public the evidence and methodologies on which judgements are based, inviting alternative interpretations, and suggesting improved studies.

I am also aware that, in an attempt to focus on certain types of lexical creativity, I have, at times, sought to isolate certain textual features from their surrounding co-text. This strategy is, of course, never completely successful, and on several occasions I have referred to the textual history of a form or collocation; on others the analysis has spilled over into grammatical analysis. This is how it should be. As neo-Firthian linguists have convincingly argued, lexis can never be completely separated from grammar, and no word is immune to its co-text. Meanings are not stored in the human mind "like so many file-cards in pigeonholes, waiting to be pulled out and plugged into sequences" (Beaugrande 1997:191). Rather they emerge on-line, as texts proceed. The analysis of each form presented in the last two Chapters could have drawn on more co-text. It could have made more of the interaction of lexis and grammar, not to mention the influence of extratextual features, but then we would not have covered the same ground. There is no doubt that any study of creativity and normalization in translation would benefit from a more holistic treatment, a treatment that would be completely consistent with the neo-Firthian approach to the study of texts, but whether such treatments will benefit from the availability of electronic text – and the corpus tools to process them – remains to be seen.

Caveats aside, the analysis of creativity presented in this and Chapter Six has suggested that certain translators may be more inclined to normalize than others, and that normalization may apply in particular to source text lexical features that draw on the more systematic processes of word formation in German – derivation and conversion to verbal nouns – and creative compounds and collocations that represent exploitations of more habitual lexical combinations. These are areas that could be explored in future, larger-scale research. As Alan Partington (1998:149) has said, the findings of corpus-based studies are in some ways always suggestions for future research.

Appendix 1
Works Included in the German-English Parallel Corpus of Literary Texts (GEPCOLT)

Note that bibliographic details given here are for the first publication of the work in each of German and English. The name of the electronic file holding each work is highlighted in bold and given in square brackets immediately after the bibliographic details of the work. These file names appear alongside bilingual examples extracted from GEPCOLT and listed in the main body of this book and in Appendix 3. The file naming convention applied enables Multiconcord, the program used to create these bilingual concordances, to match source texts with their target texts, as well as to identify which is the German text (*.de* extension) and which is the English one (*.en* extension).

Note also that Unica Zürn's *Der Mann im Jasmin* has been split into four separate electronic files, as indicated below. As well as enabling more efficient alignment and bilingual concordancing, this reflects the fact that the physical integrity of the published source text is difficult to preserve given that there are two separate publications in English (Green 1993 and 1994) for a single source text (Zürn 1977) and also that the translator translated one of the German texts, *Das Weise mit dem roten Punkt*, originally contained in Zürn (1977), not from the published version, but from the original, unamended manuscript. This original was not available in the present research and so it and its translation have been omitted from GEPCOLT. Likewise Green's translation, *In Ambush* (in Green 1994), of a 1963 text by Unica Zürn, has also been excluded from GEPCOLT as the original does not appear in Zürn (1977).

Works included in GEPCOLT:

Bayer, Konrad (1965) *der kopf des vitus bering* Vienna: ÖBV-Klett-Cotta Verlagsgesellschaft m.b.H. **[bayer.de]**
trans. Billeter, Walter (1994) *the head of vitus bering* London: Atlas Press. **[bayer.en]**

Biermann, Pieke (1990) *Violetta* Berlin: Rotbuch Verlag. **[bier.de]**
trans. Rieder, Ines & Hannum, Jill (1996) *Violetta* London and New York: Serpent's Tail. **[bier.en]**

Goldschmidt, Georges-Arthur (1991) *Die Absonderung* Zurich: Ammann Verlag AG. **[gold.de]**
trans. Kirkup, James (1993) *Worlds of Difference* London: Quartet Books Ltd. **[gold.en]**

Hofmann, Gert (1984) *Unsere Eroberung* Darmstadt and Neuwied: Hermann Luchterhand Verlag GmbH & Co KG. **[hofmann.de]**
trans. Middleton, Christopher (1987) *Our Conquest* Manchester: Carcanet Press Ltd. **[hofmann.en]**

Jelinek, Elfriede (1980) *Die Ausgesperrten* Reinbek bei Hamburg: Rowohlt Verlag GmbH. **[jelinek2.de]**
trans. Hulse, Michael (1990) *Wonderful, Wonderful Times* London: Serpent's Tail. **[jelinek2.en]**

Jelinek, Elfriede (1989) *Lust* Reinbek bei Hamburg: Rowohlt Verlag GmbH. **[jelinek1.de]**
trans. Hulse, Michael (1992) *Lust* London and New York: Serpent's Tail. **[jelinek1.en]**

Kirchhoff, Bodo (1990) *Infanta* Frankfurt am Main: Suhrkamp Verlag. **[kirchhof.de]**
trans. Brownjohn, John (1992) *Infanta* London: Harvill. **[kirchhof.en]**

Loest, Erich (1984) *Völkerschlachtdenkmal* Hamburg: Hoffmann und Campe Verlag. **[loest.de]**
trans. Mitchell, Ian (1987) *The Monument* London: Martin Secker & Warburg Ltd. **[loest.en]**

Ransmayr, Christoph (1984) *Die Schrecken des Eises und der Finsternis* Vienna: Christian Brandstätter Verlag und Edition. **[ransmayr.de]**
trans. Woods, John E. (1991) *The Terrors Of Ice And Darkness* London: George Weidenfeld and Nicholson Ltd. **[ransmayr.en]**

Roth, Gerhard (1972) *die autobiographie des albert einstein* Frankfurt am Main: Suhrkamp Verlag. **[roth1.de]**
trans. Green, Malcolm (1992) *the autobiography of albert einstein* London: Atlas Press. **[roth1.en]**

Roth, Gerhard (1986) *Am Abgrund* Frankfurt am Main: S. Fischer Verlag GmbH.**[roth2.de]**
trans. Green, Malcolm (in press) *On the Brink* London: Atlas Press. **[roth2.en]**

Wellershoff, Dieter (1983) *Der Sieger nimmt alles* Cologne: Kiepenheuer und Witsch. **[weller.de]**
trans. Knight, Paul (1986) *Winner Takes All* Manchester: Carcanet Press Ltd. **[weller.en]**

Wodin, Natascha (1983) *Die gläserne Stadt* Leipzig: Reclam Verlag. **[wodin.de]**
trans. Brownjohn, John (1986) *The Interpreter* San Diego and New York: Harcourt Brace Jovanovich. **[wodin.en]**

Zürn, Unica (1977) *Der Mann im Jasmin* Frankfurt am Main and Berlin: Verlag Ullstein GmbH.
(*Der Mann im Jasmin: Eindrücke aus einer Geisteskrankheit* **[zuern1.de]**; *Notizen zur letzten (?) Krise* **[zuern2.de]**; *Les Jeux à Deux* **[zuern3.de]**; *Das Haus der Krankheiten* **[zuern4.de]**)
trans. Green, Malcolm (1993) *The House of Illnesses* London: Atlas Press. **[zuern4.en]**
Green, Malcolm (1994) *The Man of Jasmine & Other Texts* London: Atlas Press. (*The Man of Jasmine: Impressions from a Mental Illness* **[zuern1.en]**; *Notes on Her Last (?) Crisis* **[zuern2.en]**; *Les Jeux à Deux* **[zuern3.en]**)

Appendix 2

Sample Header

```
<Header>
    <title>
        <filename>fn000026.txt</filename>
        <subcorpus>fiction</subcorpus>
        <collection>Unica Zürn</collection>
        <editor></editor>
    </title>
    <translation>
        <mode>written</mode>
        <extent></extent>
        <publisher>Atlas Press</publisher>
        <pubPlace>UK</pubPlace>
        <date>1994</date>
        <copyright>Malcom Green</copyright>
        <sponsor>The Arts Council of Great Britain</sponsor>
        <reviews></reviews>
        <comments></comments>
    </translation>
    <translator>
        <name>Malcom Green</name>
        <gender>male</gender>
        <Nationality>British</Nationality>
        <employment>Translator</employment>
        <status>full-time</status>
    </translator>
    <translationProcess>
        <direction>into mother tongue</direction>
        <mode>written from written source text</mode>
        <type>full</type>
    </translationProcess>
    <author>
        <name>Unica Zürn</name>
        <gender>female</gender>
        <sexualOrientation>heterosexual</sexualOrientation>
        <Nationality>German</Nationality>
    </author>
    <sourceText>
        <language>German</language>
        <mode>written to be read</mode>
```

<status>original</status>
<publisher>Verlag Ullstein GmbH</publisher>
<pubPlace>Germany; Austria</pubPlace>
<date>1977</date>
<comments></comments>
</sourceText>
</Header>

Appendix 3

Creative Hapax Forms in the German Subcorpus of GEPCOLT and their Translations into English

key: *Nrmlzd* = ***Normalized,*** *Comp* = ***Compensation,*** *n/a* = ***not applicable***

Table 18: Orthographically Creative Forms

	Source Segment	Target Segment	Nrmlzd	Comp
1.	wodin.de P492 S7 Die wahnwitzige russische **Aber-gläubigkeit**....	Wodin.en P492 Him and his crazy Russian **superstitions** ...	yes	no
2.	roth1.de P99 S5 a **spannungsimpulserl**, daua cirka o komma 5 millisekunden, **ambliduderl** 80 millivolt grabbelt üba de fasa von den neavn und pflanzt ihm sölba üba die nächste synapsn fuat	Roth1.en P99 a **lil impulse of 'lecktric tenshun**, takes abaart point five ovva millyseckund, **hamplytoode** ov 80 millyvolts sckrambulls 'long yer nerv fibers an' is propagaytid onna ovva siderv yer neckst synapps	no no	n/a n/a
3.	jelinek2.de P558 S8 Schreien ist nicht mehr möglich, denn Sophie hat sich geistesgegenwärtig und erstaunlich instinktsicher sofort auf seinen Mund geworfen, daß mich das Luder nur nicht beißt **haltjetztdiegoschn**, sonst haben wir auch für diesen Fall vorgesorgt und ein Messer bei uns.	Jelinek2.en P558 It is no longer possible to yell because Sophie, with great presence of mind and astonishing instinct, has instantly covered his mouth, the bastard had better not bite me **shutyertrap**, we're prepared for every eventuality and have a knife.	no	n/a
4.	jelinek2.de P406 S9 Da das Taschengeld gespart werden muß (wobei die Eltern es auch gleich behalten könnten), muß man bei der Oma oder dieser genannten Tante um Bluejeansgeld betteln und **kleinebotengängedurchführen**, was einen persönlich herabwürdigt und Raubüberfällen geradezu in die Arme treibt, weil man nicht anders kann.	Jelinek2.en P406 Since pocket money has to be saved (his parents might as well keep it themselves and have done with it), one has to go begging to Grandma or the aforementioned aunt for money to buy jeans, which means **running errands**, which robs one of one's personal dignity and practically forces one to assault and robbery, what alternative is there?	yes	no
5.	wodin.de P474 S1 ich bin das Pendel, und es geht ja längst nicht mehr um L oder Helmut, Deutschland oder Rußland, ich löse eine Menschheitsfrage, in der ich nicht mehr bin als ein Wassertropfen im Ozean, es geht um die Zahl Zwei, die in allen Dingen enthalten ist, wie nah liegt das Wort **Zwei-fel**, der über alles herrschende Gott Zweifel,	Wodin.en P474 I myself was that pendulum, and it had long ceased to oscillate between L and Helmut, Russia and Germany. I was solving a universal problem in which I represented no more than a drop in the ocean. The question at issue was the dichotomy inherent in all things, the figure **2** that formed the emblem of the Great God Doubt.	yes	yes

Table 19: Creative Derived Forms

	Source Segment	Target Segment	Nrmlzd	Comp
1.	jelinek2.de P736 S1 Hans schluckt **adamsäpfelnd**.	Jelinek2.en P736 Hans swallows. **His Adam's apple bobs**.	yes	no
2.	jelinek1.de P263 S4 Ihre empfehlenswerte **allerwerteste** Region hat er gründlich abgeerntet, da wächst so schnell kein Futter mehr.	Jelinek1.en P263 He has reaped her **high-yield** region thoroughly, it has his recommendation, and now there won't be any fodder growing there in a hurry.	yes	no
3.	wodin.de P573 S4 es sind die Hände eines Jünglings, die mich berühren, die Lippen eines Hermaphroditen, eines Wesens halb Mann, halb Frau, die mich küssen, einer Frau ohne Brüste und eines Mannes ohne Phallus, eines Wesens ohne die Schwüle und Wülste des Geschlechtlichen, nicht Vater und nicht Mutter, ausgeschlossen aus den Vorgängen **angstschweißiger** Körperlichkeit, den nie haltbaren Momenten der Lust, denen die grauenhafte Ernüchterung folgt,	Wodin.en P573 The hands that caress me are those of a youth, the lips that kiss me those of a hermaphrodite, half man, half woman, a man without a phallus and a woman without breasts, a creature without sexual protuberances, neither father nor mother, exempt from the processes of **fearful, sweating** carnality, the fleeting moments of pleasure that give way to terrible disenchantment.	yes	no
4.	jelinek1.de P195 S11 Sie leiht von oben ihr Antlitz, während er von unten aus seinem Handelskammerl heraus mit der **Doppelzunge** seines Geschlechts Versprechungen macht.	Jelinek1.en P195 Above, she puts a good face on things, while below he buries a bad face in things, hissing promises with his **forked tongue**.	yes	yes
5.	jelinek2.de P535 S3 Bei mir ist der Aktionsradius eingeschränkt, wegen **Einbeinigkeit**, aber wenn der Mensch das, was er macht, gut macht, so muß man es immer ernst nehmen.	Jelinek2.en P535 In my case the field of operations is limited on account of **oneleggedness** but if a person does what he does well you always have to take it seriously.	no	n/a
6.	bier.de P102 S8 Und leise, kaum hörbar für ihre eigenen Ohren: Nimm wenigstens den letzten Rest an Aufgeräumtheit und gesteh dir ein, daß du neidisch bist auf diese -, diese -! Jawohl, diese hirnverbrannten **Faustrechtlerinnen**, die dir voraus haben, daß sie ihren Kiez kennen, verdammt noch mal.	Bier.en P102 And softly, barely audible even to herself: "Just take the last little bit of your good mood and admit that you're jealous of these -, these crack-brained **women vigilantes** who have the advantage of knowing their patch. Damn it.	yes	no
7.	jelinek1.de P99 S3 Diese Frau steht auf den Papiersohlen der **Pantoffelheldinnen** da, die stundenlang verzweifelt Nahrung in sich herumirren lassen, die von ihren Familien verschmäht wurde.	Jelinek1.en P99 There she stands on her paper-thin soles. One of the **legion of henpeckers** who spend their lives eating leftovers spurned by the family.	yes	yes
8.	wodin.de P641 S10. Rußland riecht für mich nach Tod, es hat die Ausdünstung von L's vergifteter, **todesschweißiger** Haut.	Wodin.en P641 To me Russia now seemed redolent of death. It carried the effluvium of L's poisoned, **perspiring, moribund** flesh.	yes	no

Table 20: Creative Complex Verbal Nouns

	Source Segment	Target Segment	Nrmlzd	Comp
1.	wodin.de P11 S6 ... befand mich hier immer in der Zone der Illegalität, wie auch jetzt, immer im unklaren darüber, was im nächsten Augenblick geschehen kann, und immer wieder im Zweifel über mich selbst, ob ich nicht einem Wahn erliege, westlicher Kommunistenhetze auf den Leim gegangen bin, oder ob das alles von Anfang an nur in mir selbst liegt, mein ständiges Gefühl von Illegalität in diesem Land, von **Belangtwerdenmüssen**, weil ich die Tochter von Vaterlandsverrätern bin, weil Rußland immer eine Utopie für mich geblieben ist.	Wodin.en P11 ... I've always hovered in a twilight zone of illegality, as I do now, ever uncertain what might happen from one moment to the next, ever doubtful of myself and wondering whether I haven't succumbed to a delusion, fallen prey to Western anticommunist propaganda, or whether it was all inside me from the first, this eternal sense of illegality and **guilt**, because I'm the offspring of traitors to their country--this country--and because Russia has always remained a utopia for me.	yes	no
2.	wodin.de P147 S5 Aber es ist keine Erinnerung an Kinder, keine Gesichter, keine Stimmen, ein beständiges Abseits, ein beständiges **Dabeiseinwollen**, das nicht gelingt, bis auf das eine Mal, wo ich in der Mitte des Kreises stehe, und alle singen »flög ich zu dir« und deuten mit dem Finger auf mich.	Wodin.en P147 But even that isn't a recollection of children or faces. What I do recall is perpetual isolation, a perpetual **desire to join** in that was fulfilled only once, when I stood in the middle of the ring and everyone sang "to you" and pointed at me.	yes	no
3.	bier.de P23 S3 Auch das nonchalante **Einfachsodasitzen** ist nicht seine Stärke.	Bier.en P23 Just sitting there casually does not come easy to him.	yes	no
4.	gold.de P48 S5 soweit hatte er die Sprache schon verstanden: Zum **Geohrfeigtwerden** hatte man stramm zu stehen, mit den Händen an der Hosennaht, so hatte er auch die Zahlen gelernt, nach vier Ohrfeigen hatte man sich zu bedanken.	Gold.en P48 He had already grasped that much of the language: while **having your ears boxed** you had to stand stiffly to attention, hands held neatly against the trousers' side seams;	yes	no
5.	wodin.de P282 S4 Nicht nur das Essenkönnen, sondern auch das **Nicht-aufs-Klo-müssen** war eine deutsche Eigenschaft, eine Selbstverständlichkeit, die mir völlig, auf Gedeih und Verderb abging,	Wodin.en P282 **Not being allowed to go to the bathroom** was as German as being able to eat--a natural condition from which I was totally debarred, for better or worse.	yes	no
6.	roth2.de P233 S10 Wieder fiel Sonnenberg das Gesetz des »**Unbekannt-bleiben-Müssens**« ein, das er im Bus so stark gespürt hatte.	Roth2.en P233 Sonnenberg recalled once more the law of "**having-to-remain-unknown**" which he had felt so strongly in the bus.	no	n/a

Table 21: Other Creative Compounds

	Source Segment	Target Segment	Nrmlzd	Comp
1.	jelinek1.de P248 S6 Der Vater, für den es schon zur Jagd knallt, läßt in seinem **Abfahrergewand** bereits die Geschwindigkeit frei.	Jelinek1.en P248 Father, who is bursting to be off hunting, is already upping the tempo in his **he-man clothing**.	no	n/a
2.	jelinek1.de P96 S1 **Abgabenfest** wartet derweil der Direktor in seinem Büro und hilft uns nicht weiter, wenn wir an seine Tür pumpern.	Jelinek1.en P96 Meanwhile the Direktor is waiting in his office, and won't be any help to us if we go pounding at his door.	yes	no
3.	jelinek2.de P697 S1 Der **Abwaschwassertee** wird in Pappbecher geschöpft und für wenig Geld verkauft, das man für eine Maturareise spart.	Jelinek2.en P697 The **dishwater tea** is ladled into paper cups and sold for small sums that are being saved up for a school-leaving outing.	no	n/a
4.	roth1.de P118 S1 genug der trauer, genug des docierens, genug des zitierens, der mensch ist ja ein scheißdreck, die natur ein fäulnisprodukt, das angenehme ein eiterausschlag, die gesundheit ein furz, die liebe eine **afterlektion**, der glaube ein delirium, die arbeit eine folter, die schönheit ein gasbrand, die wissenschaft ein coitus interruptus, die gerechtigkeit eine hinrichtung, die treue impotenz, der freie wille eine hodenentzündung, die politik hämorrhoidalblut, der staat ein bordell, das mitleid heuchelei, die philosophie ein kadaver, die erziehung ist gehirnwäsche, die klugheit ist wundsekret, die weisheit fliegendreck, die ehre hundekot, der mut ein warzengeschwür, die freundschaft ist schorf, die musik eine menstrualblutung, die malerei ein abszeß, die schriftstellerei sputum, die kunst **altweiberpisse**, die hoffnung onanie, die stille ein abfallhaufen, der idealismus eine pestbeule, der fleiß latrinengestank, das leben ein kuhflattich, die soziale gesinnung eine kloake, die vorgesetzten sind arschlöcher, das theater ist bauchluft, der genuß schlangenfraß, die würdenträger sind schleimbeutel, die diskussionen analkonzerte, die demokratie fußschweiß, die freiheit wanzenbrut, die persönlichkeiten sind speichellecker, das benehmen ist eine akne, das angesehene von lepra befallen.	Roth1.en P118 enough of this sadness, enough of this lecturing, enough of these qotes, man is just a piece of shit, nature an end-product of putrescence, all that's pleasant a purulent rash, health a fart, love a **bum teaching**, faith a delirium, work torture, beauty a gas gangrene, science a coitus interruptus, justice an execution, faith impotence, free will an inflammation of the testicles, politics haemorrhoidal bleeding, the state a brothel, compassion hypocrisy, philosophy a cadaver, upbringing is brain-washing, cleverness a wound's exhudation, wisdom is fly shit, honour dog shit, courage a festering wart, friendship a scab, music menstrual bleeding, painting an abscess, writing sputum, art **old woman's piss**, hope masturbation, silence a pile of trash, idealism a plague bubo, industry the stench of latrines, life a cow pat, civic duty a sewer, bosses are arseholes, theatre is flatulence, pleasure venom, dignitaries are pustules, discussions anal concerts, democracy foot stench, freedom a verminous brood, personalities are toadies, good behaviour an acne, the well-thought-of afflicted with leprosy.	no no	n/a n/a
5.	jelinek2.de P543 S6 Halt, Anni, ich weiß etwas, um das klägliche Ergebnis zu verbessern, nämlich das **Andenkenbajonett** unseres Vaters, das er wiederum von seinem eigenen Vati hat, man glaubt nicht, daß dieses Ungeheuer Eltern besitzt, die es einmal geboren und gezeugt haben, er hat aber doch, Beweis: das Bajonett, welches noch aus dem Ersten Weltkrieg stammt.	Jelinek2.en P543 The result is pathetic. Hang on, Anni, I know how we can make it look less pathetic, Father's **souvenir bayonet**, which he in turn had from his Dad, you wouldn't believe this monster had parents who begat it and gave birth to it once upon a time, but he did, the bayonet is the proof, it dates back to the First World War.	no	n/a

6. jelinek2.de P531 S3 Die Anni wird immer dünner, und ihre Augen glühen dunkel aus ihrem verwunschenen Gesichtchen, wie Hans in einem lehrreichen Roman gelesen hat, aber manchmal fürchtet man sich entsetzlich, sieht man die Hoffnungslosigkeit dieser Generation in diesen **Annaaugen**, die keine Hinterwand haben, und so kann das scheußliche Außen direkt ins Gehirn wandern und dort gnadenlose Verheerungen anrichten.	Jelinek2.en P531 In her head, the darkness of absolutely evil deeds. These days, though, her tongue isn't exactly obeying instructions. Anni goes on getting thinner and thinner. Her eyes smoulder darkly in her bewitched face (Hans once read this in a most instructive novel), but sometimes you're terribly afraid when you glimpse the hopelessness of her generation in those **Annaeyes**, there is no wall behind them so the hideousness outside has free access to the brain and can cause pitiless devastation.	No	n/a
7. jelinek2.de P215 S3 Sie tut, als gehörte sie dahin, in Richtung **Annabrüste**.	Jelinek2.en P215 As if that were where it belonged, it ventures towards the **Annabreasts**.	No	n/a
8. jelinek2.de P40 S8 Die Mädel wälzen sich auf dem Fußboden der Gastwirtschaft, die blöde **Annakollegin**, die glaubt, aus einer Wurlitzer dringen Bachklänge und nicht das, was die Jugend liebt.	Jelinek2.en P40 The girls rolled about on the café floor, their stupid **schoolmate Anna** imagined you'd get Bach on a Wurlitzer and not what youngsters love.	Yes	no
9. jelinek2.de P558 S1 Hier ist die Einfahrt bereits, hinein und die Hand kleidunter geschoben, hier ist aber gleichzeitig auch das personifizierte Verbrechen des Diebstahls und Raubes eingetroffen, und als der Linzer unter dem **Annarock** wühlt, trifft den Linzerkopf ein harter Schlag aus einer fremden Faust, die sogar einem Arbeiter gehört: Hans.	Jelinek2.en P558 Here we are, the entry. In we go. And in goes the hand, shoved under the dress. But here comes the Crime of Robbery personified, too. And just as the fellow from Linz is rummaging about under the **Annaskirt**, his Linz-head is dealt a hard blow by an unknown fist, one that belongs to a worker at that: Hans.	No	n/a
10. jelinek2.de P144 S10 Die Lobby **Anna-Sophie-Rainer** weist derartiges zurück.	Jelinek2.en P144 The **Anna-Sophie-Rainer** lobby give stuff like this the thumbs-down.	No	n/a
11. wodin.de P582 S2 L mit seinem neuen, schlanken, verjüngten Körper, mit seinem alten **Apfeldieblachen** im Gesicht.	wodin.en P582 I couldn't take my eyes off L, with his new, slim, rejuvenated body and his old, inimitable, **mischievous smile**.	yes	no
12. roth2.de P162 S4 Ich betrachte verschwommenen Blicks mein Gesicht: eine **Mundnase**, ein **Nasenohr**, ein **Augenkinn**, ein **Lippenohr**, eine **Ohrenstirn**.	roth2.en P162 I study my face with my blurred vision: a **mouthnose**, a **noseear**, a **earlip**, an **eyechin**, an **earbrow**.	no x 5	n/a x
13. roth1.de P182 S1 ich werde in den tag hineingeschwemmt, ein stinkendes **ausgußtierchen** mit schielenden, platzenden facettenaugen,	roth1.en P182 i am washed out into the day, a stinking **little silverfish in the drain** with crossed, popping facet eyes,	yes	no
14. weller.de P810 S5 Dickere Äste, die ihre Rinde verloren hatten, waren silbergrau ausgebleicht oder fast **beinweiß**.	Weller.en P810 Thicker branches that had lost their bark had faded to silver-grey or **bone-white**.	No	n/a
15. bier.de P1623 S5 Der Hausmeister, ein hagerer junger Mann mit langen Haaren, Shorts und **Bergauf-Sandalen**, saß umringt von Redakteuren auf einem Stuhl davor, hielt die Hände auf den Unterbauch gepreßt und blutete im Gesicht.	Bier.en P1623 The caretaker, a gaunt young man with long hair, shorts and **sandals**, was sitting in front of it, with his hands pressed to his stomach, his face bleeding, and a group of editors around him.	Yes	no
16. jelinek1.de P7 S5 Die **Bergsöhne** schlafen manchmal schon um acht Uhr abends, während der Direktor mit geschickten Händen noch einmal Kunst in seinen Motor füllt.	jelinek1.en P7 At times the **sons of the mountains** are already asleep at eight in the evening, while the Direktor is adeptly filling more art into his engine.	no	n/a

	German	English		
17.	bier.de P1703 S5 Wahrscheinlich haben die sich wieder zusammengerauft, die beiden **Berufsteutonen**.	Bier.en P1703 The two **professional Teutons** have probably made up.	No	n/a
18.	jelinek2.de P406 S9 Da das Taschengeld gespart werden muß (wobei die Eltern es auch gleich behalten könnten), muß man bei der Oma oder dieser genannten Tante um **Bluejeansgeld** betteln und kleinebotengängedurchführen, was einen persönlich herabwürdigt und Raubüberfällen geradezu in die Arme treibt, weil man nicht anders kann..	jelinek2.en P406 Since pocket money has to be saved (his parents might as well keep it themselves and have done with it), one has to go begging to Grandma or the aforementioned aunt for **money to buy jeans**, which means running errands, which robs one of one's personal dignity and practically forces one to assault and robbery, what alternative is there?.	Yes	no
19.	jelinek1.de P165 S6 Wofür hätten sie sich denn und pflegten sich mit Wasser und **Duschemotionen**, als ob sie heiliggesprochen werden sollten?	Jelinek1.en P165 Why else would they have and hold each other, care for each other with water and **showers of emotion**, as if they were to be canonized?	Yes	yes
20.	bier.de P1908 S9 bloß eine Art **Eintagebärte** auf der Kopfhaut.	Bier.en P1908 They didn't have any, just a short **one-day stubble** on the scalp.	Yes	no
21.	kirchhof.de P1109 S1 Am späten Abend, nach einem weiteren verunglückten Essen, sprach er mit Butterworth über seine jüngsten, wie aus Grundschlamm aufgestiegenen **Erinnerungsbläschen**.	kirchhof.en P1109 Late that night, after another disastrous meal, he told Butterworth of his latest **recollections**, which seemed to rise **like bubbles** from primeval slime.	yes	no
22.	wodin.de P135 S5 Ich mache das Wetter. Die Jahreszeit der Erinnerung. **Erinnerungswetter**.	Wodin.en P135 I fabricate the weather, **mnemonic weather**, a season for remembering.	No	n/a
23.	wodin.de P33 S6 Die Blitze zuckten auf, erhellten sekundenlang das Zimmer, der Kirchturm vor dem Fenster leuchtete auf im **Feuerzickzack** und verlöschte.	Wodin.en P33 The church tower outside my window lit up, outlined by a **fiery zigzag**, and went out.	Yes	no
24.	wodin.de P407 S2 Sein Gesicht war eingetaucht in das bläuliche Licht der **Flammensterne**, die auf dem Gasherd brannten.	Wodin.en P407 The **gas rings** on the stove were alight, and his face was bathed in a bluish glow.	Yes	no
25.	wodin.de P499 S3 Ich wache auf, neben Helmut, in meinem **Fragen-keine-Antworten-Rad**.	Wodin.en P499 I awoke beside Helmut in my **wheel of unanswered questions**.	No	n/a
26.	jelinek2.de P364 S46 Man schwitzt mit ihr **Freizeitschweiß**, der angenehmer ist als der Arbeitsschweiß, weil er freiwillig geleistet wird.	Jelinek2.en P364 Watching her, they sweat the **sweat of leisure**, which is pleasanter than the sweat of labour because it is sweated on a voluntary basis.	No	n/a
27.	weller.de P2486 S1 »Was Sie da sagen, ist **Freizeitterrorismus**. Da lach' ich drüber.«	weller.en P2486 'That's just **armchair terrorism**. It makes me laugh.'	No	n/a
28.	wodin.de P341 S10 Und was die Karotten betrifft, an die denkst du lieber gar nicht erst, du nimmst, was du kriegst, was es gerade gibt, und es kann dir passieren, daß du plötzlich ein Kilo spottbilliger Krabben in deiner Awoska, deinem **Für-alle-Fälle-Netz**, hast.	Wodin.en P341 As for the carrots, better forget about them and use whatever you could get—whatever was going. You might conceivably come home with a couple of pounds of dirt-cheap prawns in your avoska, or **string shopping bag**.	Yes	no
29.	hofmann.de P72 S18 Ja, ruft er, während seine **Gabelfingerknochen** hart und weiß hervorstehen, was macht man nun mit ihnen?	Hofmann.en P72 Yes, he exclaims with his **fork fingerbones** sticking out hard and white, what are we going to do with you?	No	n/a
30.	roth1.de P150 S1 menschliche plasmamonstren, **gedankenchamäleone** mit krawatten, die über schultern flattern: vollhydraulisch!	roth1.en P150 human plasma-monsters, **mental chameleons** with neckties fluttering over their shoulders: completely hydraulic!	no	n/a

31. jelinek1.de P24 S14 Der Mann ergreift seinen ruhigen Binkel mit der Hand und drängt damit an die erstaunten Hintertüren seiner Frau. Die hört seinen Lendenwagen schon von fern kommen. Sie beginnt, kein Gefühl in sich wohnen zu lassen, aber wir haben ja noch einen Kofferraum! Da geht der schwere **Genitalienhaufen** hinein, nur keine Sorge wegen der Gerüche. Die Polster, überzeugend bezogen, bleiben nicht rein..	jelinek1.en P24 The Man takes hold of his wooden ding-a-ling and batters at the woman's astounded rear entry. She can hear the engine of his loins roaring closer from afar. She's beginning to banish all feeling from within her. But there's still room in the boot! And into the boot goes the heavy **genital load**, don't worry about the smell. The seats can't be kept clean anyway.	No	n/a
32. jelinek1.de P122 S3 Und auch wenn die Herren ihr Bein heben und ihr Wasser in ihre Begleiterinnen abschlagen, so dürfen sie doch nicht bleiben, müssen weitereilen, ruhelos, zum nächsten Baum, an den sich ihre **Genitalienwürmer** zornig klammern, bis jemand sie aufnimmt.	Jelinek1.en P122 And though the lordsandmasters cock their legs and slash their waters into their women, they can't remain but must hurry on, restless, to the next tree, where they waggle their **genital worms** till someone takes an interest.	No	n/a
33. jelinek1.de P168 S2 Er trägt oben den Scheitel und unten sein **Genitaltascherl**, das er seiner Frau mitgebracht hat, bis ihre Augen glänzen werden, wirst schon sehn!.	Jelinek1.en P168 He wears his hair parted, unruffled, and his **genitals in a bag** he's brought for his wife. How her eyes will light up! Wait and see!	Yes	yes
34. jelinek1.de P194 S6 Es wird ihnen auf Wunsch ins Gesicht gepißt, und still liegen sie unter dem **Geschlechtsbäumchen**, dessen Pflanzung sie noch selbst überwacht haben.	Jelinek1.en P194 If they wish it, women will piss in their faces. They lie still under the **tree of sex**, the planting of which they superintended themselves, and now they in turn are watered by the tree.	No	n/a
35. jelinek1.de P120 S6Er sieht, was er von den andren her gewöhnt ist, erkennt im Spiegel sich als seinen eigenen Gott, der in der Wassertiefe wandelt und angeln geht, spannt und kann sich schon schnurstracks die nächste Klientin zum Eindringen und Ohrfeigengeben vor den tropfenden **Geschlechtsbinkel** hängen. Die Technik ist nicht das Gemächte des Menschen, d. h. sie ist nicht das, was ihn so mächtig macht.	Jelinek1.en P120 In the mirror he sees himself reflected, his own deity. In the waters' depths. Fishing, plenty of fish in the sea, just hang out your **dripping rod** and wait for a catch, another woman to toss off your godhead in and then toss back. Ah, the privy parts and privy arts of mankind! All that's required of womankind is that she reck his rod (not wreck his rod), rock his godhead, toss his rocks off.	No	n/a
36. jelinek1.de P194 S2. Mit ihren mächtigen **Geschlechtspaketen** sind sie auf der Suche nach einem lieben Schoß, in dem sie auf Dauer wohnen möchten, diese Männer.	Jelinek1.en P194 With their mighty **packs of genitals** these men are out searching for a bosom where they can lay their heads for good..	no	n/a
37. jelinek1.de P170 S9 Nicht einmal das leise Reiben, mit dem das Wasser auf ihre **Geschlechtspinsel** rinnt, mit denen sie einander ihre Wünsche ausmalen, macht sie so milde, daß sie gut wären zu ihren lebendigen Gütern, diesen ängstlichen Angestellten in ihren Todeszellen.	Jelinek1.en P170 Not even the ever so slight friction of water on the **sex brushes** they use to paint each other's wishes can make them good to the goods and chattels they keep chattering with fear in the death cell.	No	n/a
38. jelinek1.de P29 S13 Wohlgeordnete Knechte, stehen sie vor ihren **Geschlechtswürsten** und hauen mit dem Besteck auf den Tisch, daß ihnen schneller ein Loch serviert werde, in das sie sich verziehen können, nur um wieder, noch gieriger geworden, aufzutauchen und neuen Unbedürftigen ihre Gastfreundschaft anzutragen.	Jelinek1.en P29 Well-ordered –servants, there they stand with the **sausages of their sex**, banging their cutlery on the table, wanting a hole to be served up fast, a hole to hide away in, only to re-emerge greedier than ever, to offer their hospitable services once again to those who have no need of them.	No	n/a

German	English		
39. gold.de P9 S4 Nach der weiten Fernen über Fernen aufdeckenden Norddeutschen Ebene fingen Berge an vorbeizuziehen, kleine spitze Berge, die ersten, die er gesehen hatte, als hätten **Himmelsfinger** die **Erdenhaut** stellenweise nach oben gezogen.	Gold.en P9 After the vast North German plain with its endless horizons, small pointed mountains drifted past, the first he had ever seen, looking as if **heavenly fingers** had hauled up the **earth's skin** here and there.	No no	n/a n/a
40. jelinek2.de P364 S11 Es beunruhigt ihre Zuschauer, daß diese **Hochglanzleute** auch nur ein einziges Privatleben haben, genau wie sie auch, wenn sie dieses verlieren, kriegen sie kein neues.	Jelinek2.en P364 Their viewers are disturbed at the thought that these **glossy people** have any private life at all, just like themselves, if they lose it they won't get another.	No	n/a
41. jelinek1.de P143 S16 Es ist jedoch geschickt genug, sich ans Schlüsselloch zu begeben und selber zu brüllen, wenn es mit dem Stock um der oberflächlichsten Trübung seines **Hosentürchens** willen schon gehaut wird.	jelinek1.en P143 And good at ructions of his own, too, when he's beaten for wetting his pants.	yes	no
42. jelinek2.de P179 S3 Der Gymnasiast mit dem **Hühnerarm** schaut ihn aber nur angeekelt an.	Jelinek2.en P179 However, the grammar school boy with his **scrawny arm** merely gives him a disgusted look.	Yes	no
43. wodin.de P588 S6 Alles an ihr, jede Linie in ihrem Gesicht, ist Bewegung, Wachheit, Empfindsamkeit, Wärme. Die kleinen **Ironieteufelchen** hat auch sie in den blau gesprenkelten Augen.	Wodin.en P588 Everything about her, every line of her face conveyed vivacity, warmth, and sensitivity; a little **demon of irony** lurked in the flecked blue depths of her eyes.	No	n/a
44. jelinek2.de P532 S1 Anna perlt den schnellen Satz **japanisch-zuchtperlenhaft**.	Jelinek2.en P532 Anna trickles off the pearls of the fast movement **as though they were Japanese cultured pearls**.	Yes	no
45. roth2.de P94 S3 Für meine Mutter sang ich Lieder in der **Kaulquappensprache**.	Roth2.en P94 I sang songs to my mother in the **language of the tadpoles**.	No	n/a
46. kirchhof.de P1929 S29 Eine **Kinderbibelschönheit**, wenn Sie den Ausdruck erlauben. «	kirchhof.en P1929 The one on the notorious poster – **a lovely creature like something out of a children's Bible**, if you'll pardon the comparison.	Yes	no
47. wodin.de P458 S13 Bald wird deutsches Leben nur noch im Museum zu besichtigen sein. Es leidet an Durchblutungsstörungen, seine Gefäße sind verengt. Es ist eine sklerotische Greisin, es hört und sieht nicht mehr. Es ist ein Tier, auf das man schießt, um das Interieur damit zu schmücken. Es ist eine Rechenaufgabe, ein Terminkalender, ein Sachbuch, eine **Klitorisgruppe**, ein Gesprächskreis, ein Bausparvertrag, ein Sexshop, ein Therapiewochenende, eine Hausratsversicherung.	Wodin.en P458 Before long, German life would be a museum piece only. It was suffering from circulatory disorders and hardening of the arteries. It was a sclerotic old crone, unable to see or hear, an animal to be shot for purposes of interior decoration, an arithmetic problem, a mortgage deed, a sex shop, a weekend therapy session, a home-insurance policy.	Yes	no
48. jelinek1.de P58 S2 Mißmutig wenden sich die Größeren unter ihnen ab und lassen Liftkarten über ihre wattierten **Körperfutterale** baumeln, Geschwindigkeit ist keine Hexerei.	Jelinek1.en P58 Sullenly the older ones turn away, their chair-lift tickets dangling at their **padded rotundities**.	No	n/a
49. bier.de P1398 S1 »Der Wagen mit dem **Körriewurschtfresser** is immer noch weg, wa?«	bier.en P1398 "The car with the **guy and his curry sausage**. It's still gone?"	yes	yes
50. jelinek2.de P382 S5 **Kreischgackergacker**.	jelinek2.en P382 **Screech cackle cackle**.	yes	no

51.	loest.de P316 S3 Eine perfekte **Kriegsnachtstraße** mit Schritten und fernen Stimmen, in sie hinein sagte der Mann: »Weißt du, daß der Führer am Denkmal war?«	loest.en P316 A perfect **wartime nocturnal street-scene**, with the sounds of footsteps and distant voices, into which the man said: 'Did you know, the Führer was at the Monument?'	yes	no
52.	ransmayr.de P777 S36 Dort unten stand jetzt einer, blickte hoch und schützte sich mit erhobenen Armen gegen die von den Rotorblättern hochgepeitschten **Kristallschleier**.	Ransmayr.en P777 Someone was standing down below now, looking up with arms raised to ward off the **curtain of crystals** whipped up by the rotors.	No	n/a
53.	bier.de P1428 S1 »Das kann wirklich kein Mensch ahnen, daß ausgerechnet hier jetzt eine **Kulturbeutelparade** stattfindet«, sagte Schade entschuldigend, als Lietze sich endlich zu dem Tisch im hintersten rechten Bogen der Galerie durchgezwängt hatte.	Bier.en P1428 "Nobody could've guessed there'd be some **culture vulture thing** going on here of all places," Schade apologised, after Lietze had finally forced her way through to the table in the furthest away bay on the right hand side of the gallery.	Yes	yes
54.	loest.de P295 S3 Wenn ein Grabenstück zermalmt war, brachen oben Sturmtrupps vor, aber immer noch war ein Maschinengewehr geblieben, das **ladehemmungslos** aus der Flanke den Angriff niederwarf.	Loest.en P295 Whenever a section of their trenches had crumbled, assault troops swarmed in over the top, but there was always that one machine-gun left, which **never seemed to jam**, but cut down the attack from its flank.	Yes	no
55.	jelinek1.de P96 S5 Die können von ihrem Platz aus nicht einmal den gedeckten Tisch voller Soziallasten sehen, setzen sich auf ihre Lederhosenboden und stoßen Schreie aus, weil da schon einer als ihr Abgeordneter hockt und ihr **Lebenssaftkonzentrat** frisch aus der Dose trinken möchte.	Jelinek1.en P96 From where they sit they can't even see all the social burdens that are heaped on the groaning table. There they sit, on the seats of their leather shorts, yawping to find their member of parliament already sitting there, wanting to drink their **life juice concentrate** straight from the can.	No	n/a
56.	loest.de P164 S3 Wenn in Deutschland um die Freiheit gekämpft worden war, hatte es selten an polnischen **Leihhelden** gefehlt.	Loest.en P164 Whenever there had been a struggle for freedom in Germany, there had been no lack of Polish **hired heroes**.	No	n/a
57.	wodin.de P281 S1 aber Schwester Marianne stieß mir den Löffel zwischen die Zähne, einen nach dem anderen, bevor ich zum Durchatmen kam, einen Löffel für die Mutti, einen für den Vati, einen für die Oma, einen für den Opa, ich mußte mir eine Unzahl von Tanten und Onkels anessen, essen, damit sie entstehen und dick und kugelrund werden konnten, ich wurde gemästet, genudelt mit einer gigantischen Verwandtschaft, die nicht einmal in meiner Vorstellung vorhanden war, und später spie ich sie wieder aus in hohem Bogen, graubraune **Linsenonkels** und gelbe **Puddingtanten**, deutsche Cousinen und Cousins, deren Existenz für mich ich mir so heiß wünschte, die einem Appetit und andere glückliche Eigenschaften zu verleihen schienen.	Wodin.en P281 She thrust the spoon between my teeth again and again, before I could even draw breath: "One for Mamma, one for Papa, one for Grandma, one for Grandpa ... " I had to eat for a whole host of German aunts and uncles—eat them into corpulent, potbellied existence. I was force-fed and crammed on behalf of a multitudinous family whose existence defied even my fertile imagination, only to spew them up when lunch was over: **lentil-gray uncles**, **blancmange-yellow aunts**, and a gaggle of assorted culinary cousins whose function was to impart an appetite and other desirable qualities.	No no	n/a n/a
58.	wodin.de P401 S3 Jeden Tag wollte ich abfliegen, und jeden Tag blieb ich. Aber nach zwei Wochen stand ich doch im Lufthansa-Büro am Kusnezki-Most und fragte nach dem nächsten freien Platz in einer Maschine. Der Mann in **Lufthansablau** tippte etwas in den Computer, schaute auf den Bildschirm, schaute auf mich: »Am 2. Februar um achtzehn Uhr, okay?«	wodin.en P401 Every day I yearned to leave, and every day I stayed on, but two weeks later I did go to the Lufthansa office on Kuznetski Most and ask for a seat on the next available flight. The man in **Lufthansa blue** keyed something into his computer, looked at the screen, looked at me: "February 2, six in the evening. Okay?"	no	n/a
59.	wodin.de P174 S5 mein Blick ist auf die hintere Zuhörerreihe geheftet, so habe ich das gelernt, man schaut auf die letzte Reihe, was jedem einzelnen Zuhörer das Gefühl vermittelt, sich im Blickfeld des Sprechers zu befinden, während irgendwelche zweiten Augen von mir über die Gesichter unter mir wandern, die schwarzhaarige Frau mit den russischen **Melancholieaugen**, die einen Block auf den Knien hat und sich Notizen macht, sehr akkurat, sehr ernsthaft, in einer weißen Bluse,	wodin.en P174 I kept my gaze focused on the back of the hall, the way I'd been taught, to give every listener the feeling that he was in the speaker's range of vision, while a second pair of eyes somewhere in my head wandered over the faces below me: the dark-haired, white-bloused woman with the **melancholy Russian eyes**, who had a pad on her lap and was making notes, very earnestly, very meticulously;	yes	no

	German	English		
60	wodin.de P19 S5 Er sitzt auf einer Brüstung, etwas nach hinten geneigt, sich mit den Händen hinter dem Körper abstützend, mit seinem **Mir-gehört-die-ganze-Welt-Lächeln** im gebräunten Gesicht.	Wodin.en P19 It shows him perched on a balustrade, leaning backward slightly with both hands on the rail, tanned face wearing his **world-is-my-oyster smile**.	No	n/a
61.	wodin.de P567 S6 Für mich liegt ein erster eigener Rosenkranz unter dem Weihnachtsbaum im Musikzimmer. **Mutterblaue** Perlen und ein silbernes Kreuzchen.	Wodin.en P567 On this, my very first Catholic Christmas, Sister Marie-Joseph presents me with my first-ever rosary, from beneath the Christmas tree in the music room: **blue** beads and a little silver crucifix.	Yes	no
62.	wodin.de P376 S11 Schön sieht sie aus in ihrem **mutterblauen** Seidenkleid. Sie legt den Arm um mich. «Wollen wir morgen früh, weißt du, wenn die Sonne scheint und der Schnee wie **Diamantenstaub** in der Luft aussieht, eine Skiwanderung machen? »	wodin.en P376. Bella, being "family," was also there, looking lovely in a blue silk dress. She put an arm around my shoulders. "How about coming skiing tomorrow morning--really early, when the sun's still shining and the snow looks like **diamond dust**?"	yes	no
			no	n/a
63.	wodin.de P450 S21 Sehe das Kind vor dem Schrank, sehe Kleider, die auf Bügeln hängen, blaue Kleider, **Mutterfarbe**, und das Kind zerreißt Kleider, noch eins und noch eins, das ganze Zimmer voller blauer Fetzen, und trampelt mit den Füßen darauf.	Wodin.en P450 I see myself standing in front of the wardrobe, see dresses suspended on hangers, see myself tearing them to shreds, one after another, until the whole room's full of blue wisps, see myself trample them underfoot.	Yes	no
64.	wodin.de P149 S16 Manchmal auch Ukrainisch, Ukraina, so heißt es auf Russisch, ein so weites blaues Wort, **Mutterwort**, wenn wir singen: powi witre, tischkom nischkom.	wodin.en P149 Or sometimes in Ukrainian. Ukraina, they call it in Russian. Such a blue, spacious, **maternal word**. "Povi vitre, tishkom nishkom," we sing.	no	n/a
65.	jelinek2.de P574 S1 Sophie wendet vor Rainers Geseire ihre patentierte **Ohrenzuklapptaktik** an ...	jelinek2.en P574 Sophie responds to Rainer's pesky drivel with her patented **ear-closing technique**.	No	n/a
66.	gold.de P261 S1 Mit vor Angst zu kurz gewordenen Beinen, aber ganz klarem Kopf war er **rucksackgeschultert** an dem Lastwagen vorbeigegangen, mit langen, ein wenig wippenden Bergsteigerschritten, die zeigen sollten, wie sehr er doch ein Einheimischer war.	Gold.en P261 His legs shrunken with terror, but with a clear head he had **shouldered his rucksack** as he passed the truck with long, rather rolling mountaineer's strides, intending to show how very much he was at home there.	Yes	no
67.	loest.de P39 S1 Ach, wäre ich doch bei meiner Einheit geblieben, in einem **Sachsenpulk**.	loest.en P39 Oh, if only I had stayed with my unit, in a **cluster of Saxons**.	no	n/a
68.	jelinek1.de P151 S1 Der **Schlaraffenrock** (im Reich der Mode der Reichen gekauft. In Wien!) schlenkert an der todmüden Frau herum.	Jelinek1.en P151 The **undressing-gown** flaps about the woman. She's dead tired.	No	n/a
69.	wodin.de P492 S25 Mein unfehlbarer Wochenkalender vor dem Fenster, seit fünf Jahren. Schuheputzen ist Montag, Kleiderlüften ist Dienstag, Wäscheaufhängen ist Mittwoch, Fensterputzen ist Freitag. An diesem **Schuhputz-Montag** rufe ich L an und sage, daß ich komme.	Wodin.en P492 My unerring guide to the day of the week for the past five years, right outside my window: Monday was shoe-cleaning, Tuesday clothes-airing, Wednesday laundry-drying, Friday window-cleaning. This particular **shoe-cleaning Monday** I put a call through to L and told him I was coming.	No	n/a
70.	roth1.de P150 S3 , straßenbahnleitungen, abblätternde hausmauern, **schwarzzerklüftet** von feuchtem ruß, gasrohre, tintenschwarze fensteröffnungen, medikamente essen, zigaretten rauchen, identitätslose rote ziegelwände, alte weißhaarige kriecher, toilettenschläfer, tick-tack, juckreiz, ein skelett mit augäpfeln, venenschlangen von porenlöchrigen hautsäcken verhüllt, ein mensch wie ein tintenfisch, wurmwelt, madeneier, raupengewimmel, rinnsale, dachböden, ratten, strychninköder, ein herrlich blauer zungenpömmel, salpetersäure, heroin, zentimeterlange würmer!	roth1.en P150 tram wires, flaking house walls, **black fissures** from damp soot, gas pipes, inky black window openings, eat medicaments, smoke cigarettes, red brick walls without identities, old white haired crawlers, toilet sleepers, tic-toc, itching, a skeleton with eyeballs, vein-snakes covered with pore-perforated bags of skin, a man like a sqid, worm-world, maggot eggs, teeming caterpillars, rivulets, attics, rats, strychnine bait, a wonderfully blue tassle of a tongue, nitric acid, heroin, centimetre long worms!	yes	no

71. hofmann.de P98 S22 Butterschmalz, sagt der Herr Schlachthofdirektor und spuckt, weil auch er den schlechten **Schweinehausgeschmack** ein für allemal loswerden will, ein paarmal kräftig auf den Boden, gibt es keins.	Hofmann.en P98 Butterschmalz, the director says, and because he too wants, once and for all, to be rid of the bad **pig house taste**, he spits on the ground vigorously a few times, there isn't any.	No	n/a
72. hofmann.de P98 S1 Draußen auf der Großen Viehstraße klopfen wir uns den Rock und die Hose von der **Schweinehausluft** gut ab.	Hofmann.en P98 Outside, on the Great Cattle Path, we brush the **pig house air** well and truly of our coat and trousers.	No	n/a
73. wodin.de P55 S14 Ich warf mich irgendwelchen Kadern, Gogolschen **Seelenverwesern** vor die Füße und flehte um Gnade, um Gunst, um Milde, um ihr Ja,	wodin.en P55 I threw myself at the feet of imaginary party officials, Gogolesque **bureaucrats**, and craved their mercy, their favor, their indulgence, their approval.	Yes	no
74. bier.de P1787 S1 Bei der Vorstellung, daß ausgerechnet der Biedermann Fahlenkamp dem Biedermann und Brandstifter Henke in die notorische **Seitensprungparade** gefahren war, mußte Lietze grinsen.[1]	Bier.en P1787 The idea that good citizen Fahlenkamp had crossed good citizen and arsonist Henke because of the latter's **little infidelities**, made Lietze smile.	Yes	no
75. weller.de P902 S4 Die Vögel waren plötzlich vor ihm aufgetaucht, so als wären sie flach über die Straße auf ihn zugeflogen, ein Schwarm von **Selbstmördervögeln**, zwei mußte er erwischt haben.	Weller.en P902 The birds suddenly appeared, as if they had flown at him low across the road, a flock of **suicidal birds**, he must have caught two of them.	No	n/a
76. wodin.de P134 S6 Sommer. Immer Sommer. Als hätte in der ganzen Kindheit die Sonne geschienen. Oder so: nur das, was im Sommerlicht liegt, ist noch zu sehen. Eine **Sonnen-Kindheit**. **Sonnen-Erinnerung**. Der Winter kommt nicht vor. Winterstrecken in der Erinnerung. Eingeschneite Erinnerung.	Wodin.en P134 Summer, always summer, as if the sun had shone throughout my childhood, or as if only what the light of summer illumines can still be seen. Winter never happens. Wintry expanses in the memory are clogged with snow.	Yes	no
77. bier.de P691 S3 Er versuchte ein **stinkfreundliches** Lächeln, aber es blieb im Schmerz stecken.	Bier.en P691 He attempted a **super-friendly smile**, but it faltered because of the pain.	Yes	yes
78. bier.de P229 S7 Und auch nicht **stöckelschuhfreundlich** genug.	bier.en P229 And it wasn't **high-heel-friendly** either.	no	n/a
79. ransmayr.de P538 S3 er, der **strapazenscheue** Jansen, wünsche dem japanischen Kollegen die Anerkennung der Fachwelt und trinke auf ihn als den beharrlichen Freund der Vögel Kvitøyas.	Ransmayr.en P538 He, Jansen, **disliked such rigours**, but wished his Japanese colleague the recognition due him from his peers and drank to him as the unwavering friend of the birds of Kvitøya.	Yes	no
80. kirchhof.de P1633 S30 Sie hatte mich gewissermaßen zum **Strohfreund** erkoren - ich spürte während der Zigarre förmlich die erste Schwiegersohnprüfung.	kirchhof.en P1633 She'd elected me her **dummy boyfriend**, so to speak, and I distinctly sensed, during the cigar, that I was undergoing a preliminary son-in-law inspection.	no	n/a
81. wodin.en P5 Aber während ich noch in ihr eingeschlossen bin wie im Innern einer unterirdischen Ader, naht bereits der Augenblick, wo ich dem zuvorkommen muß: wie die Helligkeit zuerst in den noch farblosen Vorhang am Fenster kriecht, dann, durch den Stoff hindurch, an der Wand entlang ins Zimmer, umherschleichend, die Gegenstände streifend, einen nach dem anderen an sich reißend, die Furie der Helligkeit, ihr magisches Theater, die Gewöhnung der Augen, der Beginn der **Super-horror-picture-show**.	wodin.en P5 But even as I lie here like a nugget in a subterranean lode, the moment of dread anticipation draws near. Light will tinge the still-colorless curtain over the window, seep through the fabric, creep along the wall and into the room, insidiously caress and possess each object in turn. Then will come the entrance of the Gorgon, daylight, and the habituation of my eyes to her magic theater, her **super-horrific picture show**.	no	n/a

[1] Example 74 also contains an allusion to Max Frisch's play *Biedermann und die Brandstifter*, an allusion that is not successfully captured in the target text.

82.	wodin.de P584 S4 Ein wesentlicher Schritt zur Normalisierung des **Tag-und-Nacht-Ablaufs**: getrennte Schlafzimmer.	Wodin.en P584 Separate rooms were a big step toward normalizing the **day-and-night cycle**.	No	n/a
83.	zuern4.de P47 S17 Ich besaß den widerlichsten Tod aller **Todespersönlichkeiten**: einen Militaristen.	Zuern4.en P47 I had the most revolting death of all: an army officer.	Yes	yes
84.	bier.de P1736 S16 Eine **Undercover-Feministin**?	bier.en P1736 An **undercover feminist**?	no	n/a
85.	wodin.de P539 S5 Die **Vatersonne** versinkt im Meer, dort drüben geht schon der **Muttermond** auf. Der Sonne. Die Mond.[2]	wodin.en P539 **Father Sun** was sinking into the sea, **Mother Moon** already rising. The sun, the moon ...	no no no	n/a n/a n/a
86.	loest.de P336 S1 Eine Mine lag in einem Hof zwischen Sparren und Ziegelschutt, ein **Wohnblockknacker** von Rang;	loest.en P336 A mine lay in a courtyard among fallen rafters and broken bricks and tiles, a **prize specimen that could have wiped out a whole block of flats**;	yes	no
87.	wodin.de P606 S11 Irgend jemand, der sie aus einzelnen, bunt zusammengewürfelten deutschen Typen zusammengesetzt hat, die deutschen Buchstaben hineingeschweißt hat in ein russisches Gestell, ein Rätsel, wie das möglich war, wie das funktioniert, aber es funktioniert. Nur meine Finger müssen sich noch ein bißchen umstellen, sich anpassen an die Idee eines russischen **Wundermechanikers** von der Typenanordnung einer deutschen Schreibmaschine.	Wodin.en P606 Just how someone had contrived to graft Roman type blocks onto a Cyrillic machine was an enigma to me, but it worked, although I did have to reeducate my fingers a little to accord with a Russian **mechanic's** notion of how the characters on a German typewriter were arranged.	Yes	no
88.	bier.de P934 S2 Bisher haben die sich jedenfalls nicht durch **Zwischen-den-Zeilen-Botschaften** profiliert.	bier.en P934 So far they haven't distinguished themselves with **between-the-lines messages**.	no	n/a

[2] In example 85, Wodin first creates the compound, *Vatersonne*, out of a head, *Sonne*, that is grammatically feminine and a modifier, *Vater*, that is naturally masculine, and then the compound *Muttermond*, out of a head, *Mond*, that is grammatically masculine and a naturally feminine modifier, *Mutter*. The clashes thus created are taken up again in the second sentence in 88, where Wodin attempts to invert the grammatical genders of *Sonne* and *Mond*. The effect cannot be carried across to English where there is no grammatical gender. Despite the loss of this effect in English translation, Wodin'' compounds are not considered to have been normalised as they are translated by the unusual collocations 'father sun' and 'mother moon'.

References

Aijmer, Karin and Bengt Altenberg (eds) (1991) *English Corpus Linguistics: Studies in Honour of Jan Svartvik,* London: Longman.

------ Bengt Altenberg and Mats Johansson (eds) (1996) *Languages in Contrast: Papers from a Symposium on Text-based Cross-linguistic Studies, Lund 4-5 March 1994,* Lund: Lund University Press.

Aitchison, Jean (1994) *Words in the Mind,* 2nd edition, Oxford and Cambridge, MA: Basil Blackwell.

Al-Shabab, Omar Sheikh (1996) *Interpretation and the Language of Translation: Creativity and Convention in Translation,* London: Janus.

al-Wadi, Doris (1994) *COSMAS Benutzerhandbuch,* Mannheim: Institut für deutsche Sprache.

Armstrong, Susan (ed) (1994) *Using Large Corpora*, Cambridge, MA and London: MIT Press.

Armstrong-Warwick, Susan (1994) 'Acquisition and Exploitation of Textual Resources for NLP', in Antonio Zampolli, Nicoletta Calzolari and Martha Palmer (eds), 451-465.

Arrojo, Rosemary (1998) 'The Revision of the Traditional Gap between Theory and Practice and the Empowerment of Translation in Postmodern Times', *The Translator* 4(1): 25-48.

Aston, Guy and Lou Burnard (1998) *The BNC Handbook: Exploring the British National Corpus with Sara,* Edinburgh: Edinburgh University Press.

Atkins, B.T.S. and Antonio Zampolli (eds) (1994) *Computational Approaches to the Lexicon,* Oxford: Oxford University Press.

------ Beth Levin and Antonio Zampolli (1994) 'Computational Approaches to the Lexicon: An Overview', in B.T.S.Atkins and Antonio Zampolli (eds), 17-45.

Atkins, Sue, Jeremy Clear and Nicholas Ostler (1992) 'Corpus Design Criteria' *Literary and Linguistic Computing* 7(2): 1-16.

Baker, Mona (1992) *In Other Words: A Coursebook on Translation,* London and New York: Routledge.

------ (1993) 'Corpus Linguistics and Translation Studies. Implications and Applications', in Mona Baker, Gill Francis and Elena Tognini-Bonelli (eds), 233-250.

------ (1995) 'Corpora in Translation Studies: An Overview and Some Suggestions for Future Research', *Target* 7(2): 223-243.

------ (1996a) 'Linguistics and Cultural Studies: Complementary or Competing Paradigms in Translation Studies?', in Angelika Lauer, Heidrun Gerzymisch-Arbogast, Johann Haller and Erich Steiner (eds) *Übersetzungswissenschaft im Umbruch: Festschrift für Wolfram Wilss zum 70. Geburtstag,* Tübingen:Gunter Narr Verlag, 9-19.

------ (1996b) 'Corpus-based Translation Studies: The Challenges that Lie Ahead', in Harold Somers (ed) *Terminology, LSP and Translation: Studies in Language Engineering, in Honour of Juan C. Sager,* Amsterdam and Philadelphia: John Benjamins, 175-186.

------ (1998a) 'Norms', in Mona Baker (ed), 163-165.

------ (ed) (1998b) *Routledge Encyclopedia of Translation Studies,* London and New York: Routledge.

------ (1999) 'The Role of Corpora in Investigating the Linguistic Behaviour of Professional Translators', *International Journal of Corpus Linguistics* 4(2): 281-298.

------ (2000) 'Linguistic Perspectives on Translation', in Peter France (ed), 20-26.

------ (in press) 'Linguistic Models & Methods in the Study of Translation', in Armin Paul Frank, Norbert Greiner, Theo Hermans, Harald Kittel, Werner Koller, José Lambert and Fritz Paul (eds) *Übersetzung * Translation * Traduction,* Berlin and New York: Walter de Gruyter.

------ (in press, 2000) 'Towards a Methodology for Investigating the Style of a Literary Translator', *Target* 12(2): 241-268.

------ and Michael McCarthy (1990) 'Multi-Word Units and Things Like That', unpublished research paper, Birmingham: University of Birmingham.

------ Gill Francis and Elena Tognini-Bonelli (eds) (1993) *Text and Technology: In Honour of John Sinclair,* Amsterdam and Philadelphia: John Benjamins.

Bakker, Matthijs, Cees Koster and Kitty Van Leuven-Zwart (1998) 'Shifts of Translation', in Mona Baker (ed), 226-231.

Barnbrook, Geoff (1996) *Language and Computers,* Edinburgh: Edinburgh University Press.

Bassnett, Susan and André Lefevere (eds) (1990) *Translation, History and Culture,* London and New York: Routledge.

Bayer, Samuel, John Aberdeen, John Burger, Lynette Hirschmann, David Palmer and Marc Vilain (1998) 'Theoretical and computational linguistics: toward a mutual understanding', in John Lawler and Helen Aristar Dry (eds), 231-255.

Bazell, C. E., J.C. Catford, M.A.K. Halliday and R.H. Robins (eds) (1966) *In Memory of J.R. Firth,* London: Longmans, Green and Co. Ltd.

Beaugrande, Robert de (1994) 'Function and form in language theory and research: The tide is turning', *Functions of Language* 1(2): 163-200.

------ (1997) 'On history and historicity in modern linguistics: Formalism versus functionalism revisited', *Functions of Language* 4(2): 169-213.

------ (1998) 'Performative speech acts in linguistic theory: The rationality of Noam Chomsky', *Journal of Pragmatics* 29: 765-803.

Bell, Roger (1991) *Translation and Translating: Theory and Practice,* London and New York: Longman.

Benson, Morton, Evelyn Benson and Robert Ilson (1986a) *The BBI combinatory dictionary of English,* Amsterdam and Philadelphia: John Benjamins.

------ (1986b) *Lexicographic Description of English,* Amsterdam and Philadelphia: John Benjamins.

Berry-Rogghe, Godelieve (1973) 'The computation of collocations and their relevance in lexical studies', in A.J. Aitken, R.W. Bailey and N. Hamilton-Smith (eds) *The Computer and Literary Studies,* Edinburgh: Edinburgh University Press, 103-112.

------ 'Automatic identification of phrasal verbs', in J.L. Mitchell (ed) *Computers in the Humanities,* Edinburgh: Edinburgh University Press, 16-26.

Biber, Douglas (1994) 'Representativeness in Corpus Design', in Antonio Zampolli, Nicoletta Calzolari and Martha Palmer (eds), 377-407.

Bloomfield, Leonard (1933) *Language,* New York: Holt.

Blum-Kulka, Shoshana (1981) 'The study of translation in view of new developments in discourse analysis: the problem of indirect speech acts', *Poetics Today* 2(4): 89-95.

------ (1986) 'Shifts of cohesion and coherence in translation', in Juliane House and Shoshana Blum-Kulka (eds) *Interlingual and Intercultural Communication: Discourse and Cognition in Translation and Second Language Acquisition Studies,* Tübingen: Gunter Narr, 17-35.

Botley, Simon, J. Glass, Tony McEnery and Andrew Wilson (eds) (1996) *Proceedings of Teaching and Language Corpora 1996,* UCREL Technical Papers 9, Lancaster: UCREL.

Bowker, Lynne (1998) 'Using specialized monolingual native-language corpora as a translation resource: a pilot study', in Sara Laviosa (ed), 632-651.

------ (1999) 'The design and development of a corpus-based aid for assessing translations', *Teanga* 18: 11-24.

------ Michael Cronin, Dorothy Kenny and Jennifer Pearson (eds) (1998) *Unity in Diversity? Current Trends in Translation Studies,* Manchester: St. Jerome.

Brown, Peter F., Jennifer C. Lai and Robert L. Mercer (1991) 'Aligning sentences in parallel corpora', *Proceedings, 29th Annual Meeting of the Association for Computational Linguistics,* Berkeley Ca., 169-176.

------ John Cocke, Stephen A. Della Pietra, Vincent J. Della Pietra, Fredrik Jelinek, John D. Lafferty, Robert, L. Mercer and Paul S. Roossin (1990) 'A Statistical Approach to Machine Translation', *Computational Linguistics* 16(2): 79-85.

------ Stephen A. Della Pietra, Vincent J. Della Pietra and Robert L. Mercer (1993) 'The Mathematics of Statistical Machine Translation: Parameter Estimation', *Computational Linguistics* 19(2): 263-311.

Burnard, Lou (1992) 'Tools and Techniques for Computer-assisted Text Processing', in Christopher S. Butler (ed), 1-28.

------ (1995a) 'The Text Encoding Initiative: an overview', in Geoffrey Leech, Greg Myers and Jenny Thomas (eds) *Spoken English on Computer,* London: Longman, 69-81.

------ (ed) (1995b) *Users Reference Guide for the British National Corpus: Version 1.0,* Oxford: Oxford University Computing Services.

Butler, Christopher S. (ed) (1992) *Computers and Written Texts,* Oxford and Cambridge, MA: Basil Blackwell.

Cahoone, Lawrence E. (1996) 'Introduction', in Lawrence E. Cahoone (ed) *From Modernism to Postmodernism: An Anthology,* Oxford and Cambridge MA: Basil Blackwell, 1-23.

Carter, Ronald (1987) *Vocabulary,* London and New York: Routledge (reprint 1994).

Catford, J. C. (1965) *A Linguistic Theory of Translation: An Essay in Applied Linguistics,* London: Oxford University Press.

Catizone, Roberta, Graham Russell and Susan Warwick (1991) 'Deriving translation data from bilingual texts', in Uri Zernik (ed) *Proceedings of the First International Lexical Acquisition Workshop,* Detroit, 1-7.

Charniak, Eugene (1993) *Statistical Language Learning,* Cambridge MA: MIT Press.

Chesterman, Andrew (1993) 'From 'Is' to 'Ought': Laws, Norms and Strategies in Translation Studies', *Target* 5(1): 1-20.

------ (1997) *Memes of Translation. The Spread of Ideas in Translation Theory,* Amsterdam and Philadelphia: John Benjamins.
Chomsky, Noam (1957) *Syntactic Structures,* The Hague: Mouton.
------ (1965) *Aspects of the Theory of Syntax,* Cambridge, MA: MIT Press.
------ (1986) *Knowledge of Language: Its Nature, Origin and Use,* New York: Praeger.
------ (1988) *Language and Problems of Knowledge: The Managua Lectures,* Cambridge MA: MIT Press.
Choueka, Yaacov (1988) 'Looking for needles in a haystack' *Proceedings, RIAO Conference on User-Oriented Context Based Text and Image Handling,* Cambridge, MA, 609-623.
Church, Kenneth and Patrick Hanks (1990) 'Word association norms, mutual information, and lexicography', *Computational Linguistics* 16(1): 22-29.
------ William Gale, Patrick Hanks and Donald Hindle (1991) 'Using Statistics in Lexical Analysis', in Uri Zernik (ed), 115-164.
Clear, Jeremy (1987) 'Overview of the Role of Computing in Cobuild', in John Sinclair (ed), 41-61.
------ (1988) 'Trawling the language: Monitor Corpora', in Mary Snell-Hornby (ed), 383-389.
------ (1993) 'From Firth Principles: computational tools for the study of collocation', in Mona Baker, Gill Francis and Elena Tognini-Bonelli (eds), 271-292.
Collier, Alex (1993) 'Issues of large-scale collocational analysis', in Jan Aarts, Pieter de Haan and Nelleke Oostdijk (eds) *English Language Corpora: Design, Analysis and Exploitation,* Amsterdam and Atlanta: Rodopi, 289-298.
Cruse, David A. (1986) *Lexical Semantics,* London, New York, New Rochelle, Melbourne and Sydney: Cambridge University Press.
Delabastita, Dirk (1996a) 'Introduction', in Dirk Delabastita (ed), 127-139.
------ (ed) (1996b) *The Translator* 2(2), Special Issue on Wordplay & Translation.
Deleuze, Gilles and Félix Guatarri (1980) *Milles Plateaux: Capitalisme et schizophrénie,* Paris: Les Editions de Minuit.
------ (1987) *A Thousand Plateaus: Capitalism and Schizophrenia,* trans. of Deleuze and Guatarri (1980) by Brian Massumi, Minneapolis MN: University of Minnesota Press.
Delisle, Jean (1980) *L'Analyse du discours comme méthode de traduction,* Ottawa: University of Ottawa Press.
------ (1993) *La traduction raisonnée: Manuel d'initiation à la traduction professionnelle de l'anglais vers le français,* (Collection Pédagogie de la traduction), Ottawa: Presses de l'Université d'Ottawa.
Dunning, Ted (1993) 'Accurate Methods for the Statistics of Surprise and Coincidence' *Computational Linguistics* 19(1): 61-74.
Durrell, Martin (1991) *Hammer's German Grammar and Usage revised 2nd edition,* London, Sydney and Auckland: Eward Arnold.
Ebeling, Jarle (1998) 'The Translation Corpus Explorer: A browser for parallel texts', in Stig Johansson and Signe Oksefjell (eds), 101-112.
Engwall, Gunnel (1994) 'Not Chance but Choice: Criteria in Corpus Creation', in B.T.S. Atkins and Antonio Zampolli (eds), 49-82.

ENPC (1997) *English-Norwegian Parallel Corpus: Manual,* http://www.hd.uib.no/enpc.html.

Even-Zohar, Itamar (1978) 'The Position of Translated Literature within the Literary Polysystem', in James Holmes, José Lambert and Raymond van den Broeck (eds), 117-127.

------ (1979, 1990) 'Polysystem Theory', *Poetics Today* 11(1): 9-26.

Facchinetti, Roberta (1998) 'Drawbacks and Pitfalls of Machine-Readable Texts for Linguistic Research', *International Journal of Corpus Linguistics* 3(2): 211-228.

Fawcett, Peter (1997) *Translation and Language: Linguistic Theories Explained,* Manchester: St. Jerome.

Fillmore, Charles J. (1992) '"Corpus linguistics" or "Computer-aided armchair linguistics"', in Jan Svartvik (ed), 35-60.

Firth, J.R. (1957) *Papers in Linguistics 1934-1951,* London, New York and Toronto: Oxford University Press.

------ (1968) *Selected Papers of J.R.Firth 1952-59,* edited by F.R. Palmer, London and Harlow: Longmans, Green and Co. Ltd.

France, Peter (ed) (2000) *The Oxford Guide to Literature in English Translation,* Oxford: Oxford University Press.

Francis, Gill (1991) 'Nominal group heads and clause structure', *Word* 42(2): 144-156.

------ (1993) 'A Corpus-Driven Approach to Grammar – Principles, Methods and Examples', in Mona Baker, Gill Francis and Elena Tognini-Bonelli (eds), 137-156.

------ and John Sinclair (1994) "I Bet He Drinks Carling Black Label': A Riposte to Owen on Corpus Grammar', *Applied Linguistics* 15(2): 190-200.

Francis, W. N. (1992) 'Language Corpora B.C.', in Jan Svartvik (ed), 17-32.

Frawley, William (1984) 'Prolegomenon to a Theory of Translation', in William Frawley (ed) *Translation: Literary, Linguistic, and Philosophical Perspectives,* London and Toronto: Associated University Presses, 159-175.

Gaddis Rose, Marilyn (1996) *Translation Horizons. Beyond the Boundaries of 'Translation Spectrum', Translation Perspectives IX,* Binghampton: State University of New York.

Gale, William A. and Kenneth W. Church (1993) 'A Program for Aligning Sentences in Bilingual Corpora', *Computational Linguistics* 19(1): 75-102.

Garside, Roger (1987) 'The CLAWS word-tagging system', in Roger Garside, Geoffrey Leech and Geoffrey Sampson (eds), 30-41.

------ Geoffrey Leech and Geoffrey Sampson (eds) (1987) *The Computational Analysis of English: A Corpus-based Approach,* London: Longman.

Gellerstam, Martin (1986) 'Translationese in Swedish novels translated from English', in Lars Wollin and Hans Lindquist (eds) *Translation Studies in Scandinavia. Proceedings from the Scandinavian Symposium on Translation Theory II,* Lund:CWK Gleerup, 88-95.

------ (1992) 'Modern Swedish text corpora', in Jan Svartvik (ed), 149-163.

Gentzler, Edwin (1993) *Contemporary Translation Theories,* London and New York: Routledge.

Godard, Barbara (1990) 'Theorizing Feminist Discourse/Translation', in Susan Bassnett and André Lefevere (eds), 87-96.

Götz, Dieter, Günther Haensch and Hans Wellmann (eds) (1997) *Langenscheidts Großwörterbuch Deutsch als Fremdsprache,* 8th edition, Berlin and Munich: Langenscheidt KG.

Graddol, David, Jenny Cheshire and Joan Swann (1994) *Describing Language*, 2nd edition, Buckingham and Bristol, Pa.: Open University Press.

Green, Malcolm (1994) 'afterword', in Konrad Bayer *the head of vitus bering,* translated by Walter Billeter, London: BCM Atlas Press, 57-61.

Greenbaum, Sidney (1970) *Verb-Intensifier Collocations in English. An experimental approach,* The Hague and Paris: Mouton.

------ (1974) 'Some Verb-Intensifier Collocations in American and British English', *American Speech* 49: 79-87.

Gregory, Michael J. (1980) 'Perspectives on Translation from the firthian tradition', *Meta* 25(4): 455-466.

Grice, H. Paul (1975) 'Logic and conversation', in L. Cole and J. L. Morgan (eds) *Syntax and Semantics* 3: *Speech Acts,* New York: Academic Press, 41-58.

Halliday, M.A.K. (1961) 'Categories of the Theory of Grammar', *Word* 17(3): 273-277.

------ (1964) 'Comparison and Translation', in M.A.K. Halliday, Angus McIntosh and Peter Strevens *The Linguistic Sciences and Language Teaching,* London: Longmans, Green and Co., 111-134.

------ (1966) 'Lexis as a Linguistic Level', in C.E. Bazell, J.C. Catford, M.A.K. Halliday and R.H. Robins (eds), 148-162.

------ (1978) *Language as social semiotic,* London: Edward Arnold.

------ (1991) 'Corpus studies and probabilistic grammar', in Karin Aijmer and Bengt Altenberg (eds), 30-43.

------ (1992) 'Language as system and language as 'instance': The corpus as a theoretical construct', in Jan Svartvik (ed), 61-77.

------ and R. Hasan (1976) *Cohesion in English,* London: Longman.

Halverson, Sandra (1998) 'Translation studies and representative corpora: establishing links between translation corpora, theoretical/descriptive categories and a conception of the object of study', in Sara Laviosa (ed), 494-514.

Hanks, Patrick (1988) 'Typicality and meaning potentials', in Mary Snell-Hornby (ed), 37-47.

------ (1996) 'Contextual Dependency and Lexical Sets', *International Journal of Corpus Linguistics* 1(1): 75-98.

------ (1997) 'Norms and exploitations in linguistic behaviour or, *baked sprouts and freshly baked ensaimadas*', in Barbara Lewandowska-Tomaszczyk and Patrick James Melia (eds), 206-224.

Harvey, Keith (1995) 'A Descriptive Framework for Compensation', *The Translator* 1(1): 65-86.

------ (1998) 'Translating Camp Talk. Gay Identities and Cultural Transfer', in *Translation and Minority,* Special issue of *The Translator* 4(2), guest-edited by Lawrence Venuti, 295-320.

Haskel, Peggy I. (1971) 'Collocations as a measure of stylistic variety', in R.A.Wisbey (ed) *The computer in literary and linguistic research - Papers from a Cambridge Symposium,* Cambridge: Cambridge University Press, 159-168.

Hatim, Basil and Ian Mason (1990) *Discourse and the Translator,* London and New York: Longman.

------ (1997) *The Translator as Communicator,* London and New York: Routledge.

Henry, Ruth (1992) 'Begegnung mit Unica (Zürn)', afterword in Unica Zürn *Der Mann im Jasmin,* revised edition, Frankfurt and Berlin: Ullstein, 171-183.

Herbst, Thomas (1996) 'What are collocations: sandy beaches or false teeth?', *English Studies* 77(4): 379-393.

Hermans, Theo (1985a) 'Translation Studies and a New Paradigm', introduction to Theo Hermans (ed), 7-15.

------ (ed) (1985b) *The Manipulation of Literature: Studies in Literary Translation,* London and Sydney: Croom Helm.

------ (1996) 'Norms and the Determination of Translation: A Theoretical Framework', in Román Álvarez and M. Carmen-África Vidal (eds) *Translation, Power, Subversion* Clevedon, Philadelphia and Adelaide: Multilingual Matters, 25-51.

------ (1999) *Translation in Systems,* Manchester: St. Jerome.

Herrnstein Smith, Barbara (trans) (1978) *On the Margins of Discourse: The Relation of Literature to Language*, Chicago: Chicago University Press.

Hockey, Susan (1998) 'Textual databases', in John M. Lawler and Helen Aristar Dry (eds), 101-137.

Hofland, Knut and Stig Johansson (1998) 'The Translation Corpus Aligner: A program for automatic alignment of parallel texts', in Stig Johansson and Signe Oksefjell (eds), 87-100.

House, Juliane (1981) *A Model for Translation Quality Assessment,* Tübingen: Gunter Narr.

------ (1997) *Translation Quality Assessment: A Model Revisited,* Tübingen: Gunter Narr.

Johansson, Stig (1980) 'The LOB Corpus of British English Texts: Presentation and Comments', *ALLC Journal* 1: 25-36.

------ (1995) '*Mens sana in corpore sano*: On the Role of Corpora in Linguistic Research', *The European English Messenger* 4(2): 19-25.

------ (1998) 'On the role of corpora in cross-linguistic research', in Stig Johansson and Signe Oksefjell (eds), 3-24.

------ and Knut Hofland (1994) 'Towards an English-Norwegian parallel corpus', in Udo Fries, Gunnel Tottie and Peter Schneider (eds) *Creating and using English language corpora: Papers from the Fourteenth International Conference on English Language Research on Computerized Corpora, Zürich 1993,* Amsterdam and Atlanta: Rodopi, 25-37.

------ Jarle Ebeling and Knut Hofland (1996) 'Coding and Aligning the English-Norwegian Parallel Corpus', in Karin Aijmer, Bengt Altenberg and Mats Johansson (eds), 87-112.

------ and Signe Oksefjell (eds) (1998) *Corpora and Cross-linguistic Research,* Amsterdam and Atlanta, GA: Rodopi.

Jones, Susan and John Sinclair (1974) 'English Lexical Collocations: A Study in Computational Linguistics', *Cahiers de Lexicologie* 24: 15-61.

Kano, Nadine (1995) *Developing International Software for Windows® 95 and Windows NT™,* Redmond, WA: Microsoft Press.

Katz, Jerrold J. and Jerry Fodor (1963) 'The structure of a semantic theory', *Language* 39: 170-210.

Keenoy, Ray, Mike Mitchell and Maren Meinhardt (1997) *The Babel Guide to German Fiction in English Translation [Austria, Germany, Switzerland]*, London: Boulevard Books.

Kelly, Louis (1979) *The True Interpreter: A History of Translation Theory and Practice in the West*, Oxford: Basil Blackwell.

Kennedy, Graeme (1998) *An Introduction to Corpus Linguistics*, London and New York: Longman.

Kenny, Dorothy (1996) 'It looks for all the world as if Günter Grass writes in English...', *Translation Ireland* 10(3): 12-13.

------ (1998a) 'Equivalence', in Mona Baker (ed), 77-80.

------ (1998b) 'Creatures of Habit? What translators usually do with words', in Sara Laviosa (ed), 515-523.

King, Philip (1997) 'Parallel corpora for translator training', in Barbara Lewandowska-Tomaszczyk and Patrick James Melia (eds), 393-402.

Kittay, Eva Feder (1987) *Metaphor: its cognitive force and linguistic structure*, Oxford: Clarendon Press.

Kjellmer, Göran (1982) 'Some Problems Relating to the Study of Collocations in the Brown Corpus', in Stig Johansson (ed) *Computer Corpora in English Language Research 1975-1981*, Bergen: The Norwegian Computing Centre for the Humanities, 25-33.

------ (1984) 'Some Thoughts on Collocational Distinctiveness', in Jan Aarts and Willem Meijs (eds) *Corpus Linguistics: Recent Developments in the Use of Computer Corpora in English Language Research*, Amsterdam: Rodopi, 163-171.

------ (1987) 'Aspects of English Collocations', in Willem Meijs (ed), 133-140.

------ (1990) 'Patterns of Collocability', in Jan Aarts and Willem Meijs (eds) *Theory and Practice in Corpus Linguistics*, Amsterdam and Atlanta: Rodopi, 163-178.

Kučera, H. and W. N. Francis (1967) *Computational Analysis of Present-Day American English*, Providence, Rhode Island: Brown University Press.

Lakoff, George and Mark Johnson (1980) *Metaphors We Live By*, Chicago: University of Chicago Press.

Laviosa, Sara (1997) 'How Comparable Can 'Comparable Corpora' Be?', *Target* 9(2): 289-319.

------ (1998a) 'The English Comparable Corpus: A Resource and a Methodology', in Lynne Bowker, Michael Cronin, Dorothy Kenny and Jennifer Pearson (eds), 101-112.

------ (1998b) 'Core patterns of lexical use in a comparable corpus of English narrative prose', in Sara Laviosa (ed), 557-570.

------ (ed) (1998c) *L'approche basée sur le corpus/The corpus-based approach*, Special issue of *Meta* 43(4).

Laviosa-Braithwaite, Sara (1996) *The English Comparable Corpus (ECC): A Resource and a Methodology for the Empirical Study of Translation*, unpublished PhD thesis, Manchester: UMIST.

------ (1998) 'Universals of translation', in Mona Baker (ed), 288-291.

Lawler, John (1998) 'The Unix™ language family', in John M. Lawler and Helen Aristar Dry (eds), 138-169.

------ and Helen Aristar Dry (eds) (1998) *Using Computers in Linguistics: a practical guide,* London and New York: Routledge.

Lawson, Ann (1997) 'English words in use: compiling a dictionary of collocation', in Barbara Lewandowska-Tomaszczyk and Patrick James Melia (eds), 225-235.

Lecercle, Jean-Jacques (1990) *The Violence of Language,* London and New York: Routledge.

Leech, Geoffrey (1991) 'The state of the art in corpus linguistics', in Karin Aijmer and Bengt Altenberg (eds), 8-29.

------ (1992) 'Corpora and theories of linguistic performance', in Jan Svartvik (ed), 105-122.

------ and Steven Fligelstone (1992) 'Computers and Corpus Analysis', in Christopher S. Butler (ed), 115-140.

Lefevere, André and Susan Bassnett (1990) 'Proust's Grandmother and the Thousand and One Nights: The 'Cultural Turn' in Translation Studies', introduction to Susan Bassnett and André Lefevere (eds), 1-13.

Lehr, Andrea (1996) *Kollokationen und maschinenlesbare Korpora: Ein operationales Analysemodell zum Aufbau lexikalischer Netze,* Tübingen: Niemeyer.

Leppihalme, Ritva (1996) 'A Target-Culture Viewpoint on Allusive Wordplay', in Delabatista (ed), 199-218.

Leuven-Zwart, Kitty van (1989) 'Translation and Original: Similarities and Dissimilarities, I', *Target* 1(2): 151-181.

------ (1990) 'Translation and Original: Similarities and Dissimilarities, II', *Target* 2(1), 69-95.

Lewandowska-Tomaszczyk, Barbara and Patrick James Melia (eds) (1997) *PALC '97: Practical Applications in Language Corpora Proceedings*, Lódz: Lódz University Press.

Louw, Bill (1993) 'Irony in the Text or Insincerity in the Writer? The Diagnostic Potential of Semantic Prosodies', in Mona Baker, Gill Francis and Elena Tognini-Bonelli (eds), 157-176.

------ (1997) 'The Role of Corpora in Critical Literary Appreciation', in Anne Wichmann, Steven Fligelstone, Tony McEnery and Gerry Knowles (eds) *Teaching and Language Corpora,* London and New York: Longman, 240-251.

Lyons, John (1977) *Semantics,* Cambridge: Cambridge University Press.

------ (1981) *Language and Linguistics: An Introduction,* Cambridge: Cambridge University Press.

Malmkjær, Kirsten (1997) 'Punctuation in Hans Christian Andersen's stories and in their translations into English', in F. Poyatos (ed) *Non-verbal Communication in Translation,* Amsterdam and Philadelphia: John Benjamins, 151-162.

------ (1998) 'Love thy neighbour: Will parallel corpora endear linguists to translators?', in Sara Laviosa (ed), 532-541.

Martin, W.J.R., B.P.F. Al and P.J.G. Sterkenburg (1983) 'On the processing of a text corpus: from textual data to lexicographical information', in R.R.K. Hartmann (ed) *Lexicography: Principles and Practice,* London: Academic Press, Inc., 77-87.

Mason, Ian (1994) 'Discourse, Ideology and Translation', in Robert de Beaugrande, Abdulla Shunnaq and Mohamed Heliel (eds) *Language, Discourse and Translation in the West and Middle East,* Amsterdam and Philadelphia: John Benjamins, 23-34.

Mason, Oliver (1996) 'Corpus Access Software: The Cue System', *TEXT Technology* 6(4): 257-266.

------ (1997) 'The weight of words: an investigation of lexical gravity', in Barbara Lewandowska-Tomaszczyk and Patrick James Melia (eds), 361-375.

May, Rachel (1997) 'Sensible Elocution: How Translation Works in & upon Punctuation', *The Translator* 3(1): 1-20.

McEnery, Tony and Andrew Wilson (1996) *Corpus Linguistics,* Edinburgh: Edinburgh University Press.

Meijs, Willem (ed) (1987) *Corpus Linguistics and Beyond,* Proceedings of the Seventh International Conference on English Language Research on Computerized Corpora, Amsterdam: Rodopi.

Mitchell, T.F. (1975) *Principles of Firthian Linguistics,* London: Longman.

Mounin, Georges (1963) *Les problèmes théoriques de la traduction,* Paris: Gallimard.

Munday, Jeremy (1998) 'A computer-assisted approach to the analysis of translation shifts', in Sara Laviosa (ed), 542-556.

Nakamura, Junsaku and John Sinclair (1995) 'The World of *Woman* in the Bank of English: Internal Criteria for the Classification of Corpora', *Literary and Linguistic Computing* 10(2): 99-110.

Neubert, Albrecht and Gregory M. Shreve (1992) *Translation as Text,* Kent, Ohio: The Kent State University Press.

Newman, Aryeh (1987) 'Translation Universals – Perspectives and Explorations', in Marilyn Gaddis Rose (ed) *Translation Perspectives III: Selected Papers 1985-86,* Binghamtom, New York: State University of New York at Binghamton, 69-83.

Newmeyer, Frederick J. (1980) *Linguistic Theory in America,* New York and London: Academic Press.

Nida, Eugene (1964) *Toward a Science of Translating,* Leiden: E.J.Brill

Nielsen, Jane and Anne Wichmann (1994) 'A Frequency Analysis of Selected Modal Expressions in German and English Legal Texts', *Hermes* 13: 145-155.

Nord, Christiane (1991) 'Scopos, Loyalty, and Translational Conventions', *Target* 3(1): 91-109.

Ó Cróinín, Donncha (1999) 'Corpus Náisiúnta na Gaeilge/National Corpus of Irish', *Teanga* 18: 65-70.

Olohan, Maeve and Mona Baker (in press, 2000) 'Reporting *that* in Translated English: Evidence for Subconscious Processes of Explicitation?', *Across Languages and Cultures* 1(2).

Olson, Gary A. and Lester Faigley (1991) 'Language, Politics, and Composition: A Conversation with Noam Chomsky', in Gary Olson and Irene Gales (eds) *Interviews: Cross-disciplinary perspectives on rhetoric and literacy,* Carbondale: Southern Illinois University Press, 61-95.

Opas, Lisa Lena and Pekka Kujamäki (1995) 'A Cross-linguistic Study of Stream-of-consciousness Techniques', *Literary and Linguistic Computing* 10(4): 287-291.

Øverås, Linn (1996) *In Search of the Third Code: An Investigation of Norms in Literary*

Translation, unpublished Cand. Philol. thesis, Oslo: University of Oslo.
------ (1998) 'In search of the third code: an investigation of norms in literary translation', in Sara Laviosa (ed), 571-588.
Packalén, Sture (1994) 'Syntagmatische Lexemstrukturen in Forschung und Lehre', *Studia Neophilogica* 66: 223-230.
Palmer, Frank Robert (1968) 'Introduction', in Firth (1968), 1-11.
Partington, Alan (1995) 'True friends are hard to find: a machine-assisted investigation of false, true and just plain unreliable 'friends'', *Perspectives: Studies in Translatology* 3(1): 99-111.
------ (1998) *Patterns and Meanings: Using Corpora for English Language Research and Teaching,* Amsterdam and Philadelphia: John Benjamins.
Pearson, Jennifer (1996) 'Electronic texts and concordances in the translation classroom', *Teanga* 16: 85-95.
------ (1998) *Terms in Context,* Amsterdam and Philadelphia: John Benjamins.
------ (1999) 'Genes go wild in the countryside: using corpora to improve translation quality', *Teanga* 18: 71-83.
Peters, Carol and Eugenio Picchi (1998) 'Bilingual Reference Corpora for Translators and Translation Studies', in Lynne Bowker, Michael Cronin, Dorothy Kenny and Jennifer Pearson (eds), 91-100.
Puurtinen, Tiina (1997) 'Syntactic Norms in Finnish Children's Literature', *Target* 9(2): 321-334.
------ (1998) 'Syntax, readability and ideology in children's literature', in Sara Laviosa (ed), 524-533.
Pym, Anthony (2000) 'Historical Development', in Peter France (ed), 73-81.
Rectanus, Mark W. (1990) *German Literature in the United States: Licensing Translations in the International Marketplace,* Wiesbaden: Otto Harrassowitz.
Renouf, Antoinette (1987a) 'Corpus Development', in John Sinclair (ed), 1-40.
------ (1987b) 'Lexical Resolution', in Willem Meijs (ed), 121-131.
------ and John Sinclair (1991) 'Collocational frameworks in English', in Karin Aijmer and Bengt Altenberg (eds), 128-144.
Russ, Charles V.J. (1994) *The German Language Today,* London and New York: Routledge.
Sager, Juan C. (1997) 'The Neutralisation of Culture-specific Concepts in Translation: Observations on G. Pontiero's translation of José Saramago's *Essay on Blindness*', in Pilar Orero and Juan C. Sager (eds) *The Translator's Dialogue. Giovanni Pontiero,* Amsterdam and Philadelphia: John Benjamins, 107-114.
Sampson, Geoffrey (1980) *Schools of Linguistics: Competition and Evolution,* London: Hutchinson.
------ (1987) 'Probabilistic Models of Analysis', in Roger Garside, Geoffrey Leech and Geoffrey Sampson (eds), 16-19.
Sarup, Madan (1988) *An Introductory Guide to Post-structuralism and Postmodernism,* Hemel Hempstead: Harvester Wheatsheaf.
Saussure, Ferdinand de (1916) *Cours de Linguistique Générale,* Paris: Payot.
Schmied, Josef and Hildegard Schäffler (1996) 'New approaches to contrastive linguistics and translation studies: bilingual corpora', unpublished research paper.

Scott, Mike (1997) *WordSmith Tools version 2.0,* Oxford: Oxford University Press.
Sebba, M. and Steven Fligelstone (1994) 'Corpora', in R.E. Asher and J.M.Y. Simpson (eds) *The Encyclopedia of Language and Linguistics,* Oxford, New York, Seoul and Tokyo: Pergamon Press, 769-773.
Shamaa, Najah (1978) *A Linguistic Analysis of some Problems of Arabic to English Translation,* unpublished PhD thesis, Oxford: Oxford University.
Shlesinger, Miriam (1989) *Simultaneous interpretation as a factor in effecting shifts in the position of texts on the oral-literate continuum,* unpublished MA thesis, Tel Aviv: Tel Aviv University.
------ (1991) 'Interpreter latitude vs. due process: simultaneous and consecutive interpretation in multilingual trials', in Sonia Tirkkonen-Condit (ed) *Empirical research in translation and intercultural studies,* Tübingen: Gunter Narr Verlag, 147-155.
------ (1998) 'Corpus-based Interpreting Studies as an Offshoot of Corpus-based Translation Studies', in Sara Laviosa (ed), 486-493.
Shreve, Gregory (1996) 'On the Nature of Scientific and Empirical Translation Studies', in Marilyn Gaddis Rose (ed), 69-86.
------ (1997) 'Prolegomena to an Empirical Translation Studies', in Gerd Wotjak and Heide Schmidt (eds) *Modelle der Translation / Models of Translation Festschrift für Albrecht Neubert*, Frankfurt:Vervuert, 41-58.
Sinclair, John (1966) 'Beginning the Study of Lexis', in C.E. Bazell, J.C. Catford, M.A.K. Halliday and R.H. Robins (eds), 410-430.
------ (ed) (1987a) *Collins Cobuild English Language Dictionary,* London: HarperCollins.
------ (1987b) 'Collocation: a progress report', in Ross Steele and Terry Treadgold (eds) *Language Topics: Essays in honour of Michael Halliday,* Amsterdam and Philadelphia: John Benjamins, 219-331.
------ (ed) (1987c) *Looking Up,* London: Harper Collins.
------ (ed) (1990) *Collins Cobuild English Grammar,* London: HarperCollins.
------ (1991) *Corpus, Concordance, Collocation,* Oxford: Oxford University Press.
------ (1992) 'The Automatic Analysis of Corpora', in Jan Svartvik (ed), 379-397.
------ (1996) 'The Search for Units of Meaning', *Textus* IX: 75-106.
------ (1997) 'The Lexical Item', unpublished manuscript received from author.
------ and R. M. Coulthard (1975) *Towards an Analysis of Discourse,* Oxford: Oxford University Press.
Smadja, Frank (1989) 'Lexical Co-occurrence: The Missing Link', *Literary and Linguistic Computing* 4(3): 163-168.
------ (1991) 'Macrocoding the Lexicon with Co-occurrence Knowledge', in Uri Zernik (ed), 165-189.
------ (1993) 'Retrieving Collocations from Text: Xtract', *Computational Linguistics* 19(1): 143-177.
------ and Kathleen McKeown (1990) 'Automatically Extracting and Representing Collocations for Language Generation', in *Proceedings of the 28th Annual Meeting of the Association for Computational Linguistics,* Pittsburgh, Pa.: Association for Computational Linguistics, 252-259.
------ Kathleen McKeown and Vasileios Hatzivassiloglou (1996) 'Translating Collocations for Bilingual Lexicons: A Statistical Approach', *Computational Linguistics* 22(1): 1-38.

Smith, Neil (1999) *Chomsky: ideas and ideals,* Cambridge: Cambridge University Press.

Snell-Hornby, Mary (1988a) *Translation Studies: An Integrated Approach,* Amsterdam and Philadelphia: John Benjamins.

------ (ed) (1988b) *Zürilex Proceedings: Papers read at the EURALEX International Congress, University of Zürich, 9-14 September 1986,* Tübingen: Francke Verlag.

------ (1990) 'Linguistic Transcoding or Cultural Transfer? A Critique of Translation Theory in Germany', in Susan Bassnett and André Lefevere (eds), 79-86.

Sperber, Dan and Deirdre Wilson (1986) *Relevance,* Oxford and Cambridge MA: Basil Blackwell.

Stubbs, Michael (1993) 'British Traditions in Text Analysis – from Firth to Sinclair', in Mona Baker, Gill Francis and Elena Tognini-Bonelli (eds), 1-33.

------ (1995a) 'Collocations and semantic profiles: on the cause of the trouble with quantitative studies', *Functions of Language* 2(1): 23-55.

------ (1995b) 'Collocations and Cultural Connotations of Common Words', *Linguistics and Education* 7: 379-390.

------ (1995c) 'Corpus evidence for norms of lexical collocation', in Guy Cook and Barbara Seidlhofer (eds) *Principle and Practice in Applied Linguistics,* London: Oxford University Press, 245-256.

------ (1996) *Text and Corpus Analysis,* Oxford and Cambridge MA: Basil Blackwell.

Svartvik, Jan (ed) (1990) *The London-Lund Corpus of Spoken English,* Lund: Lund University Press.

------ (ed) (1992a) *Directions in Corpus Linguistics,* Proceedings of Nobel Symposium 82, Stockholm, 4-8 August 1991, Berlin: Mouton de Gruyter.

------ (1992b) 'Corpus linguistics comes of age', introduction to Svartvik (ed), 7-13.

------ (1996) 'Corpora are becoming mainstream', in Jenny Thomas and Mick Short (eds) *Using Corpora for Language Research,* London and New York: Longman, 3-13.

Terrell, Peter, Veronika Schnorr, Wendy V.A. Morris and Roland Breitsprecher (eds) (1997) *Colllins German Dictionary,* 3rd edition, Glasgow and New York: HarperCollins Publishers.

Teubert, Wolfgang (1996) 'Comparable Corpora or Parallel Corpora?', *International Journal of Lexicography,* Special Issue on Corpora in Multilingual Lexicography 9(3), 238-264.

Tognini-Bonelli, Elena (1996a) *Corpus Theory and Practice,* Birmingham: TWC.

------ (1996b) 'Translation equivalence in a corpus linguistic framework', *International Journal of Lexicography,* Special Issue on Corpora in Multilingual Lexicography 9(3), 179-196.

Toury, Gideon (1978) 'The Nature and Role of Norms in Literary Translation', in James Holmes, José Lambert and Raymond van den Broeck (eds), 83-100.

------ (1980) *In Search of a Theory of Translation,* Tel Aviv: The Porter Institute for Poetics and Semiotics, Tel Aviv University.

------ (1985) 'A Rationale for Descriptive Translation Studies', in Theo Hermans (ed), 16-41.

------ (1989) 'The Meaning of Translation-Specific Lexical Items and Its Representation in the Dictionary', in Mary Snell-Hornby and E. Pöhl (eds) *Translation and Lexicography,* Amsterdam and Philadelphia: John Benjamins, 45-53.

------ (1991) 'What are Descriptive Studies into Translation Likely to Yield apart from Isolated Descriptions', in Kitty van Leuven-Zwart and Ton Naaijkens (eds) *Translation Studies:The State of the Art: Proceedings from the First James S Holmes Symposium on Translation Studies,* Amsterdam and Philadelphia: John Benjamins, 179-192.

------ (1993) 'Still in Search of Laws of Translational Behaviour: Closing in on Discourse Interference', in Kinga Klaudy, János Kohn, Katalin Molnár and Lajos Szalai (eds) *Transferre Necesse Est ... Current issues of translation theory – Aktuelle Fragen der Übersetzung,* Szombathely: Philologische Fakultät der Berzenyi-Hochschule, 21-38.

------ (1995) *Descriptive Translation Studies and Beyond,* Amsterdam and Philadelphia: John Benjamins.

Trask, R.L (1993) *A Dictionary of Grammatical Terms in Linguistics,* London and New York: Routledge.

Trudgill, Peter (1996) 'Series Editor's Preface', in Stubbs, xi-xii.

Tymoczko, Maria (1998) 'Computerized corpora and the future of translation studies', in Sara Laviosa (ed), 652-659.

Van Brederode, T. (1980) 'Towards a theory of collocations', in Wim Zonneveld and Fred Weerman (eds) *Linguistics in the Netherlands 1977-79,* Dordrecht: Foris Publications.

van der Wouden, Ton (1992) 'Prolegomena to a Multilingual Description of Collocations', in Hannu Tommola, Krista Varantola, Tarja Salmi-Tolonen and Jürgen Schopp (eds) *Euralex '92 Proceedings* studia translatologica ser. A. vol. 2, Tampere: Department of Translation Studies, University of Tampere, 449-456.

Van Doorslaer, Luc (1995) 'Quantitative and Qualitative Aspects of Corpus Selection in Translation Studies', *Target* 7(2): 245-260.

Vanderauwera, Ria (1985) *Dutch Novels Translated into English: The Transformation of a "Minority" Literature,* Amsterdam: Rodopi.

Venuti, Lawrence (1995) *The Translator's Invisibility: A History of Translation,* London and New York: Routledge.

------ (1996) 'Translation, Heterogeneity, Linguistics', *TTR* 9(1): 91-115.

------ (1997) 'Unequal Developments: Current Trends in Translation Studies' *Comparative Literature,* 49(4): 360-368.

------ (2000) *The Translation Studies Reader,* London and New York: Routledge.

Vermeer, Hans (1978) 'Ein Rahmen für eine allgemeine Translationstheorie', *Lebende Sprachen* 23(3), 99-102.

Vinay, Jean-Paul, and Jean Darbelnet (1958) *Stylistique comparée du français et de l'anglais,* Paris: Didier.

------ (1995) *Comparative Stylistics of French and English: A Methodology for Translation,* trans. of Vinay and Darbelnet (1958) by Juan Sager and Marie-Josée Hamel, Amsterdam and Philadelphia: John Benjamins.

Wahrig, Gerhard (1986) *Deutsches Wörterbuch,* Neuausgabe, Munich: Mosaik Verlag.

Weissbrod, Rachel (1992) 'Explicitation in Translations of Prose-fiction from English to Hebrew as a Function of Norms', *Multilingua* 11(2): 153-171.

Wilson Andrew and Tony McEnery (eds) (1994) *Corpora in Language Education and*

Research: a Selection of Papers from Talc 94, UCREL Technical Papers 4, Lancaster: UCREL.

Wilss, Wolfram (1977) *Übersetzungswissenschaft. Probleme und Methoden,* Stuttgart: Ernst Klett.

------ (1982) *The Science of Translation: Problems and Methods,* trans. and revised edition of Wilss (1977), Tübingen: Gunter Narr.

Woods, Anthony, Paul Fletcher and Arthur Hughes (1986) *Statistics in Language Studies,* Cambridge, New York and Melbourne: Cambridge University Press.

Woolls, David (1997) *Multiconcord version 1.5,* Birmingham: CFL Software Development.

Zampolli, Antonio, Nicoletta Calzolari and Martha Palmer (eds) (1994) *Current Issues in Computational Linguistics: In Honour of Don Walker,* Special Edition of *Linguistica Computazionale* Vol. IX-X.

Zanettin, Frederico (1998) 'Bilingual comparable corpora and the training of translators', in Sara Laviosa (ed), 616-630.

Zernik, Uri (ed) (1991) *Lexical Acquisition: Exploiting On-Line Resources to Build a Lexicon,* Hillsdale, NJ, Hove and London: Lawrence Erlbaum Associates Inc.

Zhu, Qi-bo (1989) 'A quantitative look at the Guangzhou Petroleum English Corpus', *ICAME Journal* 13: 28-38.

Subject Index

Author Index

For Product Safety Concerns and Information please contact our EU
representative GPSR@taylorandfrancis.com
Taylor & Francis Verlag GmbH, Kaufingerstraße 24, 80331 München, Germany

www.ingramcontent.com/pod-product-compliance
Lightning Source LLC
LaVergne TN
LVHW080649011026
849160LV00014B/1368

* 9 7 8 1 9 0 0 6 5 0 3 9 7 *